D1434713

About the author

Jonah Blank, formerly an editor of the *Asbai Evening News* in Tokyo, has reported for the *Dallas Morning News* and other newspapers from Sri Lanka, Sudan, the Philippines, Burma, Malaysia, Thailand and India. He was educated at Yale and Harvard and currently lives in Cambrige, Massachusetts.

Arrow of the Blue-Skinned God is his first book.

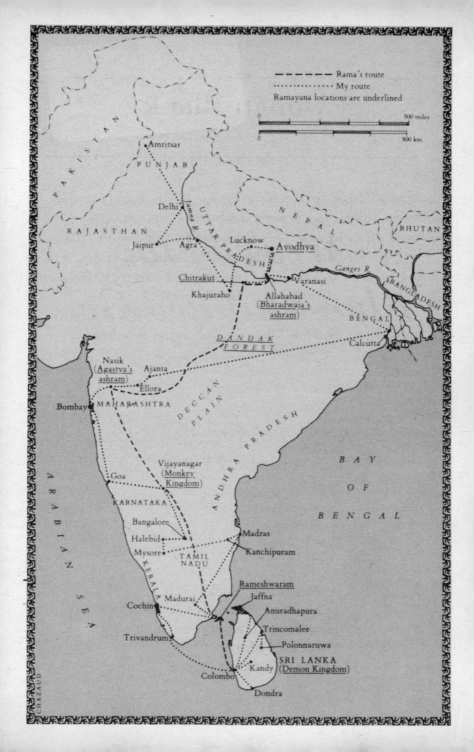

Rama's route
My route
Ramayana locations are underlined

500 miles
800 km

PAKISTAN

Amritsar

PUNJAB

Delhi

RAJASTHAN

Jumna R.

Jaipur

Agra

UTTAR PRADESH

Lucknow

Ayodhya

NEPAL

BHUTAN

Chitrakut

Khajuraho

Varanasi

Ganges R.

BANGLADESH

Allahabad
(Bharadwaja's
ashram)

BENGAL

DANDAK
FOREST

Calcutta

Nasik
(Agastya's
ashram)

Ajanta

Ellora

Bombay

MAHARASHTRA

DECCAN
PLAIN

ANDHRA PRADESH

BAY

OF

BENGAL

Vijayanagar
(Monkey
Kingdom)

Goa

KARNATAKA

ARABIAN

Bangalore

Halebid

Mysore

Madras

Kanchipuram

TAMIL
NADU

SEA

KERALA

Rameshwaram

Jaffna

Madurai

Anuradhapura

Cochin

Trincomalee

Polonnaruwa

Trivandrum

SRI LANKA
(Demon Kingdom)

Colombo

Kandy

Dondra

CHAZAUD

Jonah Blank

Arrow of the Blue-Skinned God

RETRACING THE RAMAYANA THROUGH INDIA

A Touchstone Book
Published by Simon & Schuster
New York   London
Toronto   Sydney
Tokyo   Singapore

First published in Great Britain by
Simon & Schuster Ltd in 1993
First published by Touchstone, 1994
An imprint of Simon & Schuster
A Paramount Communications Company

Copyright © Jonah Blank, 1992
published by special arrangement with
Houghton Mifflin Company

This book is copyright under the Berne Convention
No reproduction without permission
All rights reserved

The right of Jonah Blank to be identified
as the author of this work has been asserted
by him in accordance with the Copyright,
Designs and Patents Act of 1988

Simon & Schuster Ltd
West Garden Place
Kendal Street
London W2 2AQ

Simon & Schuster of Australia Pty Ltd
Sydney

A CIP catalogue record for this book is
available from the British Library

ISBN 0-671-71212-8

Printed and bound in Great Britain by
HarperCollins Manufacturing, Glasgow

Map by Jaques Chazaud

To my family

Contents

Preface

IMAGINE A STORY that is the *Odyssey,* Aesop's fables, *Romeo and Juliet,* the Bible, and *Star Wars* all at the same time. Imagine a story that combines adventure and aphorism, romance and religion, fantasy and philosophy. Imagine a story that makes young children marvel, burly men weep, and old women dream. Such a story exists in India, and it is called the Ramayana.

This best beloved of Indian epics was sung by nameless bards for ages before being written down by a poet named Valmiki in the third century B.C. It chronicles Rama's physical voyage from one end of the Indian subcontinent to the other, and his spiritual voyage from Man to God.

I followed Rama's footsteps through his first trek, and occasionally got a faint glimpse of his second one as well.

Starting my journey at the same age my forerunner had started his, I retraced Rama's path from Ayodhya to Chitrakut, from Sage Agastya's hermitage near Nasik to the Monkey Kingdom of Kiskindhya, from the bridgehead of Rameshwaram to the battlefield of Lanka. I'd expected this to be a common pilgrim's route — after all, Rama is one of the most popular deities in the Hindu pantheon — but nobody I met along the way had heard of anyone retracing the whole journey. The pious wanderers who preceded me (for surely I was not the first) were apparently modest enough to keep their mouths shut.

Although my peregrinations followed the Ramayana's plot line chronologically, I do not recount them in the order they occurred. Instead I tell the stories of the people I met along the way wholly out of sequence, introducing each vignette as it seems relevant to the themes of the epic. Often I strayed from Rama's footsteps to visit places that had no epic significance, for pilgrimage towns are not the only spots where people ask and answer eternal questions. I used the Ramayana as a framework for looking at India today.

> > >

How relevant is this ancient epic now? Well, you can open the New Delhi telephone directory at random and find pages where every single person is named Ram after the tale's hero. A two-year serialization of the Ramayana was the most widely viewed television program in Indian history. But the story's importance goes far beyond mere popularity. The issues that dominate this Sanskrit saga are the same issues that dominate modern India.

The hottest of all political hot potatoes today is a controversy over what manner of monument should stand on Rama's birthplace. In addition to helping topple three governments in barely a year, this dispute has stoked the flames of Hindu fundamentalism; it has turned the religious right wing into the most dynamic force in the nation. And, on a deeper level, the questions that Indians debate as they sip their afternoon tea are questions which were raised long ago in the Ramayana.

The central epic theme of caste, for instance, has lately thrown its shadow across the whole country. Former Prime Minister V. P. Singh's sweeping program of quotas and affirmative action for the "backward castes" unleashed a torrent of riots and self-immolations in 1990, and the flood shows no sign of subsiding.

War (like nearly every epic, the Ramayana is largely a war story) continues to wrack the Indian subcontinent from Kashmir to Assam to the Punjab. As in the saga, each battle pits one race of people against another. In Sri Lanka, the site of Rama's cataclysmic duel with the forces of evil, war is still an omnipresent, inescapable condition of life.

Religion has always been inextricably linked with Indians' identity, and it is now as much as ever. The Ramayana is a holy text, a part of the sacred Hindu canon, and today the Hindu faith is undergoing its most radical transformation in at least three centuries. The teachings of Mahatma Gandhi and the onslaught of Western secularism have forced Indians to reexamine their most cherished beliefs.

But above all, the Ramayana is a story of duty. Prince Rama is the personification of Right for the simple reason that he knows what he has to do, and he does it. In a sense, most of India's cultural quandaries boil down to a conflict between duty and individual desire. India is in the midst of a metamorphosis from a rooted, almost feudalistic society to a mobile, democratic one. Possibly for the first time ever, large numbers of people are living their lives in accordance with their own wishes rather than the rigid dictates of tradition. Ideas of fate, governance, family, even good and evil, are all bound tightly to the fast-changing notion of duty. And after eons of arranged marriages, increasing numbers of Indians are abandoning the concept of love as duty in favor of love as love. Any such transformation brings great opportunity, but also great pain.

My goal is not to "explain" India — such a task is far beyond my abilities. I suspect it would be beyond the abilities of *any* single observer, certainly any observer from across the wide ocean. My intent is to let the reader meet some of the fascinating people I have met, see some of the sights I've seen, ponder some of the philosophical mysteries I've pondered. And, of course, to retell a story that has mesmerized millions down through the ages.

My recounting of the epic tale is just that, a recounting and not a translation. I have tried to stick scrupulously close to the Ramayana's plot, and I owe a great debt to the renditions of Makhan Lal Sen, Ralph Griffith, and Romesh Dutt, but the manner of telling (with all its shortcomings) is purely my own. I felt it necessary for the reader to have some idea of the saga's story, but I make no claim to capture more than a fraction of the sweep, power, and poetic beauty of the original.

— *Cambridge, 1992*

I could not ever truly follow your footsteps, as an ass cannot imitate the pace of a horse, nor a crow the gait of a swan.

— BHARATA TO RAMA,
the Ramayana, Book VI, Chapter 86

Prologue

WHEN GURU BABA Raghunanden Das last saw the world beyond his door, George VI was the emperor of India, Mahatma Gandhi had temporarily given up politics for weaving, the Japanese ruled most of eastern China, and German panzers were preparing to roll over Poland. Guru Baba Raghunanden Das did not care. He was nine years old.

For the past half-century Guruji hasn't set foot outside his home in Hanuman Cave. From visitors he hears bits of news mixed in with village gossip, everything from the Soviet Union's disintegration to the latest scandal of the postman's lascivious daughter, but he doesn't particularly care. It is all unimportant to the hermit. Just more talk of busy people running about in furious circles. They never get anywhere, he laughs, so they try to run faster.

The guru wears a dirty white robe and a dirty white beard. He doesn't bother to wipe away the flies that are crawling all over his face, in and out of his nostrils, across his lips and eyelashes. Why should he? If he shooed them off, others would come in a moment or two, and are not flies living creatures? Outside the mouth of his cave a troop of monkeys sits chittering. A young acolyte shakes a stick at them when they try to steal the rotting pieces of fruit left as oblations on the makeshift altar.

I kneel to touch the old man's sandals, and he pours sour curd into my palms as a blessing. When I look up, he has shuffled into the dim recesses of the room to prepare a simple meal of stewed vegetables. Guruji personally cooks the food he serves to every guest. Each day his routine is exactly the same: ten hours of private worship, seven hours of public ministry, four hours of meditation, an hour for meals and bathing, and two hours of sleep. Doing the math, I find that he's spent less time asleep in his sixty years than I have in my twenty-five.

What does he ponder in his predawn yoga, while all the rest of Ayodhya lies dead in sleep? Lord Rama, the old man says with a chuckle, as if any other answer would be faintly absurd.

From all over the state of Uttar Pradesh, devotees come seeking advice. Guru Baba Raghunanden Das gives them guidance on life — he, whose knowledge of life comes from books written two millennia ago. At noon, two dozen men and women file into the dank little room, reverently kiss the guru's feet, and deposit their offerings before a big picture of Rama and Sita. It is the only ornament there.

The cave's air is thick with the greasy smell of a dozen oil lamps, whose flickers illuminate the guru as he speaks. In a patient, paternal voice he admonishes his disciples to work hard at their jobs, show kindness to others, and be diligent in their worship of the gods. Just do this, he says, and all else will follow.

Outside the cave, I talk to a teenager who had been fidgeting during the sermon. He's an apprentice auto mechanic from bustling Allahabad, out here in the boondocks to visit relatives. A pious aunt dragged him to the guru for a blessing, he says, and his knees are still stiff from sitting so long. He hasn't much time for theology and the like — his is a world of carburetors and movie houses and flirtatious cigarette girls. When I ask him who serves as his model in life, the answer comes almost automatically:

Lord Rama, the young man says with a chuckle.

One
BEGINNINGS

*W*HOEVER reads this noble tale of Rama's deeds," writes the poet Valmiki at the start of his epic, "will surely be freed from all sins and will attain heavenly bliss." Reason enough to begin.

Any fool could see that Rama was destined for great things. It wasn't just his rare beauty, his faultless character, or the powerful arms that hung down to his knees. The world at that time was full of such heroes. What made Rama extraordinary right from the start was the lustrous blue-green color of his skin. Only celestials have this aquamarine hue — celestials, and a very few mortals who are very special indeed. Had certain people taken note of this early on, a great deal of pain and bloodshed could easily have been avoided. But, of course, nothing that is fated can ever be changed.

At the time of Rama's birth his father, King Dasarastha, was nine thousand years old. The king commanded an army of several million troops, enjoyed riches beyond a usurer's imaginings, and ruled over as much of the known world as he cared to possess. Ayodhya, his imperial capital, was a place of shady gardens and mango groves, seven-story houses and marble mansions, a place where even the elephants and horses had illustrious bloodlines. All the men and women were of irreproachable character. The Brahmins earned their reverence by prayer, the Kshatriyas kept the state safe from attack, the Vaishyas did their trading honestly, and the Shudras served all without a whisper of complaint.

Rama's education was entrusted to the saint Vishvamitra, a one-time monarch who had aspired to something better. Realizing the emptiness of earthly power, Vishvamitra had resolved to turn himself into a Brahmin. He prayed earnestly for one thousand years, at the end of which time Lord Brahma Himself, the Great-Grandfather of all created beings, graced him with the title Rajarishi, King of Saints. Vishvamitra was mortified. All his penance had counted for nothing, all his efforts to expunge the vain Kshatriya caste from his being had been rebuffed: he was still a king after all.

For another thousand years Vishvamitra practiced even stricter austerities. In the blazing summer he lay upon bonfires, in the winter he stood the fury of icy tempests, in the season of monsoons he sat unperturbed at the bottom of the flood. The gods had no choice. They granted his boon and turned him into a simple Brahmin.

Now Vishvamitra the Brahmin taught Rama how to be a king. He instructed him in all the arts of war and peace. He showed him how to master an unbroken horse, how to fight with sword, mace, disc, and javelin, how to make bow and arrow sing songs of victory. He also taught him dharma, the Truth that guides the universe. Vishvamitra educated his pupil in all the Vedas and the Vedangas, in all the learned texts sacred and profane. Many rulers, reasoned the self-made Brahmin, know how to fight, but all too few know how to think.

When Rama was thirteen years old, Vishvamitra gave him a gift of divine armaments. He taught the prince all the mantras necessary to summon magical weapons at will, weapons invisible and invincible. The blades and the darts spoke to Rama with human voice: "We are your servants," they said, "merely think of us and we will appear in your right hand."

The sage and his student traveled to the land of Mithila, where King Janaka had issued a challenge: his daughter Sita was of marriageable age, and he would accept no bride-price other than pure valor. Anyone who could string an unbending bow given to the king by the god Shiva would win the hand of the princess.

Legions had tried. Monarchs and lords, knights and demons, warriors with the strength of ten bulls — not one had even been able to lift the bow up in his hands. Gods even, gods themselves, had tried, and had stormed back to the heavens in shame. At the Ayodhyan's arrival, the bow was brought out in its cast-iron box. One hundred brawny men pulled the eight-wheeled chariot with great difficulty.

Rama calmly picked up the bow and drew it so hard that he snapped it in two. Sita had found a husband.

At their wedding, all the proper rites were observed. King Dasarastha gave away 400,000 cows with horns covered in beaten gold, each accompanied by a calf and a milking vessel. Vishvamitra and the other court Brahmins built an altar decked with sweet-smelling flowers and ears of barley, urns of colored water, golden ladles, cups, spoons and saucers, incense dishes, and conch shells carried from an impossibly distant place called the ocean. They lit the sacrificial fire, and Sita was led in, all her limbs laden with the weight of sapphires, emeralds, rubies, and diamonds. King Janaka sprinkled Rama with holy water and gave up his daughter forever. Kettledrums rolled, and the heavens poured down music and flowers.

Rama and Sita lived together in perfect bliss, barely able to tolerate a moment's separation. So it was for twelve years.

> > >

King Dasarastha, now aged nine thousand and twenty-five, was tired. For some time he had wanted to set down the burdens of rule, and once Rama reached adulthood he decided to abdicate. The citizens of Ayodhya greeted his decision with heartfelt cheers — perhaps a touch too heartfelt for the old king's taste, but no matter. He ordered his courtiers to prepare for a coronation.

Dasarastha had a junior wife named Kaikeyi, who had a hunchbacked dwarf for a maid. When this maid saw the streets of Ayodhya blanketed in red lotus petals and sprinkled with fresh sandalwood oil, she knew something was afoot. Being quite clever, she quickly figured out what it was. Being completely amoral, she decided to stop it. She ran to her mistress with mock tears in her eyes.

"Cry with me, Kaikeyi," the dwarf sobbed, "for your husband is overthrown, your son is disowned, and Rama will soon be our master."

The queen was slow to rile. Like everyone else in Ayodhya, she loved and admired her stepson Rama, never thought of begrudging him his right as first-born. Her own son, Bharata, was the next in line, but there had never been any trace of rivalry.

"You will be a slave, Kaikeyi," the hunchback continued, "and I, the slave of a slave. Rama will kill Bharata, of course. Who would there be to stop him?"

The pleas and the tears went on for hours.

Jealousy is a powerful emotion, particularly in junior wives who have much to lose.

"Do not worry," said the queen at length, "Rama will never be crowned."

CRAECRAECRAECRAECRAECRAECRAECRAE

Valmiki, unlike such slackers as Homer and Virgil, begins his epic at the very beginning. No *in medias res* shortcuts for him, just the whole story, start to finish. If I were to retrace Prince Rama's steps, I would have to set out where the hero's feet first touched mortal ground. In Ayodhya, the village of his birth.

As it happens, modern-day Ayodhya provides the clearest possible example of India's continuing obsession with the Ramayana. In the space of a year and a half, one million protesters risked imprisonment, several thousand partisans suffered serious injury, more than three hundred militants or innocent bystanders were killed in riots, and three prime ministers were thrown out of office, largely on account of an epic two millennia old.

In Ayodhya there is a mosque that may, or may not, rest on the precise spot of Rama's mythical birth. Fundamentalist Hindus are clamoring to tear down the Islamic structure and build a new mandir to Rama in its place. India's political challenges are manifold: poverty, illiteracy, disease, communal violence, industrialization, at least three long-running guerrilla rebellions — and the most pressing topic on the nation's agenda is the fate of one lumpish gray building.

For millions of people this little temple is truly more important than employment, education, clean water, or peace. The Ramayana is not some ossified legend, it is the guidebook of life. It is a work for which multitudes of men and women, even now, are willing to kill and willing to die.

Rama's hometown today is no imperial capital, no seat of a world empire. It is a sleepy little village like thousands of others, its twisty, unpaved alleys full of flounder-eyed goats, creaky bullock-carts, and emaciated dogs with yellow teeth. There are maybe half a dozen cars here, and the telephone numbers have only two digits.

The pious have long flocked to Ayodhya. The town typically draws four million Hindu pilgrims a year — almost twice as many visitors as the Taj Mahal. But recently the outsiders have not all been pilgrims. Ayodhya today seethes with political intrigue just as venomous as that of Queen Kaikeyi and her dwarfish servant. The wrangling has sown rancor between Hindus and Muslims all through India.

Hari Prasad, a market vendor in Ayodhya, doesn't like Muslims. They're violent people, he says, untrustworthy people, people who kill cows, people who will cheat you any chance they get, people who never bathe. And at that lumpish gray mosque, they defile sacred soil with their arrogant prayers.

"They want everyone to worship *their* god," he complained as he pushed his cart of cooking utensils to sell in the bazaar. "Why can't they just live quietly? We do not insist that they become Hindus, but this is *our* country. If they don't like it, they should leave."

Hari Prasad doesn't personally know any Muslims. There are almost none left in Ayodhya.

Babri Masjid, the mosque at the center of the maelstrom, was built for the Mughal emperor Babur in 1528. Does it actually rest on Rama's birth site? Who's to say? Can a mythical figure whose incarnation is a matter of faith rather than history really be said to have a birthplace at all? It's rather like arguing over the location of the Garden of Eden. But until the end of the nineteenth century Westerners, from Richard the Lionheart to "Chinese" Gordon, searched long and earnestly for the grottoes of Adam and Eve. I do not know whether we are better or worse off for giving up Eden as nothing more than a legend.

For four and a half centuries, the land deed of Babri Masjid was a question only for pandits and scholars. But in 1986 the politicians came. After a court order unchained the mosque's doors for the first time since Independence, Hindu militants and Muslim mullahs drove in from Delhi to stake out their rival claims. All over the country, from Hyderabad to Aligarh, blood was spilled in the name of a little gray temple. The people of Ayodhya could only sit back and watch as their town became the national symbol of religious strife.

"We didn't ask for this fight," said Gayan Das, a resident of Ayodhya since birth; I'd struck up a conversation with him while asking directions to the temple. "We didn't ask for it, we didn't look for it, we don't want it." He ran his hand over his tonsured scalp — Gayan Das has been an ordained swami virtually all his life. "Any good Hindu tries to avoid discord, works for social harmony. This is a holy place. It is not right to make it a battleground."

Gayan Das himself is no stranger to combat. He used to be the heavyweight wrestling champion of all Uttar Pradesh. At forty-six, he still has a pugilist's build. His arms are a pair of billy clubs, his chest a keg made of oak. He has one cauliflower ear, and a nose mashed flat by an illegal sucker punch twenty years ago. The stubble on his chin has more salt than pepper, but he still looks like he could eat you for lunch.

"Wrestling has nothing at all to do with violence," he said. "It is physical, yes, and people do get hurt sometimes, but there is no anger, no malice. You always respect your foe, treat him honorably, try to minimize his pain. *That* is the proper way to fight."

He sent a boy to fetch his scrapbook, a collection of brittle yellow clippings from the local papers. There were even a few from the national press: the *Times of India,* the *Hindustan Times,* the *Indian Express,* real big stuff, man, have a look. A much younger Gayan Das, still with the cauliflower ear and mashed nose, lifts trophy after trophy above his head and mugs for the shot.

"No matter what your opponent's caste," he continued, "no matter what his faith, always you compete as equals. And after the bout you salute each other like gentlemen and live as friends. If you get hurt, what of it? People often get hurt in life, that is nothing to be upset about. Certainly no reason to get angry at your foe."

Gayan Das still enters wrestling competitions, still trains almost daily. "Only now," he said with a grin, "I don't win *every* match." Like most wrestlers he has particular reverence for the Monkey God, Hanuman, the loyal servant of Rama who helps rescue Sita from the abode of demons. What better inspiration could a grappler want than the Prince of the Apes? Gayan Das's monastery, even, is named after Hanuman. It has a reputation for being a rough-and-tumble place, a temple where monks train in ancient weaponry and all manner of martial arts. In the dusty courtyard several sadhus were practicing their holds as we spoke. "Our wrestling is a symbol," said the former champion, "a mark of our commitment and our will. This is how we keep our minds and our bodies sharp for the defense of the faith.

"But these, these . . . *politicians,*" he added with a snort, "what do they know about faith? They stir up the ordinary people to fight their battles for them, then sit back and watch in safety."

That evening I saw an impromptu wrestling match in a public park. A crowd of fifty or sixty was gathered in a tight circle around a barker who offered 150 rupees to any man who could beat the champ. That is not an enormous amount of money, and for some time nobody stepped forward. The champ wasn't particularly big or muscular, and I thought of having a go myself, but fortunately a friend shook his head. "Look first," he said. Once the prize money was raised to 200 rupees, several challengers lined up. Each stripped off his shirt, dropped some crumpled bills into a hat, and was promptly hurled to the ground. The champ did it for pocket change. I realized then that for Gayan Das wrestling was not just a symbol, it was a joy.

But Gayan Das, unlike Ayodhya's newer brawlers, knows the difference between a good fight and a bad one.

A few minutes' walk from Gayan Das's monastery is a little cold-drinks stand owned by the Sodhi family, the only Sikhs in town. They are relative newcomers to Ayodhya, having arrived a mere two hundred years ago. On a hot day (and in late March every day is hot) each passerby stops in for a bottle of Limca, and a bottle soon becomes three or four. Nowadays the afternoon talk generally turns to Rama, politics, and Babri Masjid.

"Foolish, *yaar,*" said Gurjit Singh Sodhi, the proprietor. "So much foolishness, so much to-do."

"You see the news last night?" asked Sunil, a village headman. It was an unnecessary question, since nobody else there owned a television set. "They say more MPs will come 'fact-finding' next month."

"Just what we need, eh?"

"Yes, just what we need." Like almost everybody in Ayodhya, Sunil has little use for meddling outsiders. If pressed, he vaguely supports plans for the new temple but, like his neighbors, he seems to wish the whole matter would just go away.

"What I say is, let them build the temple to Ram," said Gurjit, using Rama's Hindi rather than his Sanskrit name. "Let them build it as big and beautiful and fine as they like, but build it right *near* the mosque, without tearing it down."

"Good, good," said somebody else.

"No, man, no," another voice answered, "Ram's temple

must be in the right place, eh? Got to be there. Let the Muslims move *their* building."

"Perhaps the best solution," said Gurjit with thought, "would be if the Muslims *did* move it voluntarily." He brought out four more bottles of soda that would have been refreshingly cold had the ancient refrigerator been functioning. "But you can't just tear it down, can you? I mean, it *is* a house of worship."

"One way or the other," said Sunil, "voluntarily or not, there *will* be a temple soon. As there should be." He turned and pointed his empty bottle at me. "You should not think we have a problem here between Hindus and Muslims. At least, we didn't used to. Muslims used to study Sanskrit right alongside us at my father's school. We Hindus still hang garlands of flowers at the graves of Muslim saints."

"I never do that," said a man in the back.

"Well, I do," Sunil continued. "Why not, eh? What can it hurt? Maybe you get some good luck — maybe your girl will find a husband one of these days, eh?" A round of chuckles. "Just last week," he said, turning to me again, "two of my Muslim friends came to celebrate the festival of Holi with my family. We don't need trouble here, everything is just fine."

Sunil, Gurjit, and most of the other people of Ayodhya know something that the outsiders seem to have forgotten. Perhaps living so close to the source of the epic has given them a better understanding of the Ramayana's meaning. What they know that the politicians do not is this: Rama, the earthly avatar of God the Sustainer, would never have been a purveyor of hatred.

Three bullocks ambled lazily by the storefront, leaving three steaming piles of dung in their wake. A few minutes later an old woman waddled along, dropped to her knees, and scooped up the fresh patties with her chapped hands. She slapped them onto an already laden tin plate, and shuffled down the alley. In any small town one can see women and children picking up cow dung, kneading it with straw, shaping it into small bricks, sticking it onto the sides of their houses to bake dry in the sun. These bricks are a peasant family's most common source of fuel, but that is not the only reason the old women scrape the pavement. To an orthodox Hindu, even the cow's excrement is holy.

Is it illogical to kill and die for a myth? Is it any less illogical to have reverence for cow dung? For a phallus-shaped Shiva lingam? For the dead body and dead blood of a beggarman nailed to a cross? "It is ridiculous," wrote the second-century Christian theologian Tertullian of his own faith, "and therefore it must be true." All religion is shot through with illogic. Otherwise it would be mere science.

Anything that can be proven cannot last. We laugh at the "science" of yesterday, the Ptolemaic spheres of the universe, the balancing of choler and phlegm in the human body, the reading of a person's character by the shape of his skull. Even a hypothesis conclusively proven true soon loses its relevance: does anybody care that the earth really *is* round instead of flat? Facts falter, only ideas survive.

The Ramayana is not a fact but an idea. That is why it will continue to dominate India in a way no objectively verifiable chronicle ever could. It is beyond corroboration. It can never be confirmed, so it can never be denied.

> > >

Around the corner from the manure collector, another old woman hung a string of dried cow patties outside her door for luck. A large mound of dung sat at the step, stuck each day with newly plucked flower stems. Had I been rude enough to tell her that the custom was unhygienic, she would assuredly have laughed at my science.

The woman's name is Rampati, and her home is a temple. Her family are pandits, hereditary priests, and have little patience for the controversy engulfing their village.

"Of course we all serve Lord Ram," said Rampati. "We love God just as much as any big man from the city — my family doesn't need anyone to tell them about religion."

Her son, the current pandit, shook his head vigorously in agreement.

"Certainly we'd like to see a temple built," the woman continued, "but it is just not worth all the anger and the fighting. In Ayodhya there are already 8,500 temples — do we really need one more?"

If the traditional temple guardians are sickened by temple politics, perhaps the temple politics are more than a little bit sickening. At one point in the epic, Rama counsels his brother on the nature of various sins. Among the greatest transgressors, he says, is anyone "who quarrels with others about their respective faiths and gods, as well as anyone who listens to those disputes."

On my second day in Ayodhya, I went to the heart of the matter. To the spot where it all happened, or did not happen, or happened in a mythical sense if not a physical one. I went to the most celebrated spot outside of Bethlehem where God did (or did not) incarnate as Man.

At Babri Masjid, pilgrims clad only in loincloths are searched for concealed weapons. Ancient yogis who wouldn't know how to operate a telephone walk through airport-style metal detectors to prove they're not harboring high explosives. The plain, unassuming building is surrounded by a double row of iron fences tipped with razory tangles of barbed wire.

"Belt, belt!" a man in some sort of semiofficial uniform called out to me. "You! Belt, here!" He put out his hand.

I took off my belt and gave it to him. Leather — the hide of butchered cows — is not permitted beyond the gate.

The inside of the mosque has already been turned into a Hindu temple. There are no Qur'anic verses painted in scribbles of gilt Arabic, no prayer-clocks, no men in Abraham Lincoln beards bowing in the direction of Mecca. In their place are icons of the pudgy blue baby Rama, candles, bells, incense sticks, and bald-headed sadhus prostrating themselves before the graven images of the infant god. The site is already Ramjanam Bhumi, the Temple of Lord Ram, in fact if not yet in name.

Soldiers are on patrol everywhere. They carry heavy Sten rifles, Second World War–vintage guns inherited from the British army at Independence. The massive wooden stock on the weapon makes it awkward for firing, but ideal for bashing heads.

One young infantryman refused to give me his name, rank, or serial number, but quite cheerfully answered any other question.

"These precautions are here to safeguard the public," he said.

"Safeguard them from what?"

"Riots, bombs, any type of insurrectionary mischief."

"Have there been any riots yet?"

"No, not here yet. But the Muslims are always threatening."

"Do Muslims ever come here?"

"Oh, certainly they are free to come here."

"But *do* they?"

The soldier stomped some dust off the sole of one foot. He was dressed in full combat gear — khaki fatigues, helmet, and all — but since this is holy ground his feet were bare.

"They are free to come," he said. "If they wanted to come, nobody would stop them."

I asked who was in charge of the town.

"The legal government, of course," the soldier replied. "Not the VHP. Most assuredly not. Good day."

A few months later Babri Masjid would indeed be the site of riots, bombs, and insurrectionary mischief. Hundreds of thousands of marchers would overwhelm the security forces, push through the accordion wire without noticing the pain, break down the chain-link barriers, begin physically tearing the mosque to pieces with their bare hands. The army would restore order with lathi-poles and lead, with bamboo and bullets.

In all likelihood, a few months after our conversation this very soldier had a hot day's work. In all likelihood he spent several sweaty hours fracturing rib cages with the butt of his splintering Sten, terrified at every moment that he might be torn apart like the bricks of the mosque at his back. Perhaps he was pummeled to death, perhaps he was promoted for valor, but either way the sacred soil of Rama's birth must have taught him something about tolerance: the mob clamoring for his blood was made up not of Muslims but of his fellow Hindus.

Right next to the temple, inside the steel perimeter with its knife-edge spirals, is a large-scale model of the temple-to-be. It is under the display tent of the Vishva Hindu Parishad, as the VHP is called on those rare occasions when Indians forego initials for full names. Whatever anyone may say, the VHP is very much in charge of Ayodhya. Here at their recruiting pavilion, hundreds of visitors stop to marvel at the mock-up of a lavish architectural fantasy. If Ramjanam Bhumi is built anything like its model, it will be by far the most extravagant temple in a town full of temples, perhaps the most spectacular in the entire state. Pilgrims press their noses to the glass case and drop coins in a box to become part of the dream.

The man who really runs Ayodhya was asleep when I arrived. Mahesh Narayan Singh is the secretary of the Ramjanam Bhumi Committee of the VHP, and he was taking his midafternoon nap. An aide brought me tea, and time passed. When it became clear that the secretary would not be waking up un-prompted, the aide ushered me into his room.

Mahesh Narayan Singh, a big, beefy man with hair prema-turely white, sat up in his bed and rubbed his bleary eyes. The heavy curtains were still drawn, so there was little for him to see. He took a cup of tea from a tray at the foot of the mattress and told me of his plans.

"Ram is the most important god in the Hindu faith," he said. "And this is the very spot where he was born. How could we *not* give him every due honor?"

I asked why, with all the mandirs already standing in Ayo-dhya, he needed another. Couldn't there be some compromise, some way of honoring Rama on the site without humiliating the Muslims by razing their mosque?

The new temple, he replied, would be far more than a place to worship Rama. It would be a beacon to guide all Hindus back to their faith. "Look at the splendors of India's past," said the secretary, "Khajuraho, Ellora, Somnathpur, Kanchipuram, the list goes on and on. Each one strengthened the people's spirit, reminded them of what a wonderful thing it truly is to be a Hindu. And when was the last such temple built? Not for many hundreds of years."

He poked a pillow into a more comfortable shape and wedged it under his back.

"You see," he said, "India is our mother. That, plain and simple, is the essence of Hinduism. You must honor and cherish your parent, always. You would sacrifice anything to defend your family from harm, would you not? Of course you would. Well, our nation is our parent, and we must defend her sacred status."

It is filial obedience that sends Rama into exile. The prince of Ayodhya places his father's command above his duty to his wife, his subjects, his own birthright, even right and wrong. When the modern-day prince of modern-day Ayodhya honors his parent, he is following an illustrious example.

"But aren't the Muslims Indians as well?" I asked. "Aren't they your brothers and sisters, children of the same Mother Soil?"

"Yes, they are, but they seem to forget this. After all, who were their ancestors, these Muslims, eh? Their ancestors were Hindus just like mine. Back when the Mughals invaded our country, they forced so many good Hindus to convert to Islam at the point of a sword. So many. Not just here — everywhere in the world the Muslims gain converts by force. They are a warlike people, it is bred in the bone."

The VHP is still battling against Islamic warriors long dead. When a television serial on the eighteenth-century Muslim ruler Tipu Sultan was aired in 1990, the Hindu group staged a hunger strike in protest.

"Our Indian faith was in existence since the beginning of history," the secretary continued. "That is not dogma, mind you, that is historical fact. Hindu worship goes back two thousand years before this Prophet of theirs was even born." Undeniable — if one stretches the definition of Hinduism a bit to include archaic Brahminism. "We do not force others to accept our belief. We are the only faith that truly practices nonviolence. But simply because we eschew killing and hurting people does not mean that we're pushovers."

There are two other Mughal mosques that the VHP is pressing to take over. Babri Masjid is far and away the most celebrated, but it is only one of many sites where, fundamentalists say, Muslims destroyed existing Hindu temples over the centuries. "There are mosques on top of a Shiva temple in Varanasi and a Krishna temple in Mathura," said the secretary. "All we are demanding is the return of three holy places that originally were ours. It is not a lot to ask for."

Not a lot, or perhaps far too much. Like most things in India, it depends on your point of view.

All hatred, it has been said, comes from fear. Despite a long tradition of mutual atrocities, it is hard to believe that 690 million Hindus feel truly threatened by 90 million Muslims. I asked the secretary whether the fundamentalist revival might stem from a different fear entirely, a fear that always smolders but can never burn hot enough to enflame a people's spirit: a fear of modernity.

The secretary leaned forward on the bed to take a biscuit from the tea tray, and nibbled on it as he spoke.

"Yes indeed, we have much to worry about quite apart from the Muslims," he said. "Hindus, more and more, are forsaking their own traditions freely, without anybody forcing them. More and more, all the time, they would rather go to the movies, wear Western clothing, study abroad and move to the United States. They forget to worship the gods — how can you call yourself a Hindu if you don't worship the gods? For them the great epics Ramayana and Mahabharata are merely television programs."

"Those television programs have made the VHP successful."

"Yes, they have helped stir up interest in the grand epics. But the Indian nation must be reminded that its days of glory are not all in the past. This is why we will build a new temple. We must be reminded not merely with pretty words, but with monuments in immovable stone."

Mahesh Narayan Singh is a Kshatriya, of course — just about everyone with the name of Singh is either a Kshatriya or a Sikh, and the secretary wears neither a Sikh's turban nor a beard. His father was a "farmer," most likely in the same sense that a landed English baronet may refer to himself as an "agriculturist." As a member of the caste entrusted with the defense of faith, Mahesh Narayan Singh sees his work as a sacred crusade. "It is," he said, "my religious duty to wake my countrymen up."

Rama himself is a Kshatriya. He too is duty-bound to protect Hinduism from any attack. But the epic tells us that he goes far out of his way to avoid every battle, fights only as a last resort, never takes up arms without regret. I couldn't help but admire Mahesh Narayan Singh's pious convictions, his commitment to uphold traditions that too many consider old-fashioned. But I also couldn't help but wish that his fervor were tempered with a healthy streak of Rama's righteous restraint.

Was Babri Masjid actually built by tearing down an older Hindu shrine? The question is of vital importance to Ayodhya and of vital importance to India. The answer (like so many answers in India) is maybe, maybe not.

Emperor Babur certainly would not have spared any Hindu mandir out of kindness. He destroyed enough other temples that if he did not ruin one in Ayodhya it was only because he didn't happen to find one there. This founder of the Mughal dynasty was a highly accomplished Turki poet, a patron of the arts, a lover of fountains and gardens. He was not a particularly cruel man for his time, but his time was a cruel one. Babur's name means "tiger" in Arabic, and the blood of both Genghis Khan and Tamburlaine flowed thick in his veins.

When Babur swept into the subcontinent from the steppes of central Asia, he saw the words of God's Own Qur'an blazing before his eyes: "Slay the idolators wherever ye find them," reads chapter nine, verse five, "take them captive, besiege them, and wait for them in ambush." The Qur'an urges tolerance for Christians, Jews, and Zoroastrians (all fellow monotheists) but clearly orders the faithful to eradicate the paganism that had been Arabia's practice before Muhammad. Now, a full eight hundred years after the Prophet's death, the pagans were still triumphant throughout this vast new territory of India.

Muslim invaders, the first ones Pathans from Afghanistan, had been carving out little fiefdoms for themselves since the twelfth century. They saw their new subjects bowing down before idols, the greatest abomination Islamic minds could imagine. And not simply prostrating themselves before graven images of God (which would be blasphemy enough) or of men (a blasphemy barely fit even to be mentioned), but manifold images of beasts, birds, and biological oddities. Serpents, bulls, boars, monkeys, men with four faces, women with a hundred arms, creatures half human and half elephant or lion — why, often the idol was simply an enormous phallus! Muhammad's example was clear: he had marched right into the holy Kaaba in Mecca and personally smashed the 360 idols that his own family had adored and tended for generations.

One can see the Muslim conquerors' handiwork at Qutab Minar, about ten miles out of Delhi. The minaret itself is a fine piece of Islamic architecture, not a delicate, pencil-thin shaft like those that summon the faithful in Istanbul and Isfahan, but a massive, arrogant tower that seems to spiral right up to the heavens. What is most remarkable, however, is not the Minar itself but the now-abandoned mosque — the very first in India — at its base.

One would never guess it was a mosque to look at it. All the statuary, all the ornamentation, all the hundreds of close-packed figures on every door and lintel, seem to come straight from a Hindu temple. Which, in fact, they did. The Muslim architect tore down twenty-seven local temples and built his mosque from the pillaged stone, keeping all the fabulous decoration but purging it of any un-Islamic taint. Every single face on those thousands of figures has been carefully smashed away by iconoclastic hammers. Apsaras sing celestial songs with no mouths, gandharvas dance before stone audiences with no eyes. A headless image of the great god Vishnu — of whom Rama is a human incarnation — is identifiable only by the conch shell he holds in one of his four hands. The merry, roly-poly god Ganesh has had his elephant head hacked to oblivion, but even the most fervent of chisels could not obscure his enormous pachydermatous belly.

The invaders left one piece of the original temple intact, however. In the very center of the mosque's courtyard stands a pillar of iron, thought to date all the way back to the Gupta Empire of the fifth century. Even today scientists are utterly baffled by it: the pillar has not rusted in over 1,600 years, and at the time it was cast, much of India had scarcely entered the Iron Age.

If you stand with your back to the pillar and link your hands around it, they say, you will get your heart's fondest wish. Now day-trippers from Haryana and vacationers from Madhya Pradesh line up to attempt the backward embrace. One after the other, they lean against the cold metal and stretch their arms out behind them. Stretching and stretching, straining and reaching, just another inch, c'mon, man, you can do it, *yaar,* you can do it, just another inch, almost there, man, almost, almost. Friends try to help each other gain those few vital centimeters, sometimes two of them pulling on each arm, their feet braced against the ancient pedestal. With laughs, gasps of pain, and half-serious jokes about dislocation, they always quit. The struggle has been going on for centuries. At the height of a man's shoulders, the pillar's iron is worn from black-gray to shiny silver.

I do not attempt to span the column, I do not try to find out whether my wishes will be fulfilled. There are certain things in life it is better not to know.

Certainly the Mughals rode roughshod over their Hindu subjects and destroyed an incalculable amount of irreplaceable art. But was a temple in Ayodhya one of these casualties? The town itself was settled by 700 B.C., four hundred years before the Ramayana was written down, but scholars still don't know whether this was the Ayodhya referred to in the epic. In Valmiki's day it was a Buddhist center called Saketa — Gautama the Buddha himself lived and preached there for a time. By the fifth century after Christ, the wandering Chinese monk Fa-Hsien reported that the village boasted one hundred Buddhist monasteries by the banks of the Gogra River.

The worship of Rama as a major deity did not arise until the thirteenth century. Guru Swami Ramanand soon made this new cult one of India's most popular, but any Rama temple that Babur's army found in Ayodhya could not have been much more than two hundred years old. If a mandir was standing (there is no contemporary record for or against), it dated back not to Rama's birth or even to Valmiki's writing, but only to Swami Ramanand's preaching a millennium and a half later.

Tulsi Das, the author of an immensely popular Hindi version of the Ramayana, lived his whole life in and near Ayodhya at the very time Babri Masjid was constructed; in none of his writings is there any mention of the demolition of a venerable shrine, an event he'd hardly be likely to pass over. Still, devout pilgrims (not to mention the editors of *Encyclopaedia Britannica*) have believed Babri Masjid to sit atop Rama's birth site for as long as the most ancient of the bazaar gossips can remember. When the facts are inconclusive, truth is what you declare it to be.

For one bazaar gossip named Mrs. Sahia, the truth has never been in question. "The Muslims don't know their place," she said. "They act like they own this country. They should just be happy we let them stay here."

Mrs. Sahia is a shopkeeper on Ayodhya's central street. She came to the village ages ago, sent here as a terrified bride barely out of childhood. Now she has four sons, four grandsons, four houses, four general goods stores, and (she notes with pride) two television sets.

"Back in 'forty-seven," she said, "the Muslims got all of Pakistan for their state, and we got India for ours. Do you think Hindus are welcome in Karachi or Lahore? Of course not. Yet we let Muslims live here in peace, and they do nothing but stir up trouble. If they don't like it here they should go back to Pakistan where they belong."

"Yes, yes," said her son, "send them all back."

In the street outside, two pariah dogs fought listlessly over a chicken bone. One had the aristocratic black-and-gray markings of an English harrier hound. All over the northern part of India these uniquely speckled descendants of pampered hunting dogs scavenge along with mongrels. It was not only humans that Partition left homeless. But the dogs have shorter lives and shorter memories.

"Our whole family hates the Muslims," Mrs. Sahia said proudly. "They want special treatment — what special treatment did *we* ever get?"

"None!" said her son. "None at all!"

I asked if she had felt this way before the VHP and the politicians of the Bharatiya Janata Party came to town. Her Highness the Maharani of Gwalior, now seated as a BJP member of Parliament, has made Ayodhya's temple her own pet project.

"The politicians are just windbags," Mrs. Sahia huffed. "All of them, just in it for their own purposes. They don't really care about us at all. But the VHP we support. Before they proposed the temple, we'd never really thought about it much. They made us aware of the problem and started to do something about it. Why shouldn't good Hindus from other parts of the country help build a temple? Ram is not just for Ayodhyans, he is the god for all Hindus everywhere."

What about tolerance, I asked her, and the tradition of Hindu nonviolence.

"I know nothing of theology," she said with a dismissive toss of her hands. "What do I look like to you, a pandit? I am an ordinary woman, not some city-educated girl like today. If you want to know about theology, go ask a sadhu. There are certainly enough of them around in this town."

A small boy came up and tugged at her sari. She brushed him off without looking down.

"I will tell you this," she added, looking me straight in the eye, "if the government does not stop its foolish talking and allow the temple to be built very soon, the ordinary people will not wait. There will be a revolution."

A revolution of bitter shopkeepers, of sour-hearted matriarchs, of angry, jealous, ungenerous souls, a revolt of intolerance and bile, an uprising born not of righteousness but of hatred. It does not not seem the sort of revolution that Rama, the embodiment of charity, harmony, and all human virtues, could ever inspire.

It took me several days of hard searching to find any Muslims at all in Ayodhya. They were cloth merchants, six of them, huddled together in a small textile stall. Five were traveling salesmen from Maharashtra, just in for the week. The other was Muhammad Latif.

"My family has lived here for nine generations," he said, "ever since the time of my great-great-great-great-great-great-grandfather. Was that six 'greats'? Good. We have been here for a very long time, and we will not be forced out."

"Never," said one of the men from Maharashtra. "We Muslims from all over the nation will defend our brethren."

"If we give in here," said another of the cloth merchants, "what will be next? Maybe they'll try to close our schools, maybe take away our voting rights, who knows? You must make a stand."

I asked how many Muslims were left in town.

"Not so many," Muhammad Latif conceded. "More than a few have gotten fed up and left. We are not physically threatened, you understand, but the constant struggle is sometimes too much. Still, we have enough here to defend what is ours."

"And they do not fight alone," said the first merchant.

"Couldn't there be a way to compromise," I asked, "perhaps to move the mosque or —"

"Never," said Muhammad Latif. "Never. The house of God must remain a house of God, always." His hard, angry stare softened a shade. "We are not unreasonable people," he said, "we are quite willing to talk. If all the outsiders on both sides went away, I am certain we Ayodhyans could resolve the problem among ourselves. But the mosque must never be torn down."

I could understand the Muslims' fear. Though throughout Indian history they have been more often the oppressors than the oppressed, today the Muslims are an embattled minority in a nation that has been their home for centuries. And the desanctification of a consecrated mosque is, in their view, a sacrilege too horrible to contemplate. But Babri Masjid has no special Islamic significance, it is merely one among many thousands of mosques in India, not even a particularly important or remarkable one at that. And it happens to rest on a site that the Hindus, rightly or wrongly, cherish more dearly than just about any other scrap of land. I hoped they would not be forced to give up their house of worship, but I wished they would have the generosity of spirit to give it up anyway.

Violence is rare in Ayodhya, but the Babri Masjid controversy has unloosed bloodshed all across the subcontinent. In the two months prior to the 1989 general election, factional rioting broke out in the states of Rajasthan, Uttar Pradesh, Maharashtra, Madhya Pradesh, Gujarat, West Bengal, and Bihar. Six hundred people, mostly Muslims, were killed in this brief spurt alone. Two years earlier, shortly after a court ordered the temple "opened" to Hindu fundamentalists, partisans of the two faiths took to the streets in Meerut armed with guns, knives, gasoline bombs, stones, axes, anything they could get their hands on.

After a four-day orgy of destruction, the Indian army clamped down a round-the-clock curfew. In 1990, not long after I left the village, nationwide riots took the lives of hundreds more. Rajiv Gandhi, V. P. Singh, and Chandra Shekhar — nearly half the prime ministers in Indian history — all were dethroned in less than two years, largely because they could not give Babri Masjid to the fundamentalists.

The pot of religious discord periodically boils over into violence, but it always is quietly simmering. Even cities at peace feel the heat. All over India, communities that had forgotten the taste of turmoil now find their social harmony more precarious every day:

At the Friday Mosque in Delhi, across a twisty alleyway from a bloody-smocked butcher neatly stacking up pyramids of unskinned sheep heads, I heard a peppery old imam fulminate against Hindus. On the hard stone steps outside the mosque, goats and lepers were fighting each other for a meal of scavenged scraps. One woman covered from head to toe in strict black chador, her face shrouded without even an eye-slit, sat with a wooden begging bowl in her lap. Did she wear the thick purdah veil out of religious modesty, out of shame, or because her disfigurement was too horrible to be seen? A palsied hand stuck out of the black cloak, reaching for a coin that nobody bothered to drop. The men attending Friday prayers were too wrapped up in sectarian hatred to have time for a trifle like charity.

In the southern state of Kerala, not far from Trivandrum, I once walked through two little fishing villages clustered around a protected bay. One village is Hindu, the other Muslim. Both lie below a fanciful baby-blue mosque set on a high cliff, its eighteen minarets an asymmetric jumble of differing heights and diameters. Children from both hamlets, the fishermen told me, used to play together in the mosque's odd-shaped shadow. Now the Hindu children play near a muddy river on their own side of town.

On the black sand of the beach where I walked, women were laying out rows of fish tossed up by the night's storm with the hope that they would dry in the fickle sun. All the townswomen used to work side by side, Muslims giving their neighbors the fat prawns forbidden by Islamic dietary law, Hindus giving their friends some little red cuttlefish in exchange. Now the women do not trade fish. The black beach stinks of dead sea creatures for days after each storm, but the stink is not everywhere the same. Where the Hindu matrons spread their catch it smells only of prawns, where the Muslims toil it reeks only of cuttlefish.

The Ramayana has stirred up discord where none had existed. It is sad when strangers turn on strangers, but sadder still when friends turn on friends.

And yet. India is always on the brink of at least three civil wars, always has been, and somehow manages not to let it poison all aspects of life. Muslims and Hindus may be murdering each other's families in Kashmir but riding together peacefully on a train in Tamil Nadu.

There were six of us in the compartment (on one occasion I recall) when the afternoon began to die. We had been playing cards and exchanging newspapers and staring out the window and chatting sporadically about nothing much at all. It had already been a fairly long trip, and it would be much longer before we arrived.

"So then, I win, do I not?" asked a man with a quizzical look and a handful of face cards.

"No, my friend, your cards have no order," said his neighbor, "they do not add up to anything."

"But look — I have a king, two queens, a knave, and a ten."

"So what, man? That is a pair of queens and some garbage."

"Surely we should add up the tally of all the cards in the hand?"

"It does not work that way, boss. Come on, we try again."

To avoid having to play bridge, I had been teaching them poker.

"Don't worry," I said, "that's why we're playing for matchsticks."

"Hey, *babaji,* mind if I look at your copy of the *Express*?"

"You see this piece on Rajiv at the temple? You think he ever goes to a temple when there is not a cameraman following?"

The former prime minister, voted out of office a few months previously, was not the most popular man in India. His vacillation on the Babri Masjid issue had stirred distrust among Hindus and Muslims alike.

"Enough talk, boss, back to the cards."

The man with the quizzical look dealt, and we made our bets from little piles of matches on the shaky fold-up table. Trade in cards, another round of betting, then show and tell.

"Anyone beat a pair of aces?"

"Yes, yes, look at this — two knaves and two sevens."

"I have three deuces," said the dealer. "Is that better?"

"Sorry, boss, my knaves and sevens win."

"No," I said, "dealer takes the hand. Three of a kind beats two pair."

"But, my friend, they are only deuces."

"Pair, two pair, three of a kind, straight, flush, full house, four of a kind, straight flush," I repeated for at least the twelfth time. "All right, everybody in?"

When the sun sank below the edge of the earth, the man with the quizzical expression excused himself from the game. He moved to his own bunk and neatly covered the dusty fabric with a few spread newspapers. From his breast pocket he took out a compass to determine quiblah, the direction of Mecca, and got down on his knees. For six minutes he said his evening prayers, unsteadily standing, kneeling, and bowing his chest to the bench, often grabbing the support rail to keep his balance against the train's constant lurches.

For six minutes all the rest of us kept reverent silence. The four Hindus, who might well have viewed Islamic prayers on Rama's birth site as an abomination, here politely bowed their heads while the shahada was recited.

"Well, now," the quizzical man said, putting away the compass and folding up the newspapers, "Shall we get back to the game?"

"Could I have the order of hands once more, please?"

"Pair, two pair, three of a kind . . ."

➤ ➤ ➤

On my last evening in Ayodhya, I sat on the roof of Guru Baba Raghunanden Das's compound next to the hermitage at Hanuman Cave. Around five o'clock each day any friends, students, or visitors of the guru climb the crumbly mud-brick steps to savor the refreshing cool breeze. They lounge about, talk, sip tea, and bask in the mellowing rays of the setting sun. Guru Baba Raghunanden Das, the half-century hermit, cannot come up here from his home below. He can see the sun and hear the wind, but he will never again feel them on his face.

Those of us on the roof were discussing, naturally, Babri Masjid.

"What really matters," said Dr. Lohtia, a mathematics teacher in nearby Faizabad, "is not the place where you pray."

"The place?"

"Yes, the temple, the mosque, what-have-you. It makes no difference. Any filthy alleyway can be a mandir if your mind is right."

A woman who had been sitting quietly clucked her tongue. "Praying in an alley?" she said. "Surely you cannot mean that, baba."

"Yes, yes, in an alley, I tell you. Why not? Do you think that God will not hear?"

The woman shook her head but didn't presume to question. Dr. Lohtia is not only one of the guru's oldest pupils, he is also a close friend.

"What matters," he said, turning to me, "is how you treat others. Plain and simple. And it is the very same for Hindu, non-Hindu, even for those who have no belief in God at all. Be kind to others. Not very difficult, eh?"

"What about Babri Masjid?" I asked.

"You know, for the thirty years that the mosque was locked up we would worship Lord Ram right outside — quietly, side by side with the Muslims, without turning the place into a mandir all our own. Not just me, almost everyone in Ayodhya. Nobody seemed to mind until the VHP told them to stop it. After all, a house of God is a house of God."

The tongue-clucker broke her silence. "Guruji supports the temple," she said triumphantly.

"Yes, indeed he does," Dr. Lohtia replied. "But Guruji has helped each of us learn how to think. What sort of students would we be if we merely parroted his words?"

I had no standing to make a judgment, but I felt that Guru Baba Raghunanden Das had trained his pupil well. The militants on both sides of the Babri Masjid controversy are so caught up in the minutiae — whose shrine was built when and under what circumstances — that they forget the essence of their respective faiths. Love God and treat all humans with kindness (the guru preaches) — the rest of theology will follow from that. The Ramayana is not the stuff of petty bickering. It is an epic of self-sacrifice, of unbending morality, of trust, and of love.

In the courtyard down the crumbly mud steps, three old

women sat with their backs to the brick wall. They did not care about religious disputations. For most of the afternoon they had been lazily singing a simple refrain to the idle beat of a slow drum. It helped to pass the time of day. The song had only two words, two names that encapsulated every bit of theology the old women needed to know. One name was Sita, the other Ram.

"SitAA-RaaaaAAAm, SitaaaaaaAAAA-Ram! SitAAA-Raa-AAAaaaAAAm."

Two

FATE

King Dasarastha had three hundred wives, and he was passionately in love with each of them. Every time even the plainest of them (and he never could quite remember what her name was) looked him square in the eye, he turned right to butter. So when the spellbinding Kaikeyi herself whispered a request in his ear, the matter was as good as settled.

The night the king decided on Rama's enthronement he could not find Kaikeyi in her bedchamber. He searched all through the women's quarters, through the gardens, through the kitchens and hallways and down the back stairs. Finally a servant told him that the queen had retired to the Chamber of Wrath.

Every happy home needs a Chamber of Wrath. It is a place where people go when they are angry or sad, so that their sour mood does not infect the other members of the household. Perhaps it was even the Chamber of Wrath that made Ayodhya a city of harmony.

Dasarastha found his wife lying on the cold floor in a salty puddle of tears. He begged her to return to her suite, but she only cried. All Ayodhyans must be happy, she sobbed, so she had no choice but to stay. If necessary she would live in the Chamber of Wrath her whole life.

"Just tell me what you want," the king implored her. "Which murderer would you have me set free, which innocent person shall I put to death? All you have to do is ask."

Kaikeyi's tears dried up. She reminded her husband that years ago he had promised her two boons. Dasarastha was quick to renew his vow.

"Anything," he said.

When he heard her demands, the king fainted like a grandmother. Send Rama into exile for fourteen years and place

Bharata on the throne instead — it must be a bad dream, he thought, just a bad dream. But when he came out of his swoon Kaikeyi was still staring down at him with her hard, implacable, beautiful eyes.

For hours he beseeched her to release him from his foolish pledge, for hours she shamed him with volleys of scorn. He was a feeble doe that night, and she an impatient tiger. What is said can never be unsaid, what is done can never be undone. By midnight Kaikeyi could leave the room and rejoin the company of the well-contented, but the king had to stay in the Chamber of Wrath until a chamberlain arrived and reminded him it did not suit his dignity.

When the court musicians came to sing their customary bedtime eulogies to Dasarastha, the king told them to shut up, just shut up, shut up and get the hell out, all of you, and don't come back either. Tonight the hymns of praise would only turn his stomach.

In all of Ayodhya, the only person untroubled by the news was Rama himself. What's done is done, he said stoically, and did his best to cheer the others up. So widespread was the indignation that the Chamber of Wrath could not hold all the mourners, and citizens were permitted to be irate in public.

Most distraught of all was Rama's mother, Kausalya. She ripped handfuls of graying hair out of her head and tossed them on the ground, beat her fists against the room's stone walls until her knuckles oozed blood.

She threatened to take poison, to jump out a window, to cut out her heart with a table knife. When all the other queens began to tease her and make her wash their laundry, she told Rama, perhaps he'd wipe that smile off his face. "In some past life," she wailed, "surely I must have chopped off a cow's udders and starved the little calves of milk."

A man's father, Rama replied, is God on earth. There is no greater virtue than filial obedience, and no greater duty. He reminded her of the saintly rishi Kundu, who killed a cow on the orders of his father and was blessed for his unquestioning loyalty. He recalled the example of his own revered kinsman, a son of Jamadagni, who did not flinch when commanded to hack off his own mother's head with an axe. A father's word is even more binding than dharma itself.

Kausalya was not comforted by the last example, but she did cease her complaining.

Where the mother cried, the brother raged. Lakshman's powerful frame could scarcely contain his fury: his eyes bulged, his hair stood on end, and his skin tightened until it seemed about to explode.

"O Arya!" he said, for he took his bloodlines very seriously, "how can you give up your birthright so meekly? We will fight side by side to take back what is yours. The old man is tired and senile, his reason must be going — just give me the word and I will gleefully slaughter all his soldiers one by one, I'll become an enraged elephant, an invincible —"

Rama arced his smile a barely perceptible degree, and Lakshman fell silent. "Put aside your Aryan vanity, your Kshatriya pride," Rama admonished his brother. "Neither one can alter destiny. Why do you think Kaikeyi has plotted against me? She is a virtuous woman and has always loved both of us like her very own sons. She is merely the agent of fate. I am clearly destined for exile, so there is no point in spouting such hot-headed nonsense. Obey and accept: do it happily, and your burdens become blessings. In all honesty, I now prefer the forest to any kingdom."

Lakshman spat a gob of contempt on the ground. "Fate, fortune, doom, it is all for the weak," he said. "A strong man like you or me has no use for it. We make our fate, brother. I have wrestled with demigods, choked the immortal life out of demons, and you tell me to obey something I can't even see? Just let this Destiny show his head, and I'll knock it clean off his shoulders."

Rama had never been seen to laugh, and he did not do so, but his eyes glinted with amusement. "Destiny has no face to show," he replied, "but it is always there. You can follow its path with joy or with bitterness, but you will most certainly follow its path. Nobody can conquer fate, not you, not me, not the gods in heaven, not even Lord Brahma Himself."

Lakshman knew he would follow Rama to the barren reaches of the earth. His brow remained cast in a knotty frown, but he did not say another word.

Sita, however, said many words. When Rama told her that he would have to leave her behind, she did not cry, did not rage, did not throw a princessly tantrum. She simply refused.

"If you are exiled," she said, "I am exiled."

He tried to persuade her to stay in Ayodhya, reminded her that the forest is not a fit place for any well-bred woman, least of all for the daughter of a king.

"If you are exiled," she said, "I am exiled."

He reminded her of all the horrors of the jungle, of the ravenous beasts, the demons, the biting insects, the rats, the red ants that nibble on a girl's flesh during the night so she wakes up a mere skeleton.

"If you are exiled, I am exiled."

Finally, he had no choice but to command her to stay. Sita's answer was a crisp monosyllable.

"No?" said Rama in disbelief. "No? What do you mean by 'No'? The virtue of a woman is to obey her husband, just as that of a son is to obey his father. You know this."

"I would never think of arguing with you," Sita said calmly, "but I must disagree. A wife's virtue is to *help* her man, not simply to follow any foolish order he may choose to give. I can only serve you if I am with you, so I shall gladly go to the forest. When we were married, our two separate destinies were forged into one. If your fate is exile, mine is as well."

There was nothing for Rama to say.

Dasarastha was crying unkingly tears as he bade his son goodbye. It was not the guilt of his unjust act, the anger at his wife, the embarrassment at his weakness, or the shame at his loss of his people's respect. The king was crying because he knew he would never see his favorite son again.

Rama tried to cheer his father up. Bharata will be a fine ruler, he said, fourteen years isn't so very long, the forest is a beautiful place, and a vow is a vow.

"Maybe, perhaps," Dasarastha stammered, "perhaps I could send all Ayodhya into exile with you, have the workmen build an even more magnificent palace in the wilderness, let Bharata inherit an empty city, bring the, the . . ." The words trailed off when he heard how ridiculous it all sounded in the open air.

"Maybe," the king whispered, "maybe, you know, if you were to seize the throne from me, throw me in chains, what could I do, eh? Who would stop you, if you just —" Kaikeyi cut him short with a glance.

"I beg you not to worry so much," Rama said to his father. "We all must accept our fates gladly, welcome them with open hearts. It was your destiny to give the order, it is mine to obey. For my part, I take up the hermit's life with joy. I relish the chance to see the world, to bare my soul to nature, to live as man once lived so many ages ago. I pray to you, do not be sad for me, for I am not sad at all."

So Rama, Sita, and Lakshman stepped into the chariot that would take them as far as the holy Ganges. For hours after they'd departed, the old king stood gazing at the horses' footprints, until the afternoon wind came and swept the last traces away.

A king exiles his beloved son, because it is fated. A prince smiles as he gives up his throne, because it is fated. A wife gladly suffers banishment in the forest, because it is fated. Dasarastha, Rama, Sita, and the rest all understand that they are merely characters in a story written long ago. The men and women of the Ramayana know they are actors playing out their allotted roles, and an actor may perform well or badly, but can never alter the words of the Playwright.

We moderns like to believe we are the Authors of our own stories. We think our lives and our destinies are under our personal control. Indians of Rama's day and Indians of today have never shared this notion.

Fatalism, it may be argued, turns us into soulless automatons, mere cogs in the cosmic machine. But to most Indians, fate is a joy, the tie binding each person to the rest of humanity. It is proof that God cares for every single one of us, that each man and woman has a place in the eternal plan. What would be truly sad would be if there were no power shaping our lives, no blueprint to give our sufferings meaning, if each of us were alone in the universe, if we had perfect freedom and nothing to do with it but flounder in the void.

For most Indians fatalism isn't a matter of faith, just simple common sense. The idea that we determine our own fortunes isn't merely heretical, it's plainly untrue. A Bihari peasant, no matter how hard he works, is pretty well certain to remain a Bihari peasant. No amount of earnest labor will prevent the sun from withering his crops, the monsoon from sweeping away his home, the landlord from raping his wife. That is simply the way things are.

Justice generally waits until the hereafter. Hindus look forward to an interminable chain of reincarnations leading eventually to heaven, Muslims to a garden of eternal bliss, but both see in the afterlife an undying glimmer of hope. Justice may even take a dozen lifetimes to arrive, but arrive it always does. This predestined certainty makes every day bearable.

Far from breeding despair, fate lets us see life as a grand drama — a tragicomedy perhaps, part tearjerker and part farce. We read the script as it is given to us page by page, and have faith that the Author will write us out a good ending.

Or perhaps, as I found in the nearest city to Ayodhya, fate's mysteries are best described by walls instead of words.

There is a way through the Labyrinth. You might find it hard to believe, since every path you take seems to lead nowhere, but you go on searching because you know a way *must* exist. If it did not, the whole Maze would be nothing but a cruel joke. And that is something you can never accept.

The labyrinth is on the roof of the Great Imambara in Lucknow. In the late eighteenth century an outrageously extravagant ruler of the princely state of Awadh built it on the upper three stories of his palace as an entertainment for the women of his harem. Somebody has decided that the pleasure dome of a debauched nawab-wazir is hallowed ground, so you still must walk the dirt-strewn passageways barefoot.

Down twisty tunnels, up steep staircases, through portal after portal and round another bend, you walk and walk and wind up back where you started. Promising hallways lead only to dead ends. When the ceilings get lower and lower you have to duck to go on, and you feel you must be nearing your goal. You run into a blind wall and must retrace your steps in the dark. You're not even sure just what it is you're looking for, but you know you haven't found it. Perhaps there is not even anything for you to find.

Two young men were lost in the maze along with me. After we'd passed each other half a dozen times I stopped and pulled out a pack of cigarettes.

"Thanks, *bhai*," said the first man, leaning his head forward to the offered match. "Too much walking for one afternoon."

"Yes," said his friend, "and all in circles."

"Have you two been here before?"

"Oh, yes," said the first man. A large gap in his upper front teeth made most of his *s*'s whistle. "Many times. Sometimes we find our way to the balcony over the Grand Throne Room, sometimes we do not."

"But fun to try," said his friend.

Two cigarettes later, the whistler revealed that they were university students majoring in philosophy. Emboldened, I ran an idea by them.

"Perhaps," I ventured, "fate is a Borgesian labyrinth. We are perfectly free to wander through it at will, but the paths we tread are wholly determined by the walls of the maze. We can select any route we please, even change routes from time to time, but we still must follow the corridors wherever they may lead."

"Yes, indeed," said the whistler. He may have felt the analogy faintly absurd but was willing to play along. "If every road went where we desired, each of us would be a big movie star."

"But *bhai*," his friend addressed me earnestly, "we do not all have the same destiny."

"Quite true," I said, "the maze is different for every person."

"Why not just break through the walls?" said the whistler.

"Cannot be done," said his friend. "No way to alter fate, you know that. The walls of this maze," he said, turning back to me, "must be made of cast iron."

"*Invisible* iron," I said, spinning the trope out for all it was worth. "We can see the goals before us —"

"— the throne room," interjected the whistler, "the balcony, perhaps a pretty garden —"

"— more concretely," said his friend, "a good job, a beautiful wife, plenty of money, what have you —"

"— we can see the goals," I continued, "but we can't just step forward and reach them. We can't get there by a straight course — if we try we hit our nose on the thin air. We become angry and frustrated, because we do not realize we are in the maze at all. Instead, we should *feel* our way along the invisible borders, as we wind roundabout along our proper path."

Light was fading, I had no more cigarettes, and the student-philosophers had indulged me long enough. We went our separate ways back through the dusk-blackened maze of the Great Imambara.

As I edged forward with my hands outstretched to keep from

walking face first into a brick barrier, I heard muffled echoes of other people trying to find the exit before nightfall. We all stumbled along, each in his own personal Labyrinth, both blocked and guided by walls we could not see.

Fatalism is no call to inaction, no license for passivity. Even if your Maze has a clear path to the finish, you will never find it by merely sitting still. You cannot change the world, but you can — and must — change yourself. The Hindu faith places greater emphasis on an individual's actions than any other religion in the world. Christians, Muslims, and even many Buddhists see salvation as the free gift of God, bestowed on sinful humans as a reward for faith. For a Hindu, salvation can never come from outside. It is something you must build for yourself. Something you earn.

All of a person's future incarnations are determined by his or her karma, the eternal tally of good and bad deeds. By stoically accepting your destiny and following a strict code of ethics you can win rebirth as a millionaire, or perhaps as a Brahmin. If you accumulate enough good karma over the course of ages, you may even be able to escape the cycle of living altogether and reach blessed Nirvana. Fate governs your life, but ultimately you govern fate.

"It's no excuse for laziness," said a woman driving water buffaloes through the street of a town outside Lucknow. "You cannot simply say, 'If God intends me to eat I will be fed' — do you think that the food will just jump off the plate into your mouth? No, you must take it yourself, and first you must earn the money to buy it. You will never eat unless God so wills it, but do not expect Him to ladle you out a portion from the pot."

The shaggy yoke-horned buffaloes stomped about in the muddy road, their ludicrously long, floppy ears idly whisking away fat flies, their cylindrical chests rolling like hairy casks of wine. I asked if it bothered her to have to suffer for sins committed in a long-forgotten existence.

"Bothered, why?" she asked. "Who should I be angry at?"

"You see," said a pandit, who had been silently squatting on his heels in a doorway nearby, "it is her own karma that controls her life."

Belief in absolute destiny would be depressing only if it came from outside. If Hindus saw some external force dominating all their actions, perhaps they would wallow in despondency, but in their view destiny is a power inside our very souls. Faith is the search for the power each of us carries within.

The pandit pointed at a buffalo with wildly spiraling horns. "You see that animal over there?" he said, jabbing his finger at the beast. "You see how his horns are curved all the way back to his ears? It is not an uncommon condition among water buffaloes. In a year or two, if the brute is unlucky, the horns will slowly start to grow into his skull. They will gradually break through the bone and enter the brain.

"Each day the poor animal will experience more and more pain. He will bellow and roll about, and he will never understand why his head is splitting open. He has no mirror, he cannot see that the cause is his own twisted horn, his own body. Even if he did know, what could he do about it? He is the cause of his own torment, but he is powerless to end it."

The woman tickled the buffalo on its bristly forehead, and the pandit continued.

"But we humans can saw off the horn," he said, "cut it short before it causes injury. As you can see by looking at the herd, this woman has sawed off several horns here already. To the animal, it must seem like a miracle — in a little instant the ceaseless agony ceases.

"Likewise, we humans are often afflicted with woes and torments we cannot cure and cannot even understand. Every day this is so, and many good people suffer. But we believe that the torments come from within, whether the fruit of past misdeeds or the perfectly logical result of some other chain of events we could never even imagine. We pray to various devas, to dozens of divinities, beg them to ease our pains, and often they answer our prayers. That does not diminish the power of destiny, nor the power of God."

The ability to cut off a buffalo's horn does not make man a deity, does not make him the master of fate. It merely makes him stronger than a buffalo.

> > >

The legendary kingdom of Ayodhya was reborn in the eighteenth century. The name of the new state was Awadh, a variant pronunciation of Ayodhya, and its capital at Lucknow was less than a day's journey from the pilgrimage town of Rama's birth. For a time its royal court was again one of the most splendid in all India.

Other nations, both Hindu and Buddhist, have proclaimed themselves successors to the Ramayana's mythical empire. The kingdom of Ayutthaya, one of the most magnificent civilizations in Southeast Asia, took its name from the Siamese form of "Ayodhya." Scores of monarchs from Angkor to Annam and from Bangkok to Bali — including every ruler of Thailand for the past two hundred years — have grandly assumed the appellation of "Rama." But because Awadh physically occupied the very same lands described in the epic, it always had a special claim to the Ramayanic mantle. That may not have meant much to the Muslim overlords, but this symbolism gave the Hindu peasantry a deep feeling of pride.

I went to Lucknow to look for this history. Ayodhya's last living incarnation, its final earthly avatar, passed away just before the American Civil War. Perhaps there were still traces of it in the air, ghosts lingering among the recently deserted pavilions and pleasure domes.

The one-time capital of Awadh still wears an aura of seedy decadence, like a flashy royal cape trimmed with rabbit skin instead of ermine, stitched with tinsel instead of gold lace. Lucknow was always a place of lofty dreams never realized, of promise gone to pot.

The Great Imambara is great in size only. It is a gaudy, jerry-built mass of cheap brick and flaking plaster, but it is indeed large. Its audience chamber is painted a sickly shade of green, as if the palace itself were nauseated by its own decrepitude. Like most of the old buildings in town it was slapped up with regal impatience, abandoned with regal impatience. As one visitor wrote in the *Calcutta Review* of 1855: "It is the same everywhere in Lucknow. Money is paid for the palaces. The palaces crumble. Money is paid for the mosque. It has no readers, no teachers, no services, no books. Money is paid for the tombs. All that is not dirt in them is cob web."

Downstairs from the maze and through a few arches is the Bouli, a vast octagonal pit that, it is said, has no bottom at all. It is also said that a monarch named Asaf ad-Daulah used to toss architects who displeased him into the pit, their limbs weighed down with chunks of shoddy masonry torn from the palace walls. Nobody can see the dead architects who may lurk at the Bouli's bottomless bottom, submerged in a pool of algaed water thick as hearty bean soup, floating in the palace's flooded foundation.

Jami Masjid, the city's central mosque, looks more like a fortress than a house of worship. It was constructed by a shah named Muhammad Ali, and now it is empty even of spirits. Old men come for Friday prayers, but they do not spend their weekday afternoons languishing in the cavernous shade here. The green, yellow, and red archway sheds flakes of timeworn stucco with every rustle of the breeze. A sign posted at each entrance calls out in half-hearted approximation of English, "Non Muslem ys nt Alao." There was nobody around to stop me, but I did not enter. It seemed wrong for someone nt Alao to break the rules simply because there weren't any guards or ghosts to enforce them.

The ruins of the old British Residency are a public park now, a quiet place to have a picnic. A freshly painted placard warns visitors that out of consideration for others, they must not bring their camels or elephants inside. Four decades after Independence, the graves of the fallen Britons are still kept tidy by peasant women with rusty weed clippers.

The most prominent monument in the sprawling site is a soaring cross raised "In Memory of Major General Sir Henry Lawrence KCB & the Brave Men who Fell . . . ," etc., etc. Lawrence, the last Resident, was fatally wounded by an artillery shell just two days into the 1857 Sepoy Mutiny, which ended the East India Company's existence. His bones do not lie under the towering crucifix. They rest in an inconspicuous corner of the cemetery beneath a plain stone slab with a poignant epitaph he composed himself:

> *Here lies Henry Lawrence*
> *Who Tried to do his duty*
> *May the Lord have Mercy on his Soul*

The Residency graveyard was where Awadh died. It was here that the independent state was annexed. Lawrence's twin tombstones would be an apt commemorative for the whole kingdom: a pompous, grandiloquent memorial for posterity, overshadowing a pathetic little grave that holds the true body.

I felt nothing of epic glory in Lucknow. What I felt instead was a looming pall of decay, a mood more true to the city's actual past. From its start the princely state was destined to fall, an edifice doomed to collapse by its slipshod construction.

. . .

The history of Awadh shows the cruelty of fortune. Though blessed with a richness of soil, population, and resources that was the envy of neighboring principalities, the resurrected Ayodhya could only stagger from one indignity to the next. Her proudest years were also her most pathetic ones. For seven decades powerless tyrants ruled with stingy munificence, under the vigilantly blind eyes of foreign Residents who were not there. There was no good reason for it to be so, and yet so it was, always, year after pitiful year. Despite all the palaces and lavish processions, Awadh seemed predestined for failure.

When the Massachusetts Minutemen fired their famous shot heard round the world in 1775, the newly enthroned Asaf ad-Daulah, sitting almost directly around the world from Lexington, did not hear it. That morning he was busy vomiting into a large metal basin.

In point of fact, Asaf spent nearly every morning vomiting into a large metal basin, because he spent nearly every evening stupefying himself with liquor and opium. All night long, puffing and puffing on his long-stemmed pipe, watching the thick, black, gluey wad bubble and melt, sucking the green vapors deep into his brain, watching the welcome monsters chase each other in and out and in and out of his twisting, twirling, spiraling dreams.

When a court chronicler wrote of Asaf's reign, he prefaced his account with the note "I do not intend to record the wazir's faults, for my book would grow bulky indeed." Like most of Awadh's rulers, Asaf was not an evil man, he simply had no interest whatsoever in governing his country. Every decision was left to corrupt favorites, rapacious aristocrats, and the profit-minded proconsuls of the East India Company.

It was Asaf's father, the founder of the dynasty, who had invited the English in. He had promised them fifty lakhs of rupees to fight a war on his behalf, and the debt loomed for the rest of the kingdom's existence. No succeeding ruler could be bothered to pay it back. Year after year the British had to be bought off with chunks of sovereignty, slices of privilege, parcels of land, and insincere pledges of ever-greater sums of money.

Sometimes destiny is anything outside one's control. A crushing debt incurred by a chain of irresponsible monarchs kept in power by a meddlesome foreign army — ordinary citizens suffered great misery from each of these factors but had no way of altering their condition. Year after pitiful year, they could only watch their rulers' outrageous antics and resign themselves to the will of fate.

Asaf willingly turned the English mercenary force into a permanent garrison. They were expensive, yes, but unlike his own troops they could shoot straight. Defended from any military threat, the wazir was free to indulge his wasteful fantasies. He paid out one million rupees per year to build a string of huge, slapdash mansions, each of which he occupied for less than a week before abandoning it forever. Court records show that he employed 4,000 men simply to tend his flower gardens. But most of all, he bought animals.

He owned 3,000 horses, of which only 500 were fit to bear a saddle. Of his 1,200 elephants, only 400 were not dangerous rogues. He kept 1,000 dogs, of which only 100 were trained for hunting, and a full 300,000 pigeons and fighting cocks, for no discernible purpose at all. As the chronicler tartly noted, "All things are fondly cared for by the wazir, save man."

To pay for his extravagances Asaf stiffed all public servants of their salaries and withheld the wages of his riffraff native soldiers. Which only made matters worse. Even those officials who were honest had to resort to corruption simply to feed their families, and the nawabi army became an undisciplined mob of bandits. Elite Company troops could not legally be used to collect taxes, so fewer and fewer people bothered to pay. When the unsalaried soldiers could be coaxed into action, they lived by plunder and extortion. "They burn peasants' houses at night simply for illumination," wrote one observer, "but the subjects are so accustomed to oppression that they reckon this tyranny nothing."

Toward the end of a thoroughly dissolute reign, Asaf began to worry about his succession. There were numerous children running about the palace, but none were of royal blood. All Lucknow knew the nawab was completely impotent. Perhaps it was the opium that sapped Asaf's virility, but a British consul speculated that it was the ruler's phenomenal obesity. Such a colossal belly, the scientific Brit mused, must necessarily make the procreative act a logistic impossibility.

Whatever the cause, Asaf decided to take what he could not make. He sent his retainers into the countryside to kidnap pregnant women for his harem, then claimed their offspring as his own. Nobody was fooled. On the old nawab's death an alleged "son" tried to claim the throne, but he was quickly laughed into house arrest. After all, Asaf himself had once shouted to his whole court that the boy had been sired by a laundryman.

Asaf was succeeded by his younger brother, Sadat Ali. The East India Company was pleased to give its blessing and support — for twenty-six additional lakhs of rupees each year. Where Asaf had been profligate, weak, and irresponsible, Sadat was thrifty, strong, and conscientious. All to no avail. In 1801 an impatient governor-general forced Sadat to cede one half of the country's land, territory bringing in 135 lakhs a year, to the Company in lieu of the unpayable subsidy. Awadh seemed divinely fated for tragedy; not even a ruler of atypical competence could halt the unfolding of destiny.

The British persuaded Sadat's son Ghazi-ud-din to renounce his title of nawab-wazir to the farcical Mughal emperor and to take on the equally farcical title of shah for himself. When requesting the recognition of fellow monarch King George IV, this new emperor politely sent presents worth 100,000 pounds sterling. The British ruler sent a horse and saddle in return. An opium addict like his uncle and his son, Ghazi could only peek out of his curtained window to watch his country's decline. His name means "Holy Warrior."

Ghazi's son Nasir did his best to squander what little money remained in the palace vaults and what little loyalty remained in the people's hearts. It was not merely his enslavement to drug and drink, for a king was entitled to his entertainment. Nasir simply did not give a damn for his subjects and made no effort to hide his contempt. He dressed only in European clothes, lounged only on European furniture, even imported a barber from France to perfume his hair daily.

This French barber, named de Russet, soon became the most powerful man in Lucknow. Nasir was completely under his spell. All the ministers, clerks, and courtiers, any person who needed an audience with the king, had to see the barber first. As one disgruntled diplomat said, "It was very perceptible that the hero of the curling-tongs was, in fact, the real ruler."

De Russet knew his master's taste for cruel practical jokes, and he indulged it with glee. At a formal state dinner he once stripped the king's uncle naked and poured cold water over the old man's head. Another time he got a venerable aristocrat blind drunk and tied his flowing beard to the leg of a chair. Each morning, as soon as they were sufficiently sober, the king and the barber would plot their evening's pranks while the scissors snipped and the water pipe bubbled.

The country withered in neglect. Brutal tax-farmers, who had paid enormous bribes for their positions in expectation of future graft, bled the peasants without any fear of rebuke. Warlords carved out their own private bailiwicks. Law did not exist.

Normally such anarchy could never have lasted. Somebody with the strength (and the desire) to govern would have seized the throne and brought Awadh a measure of order. But under the terms of the 1801 treaty, Company troops protected the ruler from any possible coup, cutting off the only natural means of reform. The bureaucrats in Calcutta knew this but couldn't think of any way out. One surviving memo candidly admits, "Had it not been for our connexion with Oudh [Awadh], oppression and disorder, although they might have attained as great a height, could not have been of equal duration."

Nasir did not care that his throne was propped up by the tips of foreign bayonets. The British were like opium. They would make all your worst problems melt right away, but once you started using them you could never stop.

At his death Nasir left no treasury and no heir. An uncle took the crown, under the proud name of Muhammad Ali, but the new shah was not a fighter. A frail, elderly man, he bargained away the bare facade of sovereignty to assure British support. "I hereby declare that in the event of my being placed on the throne," reads a statement drafted for him by a zealous consul, "I will agree to sign any new treaty that the governor-general may dictate."

It was too humiliating even for the flint hearts at the Company. The Court of Directors rejected both this abject oath of submission and the onerous treaty dictated by the governor. It was a stroke of mercy, but it did not matter. Humiliation was the fate of Awadh, no act of man could change that. The governor-general was so embarrassed at being overruled that he did not let anyone know of the directors' decision. Neither the shah nor the succeeding governors ever learned of it, and twenty years later the British Resident still believed the pact to be in effect.

Muhammad Ali was too sickly to govern by himself but too suspicious to entrust any minister with real power. He went through no fewer than seven viziers during his five-year reign. His son, Umjid Ali, maintained the dynasty's traditional ineffectuality, not through hedonism or feebleness but through religious bigotry. Awadh was a state populated by Hindus, administered by Muslims, lorded over by Englishmen. Umjid Ali not only refused to deal with anyone who wasn't a Muslim, he had no use even for any Muslim who didn't belong to his own Shi'a sect. Death came to him as medicine, through a poisoned salve on an ulcerous shoulder.

The last ruler of Awadh was India's own Nero. Not so cruel, perhaps, but nearly as depraved. According to his hookah bearer, Shah Wajid Ali "spent all his time in dancing and singing and fiddling — sometimes in female, sometimes in male attire, surrounded by his wives and favorite eunuchs." He chose as his chief minister a corrupt, reactionary drunkard whom he'd met in a brothel. The opium and the wine scarcely need be mentioned — by this time they'd all but replaced the orb and scepter as recognized emblems of royalty.

Two years after Wajid's ascension a new Resident made a tour of the nation. Colonel William Sleeman was certainly the most capable Briton ever to set foot in Awadh. Fluent in Hindi, Urdu, and Bengali, well versed in India's culture, history, and religions, Sleeman had a far better understanding of the people's needs than did the sycophants of Lucknow or the account balancers of Calcutta. He had recently succeeded, almost singlehandedly, in breaking the back of the bloodthirsty Thugee cult that had terrorized all northern India with its ritual murder and human sacrifice. Today, in the state of Madhya Pradesh, there is a town named Sleemanabad. At a small temple there, an eternally tended flame still burns in his memory.

What Sleeman found should not have come as a surprise to anybody. Awadh's body politic was rotting from head to foot. The extent of the decay shows in the fractions: one quarter of the state revenue was routinely embezzled by petty local bureaucrats before it reached the king's countinghouse, another quarter was siphoned off by palace chamberlains. Anyone doing business with the government had to give corrupt clerks a standardized kickback of one third of the value of the transaction. Half the expenditure for the shah's army went to royal favorites and holders of sinecures. Price rigging and graft tripled the price of every building project.

If life in Lucknow was chaotic, existence in the countryside was positively Hobbesian. Provincial fief-holders turned into lawless warlords; they spent their money building fortresses rather than prisons, and criminals went wholly unpunished. Often the most vicious criminals were these princelings themselves. One potentate took great pleasure in smearing the beards of his peasants with moistened gunpowder, waiting until the saltpeter dried, and then lighting the men's whiskers to watch their heads explode.

In the capital itself, jails existed only to fill the wardens' purses. Any thief or killer inept enough to be arrested would walk free after paying a small bribe. Each year Wajid spent 2 million rupees more than he took in, and only 577 rupees went for law enforcement.

Colonel Sleeman presented his findings and laid out a clear-sighted, comprehensive blueprint for reform. His plan might have saved Awadh from her rulers, but it was not fated to be. It was too extreme for Wajid and not extreme enough for the Company. In a truly prophetic statement, Sleeman warned his superiors that "the annexation of Oudh would cost the British power more than the value of ten such kingdoms, and would inevitably lead to a mutiny of the sepoys."

In the Ramayana, destiny blinds its victims to the truth. The Demon King Ravana (whom we shall meet before long) is warned by his own brother that his villainies will bring him death. He knows his path leads to destruction, but he follows it anyway. It is his fate, he has no choice. The English also ignored clear omens: every Cassandra's curse is to be right and to not be believed. Seven years after Sleeman's admonition, Calcutta annexed Awadh, the sepoy soldiers of Britain's Indian army did indeed mutiny, and the East India Company itself was dissolved. They stumbled down their predestined course with eyes wide open, never seeing a thing.

All during Sleeman's term, the governor-general very much wanted to gobble the country up. A mean-minded, sharp-tempered peer, the Earl of Dalhousie was not fond of compromise. As he saw it, Awadh's government was beyond salvation. Britain could either abandon the kingdom entirely or take it over, and he was hardly a man to cut his losses. He tried long and hard to provoke Wajid into some action that could be grounds for annexation, but the shah cannily refused to take any action whatsoever. The best defense was complete inertia — a state that suited Wajid to perfection. Dalhousie complained in a letter home, "The king won't offend or quarrel with us, and will take any amount of kicking without being rebellious."

The governor's needling finally paid off. An English brigadier was attacked by his Indian troops when he rudely interfered
with a procession celebrating the holiest of all Shi'a festivals.
On February 8, 1856, the Earl of Dalhousie was able to write,
"Our gracious Queen has 5,000,000 more subjects and 1,300,000
pounds more revenue than she had yesterday."

Barely a year later Lucknow became the epicenter of the
Great Mutiny, perhaps the worst tragedy in British colonial history. The Residency compound was besieged, and during the
interminable months of grinding attrition, two out of every
three people inside met their deaths. When the British gained
the upper hand, they punished all rebellious sepoys by tying
them to the mouths of their cannons and firing bloody salutes.

Wajid Ali Shah was sent into exile in Bengal with his eunuchs
and his hookahs and his crates of women's clothing. He lived
out his life a forgotten pensioner in a foreign land, always plot-
ting his triumphal return, always knowing it was not destined
to happen.

So ended the days of the last prince of Ayodhya. So passed
the last shadow of Rama's legendary empire.

Lucknow is no longer a place of wild escapades. It is a city
where sober Shi'ites do their marketing with straight faces,
where nobody wonders what will happen next. The plastery
palaces are still there, but they are haunted by no ghosts. The
impotent lecher Asaf ad-Daulah does not shake the walls of the
Great Imambara or the Rumi Darwaza with his elephantine
tread. The Hussainabad Imambara's marble floors and garish
chandeliers do not reverberate with the dry, hacking cough of
the invalid monarch Muhammad Ali. In its audience chamber
the nawabs' step-throne of polished silver is empty even of
phantasms.

One of the quickly discarded summer mansions contains a
gallery with portraits of the rulers of Awadh. They are all here,
in faded oils: fat Asaf, leaning his hand on a chair to remain
upright; Ghazi-ud-din, preposterous in the ermine-trimmed
robe and crown he adopted when he turned from nawab to
king; Umjid Ali, eyes glaring with the contempt of narrow
faith; transvestite Wajid, so obese as to be nearly circular, here
wearing a man's ballooning pantaloons.

Nobody visits the picture gallery. I had to wake up a care-
taker who was curled asleep in a closet and put some rupees in

his palm to get the lights turned on. Nobody remembers the wazirs, he said, they're too busy with other things. Across the street is a big billboard with the advertisement: "Cenza — The Most Expensive Television Money Can Buy."

But Lucknow is still a city of gardens — laced with too many concrete walkways, cut up by too many ungainly playgrounds, but gardens nonetheless. Every spring the pampered flower beds of Asaf ad-Daulah burst once more into bloom.

> > >

On a train from Lucknow to Jhansi I sat in one of the seats that face backward rather than forward. From this position the view of the countryside isn't as good, but it's more true. The only scenery visible is what's left behind, with not even a glimpse of what lies ahead. One thunders down the track blind, seeing only the past and never the future.

Trains make a hollow, clanking sound when they go over a bridge. I always look up when I hear this clanking, crane my neck out the window to watch the women washing their crimson saris in the muddy brown water, watch the men casting hand-sewn nets for bony little fish, watch the children splashing about as if their lives had never been troubled by a shadow of pain.

On a bridge just beyond Kanpur, an hour or so out of Lucknow, I looked out on the holy Ganges for the first time. I saw five corpses floating in the slow, stately current, all of them face down, all bloated and bleached ghastly white, only one large enough to be that of a full-grown man.

I asked one of my fellow passengers why.

"Why are there bodies floating in the Ganges?" he said. We had been talking about fate for the better part of an hour, and he wasn't sure whether the conversation had suddenly switched to scenery.

"Why are *they* bobbing in the river and *we* watching them from the reserved compartment of an express train," I said.

"Who can say why? That is just the way it is."

He watched the dead drift downstream, toward what destination nobody could know.

"It's like the railway," he said. "Life, I mean. Just like the railway. You can buy a ticket for whichever train you like, but your choices are limited by the timetable. You can never go anywhere that they haven't laid down tracks — even if you had all the money in the world you could not get to, say, Khajuraho by train. It just could not happen.

"Even when you follow the timetable, the train will most likely be delayed, and there is nothing you can do about it. What can you do, eh? You are not the engineer! You have no choice, you simply sit in your seat and wait. You just be patient, and eventually you will reach your destination. You are only a passenger on the train, not the conductor."

He crinkled up his broad nose. "And wherever you go," he said, "the second-class compartments will smell of urine."

Are Indians fatalists because they cannot change their lives, or can they not change their lives because they are fatalists? Chicken or egg, *bhai,* chicken or egg, how can you answer that one, eh?

In the elite cosmopolitan spheres of Bombay and Calcutta, fate is a four-letter word. Professors and professionals don't like to think about it, seem faintly embarrassed that so many of their countrymen still cling passionately to a notion so out of step with the modern age. Predestination isn't really a part of Hindu belief, they say, the West just has this tired old image of passive, hopeless Indians — and besides (they add with a raised forefinger) you Christians have your John Calvin, your Saint Augustine, your Martin Luther.

Yes, I reply, but here people still really believe in it.

If the Indians did not have this belief they might be a little bit happier, and a great deal more sad. It comforts those who have few comforts in life, sustains a nation that has much to bear. It turns all mishaps and hard times into pieces of a divine jigsaw puzzle, a puzzle that really does fit together perfectly in the end. It lets every street sweeper and beggerwoman feel linked to the rest of Creation, for the crux of the credo is that nobody acts alone.

In the big cities, all that is changing. Not so fast as the secular elite would like to think, but changing nonetheless. For the first time in centuries, perhaps for the first time ever, Indians really can alter their lives. There has always been a limited degree of social mobility: a man running away from his village to establish a new identity, a woman marrying above her station and hiding her past, a tough, lower-caste clan gaining enough muscle to call itself Kshatriya nobility and paste all who objected.

But never before could anybody, just anybody, dream wonderful dreams.

The worst part about dreaming is the part where you wake up. It is theoretically possible for any butcher's son to become a rocket scientist, but very few actually do. Even in Bombay. A typical bazaar-wallah's life is no better, but he has that aching thought in the back of his skull that perhaps it should be. The possibility taunts him, laughs in his face as he slices the white fat from the greasy lamb shank. Of course it's possible, just look at the stories on television, at the movies, look at that runny-nosed kid down the alley who got a scholarship to medical school. The misery in life is not there as part of a divine plan, it's just there.

India is starting to trade stagnation and peace of mind for opportunity and frustration. The same is true in many other Third World countries, but nowhere is the exchange more clear-cut. When old women complain about Westernization, moan that their grandchildren are growing up like little Americans, this is what lies at the heart of their grumbles. It's easy to see what one gains from modernity: the TV sets, the waterproof tin roofs, the medicines that work like powerful magic. It's more difficult to see what one gives up.

There is nothing shameful about being a butcher. Or a street sweeper, a rickshaw-puller, a woman who scoops cow dung off the street with her bare hands. At least, there had been no shame until now. If a person's station in life is predestined it can bring no dishonor. But if one controls one's own fate, poverty becomes a mark of failure. It virtually becomes a sin.

Opportunity makes honest work seem disreputable. If anyone at all can become a business tycoon, what does that say about the janitors and busboys? Americans look down on menial labor because we're told that we can. We deem work at McDonald's demeaning, barely even fit for teenagers, certainly a disgrace for any capable adult. There are, of course, no McDonald's in India. But if there were (perhaps serving beefless lamburgers), they would never be short of willing fry-cooks.

Oddly enough, America's message — that earnest effort will bring success — is itself rooted in fatalism. The Protestant work ethic owes much to John Calvin's predestinarian belief in a small core of God's chosen elect on earth. The elect must be industrious, Calvin said, simply because it is their inherent nature; they must be materially well off, not as a result of their labor, but as a divine symbol of their election. Over the course of three centuries this evolved into the Horatio Alger myth that anybody can get ahead by simple gumption and elbow grease. This myth, true or false (for not all myths are falsehoods), has become the myth of America. From the New World to the Third World the idea has spread, perhaps the purest form of secular free will ever expressed.

It is an exhilarating concept, but a cruel one. Freedom creates winners, but losers as well. For every banker, broker, or lawyer there will be ten people to clean their clothes, mow their lawns, drain their septic tanks. "The poor," Christ said, "are always with us." Alger's book *Acres of Diamonds* urged the poor to gather up wealth in bushels, but said nothing to those who couldn't find a basket. A diamond is not only the most brilliant of stones, it is also the hardest and most cutting.

India is a poor country, and fate is a comforting doctrine. It lets bent-backed rice farmers and bent-backed garbage pickers maintain their dignity. In a Western, free-will view, society's untouchables have only themselves to blame. They're lazy, we say, they're stupid, they're incompetent, they have no get-up-and-go. But in the Hindu view, a man is not a failure for quietly doing the job he was born to do. In fact, he could be no greater success.

All over Asia, people take extraordinary pride in very ordinary work. Rickshaw-peddlers in Mandalay, dumpling-folders in Penang, sari stitchers in Lahore, they carry on their trades with religious zeal. Like the shoe-wallah in Delhi who saved my sole:

I met him among the airy colonnaded rings of Connaught Circus, among the throng of book vendors who spread their virtually identical stocks of bootleg English paperbacks across the pavement. Since India is not party to international copyright agreements, I stepped over copies of Dale Carnegie's *How to Win Friends and Influence People* stacked next to editions of a locally produced sequel, *How to Win Girls and Influence Women*. The most popular books are pirated potboilers by Jackie Collins and Danielle Steele, most with covers featuring the same scantily clad blond bombshell. One stall had a pinup calendar identifying the model as pop singer Samantha Fox in her previous incarnation as a porn queen. In India there is no escaping past lives.

When walking in the Circus I would always look down to avoid tripping over book vendors, fruit vendors, betel vendors, beggars, fortune-tellers, and shoe-wallahs. In Delhi there seem to be more people who shine and repair shoes than people who actually wear them. When a weasely-looking man tapped me on the shoulder to tell me that my shoes were stained, I chased him away: Connaught Circus con men know more tricks than you can imagine, and one of their favorites is to daub ketchup (or worse) on your shoes and then clean it off for a fee.

I found a nearby shoe-wallah who scraped the sticky mess off. He went about his business glumly, and I couldn't blame him. After all, he spent each day squatting in the dirt, pleading passersby to let him polish their footwear for two or three rupees a shot. Several weeks of route-marching had worn a large hole in the sole of my right shoe, and I asked him to repair it.

"I am not repairing," he said with a scowl, "Only polish. My brother can fix."

He took me down a back street to another colonnade where his brother was camped out on the sidewalk, then hurried back to his own spot.

"Oh, now why you wait so long to fix?" asked the brother shoe-wallah, shaking his head. "This hole goes straight through, you can stick your toe right out!"

This was not news to me. I gave him my shoes and stood barefoot on the strip of cardboard he'd set down.

"Look, look," he said, sticking his thumb through the worn leather, "Peek-a-boo! But not to worry, I can fix. Good as brand-new."

He went to work. Rummaging through piles of odds and ends around him for materials, he rebuilt the shoes from the bottom up. First he ripped off the old soles with a rusty pliers and cut new ones from the remains of a blown-out tire. He smeared out paste with a grubby forefinger, waited for it to dry just enough, scrounged about for twisted hobnails, and battered them straight with an old steel pestle. To make the heels level he glued chips of cardboard under the rubber, each chip cut to just the right thickness. He banged in the second-hand nails with a homemade hammer. He triple-stitched a gap in the leather uppers with a long, well-used tailor's needle. Finally he sharpened his matte knife by scraping it on the slate pavement and expertly trimmed away any excess tread. As he worked, he hummed a cheerily tuneless song.

"See!" he said triumphantly, "just like new!" And, appearance aside, it was.

The whole thing took forty-five minutes. We'd agreed on the price beforehand, so he could easily have slapped on a quick patch and been done. I asked him where he'd learned his craft.

"My father teach me," he said. "For years he did sit here, where I sit now, and I kneel beside him to help. I learn everything from him."

"Did you ever want to do anything else?"

"Do another job? Why should I? This is the job my father taught me. I do it well, eh, *baba*? Build the shoes like new. I do not know how to do other things, so why think of another job?"

"Don't you ever wonder?"

"I tell you something," he said. "You saw my younger brother, who cleaned your shoes. He does not like to be a shoeman. He want to be a truck driver, go all over the country. But he cannot pay for driving school, can only ask his friends to teach him a little bit. Who will hire him? So he has to work, has to be a shoe-man all the same. Still he does not like it, but what can he do? Me, I have always been a shoe-man, I am meant to be a shoe-man, and that, I say, is good enough."

> > >

Why have people always felt that the stars control our lives? Humans all over the earth have looked to the sky for guidance — from Babylon to Beijing to the Reagan White House. The marriage of Rama and Sita could not be celebrated until the heavens were auspicious, and to this day few Indians will schedule a wedding or any other important event without first consulting an astrologer. Up-to-date Americans don't believe in all that, of course, but we check our horoscopes just the same.

Perhaps the answer lies in the firmament. From certain places on earth, like the bare, cold Nubian desert or the steamy South Indian plain, the heavens still look as they must have looked when the world was just born. One stares up at the sky and understands why the ancients were drawn to astrology. The stars fairly scream for attention, far too loud to be ignored. The Egyptian writer Naguib Mafouz once speculated that God created the stars' brilliance to direct man's gaze upward.

The stars above Madurai (a city near the subcontinent's southern tip) are as brilliant as any I've seen — only fitting for one of

India's holiest pilgrimage sites. The town's gargantuan temple is dedicated to the goddess Meenakshi, a princess who was born with three perfect breasts. It was prophesied that the extra mammary would disappear when she met the man she was destined to marry, and sure enough, as soon as Meenakshi set eyes on the god Shiva, her third breast melted away. The temple at Madurai has been the haunt of seers and prophesiers ever since it was built.

In the afternoon, when the inner sanctum is closed, the fortune-tellers are the only people awake. Pilgrims and penitents, holiday-makers and holy men, all are stretched out flat for their two o'clock nap. I wandered the cavernous chambers and labyrinthine corridors alone, gazing up at the wildly painted ceilings, counting the nine hundred–odd pillars in the Thousand-Pillared Hall.

The first man who told my destiny worked strictly by the numbers. He asked me the date, year, and time of my birth, did a few calculations with a sliver of pencil on a shred of old newspaper, and came up with the timetable of my life. If he is to be believed, I will get married in the next four to seven years, have two children, reach the pinnacle of my success between the ages of thirty-two and forty-nine, and die just before senility sets in, five and a half decades from now. "Excepting," he cautioned, "that you do not engage in some sort of dangerous adventure, in which case I cannot guarantee you any great length of life."

How could he forecast my future with such mathematical specificity? Quite simple, he said, once one knows the rules. Every person's destiny is partly established at the moment of birth, by the alignment of the planets. Just as the moon's gravity invisibly affects the earth's tides, other celestial bodies invisibly affect people's inherent natures and fortunes. The laws that govern this phenomenon are no more complex or mysterious than the laws of physics or chemistry, but to the uninitiated both seem incomprehensible. It has nothing to do with karma, dharma, or any other religious concept. Astrology is not a faith, practitioners insist, it is a science.

That is not to downplay the role of karma: no good Hindu would deny that every action has its inevitable reward or punishment. But the course of karma is seldom easy to predict, while my astrologer boasted a success rate of 80 percent. What pandit can say as much?

Across the street from Meenakshi Mandir is another ancient

temple, which sometime in the past few centuries was turned into a surreal bazaar. Vendors hawk copper kitchen utensils and iron frying pans beneath towering stone statues that would be the envy of any museum. The Thousand-Pillared Hall is filled with a hundred tailors, all busily working antique foot-pedal sewing machines. A public road cuts right through the center of the building, and cars, motorbikes, and rickshaws constantly zip through with horns blazing. In one corner a squinting man sharpens scissors, knives, and machetes on a granite grindstone as red sparks leap up to the cobweb-shrouded deities on the ceiling. Nobody seems to mind conducting profane business in a place that was once holy. After all, if lived properly, ordinary existence itself is a sacrament.

Beneath the bazaar's arches another soothsayer read my character in the palm of my hand. He poked and pinched each of my fingers, the mound below the thumb, the muscle just above the wrist, and hummed to himself before delivering each pronouncement.

"Hmm," he said, "you like to learn new things, seek out new experiences, you are a very good judge of character."

Okay, who could argue?

"Hmm, your mind is always searching for new challenges, you have a passion for exploration and travel."

An easy guess — I *was* in India, after all.

"Hmm, you had a temporarily disabling accident in your late adolescence, but now enjoy excellent health."

Well, I *had* been on crutches much of freshman year . . .

"Hmmmmm," he scolded, "your principal flaw is that you are too fond of the ladies. You must be careful of this, but it is not uncommon in a young man such as yourself."

That really wasn't his business, but I let it go. I asked him how he could decipher personality traits from palm lines.

"Not very difficult," he said. "One merely reads the correct lines for life, love, money, all the rest. The answer is written right in your own flesh, if only you know how to interpret it."

How do the signs get there?

"Well, at the time of birth, the stars pull a baby in certain directions. You know this, it is a matter of science. These stellar forces carve their imprints in the baby's brain, and the brain paints clues in the palm of the hand. Why does this happen, who can say? Perhaps God lets us know a bit about our futures to help us live our lives the way we should."

Can we alter what is written?

"Change your fate, the fate to which you have been born? No, my friend, this cannot be done. It is inside us at birth. Some men will grow six feet tall, some will lose their hair early in life, some have blue or gray eyes instead of brown — can anyone control these things? Of course not. And it is not only our bodies that are destined in this way, but our minds and our souls as well. One man is blessed with a powerful physique, another is born with a clear pathway to government office. Cannot change your fate, but by knowing it you can be prepared."

I did not tell him that in the West we have anabolic steroids and silicone implants, violet contact lenses and Minoxidil. We brazenly refuse to accept fate's sway even over our physical frames. Perhaps we truly succeed in fooling destiny. Or perhaps it is not destiny that is being fooled.

On a beach near the Keralan village of Kovalam, weighty issues like destiny seem worlds away. The sand is fine and white, the waves are clear and warm, and out at sea the wooden fishing boats bob lazily like gulls resting between dives. The palm trees' rustle is disturbed only by the calls of women and young girls hawking pineapples, watermelons, bananas, and oranges, balancing the fruit on their heads as they pace up and down the shore.

But even Kovalam has its reminders of mortality. Every morning the beach is blanketed with the carcasses of crabs, shrimp, squid, and glittering silver fishes, all cruelly cast up by the night tide to choke and gasp and try to flop toward the ocean before the dawn comes and their lungs explode. The remains of a score of sea snakes litter the sand as well, each one trailing a string of bright pink intestines plucked out by hungry birds.

I was sitting on the beach drinking feni, a fiery local liquor distilled from fermented cashew nuts, when a little man with a big bird cage came out of the palms and promised to tell me things no other soothsayer could say. He asked fifteen rupees — a little less than a dollar — and I offered him twenty if he would explain all his cards beforehand.

His tarot deck was homemade, each card bearing the image of a god or goddess. Some had been cut from books or magazines, some emblazoned with window decals, some painstakingly painted by hand. Each was hidden in a little paper sheath. The fortune-teller took them out one by one.

Propitious cards included Rama and Sita ("harmonious marriage, a joyous family life"); Lakshmi, the goddess of wealth and consort of Vishnu ("get lots of money, become the rich, rich man"); Lord Vishnu himself ("power and success, *baba*"); Meenakshi, with her three breasts ("learning and education"); a mosque ("piety, godliness"); the blue baby Krishna caught with his hand in the milk jug ("healthy, strong children, many of them, and *sons!*"); Rama's faithful friend Hanuman the ape ("loyalty, pure devotion"); and round-bellied, elephant-headed Ganesh ("all good luck, all the best of every good thing, cannot ask for better").

But not every card was a lucky one. There was the bloody-mouthed goddess Kali, consort of Shiva the Destroyer, garlanded with fresh skulls ("oh, not a good sign at all, you know, very, very bad indeed"); there was Durga as well, another manifestation of the same divinity, lips curved in a serene smile as she went about her slaughter ("likewise, grave misfortune and unhappiness, no way to avoid").

Half a dozen cards showed Christian figures, and almost all were bad news. I wasn't surprised to see Christian and Hindu images intermingled — after centuries of Nestorian and Portuguese influence, Kerala still has large numbers of Christians; in a clearing below the palms, not far above the high-tide line, stands a squat stone crucifix like a gray fire hydrant, decked with yellow flowers just like a Hindu icon. But I was surprised to see Jesus Himself ranked as a symbol of hopeless woe.

"Just look, my friend," said the prophesier, "look at the pain in his face. He is bleeding, with the thorns pressed into his skull."

What about the Pietà? "The mother holding her dead son and weeping, a sign that you will lose a child too early."

And a crucifixion: "Such pain, he dies slowly, nailed to the cross like a beggarman. If you pick this card, you will die in poverty."

Still, not all is misery. The image of the Madonna and Child is a fortunate one indeed: "Ah, happy family, beautiful mother with her fine, fine son."

He put all the cards back into their brown envelopes and fanned them out on the table. In a low murmur he conferred with his parrot, then opened the wooden door and coaxed the green bird out.

"She knows," said the man. "See how she looks into your

eyes. Sometimes the animals know more than the man. And God will guide her to pick the proper card."

The parrot rifled through the spread deck carefully before making her selection. She lifted the card with her stubby black tongue, grasped it in her beak, and brought it over to her master.

"Aha!" the little man said as he slipped off the battered paper covering, "the Knight!"

It was Saint George slaying the dragon of Evil. "A glorious sign," he continued, "but with sadness as well."

The parrot squawked. He put the bird back in the cage and went on: "You have great courage and strength of purpose, powerful zeal, you fight with body and mind for what is True. That much is very good. But you see the Knight here, he is all by himself. He has many exciting adventures, but in the end no time to have a family. Always he must ride off to a new land and a new battle. That much is too unlucky."

When I was a small child, I used to pretend I was Saint George. In armor made of tin foil, with a lance that was really a broomstick, I'd slay imaginary dragons when nobody was looking. But life is full of coincidences like that.

The man with the bird told me many other things, but nothing else that mattered. I asked him, out of curiosity, what would happen if I tried again and the bird chose a different card. An impossibility, he said. He never tells a person's destiny twice, not for any amount of money. In this life we all must play the hands we're dealt.

> > >

The bus from Jalgaon to Aurangabad passes through some of the most desolate terrain on the planet. Even in April, before the full wrath of the dry season has set in, all the riverbeds are stone-bone-dry. The unblinking sun bakes the earth hard and brittle, cracks it with black spiderwebs of crevices. The land is a tinderbox on the verge of spontaneous combustion, and one hesitates to light a match for fear that the air itself will ignite.

The soil seems too barren to feed a lizard, yet 75 million people live in the state of Maharashtra. Somehow, they all get fed, most of the time. They do not live on sunflowers, but for endless stretches that is the only crop to be seen. Fields of sunflowers burst without warning out of the dead beige desert, some tall and yellow and proud, some brown, withered, fried by the sun, shriveled like overcooked rashers of bacon. Often a healthy field and a scorched field stand side by side. Sometimes an entire plot will be burned to a crisp, all except a single proud sunflower miraculously left standing, full and perfect in the midst of desolation. None of the farmers I spoke to could tell me why this happens.

Three
KINGS

WHEN he reached the banks of the Ganges, Rama sent his chariot home.

"Maharaj —" the charioteer began.

"I am not a king," Rama said, cutting him off, "I am only a man."

"Maharaj," the charioteer went on, "you must ride. How else will you make your voyage?"

"Kings ride. Men walk."

"Maharaj, with your permission, I will walk behind you."

Rama shook his head.

"If a prince must walk alone," the charioteer asked sadly, "what order is there in life?"

Rama did not answer. But when he said good-bye, the form of address he used was that of a friend rather than a master.

Just after midnight, once the moon had gone to bed behind a cloud, Rama, Sita, and Lakshman sneaked out of camp. Otherwise all the followers who had accompanied them from Ayodhya would have insisted on walking behind.

The next day, on the other side of the Ganges, the three reached a forest compound built by the hermit Bharadwaja. They gladly accepted food and lodging — the afternoon's march had been a long one, and none of them had ever before had much reason to walk. But Rama could not accept the offer of a permanent home at the monastery. Too close to the city, too close to people. He asked Bharadwaja where he might go to escape from the world.

"Chitrakut," said the sage, pointing south.

Even in his sleep Lakshman wore an implacable scowl. On the fifth night out of Ayodhya, Rama could ignore it no longer, so he shook his brother awake.

"You cannot remain angry for fourteen years," he said. "When we walk on tomorrow you must leave your bitterness here. Dig a hole in the ground and bury it forever."

Lakshman did as he was told. He wiped the soil from his hands and felt the glare vanish from his brow.

"Rest assured," Rama said, "that our father is suffering a worse torment by far. It is a hard thing for an ordinary man to face his failings, harder still for a king, and Father must live with the knowledge that he is slave to his wife. Lust is the most powerful of all human emotions, even stronger than a greed for gold. If you must be sad at all, be sad for Father. He is certainly passing a miserable night."

A miserable night indeed, and his last one on earth. Dasarastha lay on his deathbed, surrounded by his three hundred wives. They could not all push into the bedchamber and had to spill out down the hallway and into a drafty stairwell. The only one of his weeping queens that Dasarastha would speak to was Rama's mother.

"Kausalya," he gasped, "I should have known, I should have known. A king cannot escape the fruit of his actions, any more than a goatherd can. I had forgotten the source of this present misery, but it all comes back to me now when I shut my eyes:

"Ages ago, when I was little more than a boy, I committed a great sin. I did it unwittingly, but no matter. A poison does not cease to function simply because it was drunk in ignorance.

"In my younger days, as you know, the passion of my life was archery. I was the finest bowman in all the land (or so they used to tell me), so skillful that I would hunt my prey by sound alone.

"One afternoon I was in the forest by myself. I had been stalking a wary tiger all day, and I didn't even notice the fall of darkness. I heard a faint gurgling at a water hole behind a bush, and instantly sent my arrow slashing. There was a cry, but it was not the cry of a tiger. It was the cry of a human."

"*Babaji,*" his wife said as she mopped the sweat from his face with the edge of her sleeve, "you must rest. Tell me tomorrow."

"There will be no tomorrow," the king replied, "and rest will come soon enough.

"Anyway, I had shot a hermit boy, straight through the heart. With his last mouthful of breath he forgave me and begged me to bring his pitcher of water to the home of his parents nearby.

"I picked up the pitcher and slung the boy over my shoulder — his body weighed no more than that of a baby deer. I entered the little hovel to find an aged man and woman sitting by the fire. 'Why have you taken so much time?' the old man asked. 'Don't you know your mother needs that water to cook?' The old woman stared me straight in the face. 'You were down at the stream so long we began to worry.' They were both completely blind.

"I told them what had happened and offered to make any reparation they wished. They had me build a funeral bier and set the corpse on fire. 'Ours is not to forgive,' the old man said, when he had wrung all the tears from his purposeless eyes. 'King or hermit, none can change fate. You too shall lose your son, and you shall die of grief as we do now.' With that, guided only by the feel of the heat, they both dove into the flames."

Dasarastha fell back on his pillow. For the rest of the night Kausalya smoothed his feverish forehead, but the king uttered only one more word. It was the name of his treacherous junior wife.

"Kaikeyi," said the rajah, and he died.

A nation without a king, the poet tells us, is not a nation at all. There is no public order, no law, the son does not obey his father, nor the wife her husband. Men kill each other off with as little concern as cannibalistic fish.

In a nation without a king, people become lazy. Peasants sleep until noon, crops go unharvested and rot in the ground. Artists mislay their brushes or chisels and never manage to find them. Soldiers spend their time drinking and throwing dice rather than guarding their posts. Scholars abandon their recitation of the Shastras and the Vedangas for lack of an audience, eventually forgetting the unwritten texts themselves, so the lore dies in their memory.

In a nation without a king, there are none of the quiet blessings of normal life. Families do not enjoy picnics in the woods. Merchants cannot sell their goods at a fair price. Elephants do not live to be sixty years old. Girls with gold nose-rings and silver hair-combs do not drape themselves in yards of flowing red brocade to dance in the streets because they are young and happy.

In a nation without a king, Brahmins cease performing the sacrifices that maintain the balance of nature. The clouds do not yield life-giving rain. The seasons do not change, or else they change all at once and overwhelm the land with heat, chill, thunder, hailstones, and summer pestilence at the same time. Cows do not give milk. Livestock refuse to procreate. The sun does not shine in the sky.

A nation without a king is a river without water, a constellation without stars, a forest without trees.

The court Brahmins sent their quickest messenger to summon Bharata so that the throne might be empty for as little time as possible. The prince had been visiting his grandmother in a neighboring kingdom and knew nothing of the week's events.

"Monstrous!" he screamed at his mother on reaching Ayodhya. "Did you truly believe I would accept this?" Kaikeyi said nothing. "Me?" his rage spilled on, "take Rama's crown? Monstrous!"

He vowed to go find Rama, surrender the throne, and then retreat to the forest in penance for the sin that had been committed in his name. But first he offered his apologies to Queen Kausalya.

"I knew nothing of it," he said to Rama's mother. "May anyone who found joy in your son's exile damn himself by kicking a sleeping cow or by urinating in the direction of the sun. May any such person earn the divine punishment meted out to those who sell poison, befoul the public drinking water, or refuse bread to a starving traveler. May he beg like a naked nomad, with an empty skull in his hands. May he —"

"Forgiven," said the queen.

Bharata set out with a retinue of thousands. Expert trackers picked up Rama's trail across the Ganges, and an army of servants quickly fashioned a pathway worthy of a king's procession. Woodsmen hacked a highway out of the untamed jungle, a road wide enough for fifty horses to trot abreast. Masons paved the avenue with polished granite, gardeners planted beds of aromatic flowers, engineers tossed up bridges, and artisans sculpted tree trunks into statues of propitious deities. As Bharata and his court traveled through the forest, the road was carved out almost beneath the wheels of their chariots.

➤ ➤ ➤

"You see," Rama was telling Sita, "the forest is far more pleasant than the city. We have everything here we could possibly want. Plenty of fresh game to eat, a cozy cave for shelter, and river water so pure and cold it makes your head tingle. Doesn't each meal taste better when you have cooked it yourself?"

"Yes, dear," Sita said dutifully.

"Why, the good earth even provides us with cosmetics. Look!" He rubbed his fingertip on a powdery red stone, and daubed a neat bindi in the center of her forehead. "Who needs maids and servants? Every morning this reflecting pool will be your mirror, and I will be the attendent to help with your makeup."

An ape bounded out of the woods with a shrill whoop, and Sita jumped into her husband's arms. Rama shooed the animal away with a dismissive toss of a hand, but Sita did not move from his embrace. She hadn't really been all that frightened of the monkey. When they separated, Sita stepped back and began to laugh: Rama's chest was imprinted with chalky red mark at the exact height of her brow.

When he heard axemen chopping their way through the wilderness, Rama ran to string his bow, but he unstrung again at the sight of the royal banners of Ayodhya. He'd been expecting Bharata to follow him, but not this quickly.

At the news of his father's death, Rama did something he had never done before. He fainted, out like stone. It was not from weakness nor even from grief but from a surfeit of thoughts bouncing around in his head: Who will guide me, what is my fate, should I take the throne, what of my vow, who will lead the kingdom, where is my duty, can any choice be the right one — too many questions all at once.

In a minute or two he regained consciousness, and dharma was clear once again. The oath of a dead king is no less binding than that of a live one, and the debt of a father must be paid by the son. Fourteen years, minus a few weeks. Rama felt much better when the decision was made.

"But I cannot be king," Bharata protested. "It is your place by birth, yours by merit, yours by every right. A mule cannot imitate a horse, nor a goose an eagle, and I cannot sit on your throne."

"You must, and you can," Rama replied. "Just remember a few simple guidelines of government:

"Better to be served by a single wise man than a thousand fools. Choose your counselors well, give them the freedom to speak their hearts freely, and then listen carefully to everything they say.

"Scrupulously follow every rite of the faith. Not only will this win you the respect of your subjects, but the religious merit you earn will make all the land prosper.

"Select your generals solely for their martial ability, and keep the soldiers well fed at all times. A king's first duty is to defend his people from attack — he is owed loyalty by his troops, but he will not get it unearned.

"Dispense justice in perfect fairness. If a ruler takes a bribe or gives favors to friends, there is no vestige of law. He will certainly fall.

"Make yourself a moral paragon for others to follow. You must epitomize all that is best, for you are the living personification of the nation itself. You must shun the Ten Royal Vices of gambling, killing for pleasure, lying, sleeping during the day, idleness, overfondness for dancing, singing, or playing music, addiction to wine, and addiction to women. Avoid these faults, and you will make a fine king indeed."

The entire court tried to change Rama's mind. Women wept at his feet. The chief royal priest told him that his duty to Ayodhya outweighed his duty to his father. One courtier even set out the argument that the living owe nothing at all to the dead, that corpses are no more than decomposing flesh and insubstantial memories, that the holy ancestral ceremony of Astaka Sradh was nothing more than a waste of good rice.

Bharata threatened to wait his brother out. He vowed to stick by Rama's side and fast, like a Brahmin who is owed money and cannot defile himself by demanding payment, so he sits patiently as a constant reminder outside the debtor's door.

"It cannot be," said Rama. "A king cannot fast. Don't you see, whether you want to rule, whether I want to remain in the forest, none of it matters. Wants count for nothing. What counts is duty, duty alone. It is my duty, as the son of a king, to keep our father's promise. It is your duty, as his son, as my younger brother, as a prince of royal blood, to do as I tell you and govern Ayodhya. That is all."

Bharata agreed to rule, but only until his brother's exile was over. He carried Rama's sandals back on his head and placed them on the golden throne, to show that he was no more than a loyal regent. For all the fourteen years, Bharata lived as a hermit in the midst of the palace's splendor, dressing in bark while his nobles wore silk, letting his hair grow tangled and matted, consenting to eat only stony acorns and brittle leaves.

<hr>

It is not so difficult to find a king today, if you know where to look. I searched for one in a palace but found him in a five-star hotel.

The Ramayana is a story for all classes, but it is the story of a royal prince. This is not merely an epic convention: two of India's most widely worshiped heroes, Shiva and Krishna, are a holy vagrant and a simple cowherd, respectively. Rama provides an example for all men, but especially for those entrusted with rule.

In a modern democracy we demand little of our government: protection from various dangers and a few social programs. We certainly do not want the state to intrude on our lives any more than is absolutely necessary. Even the laws and regulations we support (whether they punish drunk driving or securities fraud, homicide or false advertising) are all to keep the *other* fellow in line. But in a traditional Indian view government must provide far more than bare order. The monarch is wholly responsible for the welfare, both material and spiritual, of each of his subjects. A happy nation is one with a good king.

Now that the princely states are dead, what does it mean to be a rajah? Has today's republic inherited all the sacred duties of India's traditional rulers? Nobody is better equipped to answer than His Highness the maharajah of Jaipur, so that is who I asked.

The city of Jaipur is the capital of Rajasthan, by far the most lordly state in India. Rajputs have always been aristocrats. Here Kshatriyas are as common as camels, and camels here are as common as pigeons in Venice. The state's very name means "Land of Monarchs," and even the stern, unyielding majesty of the Rajasthani desert proclaims the place to be nothing less than a kingdom of kings.

Not that the desert suggests any luxury. It is a bare land, full of herds of black-headed sheep jumbled up with herds of shaggy-legged camels, a dirty plain where dun-colored goats can scarcely be distinguished from the dun-colored earth. The only shocks of color are the clothes of the inhabitants: women drape themselves in exuberant purple saris, men wrap their heads in turbans dyed flaming red or neon green. Such flamboyance seems out of place here, but a ruler can break any rule.

I hoped to find the maharajah at his home in City Palace. It's a museum now, but the rajah still lives in a suite off the main courtyard. A soldier showed me to the gate, where a dwarf in neat blue livery led me to an aide-de-camp, who introduced me to an equerry, who told me His Highness was not in. He'd popped down to Delhi, the city I'd left that very morning.

The regal presence lingers in Jaipur even when the king himself is away. Within the old crenellated walls, all the houses are painted the same bright pink hue as the palace. Elaborately carved wooden screens, ornamental cupolas, domes and spires, delicate stucco facades with tiny shuttered windows, three-story-high murals of gaily colored princes and warriors — it is hard to tell where the rajah's home ends and those of his subjects begin.

The streets are full of cows — the royal herd, I am told. From the times of epic a monarch's status has been measured by the number of his kine. Dasarastha possessed several million of the beasts and gave away 400,000 at Rama's wedding. I do not know how many cows the present maharajah owns, but I could hardly walk five steps in Jaipur without bumping into one.

There were cows stealing melons from vendors' stalls, chased away with brutal smacks on the back. There were cows napping in the middle of the avenue, creating snarls of traffic from motorists too pious to give them a nudge. There were cows, inexplicably, on the roofs of buildings, stepping gingerly over families of spry gray monkeys playing tag among the eaves. There were cows mating hastily in closed alleyways, half-minute attacks and submissions followed immediately by unembarrassed scrounging for more food.

In point of fact, these are *not* royal cattle. The maharajah would later assure me that his own cows are all kept on farms to provide milk for the palace staff, never permitted to make a nuisance roaming the city at will. But the people of Jaipur still believe they are his, so the honor and the irritation are his as well.

Most public buildings display grateful plaques inscribed with the name of the present rajah or one of his forebears. Even after the central government took over the actual running of the state, the princes contributed to the upkeep of schools, temples, and hospitals, as if Jaipur were still their own fiefdom. At the public library, where the air hangs heavy, like vaporized cobwebs, a desiccated librarian eagerly showed me through the stacks. He pointed out the Sanskrit collection, the Hindi, English, and Urdu collections, occasionally exchanging whispered "Good days" with studious readers in hiding from the filtered rays of sunlight. In a musty, well-swept room he showed me the volumes donated by His Highness's grandfather. Many were missing spines, held together only by threads, their covers crumbling, their pages disintegrating to the touch. But the books were still in use.

The city's focal point is a palace that does not exist. Hawa Mahal, the Palace of the Winds, is a soaring pink stage set, a well-disguised row of bleachers five floors high. From the street it looks like a magnificent mansion, but there is nothing behind the luxurious facade. Inside, the dingy stucco is peeling and the floor is dotted with piles of monkey dung. The stairwells have built-in spittoons for chewers of betel nut, and each landing's corner is splattered bright red from visitors with poor aim. In one corner the splatter is not from betel: below the red stain lie the remains of a smashed pigeon, a lump of guts and bones in a flurry of gray feathers.

Two hundred years ago a rajah built Hawa Mahal to let his harem women gaze out over the bazaar without staining the propriety of their purdah. The sheltered concubines would peek through tiny slits in the thick wooden screens and live vicarious lives of active normality. They would watch the raspy-voiced hawkers describing bargains with waves of their arms, watch the children scavenging, watch the farmers pulling produce to market on carts drawn by camels, each tiny buggy slung so low that the driver could see nothing but the camel's rump in front of his face.

They would watch all manner of food and finery being bought and sold, swapped and stolen: apples, coconuts, dates, onions, garlic, green grapes, starfruit, guava, cucumbers, bananas, cauliflowers, turnips, peas, cabbages, and carrots — yellow ones, white ones, deep purple ones that probably were not carrots at all, bright pink ones as pink as the walls of the Pink City itself — oranges, potatoes, ginger, tomatoes, melons, pomegranates and persimmons; red, ocher, and golden mounds of spices, blue cones of powdered dye, teas and grains and various grades of rice; perfume and sandals and dubious gemstones, and big, brown cakes of sugar all covered with stubborn flies.

I know that is what they saw, because it is what I saw through the same windows. But nowadays the Palace of the Winds is something to be gazed at rather than gazed from.

The maharajah's name had been often mentioned in Jaipur during the past few weeks, more so even than usual. I heard cacophonous sound trucks blaring his praises at street corners, barkers with megaphones insulting him in the market. Some of the old town's medieval walls were daubed with red hammers and sickles above black antimonarchist grafitti. It was a few days before the general election, and His Highness was running for Parliament.

As it turned out, democracy was not kind to the king. He lost, and lost quite decisively. And his most vociferous foe was his own stepmother.

I caught up with him back in Delhi, at a hotel far out of my own budget. He was disappointed about the election, of course, but not bitter.

"People all tell me I should have run as an Independent," he mused. "They say I'd have won by a large margin." A philosophic shrug. Certainly His Highness's prospects hadn't been helped by Rajiv Gandhi's name at the top of the Congress party ticket. But what is done can never be undone.

Bhawani Singh, the fortieth maharajah of Jaipur, was wearing a beige V-neck sweater and well-used slippers. He's a big, stocky man, with hazel eyes and hair still streaked black. He does not feel the need for an omnipresent entourage, does not surround himself with yes-men or superfluous bodyguards. The only aide there left, cradling his motor-scooter helmet in his arms, as soon as I arrived.

The king wished his assistant a good evening, towering over the small man as he closed the door, and came back to tell me about democracy. I asked him about the posters, the bullhorns, the pandering promises, the countless silly things every politician must do to win office, asked him if he found the whole process degrading.

"No, no," he insisted, "all that nonsense is not necessary. It doesn't have to be part of the system. It's all just . . . 'gim-

micks,'" he smiled, pleased with his Americanism, "and someday the people will see right through it. Soon, I think."

I reminded him that in my country we hadn't seen through
electoral shenanigans in two hundred years.

"Ah," he said, "but India is different. We are starting with a
clean slate. Just look at us, we are the largest democracy in the
world, nearly the only true one in Asia. Just about the only state
on this continent that has never permitted military rule. Perhaps — no, *certainly* — we could do better. But I would say
this little experiment of ours has been a remarkable success."

Was it fair of his stepmother to campaign against him? The
dowager maharani had supported the right-wing Bharatiya Janata Party, part of the coalition that eventually won. "She has
her politics," said the king, looking down at his hands, "I have
mine." I didn't press him further.

After all, government in India is a family affair. Thirty years
earlier the maharani herself had been elected to Parliament by
what the *Guinness Book of World Records* still declares the largest
majority of any candidate for any national office in any democracy on earth. When another princess, the maharani of Gwalior,
ran for a lower-house seat recently, she faced attacks from her
own son, Maharajah Madhav Rao Scindia, the minister of railways. Voters cheered for the rajah but voted for "Rajmata" —
"the mother of the king." Until Rajiv Gandhi's assassination in
1991 the Nehru dynasty had governed India almost every year
since Independence, handing power from father to daughter to
son and turning the prime minister's office into a virtual hereditary monarchy. But now, every so often, people do exercise
their right to vote the king out.

If parliamentary leaders become kings, and kings lose elections for Parliament, what is a rajah to do? In essence, just be
himself.

"The people of Jaipur see me as their father," Bhawani Singh
said. "That relationship will never change. There is the same
love between us as ever. I do not rule the state in the way that
my forefathers did, but I must always try to help my people, in
every way that I can. Milk?"

He was pouring me another cup of tea from a pot on the glass
table.

"You see," he continued, "the elected government has taken
over all the day-to-day running of the state. But there is far
more than that to being a rajah. Far more, indeed.

"Like a father, I must look out for the welfare of my children. I must set a good example for them, guide them in the right direction, help smooth out any difficulties they may have. Like a father, I am treated with some degree of respect and deference." His mind drifted back to the events of recent weeks. "Usually."

In the West, whatever our politics may be, we want the government off our backs. We may want it on the backs of our neighbors — we have few qualms about regulating behavior we personally don't practice — but the only positive role we allot to the state is controlling other people's misdeeds. Perhaps we are not demanding enough.

If Hindus have seen the state as a loving father, we democrats ask nothing more of ours than pocket change and an occasional spanking. There is more to parenting than putting dinner on the table and enforcing a curfew. What we are getting is not a father but the proctor of an orphanage.

The greatest rulers, whether presidents or princes or prime ministers, have always stirred greatness in their people. John F. Kennedy awakened an idealism that Americans had let slumber for a generation. England's King Alfred forged his demoralized subjects into a spirited nation. Outside a state tax office in Bangalore, I saw a mural that showed why Jawaharlal Nehru deserves his place in the gallery of glorious leaders: it was a quote from the Pandit, reading, "I want work, work and work. I want men who work like crusaders. I want work to build up India."

Any demagogue can promise a chicken in every pot, perhaps he can even deliver it, but that is not the whole purpose of government. A great leader is one who brings his people through the sacrifices necessary to attain their goals. A great leader is one who points out the right direction and rouses his people to make the journey themselves.

The maharajah of Jaipur plays his paternal role nowadays mainly by working for the preservation of Rajput culture and heritage. He spends much of his time setting up trusts and scholarships for the traditional arts, giving lectures and luncheons, trying to keep his people from forgetting who they are. He helps Rajasthani artists enjoy the benefits of their labor by fighting against the rapacious middlemen who market their works and by searching out local talent for the restoration of the royal palaces.

Many of his ceremonial functions remain unchanged. In parades and festivals, on Rama's birthday or Independence Day or Holi, he often can be seen decked out in the imperial trappings worn by his ancestors. It is not vital, he said, but it binds all the people of Jaipur together, makes them feel like a family, gives them a tie to their own glorious history. Some of the processions are unchanged from his grandfather's day. "Only now," he said, "I don't always ride on an elephant."

Every prince is a Kshatriya first, the very apogee of the whole aristocratic caste. In Bhawani Singh, it is often difficult to separate the monarch from the knight. "A Kshatriya's duty is to guard, defend, and serve the nation," he said. "To protect the poor from oppression, to uphold religion, culture, and ethical values. God has given us so much, and we have the obligation to help those less fortunate."

I couldn't help but wonder whether the words came from Hinduism or from Harrow. That is where His Highness was educated, and he still speaks English with a distinct public school accent. These days *noblesse oblige* is a concept rarely spoken of without a snicker. We might ask ourselves what has taken its place.

When I was in school (not at Harrow but at one of its innumerable American cousins), the headmaster read the same prayer in chapel twice a week: "Lord," he'd say, trying hard to look somber, "let us see that of those to whom much is given, much is required." The students would interrupt their whisperings for a moment to mutter "Amen." But later, maybe much later, some of them might remember. Paternalism, whether of a state or of an institution, is seen as an insulting attitude. And often, to be sure, it is. But when applied with concern rather than condescension, paternalism may be just another name for leadership.

Classically, every king and every Kshatriya is a warrior first. The maharajah of Jaipur is no exception. He served eight years in the President's Bodyguard. He formed and commanded the Tenth Paratroops, a rapid-action squad modeled on Britain's Special Air Service. In the 1971 war against Pakistan he was decorated with India's highest military award. He still uses the title of lieutenant-colonel on occasion, and he advises the country's top antiterrorist team. Why did he go into the military?

"Well, of course I didn't *have* to go, but it certainly seemed the appropriate course."

A knock on the door, and two hotel maids came in to tidy up the room. Bhawani Singh offhandedly told them where to put the vase of flowers, and not to worry about the ashtrays. He did not fuss over them, and they did not fuss over him. The room was an ordinary, unpretentious businessman's suite, the same type you'd find in any Hilton or Sheraton. The hotel probably had a garish "Maharajah Suite," occupied by an ordinary, pretentious businessman.

Did His Highness model himself after that paragon of princes, Rama of Ayodhya? Surprisingly, not quite.

"Certainly everybody, not just royalty, can profit from Rama's example," he said, "but my own personal model has always been my father."

The previous maharajah was the last semiautonomous ruler of Jaipur under the British. He died in the most honorable way possible for a Rajput — playing polo.

"I've always tried to pattern my own life after his," Bhawani Singh continued. "He was one of the most forward-looking rajahs, one of the very first to open his palace to the public. He cooperated with the new democratic government, did not try to fight a foolish battle against it. One cannot blindly resist change, you know, but rather one must work hard to give that change a useful direction."

Of course, filial devotion was Rama's first virtue. By following his own father, the maharajah is, in fact, following Rama himself.

Opening the palace gave the monarchy a great burst of popularity. Perhaps it saved His Highness from joining the ranks of Bourbon pretenders, Romanov czarevitches, and self-proclaimed Hapsburg grand dukes who loiter around European spas and casinos, trying to find some sap to pick up their bar tab, praying nobody will find out that they cannot afford to stay at the Ritz. But a rajah's place goes beyond mere popularity. In India, royalty is not yet an anachronism.

"I don't mind the visitors," Bhawani Singh insisted, referring to the hordes of tourists who troop through his home every day. "Really, I don't mind at all. Two thirds of them are Indian, and they certainly deserve to see and appreciate their artistic heritage. As for the foreigners, I am proud to have them admire my family's residence."

And City Palace, I remembered from my visit there a few days earlier, is indeed thick with the shades of the king's family. One ground-floor gallery, shrouded in ponderous damask curtains to keep out the hot sun, contains life-sized portraits of all the past maharajahs; each prince mutely suffers the timeless indignity of watching pigeons nest on his gilded frame. Other rulers and courtiers, shrunk to humbler dimensions in what must surely be one of the world's finest collections of Mughal miniatures, are scattered about the old ballroom. In the pink courtyard stand two silver vessels, the largest ones on earth, each big enough to fit a Volkswagen with room to spare. They were used by one of the maharajah's ancestors on a trip to England, so that the king would not have to pollute himself by drinking foreign water.

On the second story is an armory chock-full of the fearsome weapons for which Rajput warriors were so justly famous. Basket-hilted sabers, spiky iron maces, swords with vicious hooks and claws, matchlocks, wheel locks, flintlocks, percussion-cap muzzle-loaders, double daggers called *q'atars,* all laid out in close-packed geometric designs or simply stacked up in closed rooms for lack of space. Rajput Kshatriyas wielded the tools of their trade with ferocity and great cleverness. The palace munitions hall contains guns concealed in swords, swords concealed in clubs, and clubs concealed in musical instruments. It was not solely through love or popularity that the maharajahs of Jaipur held their throne.

But City Palace was not the home of Bhawani Singh's youth. It is a venerable residence, with portions as old as Jaipur itself, but in the early twentieth century the royal family moved to the smaller Rambagh Palace to cut expenses. By the time they moved back in 1956, the place was already a museum, and the young Bhawani was off in the army. He does not trouble himself pining for the old days, when Jaipur was theoretically an independent principality.

"It is really my stepmother," he said, with not even a small grimace, "who misses that time more than I. She still misses it, even now. You see, when she came to Rambagh as a young bride, Jaipur was alive with pig-sticking and polo and parties that lasted until dawn."

Rambagh Palace is now a hotel. Tourists from Dayton and Düsseldorf stay there overnight when they come to gawk at the Hawa Mahal. Few people anywhere have gone pig-sticking since the British went home. All-night parties are nothing new, but there are few in royal mansions anymore. Polo, however, is still His Highness's burning passion. He is rated at a highly respectable two goals. The scale ranges from zero to ten, and there are fewer than a dozen ten-goal players in the world. Since a recent heart attack, however, his doctor has permitted him to ride only as a referee.

We chatted polo for a bit, whether the Argentinians would dominate the sport forever, why England hadn't produced any top players since Julian Hipwood, the pros and cons of metal faceguards. I'd played (with no great distinction) in college, which was probably the main reason His Highness took the time to meet with me. I was secretly hoping he'd invite me to join one of his matches, but he didn't, which undoubtedly saved me from deep embarrassment.

I did have one more serious question for the maharajah, and I wanted to ask it before I overstayed my welcome. What, I inquired, could India's new elective kings learn from her old hereditary ones?

"Ah," he said, "what should government do? Well, quite simply, government exists to help the people. Help them with any facet of their lives. The secular republic cannot assume the task of spiritual or moral leadership — perhaps that is where we rajahs still have a role to play — but it *can* learn to be more responsive to the citizens' needs.

"In the old days it was all quite simple: if a subject had a problem he would go to the rajah, and the rajah would try to solve it. There were many public audience days, when anybody with a complaint or a grievance could come to the palace and be heard. The system did not always run properly, and there was corruption at certain times, but the same is true for any government that has ever been. The point is, it was straightforward, direct, and it generally worked.

"Today," he continued, "what does a man do to get action on a problem? He must deal with a bureaucracy. He must fill out so many forms. He must stand in queue after queue. He must run from one ministry to another, perhaps give out a bribe here or there, and then be sent back to the first bureau. Far too much red tape. You tell me, what can we learn?"

I thanked him for his hospitality and got up to leave.

"If you're in Jaipur again," he said warmly, "be sure to look me up." As if I would need to use a telephone book.

He showed me to the door, and as he shook my hand his face grew somber.

"Do tell them about our democracy," he said. "It is something that all of us care about very deeply. After all, too many Americans think there's nothing more to India than tigers, snake charmers, and maharajahs."

When the citizens of Ayodhya beg Rama to forswear his exile, it is not mere epic puffery. In legend, and no less today, the character of the ruler is of vital concern to every subject. Dasarastha is a mediocre monarch because he pays more attention to his wives than to the welfare of his kingdom. The Ayodhyans so hunger to be governed by a virtuous man that they follow Rama to the banks of the Ganges.

Nobody will ever know whether the maharajah of Jaipur would have made a good ruler. He himself says, with apparant sincerity, that he prefers democracy to monarchy anyway. But his concept of governance — that it is a leader's duty to help his people achieve great things — is one that good democrats can take as their own.

➤ ➤ ➤

His Highness had a point about red tape: one of the worst failings of the Indian government — the greatest shortcoming of this new breed of monarch — is its impenetrable bureaucracy. In the fumbling hands of the civil service, life's simplest operations become all-day affairs. To plumb the depths of the morass one need go no farther than the post office. In 1856 a letter mailed in Lahore could reach Delhi the next day. In May of 1990 I posted a packet from Cochin, and was still waiting for it in May of 1991.

I'd bought some Keralan artworks and couldn't carry them around with me, so I undertook the arcane gnostic rituals necessary to prepare a package for the Indian mails. Here is how the drill goes: first the article must be contained in a carton custom-built to the correct size, then stitched in a shroud of white cloth. The seams must all be sealed with blobs of red wax, each blob pressed with an induplicable mark. The address and, in the case of foreigners, the passport number must be printed on the fabric in several specific places. A Customs declaration form must be pasted on, and a duplicate copy folded in just the right manner must be sewn on with white thread. Or else the post office simply won't take it.

These rites completed (having provided employment for no fewer than five people), I arrived at the office at eleven A.M. It was lunchtime, I was told, so nobody could tend to me. At two-thirty, it was still lunchtime. I persuaded a very bored man to weigh the packet, and he informed me that shipments over ten kilograms could not be accepted. A longish spate of bickering, and he looked it up in the book to find that, in fact, the limit was fifteen. To purchase stamps, fill out more forms, paste the stamps on, and pledge my adherence to every applicable guideline, I was sent to a long series of desks and stations. Each procedure involved a bounce between several windows, no two of which had the same opening hours, very few of which seemed to be open even at the appointed interval.

I wound up at the Franking Desk, where two young women spent a very long time trying to figure out how to operate their postage meter. The rate was 935 rupees. They churned out the 35-rupee stamp without much effort, but were baffled over the 900. Instead of setting the four-digit calibration for 900, or even for nine marks of 100, they opted for ninety stamps of 10 rupees each. I was sent to another desk and given a dish of paste that looked uncommonly like mucus.

I was not fast enough. The post office was shutting for the day.

I brought the package back the next morning, to have a man in uniform tell me he couldn't take it. Too heavy, the limit was ten kilograms, and my packet weighed eleven. I looked for the bored man and his magic book of regulations, but they were not to be found. Why could I mail a thirteen-kilo packet last week, and pay less than the postage they charge for eleven kilos? "Why" is not a question for the Indian mails.

I went across town to a post office in Mattancherry. They'd never heard of any weight restriction, but the woman at the counter didn't like my Customs declaration. The export limit is 50 rupees, she said. I told her she was mistaken, that it was, in fact, 500 rupees, and then I pointed to her chart, where a stain of coffee had obscured the last zero. After several phone calls and huddled conferences with her co-workers, she came up with a compromise figure of 100 rupees, the equivalent of five dollars. If my goods were worth more than that, she said, I'd have to go to the city of Ernakulam and get clearance forms from the Bank of India.

"But if I declare the package at 100 rupees," I pleaded, "and pay 935 rupees for postage, certainly Customs will impound it for fraud."

"Yes," she said pleasantly, "they most likely will."

I declared it at 500, the legal limit, and hoped that when it passed through Bombay the desk officer's chart would not be stained with coffee.

Just over a year later the packet did arrive. A large wooden icon of Vishnu's man-boar avatar seemed to have been deliberately smashed into forty-seven pieces, and a small bronze statuette had been stolen by some graft-hungry customs officer, but the rest of the contents were intact. The white shroud had been carefully sliced and restitched, out of either deception or courtesy. The Indian postal service (like the Indian government) is woefully inefficient and ridden with corruption, but one way or another it gets the job done.

In the last century, British imperialists rudely called any poorly educated Indian by the derogatory name "babu." Today that is the word Hindi-speakers use to refer to bureaucrats. A ruler's duty is the care of his people, but India's current rulers are often too busy with their foolscap forms and regurgitative regulations to pay much attention to their constituents' needs.

I tried to avoid the babus as much as possible, but when entering or leaving the country there is just no way around them. I was in India longer than the three months permitted by a standard visa, so I spent more days than I'd care to count shuttling between the various ministries and immigration departments. To get my visa extension I had to fill out forms not in duplicate, not in triplicate, but in septuplicate. An official at the airport didn't even ask to see the hard-won tax clearance certificate without which, I had been threatened, I'd surely be tossed into prison. But he did tear up my sevenfold extension papers, so I'd have to go through the process again in Sri Lanka to get back into the country.

"From which nation?" asked the babu, as he held my American passport in his hand.

"United States."

"Your profession is a . . . waiter?"

I gave a noncommittal grunt. Previous bouts with immigration officers had taught me that on government forms the word "writer" is the functional equivalent of "CIA-KGB-terrorist-hitman-spy." I'd since learned to make the "r" look like an "a" and hope for the best.

He eventually let me board. The flight from Trivandrum to Colombo took forty minutes. Check-in procedures at the state-run airline had taken two and a half hours.

For travel within the country I was able to avoid Indian Air all but twice: once I took a flight to Khajuraho, because the railway tracks are not fated to go there, and once I flew from Bombay to Goa because I'd been briefly joined by a girlfriend upon whom I did not wish to inflict the tortuous twenty-eight-hour bus ride. In the Bombay airport, while watching our flight be delayed hourly over the course of a day, we saw a fellow passenger lose his head. He was a Calcutta businessman, and he nearly throttled a desk clerk after learning his flight had been "postponed indefinitely."

"Don't get so excited, boss," said the man's friend, struggling to pull him off the bureaucrat's throat. "Just calm down. What good does it do?"

"But I *have* to be back. Tomorrow is my son's birthday."

"It does no good to get angry, *bhai*. You know how the airline is. You either put up with it, you do not fly, or you find a new country."

"But it's my boy's birthday."

"What can you do, eh? Write a letter to the *Times* if it makes you feel better. You can't change it. So next time you take the train."

"The train takes two whole days. In the monsoon, maybe more."

A man sitting next to us was a homeopathic doctor and was offering my girlfriend advice on a canker sore.

"Massage the wound with salt," he said.

"But won't that be very painful?" she asked.

"Of course," he replied. "There is always pain in life, it cannot be avoided. Especially," he cast a glance at the imbroglio before us, "when traveling on Indian Air."

The businessman from Calcutta was still ranting. He started to walk away, then turned back and threw a dispirited punch at the air in the babu's direction.

"Someday," he cried, "someday you'll see . . ."

"Calm, boss, calm, keep your temper, *yaar,*" said his friend. "What do you want, eh? Such outbursts accomplish nothing, they only make these damn-fool babus laugh at you. And besides, it is not good for the heart."

"But it's my son's birthday . . ."

The businessman's friend was quite right. When flying India's domestic carrier (or dealing with any organ of the government, for that matter) stoic detachment is a necessity. Often a flight will be rerouted in midair, and passengers headed for Agra may find themselves in Varanasi with wait-lists several weeks long for any return trip. Almost every international flight into or out of Delhi is scheduled between midnight and three A.M., a plan that leaves custom halls empty all day and crammed to overflowing during the predawn hours. A series of horrific crashes during my stay prompted the government to admit that its brand-new Airbus crafts were too complicated for pilots to understand, but the planes remained in service since there were no others to replace them. Fortunately, stoicism is India's most abundant natural resource.

Our plane arrived, and we settled in among the bare-assed kids running in the aisles, first-time fliers fanning themselves in claustrophobic panic, huge old women getting their saris caught in the lavatory doors and washing their hands in the drinking water dispenser. I don't usually read the business section of any paper, but an article in the *Indian Express* caught my eye: this year the state airline had record profits, up 68 percent, a total of over one billion rupees.

Months later, while waiting for another Indian Air flight, I sat in the Delhi airport and watched the big electric clock in the departure hall that tells passengers when to board. I thought I imagined that time was moving in fits and starts: 1:12 A.M. for fifteen minutes, then 1:27 for another twenty, 1:47 . . . Closer inspection revealed that the clock was not plugged in, and its digits were being flipped manually by a little man in gray overalls whenever the mood took him.

➤   ➤   ➤

At a run-down restaurant in a pilgrimage town, all the specials were painted on the wall. There were the usual southern thalis, northern biryanis and curries, plus a section labeled "Chinese

Dishes," the first item of which was "French Onion Soup." Above the menu a slogan was printed in big black block letters: "THE CORRUPT WILL NOT ESCAPE PUNISHMENT."

I asked the manager what it meant.

"A warning," he said, "to all politicians who take food from my table."

India's new kings often behave with an arrogance worthy of any Mughal. In the town of Chitrakut, where Rama encamped after leaving Ayodhya, I saw why so many citizens have no love for government.

It was the chief minister of Uttar Pradesh, or so rumor had it. The armed men who cordoned off the town wouldn't say. All they told the inhabitants while herding them off their own streets was that some important politician was passing through.

At noon on a Wednesday, scores of soldiers and policemen commandeered Chitrakut. They set up roadblocks on the village's only through road and turned back all traffic trying to enter or leave. Anybody walking on the road was chased away with whirling cuts of their long bamboo poles. A man tried to tell a young sergeant that he only wanted to go home, had to get home to tend to his wife who was ill with —

He doubled up and fell to the ground, a rifle butt jabbed in his belly.

Two hours later the minister still hadn't arrived. The town was still shut. I walked through alleys until I got past the roadblocks, then walked some more until I could hitch a lift to another village. Had I been Indian I would certainly have detested that politician and the republic in general for a very long time. But my home was not in Chitrakut, he was not my minister, so I, at least, could leave.

There is another reason for the government's unpopularity, of course, a reason as old as government itself. It is exemplified by a sign in my state-run Trivandrum hotel: "To every bill will be added the following: Official Service Charge, 10%. State Surcharge, 5%. Sales Tax, 10%. Additional Sales Tax, 25% of Sales Tax." In Rama's time a king was entitled to no more than one quarter of his subjects' income, and that only if he governed well.

And yet. Indians will spit venom at the babus in the tax office with one breath, then pray for their children to enter the bureaucracy with the next. Patronage is prestige here, and no job gives more opportunity for patronage than public office. Many

Asian cultures see government employment as society's highest honor, even when the governments themselves are anything but honorable. And, as the maharajah of Jaipur noted, Indians are indeed remarkably proud of their democracy.

They vote. Despite intimidation, thuggery, and murder at every election, they come out and vote. Two thirds of them cannot even read the names on the ballots, and they come out and vote. They stamp the symbol for the party of their choice: an open hand for Congress, a flower for BJP, a hammer and sickle for the Communists, a dharma wheel for Janata Dal, a bicycle, car, boat, light bulb, tiger, or crossed sabers for regional tickets from Goa, Karnataka, or Andhra Pradesh. They vote in numbers that would make any civics teacher proud.

And not all politicians consider themselves emperors, as I learned on a night train from Madras to Rameshwaram.

I was the first one in the compartment, having arrived early to escape the brewing monsoon. Two other men trickled in before the train left the station, their clothes and beards still dripping.

"Good evening," said a bucktoothed man, as he started tossing his vast collection of soaked luggage onto an upper berth.

"Sorry, *bhai*," I said, "I'm afraid that's my bunk."

"Yes," he replied, with a wide grin of utter incomprehension, "thank you very much!"

The next passenger to board, at a stop in the suburbs, looked very much like Bart Giamatti in a skullcap. His name was Abdul. Two daily commuters at another station, and the compartment was full. We exchanged the customary information on backrounds, families, and professions.

"Pharmaceutical salesman."

"Farmer."

"Writer."

"I have a small clothing company."

"Member of Parliament."

"Accountant."

"Tell me, then, what sort of pharmaceuticals do you sell?"

The member of Parliament was Abdul. Neither he nor anybody else seemed to find it at all unusual for him to be traveling home in an ordinary railway car without a retinue.

We talked sports, weather, and some politics as well. The pharmaceutical salesman was not pleased with Abdul's stance on Babri Masjid, and let him know it. The accountant, a fellow

Muslim, told him to keep up the good work. The farmer asked him why taxes were so high, but dropped off to sleep as Abdul tried to explain. The clothing manufacturer found politics dull and steered the conversation back to sports.

By the time we'd traveled a hundred miles or so, there was no more rain. Just damp, heavy heat and thick swarms of insects churned up by the storm. Each of us lay in his bunk and looked for sleep. Abdul, stripped down to his undershirt and boxers, got up to open the window wider. He stood by the bars for several minutes, slapping at the mosquitoes feeding on his belly. My mind was momentarily invaded by the image of Senator Ted Kennedy parading around an Amtrak car in his underwear, but some things are better left unimagined.

An hour before dawn, we pulled into a small station with a mob waiting by the track. They were mostly teenagers with banners and placards, and as the train screeched to a halt they started a ferocious, full-throated chant. It sounded like a blood riot. Abdul calmly put on his clothes and prepared to disembark.

"Just a few supporters," he told me modestly as he slid the corridor door. "Elections make them very . . . enthusiastic."

They had been waiting since the previous evening just to greet their member of Parliament on his return home. If this crowd could be so spirited at such an ungodly hour, I could easily imagine them following their leader to the banks of the Ganges, dogging his steps into jungly exile. Rama escaped his well-wishers by sneaking off at midnight, but MP Abdul couldn't even give his fans the slip at four in the morning.

➤ ➤ ➤

I found the maharajah of Benares not in a luxury hotel, but right next door to one. I'd been told he had very, hm, definite views on leadership and democracy, so I stopped by his office to find out.

His Highness Bikhuti Narayan Singh holds court at an old Victorian guest house in a big field near the swimming pool of the hotel Taj Ganges. Most afternoons he does paperwork there at his polished wood desk, periodically granting audiences to any of his subjects who stumble by and care to wait.

When my turn came, I was ushered in by a soldier who served as guard, chamberlain, messenger, footman, chauffeur, secretary, and aide-de-camp. The whole ground floor, with its overstuffed sofas and trophy tiger heads on the walls, looked very much like the shooting lodge it once had been. The maharajah still lives at Ramnagar, a sprawling fortress and palace across the Ganges from the rest of the city. He has his office here at the lodge partly to save visitors the inconvenience of renting a boat, partly (I suspect) to avoid the procession of shutter-snapping tourists who stream through his home daily.

His Highness deftly avoided shaking my hand, joining his palms instead and inclining his head in a small nod. I returned the gesture with a slightly deeper bow and hoped my breach of protocol hadn't been too egregious.

"You know," he said, once the introductory formalities were over, "America does not have all the answers. Far from it. You have only existed as a nation for two hundred years." There was no need for him to remind me that his own family had ruled Varanasi (the modern, and ancient, name for the holy city once called Benares) for very much longer than that.

"Yet India," he continued, "maybe even all the world, tries to follow your lead. There is much good in democracy and modernization, but much that is very bad indeed. We must not imitate America blindly, we must pick and choose with care. And *you* must recognize your responsibility to set a far better example."

He sat back in his chair, and with a thumb and forefinger twirled the tips of his gray mustache. The maharajah wore a white Nehru-collared shirt over his compact, square frame. On his head was a deep blue cap decorated with scribbles of gold.

"Just look at this 'democracy' of yours," he said petulantly. "Look at what it has produced. Who are the people who govern the United States? Are they statesmen, wise leaders, men of judgment and experience? They are movie actors!

"Your most popular president ever, Ronald Reagan — tell me truly, doesn't he make you feel embarrassed? I need not recall for you all the gaffes, all the ignorant misstatements, all the foolish lies that fooled nobody. But he is only the most shocking example. *All* your politicians are actors, merely reading scripts prepared by their, what-d'you-call-its, their . . . image makers. It's all polls and commercials, all pandering and demagoguery. This is what you say we should imitate?"

I wanted to tell him it wasn't so, but it was. He was telling me the same things I'd been telling others for years, but it was vaguely galling to hear it from the mouth of a foreign potentate. There was nothing for me to say, so I said nothing.

"Believe me," the maharajah said, "I have studied your political system well. It looks good on paper, but we do not live in a paper world. Your Constitution is a well-planned document, and there is much that India could learn from it. Most especially, we could borrow your structure of checks and balances — that was a very clever notion, for your founding fathers were wise enough to realize what sort of men might inherit their government.

"But despite many good laws and regulations, your system is rife with corruption, bribery, all manner of graft. It's the lobbyists who really govern, not the legislators, and everybody knows it, and nobody cares. I have several American newspapers delivered by air mail, and in practically every issue I see stories of more congressmen who've been bought and paid for. Look at the savings and loans scheme, my goodness, just look at Iran-Contra, the biggest embarrassment of all. You have a nice Constitution, but it hasn't done you a lot of good."

I could have mentioned any number of Indian government scandals of the past few decades, but there would have been little reason. Pointing out the blemishes of democracy in India would only have made the maharajah's case. At least he hadn't yet hit me with Dan Quayle.

"And how can you call yourself a 'democracy' anyway?" he continued, still twirling the tips of his mustache. "The word is Greek, you know, for 'rule by the people.' In America the ordinary citizens do not rule. Big businesses and wealthy pressure groups are the ones who rule. Only the rich can seek office — I read that it costs four million dollars just to mount a Senate campaign. Truman was the last man of the people, since then almost every president has been a millionaire. Even John Kennedy, whom you admire so much, he was one of the richest. America is not a democracy, it's a plutocracy."

An odd criticism from a hereditary monarch, but I let it pass. It seemed clear that His Highness was not a man who would take kindly to debate. I asked his opinion of politics in other Western nations.

"Britain, Canada, Australia, France — it is all much the same. I am more familiar with the situation in America and Britain because I sometimes travel there and I read your newspapers, but all the so-called democratic governments behave in similar fashion. There is no true democracy anywhere in the world, and perhaps there never has been."

"We do have the power to vote our rulers out."

"Yes, but we never actually do it, either in your country or in mine. We exchange one corrupt party for another, but we never change the fundamentals. That is modern-day democracy. What was it your President Lincoln (a fine man, that, a statesman in my view), what was it he said about a people getting the government they deserve?"

As long as we were quoting political icons, I trotted out Churchill:

"Another statesman put it well," I said, "when he described democracy as the worst form of government in the world — except for all the others."

"Ah," he said, "but were the old ways so very bad? I do not think so. Better than the present system — that I will not say. Perhaps, perhaps not. This, however, I do know: the rajahs cared more for their subjects than any bureaucrat ever could.

"Even now, the people of Benares are tied to me by unbreakable bonds of love and affection. We are like a family. A rajah has a sacred obligation to strive ceaselessly for the good of his subjects, always, with whatever means he may have. It is not just a job for us, the way it is for elected politicians. Why does a man run for Parliament? He'll say it is to serve his constituents, but let us be honest here. He runs for the fame, the prestige, the excitement, the power — he runs for his *own* ends. And in a few years, if he gets tired of the job, he quits and goes home. But a rajah does not seek his office. He lives his whole life with royal privileges and responsibilities, so every aspect of moral leadership is embedded deep in his heart. These lawyers and businessmen-turned-politicians, they have no tie to the people, no lifelong relationship with them. How can they care as a rajah cares?"

He let go of his mustache and straightened his gold-scribbled cap. The soldier at the door seemed anxious to show in another visitor, so I quickly asked the maharajah about Rama.

"I do indeed try to follow Rama's example," he replied, "but only because Rama himself followed the example of Manu." In Hindu tradition, Manu was the very first man on earth, and therefore also the very first king. "The Laws of Manu very clearly set out the proper path, for rajahs, for Kshatriyas, for everybody. If more of India's rajahs and other influential persons had followed the Laws of Manu, perhaps our country would not be in its present condition."

"What condition is that?"

"Hmpf!" he snorted. "You need to ask? Just look at the billboards in the streets, look at the adverts on television, look at the crime tallies in the newspapers, the shoddy merchandise in convenience stores, the rallies and riots and riffraff everywhere. We are becoming entirely too materialistic, too greedy, too secular. We are rapidly losing our ethical bearings. Unless something is done soon, we will end up every bit as self-indulgent, lazy, and amoral as the West."

I never feel so reflexively patriotic as when I hear my nation disparaged abroad. Perhaps this is because, when traveling in the Third World, I am constantly associated with every good and bad action of the American government. Punjabis have berated me for giving military aid to Pakistan, Burmese have thanked me for saving them from the Japanese army, and in the Sudan I was nearly turned back at the border for failing to justify my secretary of state's Middle East policy. Outside our own countries, we are all held personally accountable for the character of our nations and our kings.

I wanted to argue with the maharajah, but I did not want our interview to end, so I contented myself with raising a quizzical eyebrow.

"Surely you cannot deny it?" he said. "Every time I visit any American city, I dare not leave my hotel alone after sunset. Look at what happened in New York during the blackout some years ago — only the brute force of police keeps your society from lapsing into chaos. And this in the richest nation on the face of the earth. Why is it so? Because America has abandoned morality. People are too lazy to do an honest day's work, so they steal and they cheat. Not just petty criminals either, but all manner of bunko artists, get-rich-quick schemers, so-called entrepreneurs, stock manipulators, the whole bunch. There is no longer any right or wrong in your nation. There is no moral education in the schools, no moral training in the families, it's all seen as old-fashioned, outdated, even silly and laughable. I would hate to see Indians laugh at what they ought to revere."

"Perhaps," I suggested, "this is where a rajah's leadership can be of the most use."

"I have always tried to be somewhat of a moral guardian. As the rajah of Benares, the holiest of all holy cities, I feel a special sort of responsibility to uphold religious principles and values. All leaders, traditional ones such as myself and elected officials, have the duty to maintain society's spiritual well-being. But in the last resort, it is really *everybody's* responsibility."

The soldier-guard-messenger-footman-chauffeur-secretary-chamberlain-aide was now coughing loudly enough to make clear that a visitor was waiting who was more important than I.

As I got up to leave I told the rajah that despite my occasionally playing the devil's advocate, I couldn't disagree with most of what he'd said. They were unpleasant truths, but truths all the same.

"Then TELL us!" he cried, gesturing madly at my notepad. "Write about THAT! You must give India warning, so we do not copy all the West's mistakes!" His words were at once a command and a desperate plea.

It seemed to be more his task than mine, but I promised. When a maharajah (even somebody else's) asks a favor, one can't easily refuse.

Perhaps India has indeed lost something in trading monarchy for democracy. In the balance the nation has undoubtedly gained far more, but that does not diminish the value of what it has given up. From Rama's day up until the British Raj, most of India's rulers did feel a sacred tie to their subjects. Whether they governed well or poorly, their link to the people was one of blood. And bonds of blood are the strongest bonds of all. In a very real sense, a rajah *was* the paterfamilias and the state his teeming family. Some fathers abuse their children, some use the bread money to go out drinking, but that is not grounds for denigrating the institution of fatherhood.

What India has lost is a parent's guidance. Perhaps the break was long overdue. Some would say that accepting democracy marks a nation's adulthood, that people who do not govern themselves are people still in their political adolescence. Perhaps it is so. But India was already a mature, thousand-year-old civilization when the Ramayana was written. I, for one, can't bring myself to dismiss three millennia of Hindu political thought as so much childishness. And Rama, the prince of all princes, felt it no dishonor to be led by his father.

Four
SWAMIS

LAKSHMAN grimaced as he smeared the gum of the banyan tree into his hair, but Rama grinned. He enjoyed feeling the sap thicken, turning his luxuriant princely mane into a pasty, tangled bird's nest. He ran his hand over his scalp gleefully, still not used to finding an ascetic's mop in place of the proud strands of black silk.

It was not discomfort that made Lakshman twist his face into an unflattering scowl. He did not even notice how the loincloth of freshly peeled bark chafed his skin. If he had noticed, he would not have cared. But he still could not understand his brother's eagerness for debasement.

They lived quietly at Chitrakut, bathing each morning and evening in the river's delicious coolness, sleeping on beds of soft, sweet moss, dining on whatever the generous forest provided. Rama did not enjoy hunting; he felt a sharp pang of sadness every time his arrow brought down a strapping buck for dinner. But, he reasoned, a man cannot transform himself from a carnivorous Aryan warrior to an air-eating yogi overnight.

Lakshman reveled in the hunt. It was the only real pleasure left for him. He liked nothing better than to chase a wild boar into the thick brush, wrestle it to the ground, and kill it with a single blow just above the neck. He would stand over the dying animal proudly, wiping stiff bristles off his sweaty hands as blood poured from the beast's hairy snout. Rama just shook his head.

"What is the matter?" Lakshman asked once, losing his patience.

"It sickens me," his brother replied. "All the warlike pursuits we have been taught to love, what good are they? We must kill in order to eat, perhaps. We sometimes must kill to defend our people, certainly. But we must never enjoy it."

Lakshman tried to avoid rolling his eyes.

"Truth, humility, penance," Rama continued, "charity, right speech, worship of the gods, hospitality — these are the path to happiness."

Lakshman had heard the same words from the palace sages since he was a boy. He hadn't listened then either.

Eventually they decided to leave Chitrakut. So many hermits were settling there that it threatened to become a new metropolis. This pack of unready swamis had nothing to teach Rama and no willingness to learn from him. He led his wife and his brother deeper, ever deeper, into the heart of the Dandak forest.

From cave to cave they wandered, from ashram to ashram, always seeking out the wisest sages for instruction. Rama would sit bowed at their feet, hungrily devouring each guru's holy teaching. But soon, too soon, he would exhaust each master's font of knowledge and would push farther into the dark jungle in search of illumination.

One morning Rama's new-found pacifism was sorely tested. A Rakshasa ambled past their encampment, killing every living thing in its path. The demon was enormous, dressed only in a string of bloodstained tiger skins, his cavernous belly bloated with the corpses of freshly slain animals. The Rakshasa gobbled up three lions, two panthers, four tigers, ten deer, and an old bull elephant before discovering more succulent prey.

Demons, it is well known, like no meal better than raw human flesh. The Rakshasa caught a glimpse of Sita, and his stomach roared with a rekindled appetite. He grabbed her around the waist and started pawing her limbs, trying to decide whether to start his feast with a succulent leg, a tender breast, or perhaps a morsel of tasty neck meat.

"Put her down," Rama said.

The Rakshasa laughed so hard he nearly dropped his prize.

"Who tells me this?" he bellowed, still shaking with mirth. "Some little forest hermit? What will you do, little naked beggarman, will you pray at me?"

"Please," Lakshman hissed to his brother, "please let me kill him. Please let me have this one, and I won't hunt for a week."

"Put her down," Rama said. "Now."

The Rakshasa wiped tears of laugher from his yellowed eyes.

"Look at 'em, poor little weaklings," he taunted. "I'd eat you too, but your skinny little bodies aren't worth the effort of chewing."

"Please," Lakshman hissed.

"Even if you could fight me," the Rakshasa mocked, "what would you do? No little forest sadhu would dream of killing any creature."

"You are quite right," Rama said, "I cannot kill you." Then he smashed both the demon's arms and legs and buried him up to his neck in the earth.

Rama's fame spread throughout the Dandak forest. Sadhus from every part of the jungle came to seek his protection, for all were oppressed by the evil Rakshasas.

They came by the dozens, they came by the hundreds, holy saints clothed in bark and dry leaves.

"Help us," said a swami named He-Who-Eats-Only-Water. "Help us fend off the demons of the night."

"Help us," said a swami named He-Who-Eats-Only-Air. "Help us keep away the worst phantoms of evil."

Rama hesitated. He did not want to fight.

"Help us," said He-Who-Eats-Only-Water. "Remember, a king earns one fourth of the merit generated by saints under his protection."

"Help us," said He-Who-Eats-Only-Air. "It is your duty."

"It is late," said Rama, "and we must leave. Please give us permission to go, before the sun takes on a haughty look like a lowly person who has acquired wealth by evil means."

Rama was torn. He did not want to fight, but he could hardly refuse. It seemed that everyone was conspiring to prevent him from following the path of Truth. Everyone, that is, except Sita.

"My husband," she said, "let me tell you a story.

"Once there was a sage, the purest sadhu in the land, a man absolutely untouched by any contagion of violence or lust. He was so pure, in fact, that the gods feared the power of his devotion. So Indra, the mighty Lord of the Thunderbolts Himself, Indra came down to earth and visited the swami.

"He came down to the sage and corrupted him with a simple request. He asked the sadhu for a favor, and destroyed his sanctity. Indra gave the saint his very own sword, told him to keep it safe.

"The sage, of course, guarded the weapon with his life. He

kept it with him every moment of the day and night, never let it out of his sight. It was such a fine blade that from time to time disreputable people tried to steal it. The sadhu had no choice but to kill them. Soon, very soon, all the merit he had amassed through years of hard suffering was instantly obliterated.

"Do you not see, my husband, do you not see that you cannot tread two paths at the same time? You cannot be a sadhu and a Kshatriya at once, you cannot renounce all violence and still live by the sword. You must choose — will you be a swami or will you be a soldier? If you'd like my advice, give up all knightly vanity for fourteen years. Embrace the hermit's life while you live in exile and worry about princely duties later."

Rama said nothing. His face showed nothing. He left the deputation of sages without promising them yes or no.

"I know that they could defend themselves," he said to Sita as they trekked into the forest. "These holy men could destroy any Rakshasas with a mere wish. But to do this they would have to expend so much stored merit. How can I permit it?"

She did not answer. It was not her responsibility.

Rama did not refuse to help the sadhus, but he kept his sword in his scabbard. If they truly need me, he said, I will be there to protect them.

They wandered through the Dandak forest, through the broad Deccan plain, always searching out new masters, always consuming each teacher's stock of lore. So it went, for ten years.

➤ ➤ ➤

At one remote ashram Rama was disturbed during his afternoon meditation. Every time he tried to clear his mind of all distraction, he heard the faint sound of feminine laughter. It seemed far off, but pealed out like the notes of a silver tambourine. He asked the hermitage's abbot what it could mean.

"A very sad tale," the abbot replied. "A tale of virtue wasted, of frailty even among men of great power, of ages of hard labor cruelly turned to nothing.

"Many eons ago, a highly devout rishi lived in these woods. He was earnest, faithful, and single-minded. He performed austerities of incredible rigor, spent ten thousand years in unbroken penance. The gods themselves began to fear him. They worried that with his stored spiritual energy he might storm the gates of Heaven, and they decided to stop him while they were still able.

"The gods sent five nymphs to where the rishi was sitting. He had not seen another human being since beginning his meditation, and now he opened his eyes to find five celestial maidens whose beauty cannot be described in mortal speech.

"The saint's stock of metaphysical power was soon expended. He used the last of his merit to make his body eternally young and vigorous, and he is still sporting with the five nymphs to this day.

"Those are the sounds that you hear in the distance. Let them serve as a warning, for the poor man will never find true happiness now."

Rama bowed his head. "May we all be saved," he said solemnly, "from such a sad, sad fate."

Rama had learned some truths from experience, some from meditation, and some from the lessons of gurus. But as he tore through the teachings of successive masters, there was one sage for whom he was always searching. He found that sage, Agastya by name, in a hermitage near Nasik, by the banks of the Godavari.

Agastya was a maharishi of such power that even the Vindhya Mountains shrank from his glare. The haughty Himalayas bowed their snow-capped peaks when he walked by, shifted on their foundations to avoid casting him in shade. Once Agastya, answering a plea from the gods, saved the entire Brahmin caste from extinction:

There were two demon brothers named Ilval and Vatapi, who went through the world killing Brahmins. Their technique was always the same. They would meet a holy man on the road, greet him in priestly Sanskrit rather than the coarse vernacular, and invite him home for dinner. Ilval would serve a freshly slaughtered sheep, for at that time Brahmins were still permitted to eat meat. But the sheep was no sheep, it was Vatapi in animal form. After the meal, Ilval would shout, "Come out, Vatapi!" and his brother would tear through the holy man's flesh, eating the Brahmin as the Brahmin had eaten him, but from the inside out.

The demons had received a boon that they could not be killed by any warrior, mortal or divine. The gods and the Kshatriyas were helpless, so they called on the maharishi for help.

Agastya allowed himself to become the brothers' victim. He permitted them to take him home, entertain him, serve him the customary dinner of mutton. But when Ilval stood up and cried, "Come out, Vatapi!" nothing happened. Vatapi could not rip through the rishi's belly, and he was slowly digested into nothing. When Ilval grabbed a carving knife to free his brother, Agastya incinerated him with a glance. In the face of such devastating holiness, evil has no choice but to vanish.

Agastya greeted Rama with a generous feast.

"Please, please," said the saint, waving off any thanks, "it is merely my duty. Any host who fails to provide hospitality is doomed in the afterlife to dine only on his own flesh."

He offered no magic words of guidance. He cast no lightning bolt of illumination. He advised Rama to set up a hermitage of his own and think.

"What can I tell you?" the maharishi asked. "All Truth comes from within — of this you are certainly aware. I cannot teach you anything that you do not already know."

Rama did not protest. He merely listened.

"The search for Truth," Agastya continued, "is the search for one's self. When a man truly understands who he is, he will realize that he is part of God. This understanding cannot come from the intellect, it comes from a place far deeper. Know yourself, my friend, and you will see that you are none other than the Lord."

A shadow of confusion ran across Rama's brow.

"I cannot give you the answer," the sage said, "but I can give you a gift." He went into his hut and came back with three objects in his hands. They were not (as Rama had expected) a begging bowl, a scourge, and a rough-hewn walking stick. They were a divine bow studded with diamonds, an inexhaustible quiver of arrows, and a golden sword with a golden hilt in a scabbard all of gold.

"Know yourself," the sage said again. "This is who you are."

* * *

Rama's eagerness to shuck off his high station and become a sadhu is not seen as eccentricity. Indians revere him for it, just as they revere him for his knightly prowess. A perfect man should triumph in secular life, and then abandon it altogether. Rama's mistake, the reason he eventually must set aside his hermit's staff, is that he gets the order wrong. He is a Kshatriya, and until he has fulfilled the martial duties to which he was born, he cannot in good conscience retreat to the caves. He cannot live as a swami until he has lived as himself.

Indians still hear the call of the hermitage, and still they obey. Every year thousands upon thousands upon thousands of them renounce the world to look for something greater. Spiritual values are besieged by secularism and Western materialism, but even the crassest and most cynical Bombay businessman feels the pull of the forest. The most august title a man can hope to bear, today as much as in epic times, is not "maharajah" but "maharishi."

Dressed in robes of saffron, dressed in robes of crimson, dressed in loincloths, dressed in rags, dressed in nothing at all, sadhus wander the world in search of Truth. They usually own nothing more than a few scraps of clothing, a stout stick to help them walk, and a bushy gray beard heavy with dirt, dust, and insects. They are addressed as "Swamiji" — masters of the self — and given alms as acts of merit.

Theirs is still, to 690 million Hindus, the ideal life. Not everyone can follow it. Not everyone wishes to. Not everyone is able to sever all ties of family, caste, position, and comfort. But every Hindu man (for sadhus are almost exclusively men) knows deep in his soul that it would be better if he could.

Sadhus live together in ashrams or ramble at will by themselves, from one side of the subcontinent to the other and from top to bottom. They are quite naturally thickest in pilgrimage towns, of which India has thousands. Drawn to the aura of holiness and the fellowship of other swamis, they arrive in droves. At urban sites like Varanasi or Madurai they are merely one more ingredient in the metropolitan stew, but at small villages like Chitrakut they seem to make up the bulk of the population.

It is easy to see why Rama decided to stop at Chitrakut. In all the bleak, beige Gangetic plain it is one of the few spots of true natural beauty. The river still runs cool here, and clear as winter air. Its banks are carpeted in grass so green and soft you have no choice but to walk barefoot. The shade-laden forest does not extend far beyond the river, but its very existence is a pleasant surprise: throughout Uttar Pradesh, throughout India, most trees have long since been chopped down for firewood.

Pure white egrets perch tranquilly in the water, while monkeys laugh and chase one another through the leafy canopy. All the way from Ram Ghat to the outskirts of town, the only humans by the Yamuna River are a few dhobi-wallahs beating their laundry on slick black rocks, and (of course) the sadhus.

They have come from close by and from very far away. They have lived all sorts of lives. They willingly tell me how they became hermits, but are baffled when I ask them why.

Why? Why turn sadhu? They laugh, because it is a foolish question, and they are too charitable to call me a fool. Why give up a world that everybody knows is miserable and corrupt to seek blessed union with God? Why recognize that luxury is unnecessary and frivolous? Why look for peace in the only place it can be found, within one's heart? One might as well ask a starving man why he wants bread. The sadhus do not care where their spiritual hunger comes from, only that it is there and must be satisfied.

A man bent double on his staff walks along the riverbank with an even pace. It is the same pace he has kept for two decades. He lives in the forest alone, he tells me, has done so ever since he abandoned his family to find the Way. He had been a milkman, "like Lord Krishna." Every morning his wife milked the hairy water buffaloes, and he walked the streets lugging his two big tin jugs. He sold the warm, yellowish milk by the spoon, by the cup, or by the pitcher, and never considered his life at all unhappy. Then one morning, while his wife was squatting beneath the cow's udders, he ran away to the forest and never came back. It wasn't a choice, just something he had to do. His wife was strong, and his children were old enough to tote the tin jugs themselves.

Since that time he has watched the forest shrink month by month. He has no anger toward the villagers who come with axes in the dead of night. They must have fuel for their fires, he says, or else how could they cook the food? He is saddened only for the animals who must find another home.

Sometimes he wonders what has happened to his family, but he has never gone back to find out.

Another swami who lives in the woods is only passing through. He has passed through more towns than he could ever count, and he will pass through many more yet. Sometimes, on particularly long trips, he scrapes together a few rupees for a train ticket. Usually he just walks. He shows me the soles of his feet, calloused like weathered oak. This sadhu never begs, not even for food, but the kitchens of local ashrams have never let him go hungry.

Through all his roamings he is driven onward by a search for something he can't quite describe. He is looking for one particular spot in this world of illusion, the one spot where he will be at peace with his spirit. When he finds the right place, his travels will cease.

Each morning the sadhus bathe in Janaki Pool. This calm green lagoon is more than an idyllic swimming hole. It is believed to be the very site where Sita performed her daily ablutions. Mendicant Shaivites, swamis devoted to the god Shiva, festoon tree limbs with the scarlet shrouds and trident staffs that are the emblems of their sect. They wear long, tangled dreadlocks and smoke marijuana in imitation of their deity, but they look less like gods than like aged Rasta-men. Shiva, it is said, was the very first sadhu of all. He has wandered the earth disguised as a hermit since time before time, using his anonymity to keep tabs on Creation. Perhaps he is here today, bathing with his unknowing worshipers in the crisp water of Janaki Pool.

One of the sadhus is washing apart from the others. He does not bother with scarlet robes, but simply wraps his body in cast-off clothes he has picked out of the trash. He speaks with me once he has put on his rags, and I drop a few notes in his well-worn begging bowl. He cannot rely on ashrams for food — he is too low-born. Sadhus leave behind all caste, but only Brahmins and Kshatriyas can be officially ordained by a guru.

For the masses, spiritual growth generally comes through hard work and a better reincarnation. Nevertheless, there have always been a few members of lower castes who flouted convention and lived as forest ascetics. In the Ramayana, the hermit boy slain by King Dasarastha is the son of a Vaishya father and a Shudra mother; after death he ascends straight to Paradise. Valmiki himself, it is said, was a Shudra who lost even this lowly rank for killing a Brahmin.

The man by the river says his father was a Vaishya, a vendor of oily smelts who used to beat him viciously for crying that the house reeked of fish. His mother he does not remember, for she died in childbirth. He ran away from home at the age of five and has been begging ever since. Does this make him a swami or just another vagrant? What is the difference, he asks. One relies on charity to avoid polluting himself with work, the other does so out of laziness. He hopes he is not a lazy man, but God will be the judge of that. His only possession, after fifty years of mendicancy, is a battered old portable radio. He uses it to listen to his favorite program, a daily recitation of the Ramayana.

No less a philosopher than Johnny Rotten used to say, "Don't know what I want, but I know how to get it." Very few of India's swamis have ever been near a London punk club, but all of them could take the Pistol's lyric as their own. They do not know just what they are looking for, they have no idea what lies at the end of their path. But they know for certain that their path is the right one, and they will follow it faithfully wherever it may lead.

It's the Western dream turned inside out. We Americans know what we want: a big house, a fast car, a comfortable, well-tended family, plenty of electronic gadgets, and a yearly vacation on a nice, warm beach. Some demand more, some would be happy with less, but most of us feel we could be happy if only we had enough of life's physical and material pleasures. We know what we are reaching for, we just don't know how to catch hold of it.

Perhaps this is inevitable when our goals are so easily measured. There will aways be a bigger house, a faster car, a beach that looks even more enticing in the glossy travel brochure. Perhaps that is why we are so seldom satisfied with whatever we have. Perhaps we are discontented not because our sights are too high but because they are too low.

Johnny Rotten now goes by the name of John Lydon, which a respectable English suburban couple gave him at birth. I have no idea whether he was happier fifteen years ago when he shrieked his rejection of all the tired values of a tired society. But in India I met many people who calmly spurn everything that modern society holds dear, and they are quite possibly the happiest people I know.

➤ ➤ ➤

Not all of Rama's stopping places are still frequented by sadhus. The first of his many forest retreats is completely ignored today, buried in a city that has little air of sanctity.

The hermitage of Bharadwaja now lies beneath the foundations of Allahabad University. The name Allahabad means "God's Town," but it has no feel of godliness. It was so labeled by a Muslim invader, to honor a very different vision of God. Hindus who come to bathe in the sacred confluence of the Ganges and Yamuna rivers at the city's southeast corner complain of the traffic and the smog. Once every twelve years the Kumbh Mela festival draws millions of pilgrims from all over the country. For the other eleven, however, the town built atop a hermit's retreat is now remarkable only for harboring more gun and ammunition shops than anyplace else I've seen in India.

There is no forest left around Allahabad, no place for solitary ascetics to meditate even if they still were here. Just dry moonscape, the ground torn up by strip excavation. For long stretches between the city and Chitrakut there are no farms, only shallow rock quarries; the peasants cannot coax any crop at all from the hard terrain and must carve up the very earth itself. Men swing heavy pickaxes while women cart away the rubble, and small children use makeshift hammers to chip the fresh boulders into more manageable pieces. Occasionally one sees an elephant or even a camel, looking confused and lost so far from the deserts of Rajasthan.

Sometimes pilgrims who have traveled to Varanasi, a few hours away, make a sidetrip to God's Town. They are usually disappointed. When the train crosses the Ganges, luck-seeking passengers toss coins and floral garlands out the windows with high hopes. The power lines below the bridge are laden with burnt black flowers that never made it to the river, some twisting in the breeze, some long since incinerated but not yet decayed, some still sizzling with each volt of current. There is no telling which prayers are answered, whether it makes any difference whose flowers land safely in the holy river and whose fry in limbo.

Not all wishes in life are granted. People can pray and plan and hope and labor and still not have their longings satisfied. Anyone who seeks happiness from worldly things is bound to be disappointed most of the time. The realization of this truth is what prompts many ordinary men to become sadhus.

·   ·   ·

Rama's birthplace still brims with swamis, and the swamis of Ayodhya are living a paradox. Having forsaken their homes to escape the discord and bitterness of ordinary life, they find themselves in what may be the country's bitterest and most discordant village. They have no use for politics, by and large, and wish all the commotion would just vanish. In the eye of a national tornado, they still seek the calm of a hermitage.

The abbot of Valmiki Bhavan tries hard to preserve this serenity. He is called "Dancing" Gopal Das, but he won't tell me where he got the nickname. When I ask he just laughs and shakes his head. He laughs often, and the sound comes from deep in the back of his throat.

"Ayodhya is a holy place," he says, "we have all come here out of devotion to Lord Rama, to follow his example of peace and kindness. Unfortunately, these days Ayodhya is also a place of so much anger. We are saddened by this, but we try not to let it trouble our minds. After all, is there any place in the world that is not ravaged by disharmony?"

He laughs a thick laugh at the foolishness of the idea.

Gopal Das built the ashram here in Ayodhya specifically to celebrate the glories of the Ramayana. The sadhus under his guidance are a living testament, and the building itself is a tribute in undying stone. It is a cavernous two-story structure with only one room the size of a basketball court. The walls are smooth marble, every inch engraved with neat *devanagari* script no larger than the first digit of a young girl's forefinger. The pilgrims whose donations keep the temple running pore piously over the flowing black characters — all of the epic's 24,000 verses.

"You might well say," Dancing Gopal Das chuckles, "that our house is the largest book in the world!"

I try to read the writing carved in the white stone and wish I'd skipped fewer of my college Sanskrit classes. The segment over which I am laboring tells of Rama's first meeting with the Monkey King, Sugriva, but I can't make out most of the details without a dictionary.

"Such poetry," says the abbot. "Valmiki's version is most surely the best. Many people know only Tulsi Das, so I wanted to show them the grandeur of the original epic. Sanskrit is so much more beautiful than Hindi."

A bull shuffles by in the street outside, its hump broken and sagging. The sack full of lumpy cartilage hangs over one shoulder, gently swinging with the animal's every step.

"Of course," says Gopal Das, "it is not necessary for a sadhu to be a scholar. A proper spirit is far more important than knowledge of scripture or language. Most of us led perfectly ordinary secular lives before joining the ashram."

The abbot, for his part, served out a full career as a mid-level civil servant. For a quarter of a century he worked in the Indian railway, eventually holding the title of local assistant claims supervisor. When his wife died childless he felt no reason to remain in the world, all alone each day amid thousands of teeming passengers. It was then, at the age of fifty-five, that he became a sadhu and found his peace.

"Not a step to be taken lightly," he says. "One must perform various rites of penance and preparation to be ordained by a guru. One cannot merely dye one's clothes orange and set out. Yes, there are those who do, but are they truly sadhus? I greatly fear that many of them are only beggars dressed up like holy men. But that is not for you or me to decide."

Unconsciously his hand strays to the janneu-thread strung across his chest.

"For so many today," he goes on, "the most difficult step is not the spiritual preparation, but merely the abandonment of worldly comforts. Why should this be so, eh? We Hindus are not a people of luxury. In the West, I am told, everyone tries to be a rich man with a big mansion and so many electrical appliances. But here, in the old days at least, we did not care about money so much. There were always rajahs and other wealthy men, but most of us had no desire for it. Our grandfathers *shunned* luxury, they liked an honest, simple life. Perhaps now it is only the sadhus who remain truly Indian."

Another thick laugh from below the larynx.

"Our schedule," he says, "is precisely the same as if all the politicians had never come and the Babri Masjid controversy never existed. Each morning we arise at four and walk to the river to take our morning bath. Then we meditate for three hours, or else read holy scriptures, or simply recite mantras and work our rosaries." He reaches into his robes and pulls out a string of prayer beads, the rosewood cylinders all thumbed into irregular ellipses.

"In the afternoon the sadhus perform the sacred ceremonies

and eat dinner together with any pilgrims who may wish to join us. At sunset we take another bath, for it is so very important that a sadhu keep himself clean. These road-wandering fellows may let their beards grow filthy, but that is not our way.

"At night the men may listen to religious discourses held all around town. Each ashram has lectures on different subjects, and the sadhus are free to attend whichever they wish. On their return they pay respects to the gods and go to sleep. Right over there."

He points across the road to the sadhus' dormitory. It is a big, breezy courtyard with frayed canvas roofing and no outer walls at all. Each swami has a few feet of floor space for his body, and for his few possessions a small locker without a lock.

"A good sadhu does not go to the cinema," says Dancing Gopal Das. "He has no need for idle entertainment. A good sadhu never stays in a hotel, or eats in a restaurant, or does so many other things that lay people can do. And a true sadhu never, ever begs. He takes his meals at the ashram, which is funded by many generous donors. It is a simple life, but one which pleases us."

In the ashram's courtyard, a sadhu named Mihthila is peeling potatoes. He is fifteen years old and has never wanted a life of ease. The son of a poor Brahmin sharecropper, he is used to hard work. It was not the drudgery of the farm that prompted him to join the hermitage. Mihthila ran away from home because his parents did not care enough about God.

"One must obey one's parents," the boy sadhu says, "but first one must obey God. When He calls, there is no choosing. Just like Sri Gautama!"

Gautama the Buddha, revered by Buddhists as the founder of their religion, is also worshiped by Hindus as an incarnation of the god Vishnu. He abandoned his family, throne, and home to roam the earth as a sadhu in search of Enlightenment. Few would doubt that he found it.

The young hermit's model, of course, is Rama — in Ayodhya, what other model could one have? His guru has told him to pattern all his actions on Rama's example, and like a good disciple Mihthila hangs on his guru's every word. But would Rama, the perfection of filial devotion, ever condone running away from one's father?

"Gautama, Ram, both are avatars of Vishnu," the boy replies, "both different faces of the same God. When I follow Gautama, I follow Ram as well." He says it sheepishly, aware that his theology is a bit shaky. "When I left home," he adds, "I did not simply up and run off. I wrote a note to say where I had gone." But when his family made the trip to the ashram to visit, he would not even come out to speak with them.

"They only wanted to take me away," he says. "For two years I studied hard for ordination. My father, he is a Brahmin, but he cares nothing for religion. Eating, working, drinking, working more, sleeping — is that all life means? Here at the ashram, I have found there is so much more."

Children all over the world run away from home, for any number of reasons. Some have been abused, some are addicts, some dream of stardom and success, some just want unlimited freedom, some don't know what they want and don't know how to get it. In America, even teens who join the Moonies or the Hare Krishnas are generally not running to the cult's philosophy but away from their problems at home.

In India, religious fugitives are generally quite aware what direction they are running. Hermitage is not merely a refuge from an unkind world but a definite goal in itself. I don't know what Mihthila's family life was like, but I have no trouble believing that he left home out of spiritual longing, because he felt it was simply the right thing to do.

"More to life, yes, yes," another sadhu chimes in, "so very much more. How could anyone doubt this?" An old man, he sits beside Mihthila working his prayer beads while the teenager works his peeling knife. "Until you realize that God is life, you are merely dreaming. And not a good dream either, my friend. I am grateful that I discovered this truth early in life, so that I did not go wasting whatever years I have."

His family gave him up for ordination at another hermitage when he was only ten. It is not an uncommon practice, for one son delivered early to religious orders can bring the entire clan salvation for seven generations. The old man has not seen his parents since that day.

"Far better," he says, "for now Rama is my whole family. Rama is my father, he is my mother, my brothers, sisters, grandparents, uncles, and aunts. Most of us are so blinded by the earthly pleasures that we do not see that there is nothing in this earth, no joy and no pain, nothing but God."

Every day the old man whispers Rama's name one hundred thousand times. He says that the mantra never fails to bring him peace.

I've never felt drawn to join a monastery, and after an afternoon at Valmiki Bhavan I still have no intention of doing so. But Dancing Gopal Das and his monks have made the idea seem much less far fetched.

At times in my life I have sought hermitage, generally by running off to foreign countries where nobody knew my name, places where I could go many days without speaking to a soul and many weeks without hearing my native language. Whether prompted by a dull job, a romance gone sour, or a general feeling of all-encompassing malaise, each trek has been a welcome escape. And each time I travel I see enough fascinating things to reignite my appreciation for the beauty of life.

But I have always fled society out of anger rather than joy. It is not a calm, reasoned rejection of the World of Illusion but frustration when the illusion isn't pleasing enough. Perhaps that is why, when the anger has burnt itself out, I have always come back.

I know rationally that these flights to the forest are not true renunciation, that they solve nothing, that the solitude eventually makes me hunger again for the world I've left behind. Yet whenever I am dissatisfied with the course of my life, I console myself with the perverse daydream of leaving everything behind and fleeing to the harsh, untainted austerity of a Mongolian steppe.

I've got it all backward, of course. I sever all attachments, slough off possessions and home and friends and family, tread the road with no destination in mind — but only for a time. I use hermitage to restore my love for the world, not to break free of its hold. The sadhus of India have no bitterness toward society; they abandon it not because they detest it but because they are seeking something greater. That is why their renunciation succeeds. Their real flight is within.

➤ ➤ ➤

The holiest place in the world, to a Hindu, is Varanasi. Many still call it Benares, but by any name the city of the sacred Ganges will always draw sadhus and pilgrims like a lodestone of the spirit. It is the waiting room for Paradise, since anyone who dies here goes directly to Nirvana. Only God knows how many have found true enlightenment in Varanasi, but I did gain a small ray of illumination. The holy city taught me that holiness is wholly in the soul of the beholder.

Stream of Nectar, the river is called. The Light in the Darkness, the Pure, the Eternal, the Giver of Food, the Cleanser of Sins, the Friend of the Poor and the Helpless.

The Ganges is a stagnant pool of dirty green, its opaque, malodorous water thick with sanctity and raw sewage. Varanasi, strung out along its western bank, relies on the befouled river for all its basic needs. The Ganges is the city's main avenue, its public square, its source of drinking water, its sewer, its bathhouse, its cemetery. Every day Varanasi dumps 60 million liters of refuse into the river. It is estimated that 90 percent of the residents who live by the ghats suffer from some variety of gastrointestinal disease.

Wooden boats crawl down or up the shore, not aided in either direction by any trace of a current. The oarsmen generally charge by the distance rather than the number of passengers, and each craft is piled so high with bodies that brackish water seeps over the gunwales. On one small skiff I count thirty-two people, propelled by a single straining oarsman.

Water buffaloes loll happily in the slimy tide, while human mothers wash their pans and children in the animals' wake. Mud-caked herders guide the cows by their hairy tails, then wade into the river for their own morning bath. Dhobis soak their laundry and beat it with vigor, then soak it again in the river's filth. Fishermen cast their carefully stitched nets, each time dredging up nothing but a few sickly minnows, each time tossing the net out with fresh hopes of a catch. It seems preposterous to look for life in the Ganges' septic flow, but perhaps, in this holy city, they are actually Fishers of Souls.

Donkeys on neighboring ghats exchange brays. The ghats — stone steps descending deep into the water — stretch the whole length of the city. They are always a flurry of activity sacred and profane. The walls and stairs are covered with laundry laid out to dry, fishnets laid out to dry, dung patties laid out to dry in the battering sun. Pigeons, crows, and sparrows pick among the rubbish heaps for bits of food overlooked by the dogs and the beggars. Teenage boys have contests to see whose stream of urine can reach farthest into the holy river.

A family on pilgrimage performs ritual ablutions in the water. The men's heads are shaved close, with only a tiny curl of hair left at the nape of the neck. Men and women alike carry staffs, wear white robes, and have daubs of ocher sandalwood paste smeared on their foreheads. They have traveled all the way from Tamil Nadu in the south, the father tells me. This is the clan's fifth pilgrimage to Varanasi, and it will not be their last. One of the children carries a knapsack with a faded plastic decal of what looks like Baba Sai, an enormously popular sadhu from Bangalore. On closer inspection the image is that of Obi-Wan Kenobi, the inscrutable sage of *Star Wars*.

The ghat on which they are standing, Scindia Ghat, fell into the river shortly after it was built. Vertical piers and skewed pilings, sunken flagstones and a grand temple half-submerged jut drunkenly out of the ground. The product of a rajah's arrogance, its presence is a religious lesson still. In the early nineteenth century a king bragged that his personal bathing platform would be the most magnificent in the whole city, but his faith (it is rumored) lacked a firm foundation, and the structure was swallowed up by the undauntable river. The pilgrims from Tamil Nadu have chosen this spot to bathe simply because it has relatively thin crowds.

The water-level scale painted on a yellow wall shows that on one August day in 1978 every step of every ghat was completely engulfed. All of the holiest ground in India lay deep beneath the flood. The scale serves as a reminder to any who think that the Giver of Life, the Granter of Wishes can ever be subject to the expectations of man.

Below the wall and its three-story-high calibration, young children are playing a game of cricket. The red plastic bat bears a picture of that most famous of all cricketeers, Bruce Lee. The players had not been born when their cricket pitch lay beneath the water, they have no memory of the river's unpredictable wrath.

At bustling Dasaswamedh Ghat, a man whose face and naked limbs are painted chalk-white is performing a frenzied dance while holding a skull and bones. Passersby stop to watch, to laugh, or to toss coins in hopes that somehow they'll gain merit. I exchange mystified glances with a Tibetan monk who has come to study Sanskrit with a local guru.

The sanctity of Varanasi does not end at the river's edge. The old Chowk section of town is a twisty rabbit warren of alleys, all so narrow they seem designed solely for emaciated flagellants and skeletal rishis. The passageways between the buildings are like crevices in a brick mountain, with barely enough space for people to walk in single file. When a cow comes ambling from the other direction, the whole line of humans has no choice but to retrace its steps quickly.

Around each bend in this cramped labyrinth are signs of divinity. Small niches with votive icons, shrines with room for only two worshipers at a time, temples with musty courtyards reached through creaky half-doors, murals of gods and goddesses, demigods and demons. Each sanctum is a few centuries old, or perhaps a few decades, or maybe a millennium or so. It is often impossible to tell. Here past and present are separated only by time.

The godly and ungodly alike squeeze into the sacred squalor of the Golden Temple. Swamis and lepers squat on the muddy marble floor, betel chewers spit red saliva on the walls, amulet vendors thrust their wares into your palm, serene sages travel yogic roads to oblivion, dirty-faced children try to extort rupees for not stealing your shoes — all beneath three quarters of a ton of pure gold.

Non-Hindus are not permitted inside, but before I know what is happening, a quick-talking man is leading me in by the arm.

"No worry, no worry," he says, "is no problem."

He angrily fends off some objecting matrons and ushers me past the gate, then tells me I should give him money. I slip him a few rupees, which he grudgingly pockets.

A sadhu with a beatific grin plastered on his round face comes up before me and nods. "You must give me money for him," the quick talker says quickly. I give a few coins directly to the sadhu, who grins beatifically and saunters off. The quick talker only scowls.

"All visitors, they must give money," he says, whipping out a floppy ledger from the recesses of his shirt. "See here, so many foreigners give, to feed the sadhus. Look, Australia, Enga-land, France, Amrika, Amrika, all they give. One hundred rupees, fifty, seventy, how much you give?"

I look in his book. Each entry has an extra zero ineptly tacked on, to shame the next donor into dealing out more than five or ten rupees. It's a common ruse, and a rather effective one. After all, who wants to have his name attached to a bequest one-tenth that of the next fellow?

"It cost fifty rupees for one sadhu one day," says the quick talker. "How many sadhu how many day you want to feed?"

I ask him why I, a naive foreigner, can eat for ten rupees a day while an ascetic needs fifty. He scowls, and talks so quickly that I cannot understand what he says. He scurries away in search of fresh prey, while I look around the Golden Temple and leave. Like so many temple-wallahs, he apparently sees no sin in using a mandir's sanctity as bait for con games. At the gateway a boy demands two rupees to tell me where he has hidden my shoes.

In the alley outside I see a sadhu unlike any I've seen in a while. This holy man is a woman. There are a few (very few) female swamis, and they do not belong to any ashram. They crop their hair short, and they stumble through the streets mumbling to themselves, barely noticing the outside world at all, generally appearing to be not wholly sane. This woman has a begging bowl set in front of her as she mutters prayers or curses, but few people stop to give alms. I drop a few coins out of pity, and she does not look up from her litany.

At Town Hall, meanwhile, people are gathering for a special event. Saints and pilgrims wend their way through Varanasi's snarled streets, between ruthless pedicab peddlers and children defecating merrily in the road's open sewer, wend their way through the righteous chaos of Varanasi to seize a piece of tranquility. Every day from eight o'clock in the morning until one in the afternoon (during certain weeks) there is a recitation of the Ramayana. A blind old reader and two dozen orchestrated Brahmins chant the verses of the epic in harmonized antiphony. Every evening a revered guru delivers a lecture on the meaning of the story to modern man. As one might expect, the audience is mostly made up of sadhus, but all sorts of people turn out to hear the spiritual message. In Varanasi, everyone seems to have a touch of the swami.

Varanasi is a city more of Shiva than of Vishnu, but at Ram Ghat the worshipers might as well be in Ayodhya. The penitents bathing here are devoted to Rama, and Vaishnavite sadhus offer up prayers for a price. A back-country Brahmin wears a red thread looped under his ears and across his forehead, strung with tiny silver phylacteries containing sacred kusha grass. He sports a serene smile as he steps into the Ganges, a smile that comes from knowing he will emerge cleansed of any sin. The polluted river can wash away all mortal pollution.

At Ram Ghat I too pour Ganges water over my head, faces, hands, and feet. But as I do so I do not smile. "The crystal flow of the Ganga," Valmiki wrote two millennia ago, "is cool and transparent as shining gems." Reality exists only in the mind, the sadhus say, what is true is only what one chooses to believe. To the holy men of Varanasi, the Ganges is still pure and diamond-clear.

➤ ➤ ➤

The most respected people in Indian society are those who have devoted themselves wholly to faith. Prime ministers are tolerated, generals are obeyed, business tycoons are envied, but sadhus are revered. So deep is the Indian veneration for sages that it even extends to those of other religions.

The most widely adored sage in Calcutta is Mother Teresa. Indians and foreigners, Hindus and Christians, devout and merely curious, all regard her as a living saint. When I go to her mission at five-thirty one evening I half-believe I've stepped back to the retreat of Guru Baba Raghunanden Das.

A dozen or so visitors are standing outside the door to her private office, patiently waiting for the daily audience. An impossibly ancient woman next to me is lost in a pious reverie, repeating to herself over and over, "She is the Incarnate Mother, the only Incarnate Mother." The woman looks old enough to be Teresa's own mother herself.

When the nun comes out, all drop to their knees. Help us, Mata, they say, help us and pray for us, Mata, tell us what to do, give us your blessing, Mata, help us.

Mother Teresa shuffles about, lifting them up, embarrassed (but certainly not surprised) by the adulation. She can't be much more than four feet tall and is hunched over so severely she seems no larger than an eight-year-old. She wears the same blue-trimmed white robes as all the other nuns at the convent. She is light-skinned despite all her years in the tropical sun, and moves with a birdlike energy that belies her age. She speaks Bengali, Hindi, and English with equal fluency, although none of these is her first language, or even her second.

A woman, her hands tattooed with the spidery blue markings of a Hindu bride from Rajasthan, asks how to make God listen to prayers for the sick. A round-faced man asks how to feed his family now that he has no job. A teenage girl asks Teresa to pray for her father, who refuses to accept Christianity, but is truly a good man, Mata, will he go to Hell, please, Mata, please don't let him go to Hell.

She gives them her blessing and what scraps of guidance she can muster, and they back away with palms pressed worshipfully together at their chests. All this time the impossibly ancient woman has not let go of Teresa's legs, has been ecstatically kissing the nun's feet and murmuring, "The Incarnate Mother, Incarnate Mother of Everything."

My question is more complex than a request for a blessing, so she asks me to wait until the others have left. What I want to know is whether she considers herself a good Hindu.

It's not as absurd as it might sound. Mother Teresa's life is a chronicle of good deeds, and deeds play a far larger part in Hinduism than they do in Christianity. I wouldn't want to cast any doubts on her impeccable credentials as a future Catholic saint, but Mother Teresa may qualify as a Hindu rishi as well.

"Though I have all faith, so that I could remove mountains," wrote Saint Paul to the Corinthians, "and have not charity, I am nothing." Charity is the duty of all good Christians, but it is not (of itself) the path to Heaven. Both Protestants and Catholics firmly rejected the doctrine of justification by works during the sixteenth and seventeenth centuries. In a modern Christian view, acts of goodness are the natural *result* of grace, not the means of obtaining it. Salvation is always the free, unmerited gift of an infinitely generous God; if Heaven could be "earned" by good deeds alone, Christ's death would not have been necessary. "By grace are ye saved through faith," wrote Saint Paul to the Ephesians. "It is the gift of God: Not of works, lest any man should boast."

Hinduism, however, perhaps more than any other major religion, is based on action. What one *does* is just as important as what one thinks. A Christian can commit the most heinous of crimes and (if he truly repents afterward) go straight to Heaven. A Hindu, however, cannot escape the inevitable consequences of his acts. Successful reincarnation and eventual release from the cycle of rebirth come from the accumulation of positive karma, principally by doing good deeds. If this is true, Mother Teresa has built up a better stock of karma than just about anybody on the planet.

To be a good Hindu one must also worship the deities, but as Mother Teresa explains, the God of Christianity may well be the same divinity manifested by Vishnu, Shiva, and the rest. Many thoroughly orthodox Brahmins have told me the same.

The nun laughs off my labeling her a prospective rishi but grows serious at the question of how she has been influenced by living in India.

"Why . . . in every way!" she says with a shrug. "I have learned so much here. So much about fidelity, honesty, strength of devotion."

She apologizes for not being more knowledgeable about theology and self-effacingly offers to refer me to a local Jesuit scholar. It is nearly six o'clock now, time for her to say the rosary.

A few dozen nuns and visitors are gathered in a plain, bare room. Mother Teresa kneels in the back row, her voice (and those of her sisters) virtually inaudible over the blare of the traffic outside. My knees grow tired after twenty minutes, but she, a withered crayfish of a woman, maintains her weariless genuflection for the entire hour.

Perhaps her strength comes from the simple purity of her faith. It is a faith uncluttered by unnecessary speculations, unpolluted by unanswerable questionings. Like so many of the Indians she helps — Hindus, Muslims, Christians, Jains, unified only by poverty and need — she does not ponder the underpinnings of her beliefs. Hers, like theirs, is an uncomplicated creed: worship God and do good. Simple, and as powerful as any idea in the world.

Pandits and priests, scholarly divines and doctors of divinity, theologians of every stripe and all faiths may mull over the unanswerable questions of existence. They write learned treatises on the specific metaphysical nature of each Person in the Trinity, on the exact mechanism by which souls transmigrate to different temporal bodies, on the precise meaning of God's terrestrial incarnation as Christ or as Rama. It is a worthy pursuit, but it is not the essence of religion. Philosophy comes from the head, religion from the heart. Faiths differ in dogma, but their hearts beat the same rhythm.

The visitors sit off to one side during the rosary, and even the Hindus try to imitate Mother Teresa each time she makes the stations of the cross. They do not care by what name she calls God, they are certain their prayers will be answered. Mata, Mata, they mumble, holy Mata, blessed art Thou among women . . .

I am watching the visitors rather than the nuns. Their eyes tear up, their voices crack, sometimes they unconsciously press their palms together and bow. If I couldn't see the rest of the room, I'd have no way of knowing they weren't reciting mantras with their guru.

My mind wanders back to the sadhus, to the thousands of raggedy men with unkempt beards and tattered clothes who tread the roads of India looking for Truth. My eye notices the crucifix on the altar, and the man on the crucifix. When the Christian God chose to take the form of a man, He did not pick a king or a priest or even an upstanding member of society. He came to earth as a raggedy man with an unkempt beard and tattered clothes, who trod the roads to help others find Truth.

It is not only saints-to-be like Mother Teresa who earn reverence in India. What other nation could tolerate the masses of German self-styled bhikkus and smug Australian yogurt-yogis who still trek the hippie trail? In India they are winked at, even (occasionally) admired. Spirituality is more highly honored here than any other virtue. Anybody who seems devoted to God is looked at with awe. For example, the Tamil ticket collector on a train I took in Kerala.

He was a first-generation Baptist, and very anxious for me to be one as well. It was late at night, and I was not in the mood to debate theology, but he hadn't seen a white person in a very long time.

"Might you be a Baptist?" he asks.

I tell him I am not, and he urges me to be rebaptized as soon as possible. He even offers his services as a lay minister. I politely decline.

"But my brother," he says, "it is absolutely essential."

He tells me that infant baptism is an abomination. I am in no mood to argue.

"Uh-huh," I say.

"None can enter Heaven, save they bathe in the water of Life," he says, misquoting the Gospel of St. John.

I remind him of the thief on the cross, who was saved at the very last instant, after a life of unspeakable perfidy.

"No," the collector says, "that man, he went to Paradise."

Are not Paradise and Heaven the same place?

"Not at all," he says, smirking. "Paradise is below the ground, where Jesus went to save the Old Testament prophets."

"Odd, I was taught *that* place was Hell. As in the Harrowing of Hell."

"No, no, it was Paradise. Paradise is beneath the earth, Heaven is above the sky."

We carry on a rather pointless theological discussion, in which he quotes scripture he doesn't really understand, and I say "uh-huh" in hopes that it will end the conversation. He won't tell me what caste he comes from, since caste is a heathenish abomination. He asks my opinion of Oral Roberts, and I can think of no way to answer his question without snickering. We come back to infant baptism, and he remembers another verse to buttress his argument.

"The little children," he says, misquoting the Gospel of St. Luke, "they must not suffer to come near."

He tells me it means that children who die before they are baptized go straight to Heaven. I want to ask him if that means original sin doesn't kick in until voting age. But he is still holding my ticket, so I content myself with another "Uh-huh."

"You see," he says, "before I was saved by our Lord, I was the worst sort of pagan and heathen. I was a thief, a liar, a murderer, a brigand, and a cheat. Now, thanks be to God, I am living a moral life."

There are (by his definition) three Hindu pagans and heathens in the compartment. When the ticket collector has nothing more to say, one of the idolators puts a hand on his shoulder.

"My friend," he says, "I am an old man. You are young, in the full bloom of youth. Yet I look up to you for your piety, your learning, and your earnest devotion to God."

There is not a trace of irony in the Hindu's voice. The ticket collector thanks him, and seems a little chagrined.

➤   ➤   ➤

Ascetics have long been the guardians of India's soul. Some cultures are defined by their warriors, some by their poets, some by their artists, chefs, or shopkeepers. India's civilization has always been defined, to a great degree, by its swamis.

Almost every Indian hero is a holy man at heart. Rama must live as a sadhu for ten long years to earn his status as a worthy object of reverence. Lakshman is cherished not for his warlike prowess but for his unquestioning obedience to his brother. Hanuman, the Monkey Prince, is honored not for setting all of Lanka on fire but for his pious devotion to Rama and Sita.

Westerners love a paladin too, but we do not like our heroes to be too much holier than ourselves. We identify not with Sir Galahad, the saintly knight who finds the Holy Grail, but with Sir Lancelot, his adulterous father, whose only virtue is an invincible right arm. In the Mahabharata, by contrast, just before plunging into the greatest slaughter the world has seen, both armies pause while Krishna and Arjuna discuss theology. Arjuna's brother Bhima — the Arnold Schwarzenegger of Indian epic — is seen as somewhat of a buffoon. An unholy warrior is no more than a bullyboy. Indians have little respect for muscle without morality.

It was rishis — sages of exceptional holiness — who told the stories that became the Ramayana, and the rishi Valmiki who wrote them all down. It was rishis who created the other great Indian epic, the Mahabharata, a thousand years before Valmiki was born. And it was rishis who fashioned the Upanishads, the philosophical odes that transformed archaic Vedic polytheism into the more sophisticated Hindu religion.

It was iconoclastic rishis and swamis rather than stodgy Brahmins and conservative priests who ushered in each revolution of thought. The cult of Shiva, the cult of Vishnu, the entire Buddhist faith — all were products of rishis searching for Truth. The sadhus have always been India's teachers, her gurus, the shapers of her views on life. Kings may govern the people's actions, but it is sages who command their minds.

About fourteen hundred years ago, even the country's art was in the hands of the sadhus. They lived in caves dug out of remote mountainsides and created some of the most magnificent painting and sculpture the world has ever seen. At Ellora and Ajanta, deep in the wasteland of Maharashtra, one can still climb up to these stony hermitages and wonder at what has passed.

Ellora's most spectacular site is Kailasha Temple, a depiction of the Himalayan home of the divine mendicant Shiva. The structure, twice the area of the Parthenon, has been painstakingly whittled from the living cliff inch by inch, like an ivory statuette hidden in a bar of soap. The profusion of detailed deities is awe-inspiring, and hardly less awe-inspiring is the fact that each minute carving was once painted with an exuberance of shouting colors.

But of the thirty-odd shrines at Ellora, it is not Kailasha that moves me most. It's too close to the main road, too easily reached by visitors. Here the silent solemnity of the centuries is constantly ripped to shreds. Entire families come to gawk: aunts huffing and puffing, complaining about the dust, uncles rehashing last night's cricket match, nephews and nieces shrieking as they play tag between the frescoed pillars. India's present will not let her past rest in peace. There is much that is well worth gawking at, of course, but the very act of staring seems a denial of the gawkers' heritage. That is not why the sadhus crafted this temple. Kailasha is a gilt-framed mirror in which India cannot recognize its own reflection, but is quite content to admire the golden trimming.

It is the same at the older caves of Ajanta, an afternoon's travel away. The hermitages are strung in a horseshoe across the side of a mountain, but one needn't actually climb to get there. The path is wide and paved, so that overdressed Bombay matrons can ride up in wooden sedan-chairs, each hefted by four stoic bearers. At the cave mouth a servant holds an enormous mirror of polished tin, directing the sun's rays in to illuminate the chamber and slowly burn the frescoes into oblivion.

I marvel that all these murals — the red and white elephants, the monkeys playing peek-a-boo with water buffaloes, the fat, pale dwarfs supporting the weight of stone ceilings on their pudgy shoulders — were never meant to be seen. At least, not seen in any light stronger than the flicker of an oily torch or the glow of a waxy candle. I am thankful for my flashlight: the sadhus who painted these walls never saw them as clearly as I do. Then another palanquin lumbers up the steps, and the sanctuary is no longer mine.

The caves I like the most are ones that require more work. There are five hermitages at Ellora that can be reached only by a crumbling path two feet wide, a track chiseled out of the mountain face, which drops thirty yards to bare rock pits below. The path looks more difficult than it actually is, so the family picnickers stay away. There the spirits of long-dead sadhus seem almost alive.

They huddle together in the dim, dirty corners, chanting mantras that never reach my ears. They sit absolutely still, wholly invisible, but I feel their presence. So many prayers have been uttered here over the ages that the claustrophobic chambers still seem laden with entrapped piety.

Sometimes, when I am in a cave all alone, I hear shrill whispers. It's a rapid, indecipherable chittering that comes from nowhere I can identify. I turn my head left and right straining to pinpoint the source, but always it is somewhere else. That is, until I let my flashlight beam stray to the cavern's ceiling, and see that it is encrusted with hundreds of evil-looking bats. Now I recognize the musky animal smell that permeates every cave, an odor I assumed was simply the odor of death. They swoop about and complain bitterly at the intrusion, then rejoin the furry brown blanket squirming upside down from the roof. The old hermitages are still home to many hermits.

Every now and then in a temple's inner recesses, I come across a well-polished stone lingam, the phallic symbol sacred to Shiva. Often it is garlanded with the fresh flowers and ashes of a recent offering. I brighten when I see this. It proves that not all the visitors to Ellora are rowdy teenage boys shouting across the valley to hear their voices echo.

I hike back over the mountain, a hill composed primarily of semiprecious green malachite, and hear nothing but the sunburnt rustling of leaves and the subliminal humming of insects. Perhaps the well-traveled sites like Kailasha are home to spirits as well, spirits I just haven't noticed. Ghosts come out only when one is all alone.

Solitude and seclusion do indeed open up another world, a world of spirit. I have never spent a long enough time in isolation to get more than a peek into this world. The sadhus who devote their lives to it must be good friends with the spirits most of us never see.

In all the caves at Ajanta, there is not a single Hindu image. At the time these shrines were hewn from the cliff, Hinduism was no longer the land's dominant faith. But India's hermit tradition is too deeply ingrained to be washed away by a mere change of religion. This spiritual revolution, in fact, helped make India's sadhus what they are today.

In 262 B.C. India converted to Buddhism. Or, more properly, that year saw the conversion of Ashoka, the world emperor who ruled more of the subcontinent than any king before or since. Everything from what is now Pakistan to what is now Madras fell under his sway, the only time before the British Raj when nearly all of India was one unified nation.

The Buddha himself had lived three centuries earlier and was probably the most celebrated sadhu of all time. Hindus believe he was an avatar of the god Vishnu, just like Rama himself, and that he came to earth to revitalize a dying faith. His name was Siddhartha Gautama — the title Buddha, "One Who Has Awakened," can be applied to anybody who has attained enlightenment. Until the age of twenty-nine Gautama never set foot outside his house. The son of a minor Nepalese monarch, he'd had an extraordinary fate foretold at birth. One hundred and eight learned Brahmins consulted all manner of oracles, and proclaimed that the baby would either rule the whole earth or discover the Truth.

To wield limitless power or to beg scraps from the tables of street sweepers — for Gautama's father the choice was easy. He locked his son inside the palace and carefully controlled every sight, sound, and scent of the young prince's world, kept him strictly quarantined from any thought or influence that might lead him down the road of philosophy.

But in his twenty-ninth year Gautama grew curious. He sneaked out of the palace alone, and what he saw in the world outside changed his life. He saw a man wracked by disease, a corpse dumped unceremoniously in the gutter, an old man barely able to move from senility, and a holy mendicant wandering without a care in the world. The first three sights taught him the transience of all earthly joy, while the last showed him the path he had to follow.

Gautama sought enlightenment in the manner prescribed for swamis since Vedic times: he mortified his body with unspeakable austerities, hoping to purge all corporeal grossness from his incorporeal soul. In the Tripitaka, one of the oldest works of the Buddhist canon, Gautama himself describes his saintly condition:

Because of so little nourishment, all my limbs became like some withered creepers with knotted joints. My buttocks were like a buffalo's horn, my backbone protruding like a string of balls, my ribs like rafters of a dilapidated shed, the pupils of my eyes appeared sunk deep in their sockets as water appears shining at the bottom of a deep well. When I stroked my limbs with my hand, hairs rotted at the roots fell away from my body.

And then one day, his frame nearly disintegrating from ceaseless abuse, Gautama sat down beneath a boh tree and resolved not to get up until he had attained enlightenment. For a long, long time he sat, thinking, and then not thinking, and then going even beyond nonthought to a state I wouldn't be able to describe even if I'd experienced it myself. Mara, the Lord of the Demons, came before him as he sat in meditation, tempted him with wealth, power, and worldly bliss beyond imagining, but Gautama did not even look up. Finally, on a night of the full moon in May, 528 B.C., he understood what it all meant. Everything. In the entire universe.

Past generations of swamis had got it all wrong, he realized. Yes, a spiritual man must eliminate desire, but the way to do that is not by whips and thorns and diets of bark. Such scourging of the flesh is just as bad as wallowing in luxury. Both approaches make material things far too important. The physical world, Gautama realized, is utterly insignificant, so petty, changing, and insubstantial that it can hardly be said to exist at all — a mere dream, perhaps, dreamt by God Himself. One should not hate the transitory comforts of life, for hate of any sort pollutes the soul; one must treat them instead with utter indifference. The true course lies not in degrading the body but in uplifting the mind.

The Buddha was hardly alone in challenging the old faith. Many of his fellow swamis were reaching similar conclusions and forming the bhakti movement that created the Upanishads and revolutionized Hindu doctrine. But the abstruse philosophical speculation of these theologians never had much resonance with the masses. Their complex musings were conducted in Sanskirt, the holy language of the Brahmins, while Gautama taught in the vernacular tongue Pali. As Buddhism spread throughout India — from the time of Ashoka to the Gupta empire five hundred years later to the era of the last Ajanta caves two centuries later still — it was Gautama's concept of sadhuhood that flourished.

It has been over a millennium since Hinduism (primarily through the cults of Shiva and Vishnu) recaptured the souls of the Indian people. Outside of the Himalayas, there are virtually no native Buddhists left in the country. But today few swamis can be found scourging their flesh. There will always be the rare fakir who tests his iron will on a bed of nails, but most of India's sages seek a more peaceful path. The Truth they seek is not wrenched from the soul by violence but cajoled out through years of patient coaxing. Gautama the Buddha and Gautama the brother-avatar of Rama are indeed one and the same. It was sadhus who defined India's past, sadhus who determined her present.

Five

CASTE

SITA was doing her morning's laundry when the crow came along.

"Caw!" said the crow, and attempted to peck out Sita's eyes. She tried to shoo him away, but he would not leave.

"Go!" she said.

"Caw!" said the crow, as its beak darted toward her face.

"Go!" she said. "My husband is Prince Rama, and he will kill you for sure."

"Caw!" said the crow. He would have grinned, if birds had lips.

When Rama arrived, he politely asked the crow to stop.

The bird laughed an avian laugh and continued biting at Sita's head.

"Crow," said Rama, "you are leaving me little choice. If you do not stop, I will have to kill you."

"I am the son of Indra," cawed the crow. "You have no power to harm me." But Rama plucked a blade of grass from the ground, then turned it into an invincible arrow by recitation of a mantra from Brahma Himself.

The bird flew above the treetops, over the mountains, across the Five Worlds, even up through the Seven Heavens, always a single wing flap ahead of the missile, and tiring fast. He flew to men of power, to holy sages, even to his father Indra, but none could protect him from the relentless dart. In desperation he swooped back to Rama and begged for his life.

"Please," said the crow, "you who protect all, please spare me."

Rama's brow darkened. "It is too late," he said. "Once the bolt is drawn, it cannot help but speed to its target. A holy arrow cannot be unshot. But you may choose the part of your body you wish to lose."

The crow gave up his left eye and went on his way.

Sita did not have to rebuke her husband for resorting to violence. They both knew this was the act of a warrior rather than a hermit.

"It is destined, cannot be changed," Rama said. "I am what I am, there is no point in denying it."

As everyone knows, the human race is all descended from a single man named Manu. Those who came from his mouth are the Brahmins, those from his arms are the Kshatriyas, from his thighs the Vaishyas, and from his feet the Shudras. Caste is eternal, of that there can be no doubt. Rama came from the very biceps of Manu and had no choice but to fight for Truth.

Not long after Rama set up camp by the Godivari River, in the depths of the Panchavati forest, he was visited by a demon. She was old, fat, ugly, and had a voice that grated like a rusty nail. Her name was Surpanakha, and she immediately fell in love with the prince of Ayodhya. She offered to gobble up Sita and take Rama for her husband.

"I am very sorry," joked the prince, "but marriage bonds are unbreakable. The loss is all mine. Perhaps you should pursue my brother instead."

The hideous Rakshasi turned her gaze to Lakshman.

"My abject apologies," Lakshman said, continuing the jest, "but I could never accept such an honor. I am only my brother's miserable servant, hardly a worthy mate for you. But if you become Rama's secondary wife, surely he would be so enthralled by your beauty that he would ignore Sita as if she were not even there."

Surpanakha had no sense of humor. She rose up above Sita, slicing the air with her razory talons and prepared to swoop down on her supposed rival.

"Never jest with stupid creatures," Rama said to his brother, and nodded permission to fight.

Lakshman pulled out his sword and quickly lopped off the Rakshasi's nose and ears. His action could hardly have made the demon uglier. If anything, the monster's visage was less loathsome after the blows because there was less of it left.

Surpanakha flew off to her lair and came back with fourteen huge demons in tow.

"You are mine," she said to Rama, "as husband by my side or dinner in my belly. Take your pick."

"We are simple hermits," Rama replied. "We mean no harm to anybody. Please go, for we desire no violence." But as he spoke, he conspicuously strung his bow.

The fourteen demons all at once hurled fourteen lances, which Rama cut down with fourteen arrows fired as fast as a mouse can blink. Then he shot fourteen more bolts, and slew the demons cold. Surpanakha fled crying, soaked in the black blood of her henchmen. Rama let her go, because it is taboo for a Kshatriya to kill a woman.

"Cheer up," Lakshman said. "There is no shame in enjoying the pleasures of battle. I, for one, am glad to have you back. The real you — my brother, my prince, my comrade-at-arms. Not some bark-eating, beard-scratching, prayer-saying, barefooty, berry-picking little hermity fellow. Be proud, my brother, be proud of who you are."

"No cause for pride," Rama replied. "I am a born warrior, it is true, but one ought not exult in one's birth. Nevertheless, though a man cannot glory in his innate nature, he also cannot deny it.

"You are quite right, Lakshman. We are both Kshatriya fighters, there is no escaping that. Only you have known this all along, while I took a decade to learn the truth."

That afternoon the bright sky became overcast with storm-heavy clouds. Jackals began to howl, birds sought safety in tree nooks, fish dove deep under the water and rested fearfully on the riverbeds. A hot wind like a blacksmith's bellows blew across the land.

It was not a storm but a vast army of demons. Surpanakha had summoned up all the Rakshasas of the forest, and they had all answered her call. Fourteen thousand of them filled the air. They were hungry and horrible, armed for slaughter and thirsty for gore. They carried double-headed battle-axes, freshly honed sabers, crushing mallets and maces, unbreakable lances, gleaming bronze discuses aching for war. They drew up their massed legions across the whole sky and readied themselves for the fight.

"Poor fools," Rama said sadly, and killed them all.

➤ ➤ ➤

The hermits of the forest came before Rama with joined palms. They offered their most heartfelt blessings and prayers, thanked him again and again for removing the threat to their lives.

Rama, embarrassed, picked the sadhus up off their knees.

"It is not right for a holy man to bow to a warrior," he said. "It is my duty as a Kshatriya to serve you. It is my place, it is my purpose, it is the essence of my caste."

Meanwhile, Surpanakha had fled to the island of Lanka, where her brother Ravana was king. She pressed her noseless, earless face against the demon's feet, told him how fourteen thousand Rakshasas had been massacred in an hour, and demanded vengeance.

"I was only trying to bring back Sita as your concubine," she lied. With sugary words she conjured up every detail of Sita's matchless form, her almond eyes, her butter-smooth skin, her waist, breasts, legs, and delicate fingers, like an apsara that dances in the throne-room of the gods.

"Yes," said the Lord of All Demons. "Yes, indeed."

ᎦᏪᎦᏪᎦᏪᎦᏪᎦᏪᎦᏪᎦᏪᎦᏪ

Caste is dead. Or, at the very least, it has received its fatal blow and is merely taking a while to die. So say urban sophisticates and others who ought to know. One well-respected scholar at the country's most prestigious university told me that caste has been extinct for over one hundred years. Some people honestly believe this is true. Some people are very wrong.

When India became a secular democracy at Independence, caste was declared moribund; Article 17 of the new constitution outlawed its most notorious manifestation: "Untouchability is abolished and its practice in any form is forbidden." But Hinduism is an integral part of India, and caste is an integral part of Hinduism. It is embedded too deeply in the national psyche to be dug out anytime soon, least of all with a shovel made of official paper.

"He will make each of the four castes stick to its duties," wrote Valmiki of Prince Rama. Why do Indians of all classes still cherish a hero whose avowed aim is to keep them in their place? In essence, because they feel that their place means something.

The jati system, like the doctrine of predestination, gives each member of society some measure of dignity. In theory, certain castes are more privileged than others, but all are equally honorable. "Brahmins and scavengers," Gandhi wrote, "are absolutely on a par in the eyes of God." People of all classes serve humanity in different ways. Priests and kings may be treated with deference, but it is farmers and craftsmen who keep a country alive.

Rama uses a bow, the sweeper a broom, but both are doing the same job: they are working to uphold eternal dharma, the order of the universe. That is why even the lowliest garbage picker can personally identify with the Ramayana's princely hero. Caste binds all people together with a single purpose. All members of society are players on the same team, and every petty bench warmer can share in the reflected glory of the star batsman.

No, caste is not dead. It is merely experiencing a change of life. Particularly in the big cities it is evolving so fast that orthodox traditionalists are starting to look like brontosauruses. The end product of this transformation is anybody's guess. At best it will be a social system based on merit rather than birth, a system that may still be stratified but not preordained. At worst it will be a hierarchy just as rigid as before but stripped of its moral underpinnings, a power structure built upon raw politics instead of religion.

One might think that Brahmins, the top figures on the traditional totem pole, would be the least inclined to modify the caste system. As it happens, they are often in the forefront of reform. Brahmins are still the best-educated class, arguably the most cosmopolitan and socially progressive as well. They tend to dominate India's intellectual life, and when the battle over caste is fought with words rather than weapons, the Brahmins are first in the trenches.

Cho Ramaswamy, a Brahmin from Madras, has spent most of his life waging various intellectual wars, on enough different fronts to confound Sun-tzu. His résumé is so tightly crammed that one wonders when he finds time to sit down.

He is a journalist. He is a critic. He has written twenty-three Tamil-language plays, which have been staged 3,500 times, and he has acted in every performance. He is a lawyer. He is the editor of India's only magazine devoted entirely to political analysis, a satirical journal with a circulation higher than that of *Harpers'* or *The New Republic.* He has directed four movies, scripted fourteen, starred in one hundred and eighty. Then there were the television serials, three of them . . .

"Caste has been thoroughly corrupted," he said when I visited his office. "Lost its true meaning. Once it was a set of duties and obligations that allowed people to live in harmony. Today it is all mere snobbery on the part of the haves and opportunism on the part of the have-nots. Once caste bound us together, now it tears us apart."

He licked his purple lips and ran a hand across his melon-smooth head.

"Yes, there are still divisions," he continued, "but they have lost all their moral essence. Every society in the world has different classes — some men will always be more powerful and more privileged than others. But in India our system *used* to have a spiritual foundation. Today people think only of caste privileges, never of responsibilities."

I asked if that was true even of his own priestly caste.

"Certainly," he said. "The Brahmins are no exception. Formerly we prayed for all of society, we taught and studied and wrote for the good of all. Now, with the exception of pandits and sadhus who have devoted their whole lives to religion, we pray only for ourselves. If we pray at all. There is no longer a class of people to be the spiritual guides for the country, to provide a moral touchstone, to instruct, investigate, criticize, encourage, or create."

The Brahmins once were the watchdogs of the Indian soul. But now, it seems, they are too busy chasing sticks.

"We are so concerned with material things," Ramaswamy said. "In past ages such greed among Brahmins would have been seen as blasphemy, now it is positively encouraged. I do not claim to be any purer myself. I am only a Brahmin by today's definition — that is, I happen to have been born into the proper family. But in the past, a long time ago, caste was based more on character than on heredity."

"Character?"

"Yes, how a man lives his life. In epic times, an unworthy Brahmin could find himself demoted to the rank of Shudra, and a Kshatriya or even a Vaishya could become a Brahmin by earnest devotion. Both the Ramayana and the Mahabharata are laced with such examples."

When Rama's mentor, Vishvamitra, chooses to set aside his aristocratic caste and perform superhuman austerities, he is finally able to transform himself into a Brahmin. But it takes him two thousand long years.

"Even at that time," I asked, "weren't such cases extremely rare?"

He removed his heavy glasses and wiped a handkerchief across his forehead. His eyebrows were two delicate black arcs that seemed to be sketched on with cosmetic pencil.

"Who can say?" he said. "Rare or not, they did occur. I do not know when caste became ossified, turned into a purely hereditary institution, but it was certainly much later than the days of Rama. There is a tale which goes all the way back to epic times, of a learned rishi and an honest pupil, that puts the issue in perspective."

Ramaswamy, pointing his finger like a teacher himself, told me the ancient story. It went like this:

Once there was a very wise guru, teaching his students all the elements of theology. When the time came to explain the caste system, he asked each boy to stand up and tell his caste. Every child announced his station, either with pride or a touch of embarrassment.

("I should also point out," Ramaswamy interrupted himself to say, "this shows that in ancient times the youth of all jatis had some hope of education and mixed together in class — a thing that would not happen again for many hundreds of years. But I digress.")

Each student stepped forth and told his caste, all except one little boy, who said he did not know.

"Don't know?" the guru asked. "But surely you know your father's job?"

"I am sorry," the boy said, "no, I do not know it. I have never seen my father, and my mother has never told me anything about him." The rishi told his student to run right home and ask his mother, for it was a very important thing.

The boy did as he was told and came back to class. "I am sorry," he said, "but I still do not know my caste. My mother said that she had been with so very many different men that she could not even guess which of them was my father."

The other students, of course, broke out in a chorus of laughter. They called him a bastard, a son of a whore, and many other cruel names that happened to be true.

The rishi quieted them all down. He took off his own sacred janneu-thread and put it around the boy's chest. "My lad," he said, "it does not matter who your father was. You are a Brahmin, because you have told the truth."

I asked Ramaswamy about caste relations today in his own state of Tamil Nadu. The polymath gave a *tsk*-ing sound of mild disgust.

"All a game," he said, "or even worse, caste is now merely the means to an end. For Brahmins, a means of holding on to their status, for others a means of gaining new power. But the quarrels are mostly within the Shudra class, between the various jatis struggling to divvy up the pie."

Throughout India, less than one fifth of the population belongs to the "twice-born" classes — the Brahmins, Kshatriyas, and Vaishyas. Slightly more than half are Shudras, and the rest are Untouchables, tribals, and non-Hindus outside the caste system entirely. In the south there are virtually no Kshatriyas or Vaishyas at all, and only 4 percent of the people are Brahmins. The word "caste" is most appropriately applied not to the four great classes (these are termed *varnas,* literally "colors") but to the thousands of specialized subclans within them called jatis. Each part of India has its own assortment of jatis, thousands of them, all locked in rivalries that have no start or finish.

"Every jati," Ramaswamy said, "lobbies hard to be put on the government's list of so-called backward castes. That way they become eligible for special job quotas, development grants, and set-asides. Then, once on the list, each jati fights for the 'honor' of a 'most backward' classification. So far no fewer than 290 castes have won this distinction, and the number grows every day. For all we know, it may have grown in the time we have been sitting here talking."

"Isn't the classification a religious one?"

"Who is Shudra, who is Harijan — it is all decided by politicians rather than religion. They squabble over who deserves the privileges set aside for the lowest of the low. It is a hierarchy just as strict as ever, only now turned upside down. The government's affirmative action programs are well intentioned, but they have the effect of *perpetuating* caste divisions, even of strengthening them."

The last shall be first and the first shall be last, said a god from the West long ago. A revolutionary creed, but every revolution must know when to stop. Too much revolving is no more than spinning in place. After all, a complete 360-degree revolution puts you right back where you began.

"Below even the lowest Shudras are the Harijans," he said, using the polite term for people once deemed Untouchable. "It is quite true that in the past Harijans were treated most shabbily by Hindus. They were denied all opportunities, all the best things in life. This went on for centuries, and there is no excusing it. But today redress has been carried to unreasonable extremes."

I asked if Harijans weren't still a socially disadvantaged group. He shook his head, said that was not the issue.

"It is no longer a matter of righting past wrongs," he said. "The lower classes still need help, but their advocates are concerned only with power. The leaders have no interest in eliminating caste divisions — they want to keep each jati at the next one's throat to build their own constituencies. Politicians pander shamelessly to the Harijans, who form a veritable vote-bank. The quotas and set-asides, I believe, should be phased out gradually, a little bit each year, but this is not likely to happen. As long as people are kept poor, illiterate, dependent on government jobs, and bound tight to their caste, they will always be used and misled by the unscrupulous."

He looked up at a large painting of the Elephant God, Ganesh, on the wall across from his desk. The office was filled with icons and pictures of deities, mostly Ganesh, but Shiva and Vishnu as well. The only image of a mortal that I saw was a huge photograph of Mahatma Gandhi in the downstairs entrance hall.

"Jobs, funds, seats on committees, slots in colleges," Ramaswamy continued, "all are the new privileges of belonging to the 'proper' downtrodden caste. But they are granted simply by force, not earned by behavior. When Brahmins were the officially privileged class, we had to live up to a high ethical standard as the price for our position. Any Brahmin convicted of a crime would receive twice the punishment of a Kshatriya, four times that of a Shudra. The status was not given for free."

"So caste survives," I asked, "because people see it as expedient rather than True?"

"No, no," he replied. "India is not so jaded just yet. Belief in karma is still almost universal, and karma is what determines one's caste, you know. That is why people are willing to accept a low station in life, because they believe it is the fair punishment for sins in a previous incarnation. Without this doctrine caste would crumble, but Indians will never give up this belief.

I accept it myself, not from blind adherence to tradition, but because it is the only worthwhile explanation I've heard for why so many good people suffer so much hardship. After all, Christianity and Islam can say only that it is all the fault of the victims themselves, or that God's ways are inexplicable. The caste system — in its ancient form, not the way it is now — provides a logical framework for rewarding good and punishing evil over the course of many lives."

So what would he like Indian society to become?

"I would favor an end to all caste," he said. "We can never get back to a system based on character, so it is far better just to scrap the whole thing. *Varna dharma,* or duties specific to each caste, are being ignored in any case. All men and women should have the very same rights and the same obligations."

What are these obligations?

"First is public-mindedness. Every citizen must contribute to the growth of the nation by hard work. We are far too selfish, we must look out for the good of the community rather than merely our own interests.

"Second is truthfulness. We must deal with others honestly, always. According to tradition, this is a man's most important duty.

"Third, we must not covet others' wealth. Fourth, we must be kind to all living creatures, human and animal alike. Fifth, we must banish jealousy and anger. These are all difficult tasks, but they all must be accomplished every day.

"Sixth, each of us must constantly strive to realize God. If we can do this, all the rest will fall into place."

Ramaswamy's views are colored by the fact that the anti-Brahmin backlash has been greater in Tamil Nadu than anyplace else in India. That does not make his criticism of the cynical, abusive caste politics any less valid. Perhaps in some cases the pendulum *has* swung too far in the other direction. But it is a pendulum's constant back-and-forth swing that keeps the clock ticking and drives time forward.

Not every Brahmin takes his caste quite so seriously as Ramaswamy. Many members of the secular intelligentsia see no use for the jati system and look forward to its withering away. They understand the artificiality of their high social station but are not ashamed to enjoy the privileges of birth and schooling. If America has limousine liberals, India has BMW Brahmins.

"I am a godless creature," said Dr. Sarasvata with a wry grin. "Never been actively hostile to religion, you understand, just never really had any use for it."

A Kashmiri librarian, Dr. Sarasvata lives an eminently Brahminical existence. His life is devoted to scholarship and learning, he savors sparking the love of study in other minds, and he spends most of his waking hours surrounded by more books than anyone could ever hope to read. He does not drive a BMW (foreign cars are virtually unknown outside of Bombay) but is chauffeured in a well-polished Ambassador.

"Caste and all that sort of thing," he said, "have long seemed pretty much irrelevant to me. In a big city like Delhi, the divisions just don't matter any more."

Much has changed, there is no denying that. Today people of all castes mix freely in the offices, colleges, streets, and trains; they shop in the same stores, even eat in the same restaurants. Until Mahatma Gandhi began his campaign for caste liberalization, Brahmins considered themselves defiled if they accidentally consumed food that had been prepared by a cook of a lower order. There are still eateries promising "Brahmin Refreshment," but they are few and far between.

Earlier in this century Brahmins would shun any physical contact with Shudras (let alone Untouchables), as if the lightest brush could transmit some disease fatal to the soul. Today they wrestle on the same university teams, grappling each other into armlocks and half nelsons, mingling their sweat with no thought of corruption.

But after the bout is over, after the showers and the friendly slaps on the back, each wrestler goes back to his own home. There caste commingling ends. A Brahmin may have Shudra friends over to visit, may even invite them for dinner, but will seldom invite them to join the family. After all, *bhai,* we're as liberal as anybody, you know, but would you really want your pretty little daughter *marrying* one of them?

"Marriage," said Dr. Sarasvata, "more than anything else, that is what keeps caste alive. Very few indeed will marry outside their jati, very few. This is true of arranged marriages, of course, but equally so in love matches. Young people look for a mate with whom they have things in common, a similar upbringing and mindset."

A quick glance through the matrimonial section of any newspaper shows just how desperate people are to preserve their family's caste purity. Page after page of advertisements, with prospective brides, grooms, and parents zealously searching for a match with the proper credentials.

"Though being a Brahmin is not important to me personally," the librarian continued, "I fear the destruction of the caste system would be a dangerous thing. Very dangerous indeed. Despite its injustices, the structure does function. Each subclan looks after its own, takes care of every person, provides a kind of safety net. Without this order, life would be sheer chaos.

"I would rather see caste replaced by a comprehensive welfare system, that would be the ideal solution. But that will never happen, and anything is better than anarchy."

He looked out his window at a wall across the street painted with several gaudy divinities. He pointed at one of them, a figure of a buxom woman decked out in luxurious finery.

"Indians now worship many gods," he said. "When caste ends, I do fear we will worship only one, and it will be her." The deity to which he was pointing was Lakshmi, the Goddess of Wealth.

At the point in the Ramayana where Rama gives his brother Bharata advice on how to be a king, he sternly warns the young man: "Do not concern yourself with atheistic Brahmins. All those puerile persons proud of their learning can only bring evil to others, and in spite of the existence of excellent religious literature, they vainly engage themselves in vain sophistical arguments."

But even an atheistic Brahmin, a godless creature indeed, sees some value in the caste system today. Not merely for self-preservation — Dr. Sarasvata could do without his chauffeured car if he had to, and there is little reason to think that he (Brahmin or not) would ever have to. But, like most of his countrymen, he has seen enough chaos not to want any more. Everyone of his generation remembers the horrors of Partition, when Muslim Pakistan was wrenched away from the Hindu subcontinent, and over one million people died in the bloody conflict. In Sarasvata's native Kashmir and other states violently battling for autonomy, in the riot-torn streets of Aligarh, Hyderabad, or Amritsar, in every quiet village that could explode at the slightest provocation, Indians fear anarchy — with good reason.

India has never been more than half a step from civil war. This is only natural for a land that is really several dozen distinct nations stitched together. Where deathly turmoil is a looming terror, Western ideas of boundless freedom and social mobility have far less resonance.

Even removed from its spiritual roots, caste brings the country a modicum of order. Until some substitute can be found, it is an anchor of stability that India cannot (and will not) reel in. The challenge is to make sure that caste remains an anchor and not a millstone — that it serves to stabilize rather than submerge.

Not every Brahmin has a chauffeur. Most don't, in fact. Some can't even read a road sign. Some not only are not driven in fancy cars, they must themselves transport others. Sometimes without even the benefit of an automobile.

My rickshaw-wallah in Faizabad was a Brahmin. He mentioned it out of the blue, for no apparent reason. Perhaps it was because I was a foreigner and he knew he'd never see me again.

"It is not right," he said as he pedaled, struggling up a steep slope. "Not how it should be."

He was a small, thin, ill-shaven man, with an unhealthy-sounding cough. I asked how he'd come to be a rickshaw-wallah.

"My father," he said sadly, "was a big landowner. Owned several different farms. But business grew bad, and he lost all his money, and he died. I had to leave school to work. Work at any job at all, but never get anywhere."

I tried to cheer him up by asking about his family. His face was turned forward toward the traffic, but his voice sounded more melancholy than before.

"Two boys, and my wife is pregnant with another child. There is no money for schooling, hardly even enough money for food. And what will I do if I get sick, eh, how will they survive?"

His pace did not vary, but as I listened to his stammered words I knew he was starting to cry.

"It . . . it . . . it is not *right* for a Brahmin to live like this," he gasped. "I cannot look my sons in the eye, what kind of life can I give them, eh? But what can I do? A man must eat, must feed his family."

We reached my destination, and I got out. I wanted to help him, but there was nothing to be done. I thought of giving him money, but that would have been the cruelest act of all. When a man's pride has been crushed, you do not turn him into a beggar.

Caste may be a millstone for members of lower jatis, a dead-weight that prevents them from rising in society. But even for Brahmins it can be an anvil around the neck. Not necessarily in a material sense — though there are many examples of reverse discrimination and unfair quotas, Brahmins still are far from being a disadvantaged class — but in an emotional one. High caste no longer guarantees prestige, comfort, or respect, yet it does make failure all the more shameful. There have always been Brahmins engaged in menial labor, including some characters in the Ramayana. But never before have caste and station been so ruthlessly separated.

What struck me most about my rickshaw-wallah was not his situation but his complaint. Most Indians don't moan about hardships. I've met many people in India who are far more destitute, far unluckier, far more worthy of pity. But I have met very few human beings, in any country in the world, filled with more profound misery.

Across the street an overweight man with a Shudra's dark complexion held up his hand.

"Hey, rickshaw!" he called out.

I paid the Brahmin and stepped into the street. The kindest thing, it seemed, was to let him go earn his unhappy rupees.

➤ ➤ ➤

I went looking for Kshatriyas in the quiet lanes of Defence Colony. Many, if not most, of the houses in this wealthy Delhi suburb belong to retired military officers, and the names on the mailboxes are a roll call of generals, colonels, majors, and brigadiers.

Colonel Virasena never even considered a civilian career. It wouldn't have mattered anyway, since his father was determined that all the children join the military. The colonel's eldest brother became a lieutenant commander in the navy, his second brother led a tank brigade, and his sister still serves as an army major. A fourth brother manufactures sporting goods, "because *one* of us had to stay home and take care of Mother."

Like Rama, the most famous of all Kshatriyas, the colonel never thought of ignoring his father's wishes.

"Filial duty is important for everybody," he said, "but for Kshatriyas it is second nature. A man's father is his commander, he must be obeyed. Lord Rama knew this, he did not flinch for an instant. It was an unjust order, the order to go into exile and live like an animal. But he did not question, did not complain, he simply complied."

Colonel Virasena noticed that one of his trouser cuffs had come loose, so he quickly folded it back to regulation length.

"All manner of persons can learn from Rama's example," he continued, "but none more than Kshatriyas. He was the perfection of our caste. He fought bravely to defend the innocent, did his duty, and never shrank from necessary hardships. Life in the jungle was terribly rough for him. Fourteen years in exile is a very long time. It was not fourteen days, you know. Many of us who fought in the jungle, whether in Kashmir, Bengal, or the Himalayas, know just how difficult that must have been."

The Indian military has a much higher degree of professionalism and discipline than most other Third World armies. It is almost unique among the forces of developing nations in never having attempted a coup d'état. Pakistan, Bangladesh, and Burma, all formerly part of the unified British Raj, practice religions that do not recognize caste; all have been ruled by generals for most of the years since Independence. By contrast, even during the darkest days of Indira Gandhi's dictatorial "Emergency," India's civilian government was never seriously threatened. I asked the colonel if this had anything to do with Kshatriya values.

"It is certainly no coincidence," he replied. "After all, a conscientious Kshatriya knows that it is his dharma to protect. It is his role in life, the reason he was put on this earth. If he turns rebel he faces not only a court-martial but the judgment of God. His caste obligations and military training point the same way.

"But that is not the whole reason for the troops' good order. Let us be frank — in training, rules, and discipline this is still the British army."

The British might have become Kshatriyas themselves if they'd been willing. Throughout Indian history, succeeding waves of non-Hindu invaders swept into the land, settled down, and were assimilated into society. As warriors, they were generally accorded the high status of Kshatriyas. The proudest lords of the Hindu aristocracy, the soldierly Rajputs of Rajasthan, are descended from barbaric Huns.

"The English system is a fine one," the colonel continued, "none better in the world, but it is quite rigid. In this army a soldier simply cannot question orders. He cannot decide which commands to obey, heed only the charges that he happens to find reasonable. No, it is the general's job to lead, the soldier's to follow. Absolutely. And in that respect it fits quite nicely with Kshatriya values."

Courage, decisiveness, iron nerves, physical prowess — all are fine qualities, but not one makes a soldier. Any of these traits could as easily serve an assassin or a thief. What makes a soldier, above all, is obedience.

This is more true today than ever before. In a modern army, technology has taken over most of the heavy lifting. As swords have given way to rifles and rifles to guided missiles, raw brawn has become virtually irrelevant. The machine-gun is a great equalizer of men, and even the machine-gun is becoming obsolete. The weapons of war that count are now fired electronically, by men sitting in jets, tanks, or even bunkers far away from the scene of any battle.

With so much power concentrated in so few hands, it is the steadiness of those hands that matters most. The best soldier today is not the one who can wreak the greatest devastation — *any* warrior can raise a whirlwind of death if his finger is on the right trigger. The best soldier today is the one who has the self-control to obey. But even this righteous restraint is meaningless unless the men (and women) giving the orders are also bound by a moral code. Perhaps the most difficult decision any soldier must face is how to deal with an unjust command.

"One of my classmates," Colonel Virasena said by way of illustration, "was a Sikh. And they put him in charge of Operation Blue Star."

In 1984 Indira Gandhi commanded her army to storm the Golden Temple in Amritsar, the holiest site in the Sikh religion, to root out the militants holed up inside. The name of this unholy operation was Blue Star. Putting a Sikh in charge was like telling a pious Catholic to bombard Saint Peter's or the Church of the Nativity.

"My school chum," the colonel continued, "he knew it was sacrilege. But what option did he have? He was a soldier, a professional, it was not his place to question the dictates of a superior. He was a Sikh rather than a caste Hindu, but he acted as any true Kshatriya would have. I am sure the decision still weighs heavy on his soul, but I am equally certain that he does not lie awake at night rehashing his choice."

On the wall above the colonel's chair was a large oil painting of an idyllic village scene. I asked him where it was.

"Ah, yes, that," he said. "My wife's painting. She's quite good, don't you think? When she was a young woman she used to go on sketching tours all over the country. Such wonderful colors, excellent eye for shades she has. None of this modern blotches of paint smudged about."

For a few minutes our conversation turned to the shortcomings of most abstract art. Colonel Virasena thumped his armrest appreciatively at my speculation that Jackson Pollock and Piet Mondrian might be punished in Hell by having to stare at each other's paintings for all eternity.

"At any rate," he said, bringing the talk back to the matter at hand, "that picture is of my family home, about eighty miles from Lahore. In what is now Pakistan. We all had to flee in 'forty-seven, of course, all Hindus did. The very next year I was called upon to fight in the war against the Muslim state. I had no wish to kill my former neighbors, my own childhood friends, but I joined a Rajput regiment and did my duty. In 'sixty-five we again fought the Pakistanis, and I again did what I had to. But I keep this picture in the living room to remind me of my home."

The colonel may have found his job as bitter as that of his Sikh friend, but he too sleeps well at night.

"After all," he added, his tone brightening, "the military life is not right for everyone. It is meant only for those who are straight-thinking. No second-guessers, no worrywarts, only solid, to-the-point fellows. Any clever johnnies who try to cut corners, bend the rules, make excuses, they'll all be caught out in no time."

Soldiering is no longer the prerogative of the Kshatriyas, and it is no longer what it once was. In theory, at least, the military arts used to be a sacred trust. Warriors were the moral guardians of the people. They did not take up arms as a career path to prestige and privilege, although these have always been strong incentives. They risked their lives because it was their appointed station in life, their holy responsibility.

"So many ignore their *varna dharma*," the colonel said. "They set no stock in the duties of their caste. Now that people can select what line of work they wish to pursue, they think jati obligations no longer apply. But caste is eternal, it cannot be whisked away by some government edict. It is a Kshatriya's duty to protect and serve the rest of society — always has been, always will be. Perhaps he can do this as a tank commander, perhaps as a member of Parliament, perhaps merely as a postal inspector if he does the job diligently."

"What has replaced the caste values?"

"So many Kshatriyas today care only for themselves. No public-mindedness at all. Like other Indians, we are becoming far too materialistic. Men go into business rather than civil service, they just want to get rich. 'I want a color television,' they say, 'I want a big refrigerator, I want, I want.' The measure, unfortunately, is money alone. All Hindus, and those of high caste in particular, should follow the same ethical rules: be honest, help others, work hard, etcetera. But now people of all castes behave properly only if it happens to be convenient."

He smoothed the ends of his trim white mustache and went on.

"Today people of any class can become military officers, and that is as it should be. But they should not do it for the wrong reasons. Today most think only of themselves when they sign up, they seek out their commission for their own benefit, not that of society."

"So the spiritual burdens of the caste still matter?"

"I believe that the proper Kshatriya duties haven't changed, but the caste's definition has. Now I think anybody who does the *job* of a Kshatriya — that is, any soldier or government official — must take on all the Kshatriyas' moral and spiritual responsibilities as well."

Caste may last forever, but can it matter if nobody observes it? If the day comes when it is universally ignored, will it still truly exist? If a Brahmin chants in the forest where there is nobody else to hear, does he truly make a sound?

"Even in its most narrow, hereditary definition," said the colonel, "caste is *not* disappearing. The government sees to that. All these quotas and aid programs for lower jatis, they ensure the continuation of the system far into the future. How can we have a class-blind society when most civil service jobs are specifically set aside for members of certain castes?"

He looked at me to argue with him, but I could not. Quotas sometimes are a necessary evil in restructuring society, but they do tend to perpetuate the very class and race divisions they were designed to destroy. What's more, they insult the inherent abilities of the people they were meant to uplift — but that was not the colonel's complaint.

"Such reverse discrimination provokes great resentment, I can tell you," he went on. "Even when Kshatriyas try to answer their traditional call to public service, they often find every avenue blocked by the quotas. Is it any wonder our sense of purpose lags? Many take up lower occupations, but more profitable ones. I cannot see why other castes even *want* to do Kshatriya work — plumbers or carpenters are doing jolly well for themselves, making far more money than you or I."

The colonel slowly drummed his fingertips on the arm of his chair.

"Equal opportunity for all, that's what I would like. Just like we have in the military. Those who happen to have been born Kshatriya have a special responsibility, perhaps, but so does anyone who wears a uniform. People of any caste should be free to serve in government, with no special treatment, and once accepted, all should live by the Kshatriya code."

His white mustache twitched with a wry grin.

"But," he said, "politics is a vicious game, always has been."

The colonel was quite right to say that caste is eternal. His statement stemmed from Hindu piety, but it was true in a secular sense as well. Every society in the history of the world has had some degree of hierarchy. From members of the landed gentry in England to members of the Communist Party in China, each nation has its privileged classes. Even in America our castes are largely hereditary — few sons of garbagemen become millionaires, and few sons of millionaires become garbagemen.

India's class system differs from all the rest in two respects: its divisions are based strictly on birth, and they are founded upon spiritual belief rather than brute force or dumb luck. Fortunately, the first trait is changing. Unfortunately, the second is as well.

Today Indians enjoy greater social mobility than at any time in the past. Shudras can become doctors and lawyers. Untouchables can sit in Parliament, and do. In more and more localities, a Harijan whose father cleaned gutters may be the most powerful man in town. No longer is "low" birth an insurmountable barrier to advancement.

This new mobility brings new hardships. The country's woefully inefficient bureaucracy has been packed with barely qualified (sometimes barely literate) employees, hired solely to fill quotas. At the same time, thousands of well-educated Brahmins and Kshatriyas must emigrate to America and Europe every year just to find decent jobs. The ranks of unemployed with college educations number 17 million. India is experiencing a dangerous brain drain, and its solution has been to pull out the stopper.

In August of 1990, then-Premier V. P. Singh set aside 27 percent of all government jobs and university slots for members of 3,743 "backward castes," essentially the entire Shudra class. Combined with the slots previously reserved for Harijans and tribal peoples, this meant that fully half of the most coveted positions in the country were permanently off limits to those best able to fill them. In a single autumn week, seventy high-caste students publicly burned themselves to death in despair.

On the whole, though, the nation is stumbling toward a far more equitable order. No transformation on that scale can come without pain. In some states, such as Tamil Nadu, the anti-Brahmin backlash has been vicious enough to qualify as repression, but in general high-caste grumblings sound much like those of some white Protestants in America. Reverse discrimination certainly hurts, but life is still easier for Bombay Brahmins than for Bihari Shudras, society kinder to Boston Brahmins than to East LA Chicanos.

Far more disturbing than any individual setbacks, India's whole social system is losing its heart. It is not merely repression that has kept the subcontinent's masses down. Caste has survived the millennia because all Indians, not just privileged ones, believed it meant something. Something more than just the way things are: the way things should be.

Caste was created by force, it is true. About 3,500 years ago India was invaded by the Aryans, a race of light-skinned warriors from the harsh foothills of the Caucasian mountains. The conquerors built a thick wall to separate themselves from the land's subjugated natives, a wall that stretched the length of the subcontinent. It was a solid wall of ideas, a wall unbreachable by any weapon because it existed in people's minds. The Aryan men-at-arms became the Kshatriyas, the priests they brought with them became the Brahmins, and the indigenous multitudes who now served them became the Shudras. Later, once trade joined war and farming as a major way of life, the new class of merchants and shopkeepers became the Vaishyas.

Once the sting of invasion faded to a faint memory, caste developed into a central tenet of the nascent Hindu faith. The children of victors and vanquished alike subscribed to the evolving belief. Since that time Indians have accepted their station in life not simply because it was imposed upon them — all social demarcations in the world were imposed at one time or another, and nobody has ever chosen the class into which he or she was born. But the Indians saw in these ranks the work of God rather than man.

It is easier, far easier, to accept a humble position if it is divinely ordained. To a Hindu, each person's place in the world is not determined by chance. A Brahmin is a Brahmin as a reward for the virtues of a previous life, and a Shudra is a Shudra for past sins. It is all perfectly just. Over the course of several incarnations, even the lowest peasant can rise to the top of the heap.

Until the present, this belief made social inequities tolerable. But when the order of the world is no longer changeless, it is no longer wholly divine. Class is increasingly determined by money rather than by God. Indians have traditionally seen caste as a means of cooperation, a way of structuring society so that all members can work together in harmony. But if the system is stripped of its religious meaning, class becomes a struggle of each person against every other. If stratification has no basis in morality, it becomes a prison.

The cruelest prison of all is one with a half-open door. Rays of light filter into the darkness, and the inmates can glimpse the world outside. If the guards let a few men out, incarceration becomes all the more galling for the rest. The prisoners are no longer bound together by a common condition. Each one schemes, plots, and betrays his comrades in hope of winning early release.

That is not to say Indians should slam the door shut. Far better to open it wide, but the gate is too rusty for that. There is simply no way for three quarters of a billion souls all to escape the confines of poverty and degradation. There is nothing at all wrong with these souls attempting to work for a better life. But they should not forget the code that made their confinement bearable, should not seek parole merely by turning themselves into quislings.

> > >

"We are all Vaishyas now," said Prakesh Anand. "Whatever people's original caste, they have all become Vaishya."

We were standing under a cinema marquee in Calcutta, waiting for the rain to stop. It had blown up out of nowhere and was pounding down like a gray liquid fist. The downpour punched the pavement so hard that no rickshaw or taxi would halt for a fare, and there was nothing to do but wait.

"I say this not as an insult," he continued. "I am Vaishya myself. Born Vaishya, you understand, not merely become one. But now everybody lives by the code of *our* caste — or, worse, does not live by it."

He shook a small pool of rainwater out of his collar and went on.

"To make money, that is our dharma," he said. "That is our role. And persons of every class are now concerned only with material things. But the virtue of a Vaishya is to make his profits *honestly,* and that is all too often forgotten."

The Laws of Manu, that ancient text spelling out all rules for Hindu existence, speaks of four types of holy man. There is the *brahmacharya* (one who has taken a vow of celibacy), the *bhikku* (wandering mendicant), the *vanaprastha* (forest hermit renouncing worldly things), and the *grahastha* (simple householder). The householder, Manu says, is the highest of all. By his honest trade and industry he keeps all the others alive. Without him, society could not exist.

"A Vaishya is not a cheat," Mr. Anand continued, "he does not take advantage of others for personal gain. Those born to the class understand the ethics of business, or used to. The others, they think that business and morality are two different things."

Mr. Anand is an office manager at a company that manufactures women's clothing. He has worked there for twelve years. If his career continues on track, he could one day become the head of the outergarments division. At any rate, he makes a good salary and can expect an ample pension.

"The old caste distinctions," he said, "have less and less meaning today. In the big cities, most of us have jobs that do not fit anywhere in the orthodox Hindu framework. After all, the Vedas don't contain any mention of computer programmers."

Traditionally, every Hindu could be neatly pigeonholed in his own occupational jati within the overall structure of the four

Vedic classes. A rapidly changing world, however, is giving birth to brand-new jatis every day. There is, in effect, a special caste for engineers, one for journalists, one for management consultants, and one for insurance salesmen.

"It is evolving right before our eyes," Mr. Anand said, "and each new jati has its own privileges and rules of conduct. Many of these castes would normally fall within the framework of the Brahmin class — after all, lawyers, accountants, psychiatrists, and the like all require special training and education. But in my view most of these groups now fall under the Vaishya aegis, because their main goal in life is to make money. They do not perform their tasks to serve society but to serve themselves. That is quite appropriate for a Vaishya, but Vaishya should not be the only class in India."

He stuck an arm out from under the marquee to test the rain. It hadn't lessened, but the action served to ease his impatience.

"Should have brought an umbrella," he said. "Then I could have walked. Now if I walk I will catch a chill for certain, perhaps even pneumonia. If I wait, the wife will complain that I've let dinner get cold."

"Nothing to be done," I said, "so no point in worrying."

"Quite," he said. "You know, that is how most people used to view caste. Nothing can be done, so no use worrying. We used to believe in fate absolutely, trust that our caste was the only proper one for us. It's a very comforting thought, you understand, designed to keep a man going on in hopeless situations."

"And you?"

"Me? Do I believe in fate? No, no." He paused. "Well, perhaps a little. I mean, of course a person can rise or fall in the world, can find any number of jobs, be rich or poor, but there will always be one type of work that is specially right for him. Today too many people are atheists. If they pray at all it is only for material things. A man should *work* for material things, pray for spiritual ones."

It was beginning to look as if the storm would not pass that evening, and I did not want to spend the night standing outside a cinema. Mr. Anand and I both decided to make a dash through the downpour. As we rolled up our cuffs, I asked if spiritual longings were part of the Vaishya ethos.

"Oh my, yes," he said, "part of *every* man's desire. Why, Mahatma Gandhi himself — the greatest saint India has had for centuries — he himself was born a Vaishya. But today nobody remembers this."

We shook hands, divided a newspaper to hold over our heads, and sprinted through the rain in opposite directions.

All India turned to one universal caste, and that caste the Vaishya — it was an amusing thought, and a disturbing one as well. For ages, I thought as I dashed through the storm, the ideal Indian was a man like Rama: pious, brave, a duty-driven battler for the peace and order of his world. Today, if Prakesh Anand is correct, the ideal Indian is a bazaari merchant haggling over the price of dyed broadlooms so he can afford a new VCR for his color television.

➤ ➤ ➤

By the banks of the Ganges, Manju Dhobi thwacks her laundry against the rock. Scrub, rinse, and *thwack, thwack, thwack,* scrub, rinse, *thwack, thwack, thwack,* over and over again, every day. She is a washerwoman, and spends most of her waking hours down at the ghats.

Manju's caste is so much a part of her identity that she uses it for her last name. The practice is extremely common among the lower orders. Dhobis, or clothes washers, are a large and important jati within the Shudra class. Without them, everyone from truck drivers in Assam to the prime minister in Delhi would walk around in dirty shirts.

Scrub, rinse, *thwack, thwack, thwack.* Soak the clothes in the sacred sewer, let them absorb the leaden water full of yesterday's dinners and last week's funerals, then slap the sheets fiercely and spread them out to dry in the sun. No matter how dirty the river may be, dhobis seem to believe any garment can be cleaned in it if beaten with sufficient violence.

Once a month, Manju Dhobi is happy. The eleventh day of each month is a holiday, and that is the only day Manju Dhobi does not have to work. On that day she can sleep late, to eight o'clock in the morning, and then drink young beer until night.

Each evening when she goes to bed, Manju Dhobi prays that the next morning will be cloudy. If the morning is cloudy, few people will send out their laundry, for they know that it will not be dried by afternoon. If few people put out their laundry, Manju Dhobi will have an easier time.

But most days in Uttar Pradesh are sunny, and most days Manju Dhobi works hard with her sons.

"My boys," she said, "I wanted them to take the examination for the government job. I wanted them to get good positions, to rise to a new station. But they had no free time to study — how could they? And my husband had no money to bribe the examiners, the way the other parents do. What choice do the boys have? How can they ever make a good life for themselves?"

I watched her sons go about their business with sullen stoicism, strenuously beating their laundry with large wooden clubs.

I asked what keeps her going.

"Faith," she said. "Faith in God. One must believe in God and be honest. God has fated every one of us for our place in life, there is no avoiding it. Honesty brings unhappiness, that much is true. Virtuous people do not get ahead in this world. But someday, perhaps in the next life, all wrongs will be righted. One must be honest, if only for the sake of one's children. God punishes an entire family for the sins of one member."

A few yards away, her husband grunted as he beat the clothes savagely against the stones. Black bruises around Manju Dhobi's eyes show that laundry is not the only thing he beats.

Manju Dhobi is not yet thirty, but she looks fifty. By forty she will look seventy. By forty-five she will be dead.

For many Shudras like Manju Dhobi, faith is an anchor whose chain slips through their fingers. They struggle hard to hang on to the belief that gives their misery meaning. But faith cannot be grabbed, bound, hauled in, and tied fast to be kept from falling. A faith that is forced brings only cold comfort.

For many others, however, belief requires no effort. It comes uninvited, and remains of its own accord. These people need no festivals to be happy.

Fagul Sharma is a carpenter, the son of a carpenter, with sawdust under his fingernails. He plans to teach the trade to his three sons as well — why not? It's good work. On an average day, he told me proudly, he gets paid 45 rupees. Cash. How much more could an honest man want?

Those teeth Fagul Sharma still has in his head are all brown. He must chew carefully to keep them from falling out, but he always has enough food to chew. In fact, he has even had Brahmins over to his home for dinner. Relations between the castes are fine, he said.

Every night Fagul Sharma sleeps soundly. He has never worried about his place in the world, not for one moment. His station is predestined, and this assurance makes him content.

Fagul Sharma is proud of his work. "Both front doors on Valmiki Bhavan," he said, "both are mine. People come from all over to pray there, and every one of them must pass through my doors." I had indeed been impressed by the finely carved portals when I'd visited the Bhavan in Ayodhya before meeting Fagul, and I was doubly impressed now. For him, fashioning the doors was not mere labor. It was a sacrament.

Down in the south, in a town populated only by Shudras, I once passed a shoe factory. A big sign over the entrance read: WORK IS OUR WORSHIP. That traditionally has been the motto for all Shudras. Members of this class must believe in the gods, but all the arcane rituals of the religion are really not their concern. A Shudra fulfills all his obligations as a Hindu simply by working hard and honestly at the task he's been assigned by fate. It is not an exciting life, it offers virtually no opportunity for advancement, but it does have this merit: more than most paths one can tread, it provides peace of mind, basic contentment, and the promise of eventual salvation.

Fagul Sharma does not often go to temples, but there is one god to whom he pays particular reverence. On holy days he sets out garlands for Vishvakarma, the workman of the gods. In the Ramayana, Vishvakarma is the heavenly builder, the immortal carpenter who constructs the city of Lanka, who assembles Rama's magical chariot, who forges King Janaka's bow.

"I worship him in my heart every day," said Fagul Sharma. "For through him even a poor wood-carver can truly become a god."

The God of the West was a poor man as well. A carpenter, the son of a carpenter, with sawdust under his fingernails.

> > >

Anyone who doubts the pervasiveness of caste and Untouchability need only pick up a newspaper to be set right. Some items from the *Indian Express,* May Day, 1990:

Page 1: A village of Untouchables near Bellary was burned to the ground during the night. The number of injured and killed is not known. A mob of 150 caste Hindus torched the easily kindled thatch huts and ran off into the darkness. They had been provoked: that morning, five Harijans had asked for drinking water at a local restaurant.

Page 4: In the town of Vallur near Pavagada, caste Hindus have launched a boycott in an attempt to drive the Untouchables from their community. No merchant will sell them the necessities of life, and they are leaving their homes to avoid starvation. Any Harijan shopper or Hindu vendor who breaks the embargo is routinely assaulted.

Page 5: High-caste Uttar Pradesh landowners were accused of anti-Harijan atrocities in the Upper House of Parliament. The charge was sparked by a murder in the Fatehpur district, where local custom had permitted a landlord to seize and deflower the bride of any of his Harijan tenants. One Untouchable groom objected and was killed by his master's henchmen. Fatehpur is then–Prime Minister V. P. Singh's own constituency.

If May Day stands for anything in a post-Communist world, it stands for the hope of equality. There was a time when millions, possibly even billions, of people around the globe would join on the first of May to work for a classless society. It was a fine dream. Unrealizable, perhaps, but a dream that may be communism's only lasting legacy.

In 1990 most of the world's socialist countries realized that a truly classless society can probably never exist.

In 1990 India declared May Day a national holiday.

The Untouchables would seem perfect grist for the mill of revolution. For most of recorded history they have been among the worst-oppressed classes of people on earth. It was not until this century that Untouchables were even permitted inside most Hindu temples. Mahatma Gandhi led the campaign to make them part of the religion, and gave them the name Harijans — "Children of God." Although nearly one in five Indians is a Harijan, many people of all castes still refuse to accept them as Hindus. There are still Brahmins who feel polluted if touched even by a Harijan's shadow.

The ideal of social equality for all people — a twentieth-century innovation for India — would seem to be the Harijans' natural rallying cry. Many of their advocates even use the term "Dalits" ("the Oppressed") instead of Harijans, arguing that "Children of God" once was a euphemism for the offspring of temple prostitutes. They seek legal privileges, but class divisions will not be ended by government sinecures or the tokenism of quotas. Far too few are helped, and they are helped for the wrong reasons.

During the 1960s civil rights movement in America, the state opened doors with legislation and court rulings, but black citizens themselves won their real equality. It was not handed to them from on high, they fought for it and worked for it by simply refusing to accept subordinate status any longer. Deep divisions still exist in the United States, but in three decades we as a nation have come a very long way. True change comes not in laws but in people's hearts. That is why Martin Luther King, Jr., was a greater leader than Lyndon Johnson, why Mahatma Gandhi is more widely revered than Pandit Nehru. Laws can be made and unmade with a stroke of a fountain pen, but attitudes must be crafted with time and unflagging will.

In India the greatest barrier to class integration may well be the attitude of the Untouchables themselves. The poorest and least-educated members of society, Harijans are often the most conservative as well. At election time they may vote to shake the tree in hopes of dislodging choicer fruit, but most would never consider chopping the tree down. They may use government programs to get more out of the caste system, but they have little desire to abolish the system entirely. For most of them, caste is a fact of life not even worth thinking about. Something that always has been, something that always will be.

The lowest, most contemptible wretch in all India is the charnel man. Thieves, whores, and garbage pickers look down their noses at him. The only person as detested is the tanner of leather, who cuts up dead cows and sells their hides for tainted money. But almost all Hindus are cremated when they die, and somebody has to do the burning.

When I walked up to the Harishchandra Ghat in Varanasi, Suraj Chaudhri had long since set the morning's corpses in a row. He and his fellow doams were now working on a middle-aged man, making sure the limbs were properly arranged for incineration. The other bodies lay unattended by the bank of the Ganges, all waiting their turn patiently under the hot noonday sun.

Each body had been brought here on a stretcher of green bamboo borne by close kin. Each had been lovingly wrapped in white cloth, then swathed in gaudy silk brocade laced with threads of spun gold, then lashed to the palanquin with rough twine and covered with orange garlands. Now each was alone. Each band of mourners, with flutes and drums and women singing through their tears, had gone home. The only people left on the ghat were a few midday idlers, the charnel men, and the cadavers themselves.

Suraj Chaudhri was sawing away at the bamboo poles, cutting them down to the same size as the body they carried. It makes the fire neater. As a doam — the Untouchable clan responsible for burning corpses — Suraj works from four A.M. until midnight every single day. There is no time for a holiday. What could he do, ask people to stop dying merely because he wanted a rest?

It is his job, it is his life, it is him. There is no point in searching for any other way. When I ask what he thinks about caste, Suraj shakes his head. He does not think about it at all. He never asks why he is a Harijan, any more than he asks why his hair is black and his eyes brown.

His place in the universe, Suraj knows, is to burn bodies. That is why he was put on the earth. It is an important task, a necessary task, a task vital to the survival of society. He fully supports the caste system, although technically he is not even a part of it. How (he asks) could he feel otherwise? The system was instituted by God Himself — who is Suraj Chaudhri to challenge fate?

By working hard and living an honest life, Suraj hopes to scale the rungs of caste and one day reach Nirvana. It is not an impossible dream. The Ramayana provides him inspiration. He cannot read and has no television or radio, but he knows the stories well. When Rama was ferried across the Ganges, he embraced the low-born boatman as a friend. The episode gives Suraj comfort, for it shows that even a Harijan can be loved by God.

A goat ambles over to the row of corpses and starts nibbling on one of the flowery garlands. Eventually an idler gently chases the animal away.

It is not only Suraj's father and grandfather who were charnel men. Every member of his family, those still living and those dead for centuries, has worked the Burning Ghats of Varanasi. It binds them together, makes them one. A harmonious home, Suraj says, is the greatest blessing any man can have.

A boy of six or seven, Suraj's son, is hopping among the cadavers. Here he straightens an arm, there he tucks in a brocade shroud, proudly helping out as best he can. One day father and son will work side by side, one day the son will take the father's place, one day the son may even burn the father on his own bier. Today the boy is whistling cheerfully as he picks his way through the corpses.

I ask Suraj if he is happy with his life.

Happy, not happy, he says, the question has no meaning. A man's life is his life, nothing more, nothing less.

An old woman is burning on the pyre Suraj has built. She lies on top of four cross-stacked logs, with smaller sticks piled tidily on her chest. The fire melts the air, blurring all the scenery behind it, like the jet flow from an airplane. Downwind, the stench of fleshly corruption is almost intolerable. Much of the woman's skin is charred, some of it is flaking off, and a bright white bone is all that is left of her leg. But the flames have not yet reached the head. Eyes shut, lips slightly parted, moisture just beginning to bead on the forehead — she could as easily be basking on a beach. When her scanty hair finally catches fire, her lips twitch without losing their serenity. The woman greets oblivion with an involuntary smile.

There is no way to know anything about the woman's life. Perhaps she had been born a Brahmin, perhaps a Shudra. Perhaps she had been the wife of a fisherman, perhaps a cabinet minister in her own right. She entered the world nothing more than a body, left it a body and nothing more. In the end, fire burns away all class, all caste, all wealth, all luck, all social distinction, all human inequality.

Death is the only leveler, for there is none in life.

Six
ILLUSION

A DEER ran through the Dandak forest, a magical deer that seemed to be made of gleaming gold and shining silver. The other animals scampered away in fear, for this buck had the foul odor of a demon. Maricha, for that was the disguised Rakshasa's name, normally savored fresh venison, but he did not pursue the fleeing herd. He had a job to do.

"Oh, look!" cried Sita, when the deer coyly pranced through their encampment. "It glitters like a jewel box!"

Lakshman did not have the animals' keen sense of scent, but he could still smell a rat.

"I do not believe in golden stags," he said. "A living deer made of precious metal, its hide studded with gems — such a thing cannot exist. We live in the world of reality, not of make-believe. It must be some sort of demon."

Sita would not be convinced. She could not tear her eyes from the marvelous deer, stood transfixed by its miraculous spell. She had never seen anything so enticing, and begged her husband to catch it for a pet.

"Appearances can deceive," Rama said, "that is true enough. But no matter. If it is a deer, I'll capture it. If a demon, I'll kill it."

As he took a step forward, the buck bounded off into the woods. Rama ran after in hot pursuit, deeper and deeper into the forest, farther and farther from camp, until he caught up with the stag in a clearing by a brook. The effort of flight had sapped every ounce of Maricha's strength, and he could no longer maintain the veil of illusion. While Rama recovered his breath, the golden deer was transformed into a hideous fat-bellied Rakshasa.

An arrow from Rama's quiver instantly found its mark. As Maricha watched the black blood flow from his gut, he carried out the last order given to him by the Demon King back in Lanka.

"Lakshman! Help me!" The voice was Rama's but the words did not come from Rama's mouth.

"Help me, Lakshman! Help me, or I die!"

Back in the camp, Lakshman and Sita heard the shouted plea.

"How can you sit there?" Sita demanded. "Your brother is in danger!"

Lakshman did not take his gaze off the treeline. "It's a trick," he said. "The ear can deceive, like the eye or the tongue. That voice we hear is not truly Rama."

"He's in trouble! There is no time —"

"Our senses lie to us, we cannot know what is real and what is false. A demon can take the shape of a deer, a demon can take the speech of Rama. But this I do know: my brother would not be crying for help. There is no Rakshasa alive who could defeat Rama in battle."

From the depths of the jungle, the dying cry grew fainter.

"Help me, Lakshman! Pleaaaase!"

Sita bit her lip with rage.

"You want me — that's it, isn't it?" she screamed. "After all these years, I should have guessed. You want my husband to die, so that there will be nobody to —"

"Women are irrational," Lakshman said coolly, "so I will forgive your unjust slander. Rama ordered me to keep you safe, told me to stay with you no matter what. He, too, feared a trick."

Sita grabbed a dagger from her husband's spare belt.

"Go help him," she said. "Go, or I swear I will kill myself this instant."

Lakshman had no choice. He led Sita to the safety of a cave and, shaking his head, plunged off into the woods.

Ravana, King of the Demons, had crossed the ocean in a chariot drawn by mules. On reaching land, he wrapped the steeds' hooves in soft cloth and approached Sita's hiding place in silky silence.

The Lord of Rakshasas had ten heads and twenty arms. His mighty chest bore the scars of Indra's thunderbolt and Vishnu's disk — no other man or demon could claim to have fought the most powerful gods in Heaven and lived to see his wounds heal.

Ravana was hated and feared throughout the Five Worlds as a destroyer of sacrifices, eater of Brahmins, violator of other men's wives. But he possessed a boon, and that boon made him invincible.

Long ago Ravana had spent thousands of years in penance seeking the ultimate source of power. After nearly a full Age of Mankind had passed, he found it. Power comes from sacrifice, and the most efficacious offering of all is the sacrifice of one's self. Unhesitatingly, he cut off each of his ten heads and presented them as a gift to the all-powerful Brahma. Had he understood better, had he offered his *true* self — his invisible soul — Ravana might have won eternal salvation. But by courageously offering up his flesh and bone, he earned virtual immortality. Brahma caused all ten heads to grow back and asked the Rakshasa to name his boon.

Invulnerability, Ravana replied. Make me invulnerable to any attack by gods, demons, gandharvas, fierce reptiles, or birds.

The Rakshasa, in his pride, did not bother to include immunity from so petty and powerless a creature as man.

He came to Sita without royal finery, he came without his army or train of courtiers, he came with only one head on his shoulders, and that lacking even the plainest gold earrings. He came to her old and feeble, his lordly frame shrunken and wizened. He came to her cloaked in a costume of illusion, masked as a humble sadhu alone on the road.

Sita let him into her cave without question. It is the nature of the guileless to assume that others are guileless as well. She did not believe that the golden deer, her husband's shout, and now this harmless old bhikku could all be deception. Unfortunately, the world of mortals has always been a world of deception. And Sita, once again, was deceived.

Ravana dragged her, kicking and screaming, to his magic chariot, and the mules leapt into the sky. Sita cried for Rama to save her, cried for Lakshman, cried for all the animals of the forest to come to her rescue. But by that time the flying car was so high in the atmosphere that no creature on the ground could hear her pleas.

Jatayu, the King of the Birds, did hear. He was weak of wing and decrepit from age, but he flew after Sita as fast as his weary bones could beat the air.

"Stop!" he wheezed.

Ravana laughed the arrogant laugh of one who never loses.

"Hah! Hah! Hah!"

Jatayu was sixty thousand years old. He had few feathers left, and his loose skin was an unhealthy gray. But he dove at Ravana with a violence he'd not shown in centuries and bit off the demon's ten right hands.

"Hah! Hah! Hah!" bellowed Ravana.

Ten new hands sprang fresh from the bleeding stumps, and one of them picked up a sword. With a slice and a backswing he chopped off Jatayu's withered wings. The Bird King, unlike his foe, could not regenerate. He plummeted to his death, like a clam dropped on the stony shore by a hungry sea hawk.

Sita shut her eyes to avoid seeing Jatayu hit. She kept her eyes closed until the chariot was leagues away, but she refused to weep either for Jatayu or for herself.

"You have made a grave error," she calmly told her captor. "In challenging Rama, you have drunk fatal poison. There is no antidote in all the world. The poison may kill quick, it may kill slow, but your death is already assured."

"Hah! Hah! Hah!"

They sped across the Southern Sea, and Sita was amazed that such a vast body of water could possibly exist. Between the waves she saw sharks, whales, and enormous ocean crocodiles.

When they alit in Lanka, Ravana brought her to a luxurious guest-house. He ordered the servants to gratify her slightest whim, commanded that any person who offended her by so much as an insolent glance be instantly put to death. He politely ushered her through each of the splendid rooms and gardens, personally brought trays of choicest delicacies for her to eat.

"Your husband gives you poverty, hardship, and exile," he said. "He makes you cook rude herbs and sleep in a cave. I offer you wealth, comfort, and power beyond your wildest imagining. Please, fairest lady, do me the great honor of becoming my wife."

Sita was flabbergasted. At home the ruthless demon was a paragon of chivalry. Although she turned him down, of course, she could not help but ask about his abrupt change of manner.

"Do not be fooled by appearances," he said. "I may have the face of a fearsome Rakshasa. I may look like a death-dealing demon, and my prowess in battle is certainly unequaled. But I am, above all else, a perfect gentleman. Things are not always what they seem."

Sita did not soften at his words. She had been fooled by appearances three times that day and was not about to let that happen again.

God sat before me on the sofa, clad in a poorly fitting sweat-suit, puffing down a cigarette.

I was in the Bombay living room of Arun Govil, the actor who had played Lord Rama on television. For two and a half years all India had watched a serialized version of the Ramayana every Sunday. It was far more than the most popular program in the subcontinent's history — it was a national event. Once a week, between nine-thirty and ten in the morning, all action ceased. Shops closed, workmen took a break, bus drivers pulled over to any chai shop that had a television, and all the passengers jostled to watch a story they already knew. Marriages were postponed, trains were delayed, even meetings of the Indian Cabinet were rescheduled.

Gods and demons were portrayed by ordinary human beings, the epic that defines India was staged with arc lights, makeup, and camera tricks. There can be nothing more artificial, more false, more deceptive than filmmaking. An actor is, after all, simply a person pretending to be somebody else. But often illusion can lead to truth. For hundreds of millions of souls, the television serial made the Ramayana far more real than any written version ever could.

The demon Maricha uses illusion to draw Rama away from his wife. The diabolic monarch Ravana uses illusion to spirit Sita off across the ocean. If the earthly avatar of Lord Vishnu himself is so easily deceived, how can mere mortals ever know what is true?

We can't. There are no absolute certainties in life. Not even (thanks to cryonics and tricky accountants) death and taxes. The line between truth and fiction, between myth and history, changes every minute.

As the yogis teach their pupils, and as the Upanishads teach the yogis, the senses cannot be trusted. Never has this been more true than today. Sight, smell, taste, touch, hearing — all are lied to all the time. Advertisements give false promises, tofu patties masquerade as hamburgers, pop stars lip-synch songs in concert that they didn't perform even in the studio. Deception is even welcomed, for it can make our lives more pleasant; it is the false burst of air freshener that leaves our bathrooms scented like pine forests. Every leap of technology, from holographs to genetic engineering to computer-generated voice imprints, increases the possibilities for illusion. Is it live, we must ask ourselves, or is it Memorex?

At some stage, perception is more important than reality. It doesn't matter whether George Washington actually chopped down the cherry tree and couldn't tell a lie; the story has taken on a life of its own, become part of America's identity. It doesn't matter that the village of Ayodhya does not date back to ancient times and is probably not the site of epic fame; in the hearts of the pious, Ayodhya is Ayodhya. What really is true often is less important than what people believe to be true.

Arun Govil has a unique perspective on truth and illusion, reality and unreality, verity and falsehood. Each day on the set he had to transform himself into God Incarnate.

"In the minds of many people," he said, "I really am Rama. I may be walking down the street, wearing dungarees and a T-shirt, and still people will drop to their knees. Even now, more than two years after the show ended, they call out, 'Sri Ram, Sri Ram,' they kiss my feet, they ask for my blessing. What can I tell them?"

To many Indians, particularly older people and those who live far from cities, television is a mystifying novelty. It is magic. When you think about it, the notion of moving pictures materializing out of nowhere *is* quite amazing. After decades of familiarity with TV, there are still Americans who think that "Gilligan's Island" is a real place. It is hardly surprising to find Indians who accept what they see on their mystical box as the literal truth.

"At first I was embarrassed," Govil continued. "I'd pull them up, tell them I was no god. They would always look crushed. Once I was at a fancy dinner party given by a rich industrialist, with many of the most important people in Bombay. The tycoon's elderly father came into the room, and when he saw me he bowed his head to the ground right in front of all the guests. I felt terrible."

In India, as in all Asian countries, youth venerates age rather than the other way around.

"He asked me for spiritual guidance — he, a man who could

have been my grandfather! When I tell people I am merely an actor, often they do not believe me. They continue begging me for blessings, nothing I say matters. So now when devotees approach me I remind them I am not Rama, but I do say a small prayer for them just as I would for anyone I wished well."

Illusion can be more powerful than reality:

"Once, in a small village," Govil said, "a woman ran up to me in tears. She implored me to bless her little girl, who was desperately ill. What could I do? I gave my benediction, to calm the woman's nerves. Four days later she came back and told me her child had been cured.

"Now, did I save that sick girl? No, of course not. But the mother, she had the power of faith, and perhaps her prayers were answered. My only contribution was possibly to strengthen the faith she already possessed."

There is remarkably little pretense in the man who plays God. I'd expected a slick jet-setter, full of show-biz glitter and vanity. I'd expected to go through a press rep, an agent, and five secretaries before speaking to the star himself. Instead he had answered his own phone and invited me to his home. On a Saturday night, no less.

India's most famous TV idol lives in a modest apartment complex of concrete and cinder block, with a tiny elevator that consents to move only grudgingly, after much banging of buttons. Television in India is government-owned, so actors can't afford the extravagant lifestyles of their film counterparts.

Govil was not there when I arrived, but his wife greeted me with a glass of bright pink rose milk. "Arun has been held up at the studio," she said. Their seven-year-old son was beginning the same style of karate I had practiced back home, so we sat in the well-worn armchairs and talked about roundhouse kicks and hammerfist punches until the prince of Ayodhya came home.

"Rama is a straightforward character," Govil said, easing himself onto the threadbare sofa. "He is reasonable, logical, and completely bound by duty. The only problems arise when he must choose between two conflicting obligations."

Rama experiences doubt solely when his responsibilities pull him in opposite directions: commitment to parents versus commitment to truth, vow of hermitage versus burden of caste, duty to wife versus duty to subjects — but that is looking too far ahead in the story.

"He represents universal virtues," Govil said, "not just the morality for Kshatriyas, or even for Hindus, but for everyone in the world. Principally, that each of us must do his duty and treat all others with kindness. Even enemies. Rama has no hatred for the Demon King he must fight, and gives him all proper respect. Today, with so many people at each other's throats all the time, it is a lesson well worth learning."

Govil's understanding of Rama is more important than that of any scholar. It carries more weight than any pandit's pronouncement or swami's sermon. The vast majority of Indians are illiterate, and the TV serial is the only real chance they've had to experience the Ramayana firsthand. There have always been recitations and village plays, but seeing the fishmonger's son decked out in fake armor is hardly the same thing. There have even been Ramayana movies, but none distributed throughout the whole country, none reaching beyond the audience of its local language. With television, hundreds of millions who could not read Valmiki, could not read Tulsi Das, could not read the dozens of local versions in Tamil, Bengali, or Malayalam, all were for the first time sharing the same story.

When these millions think of what Rama means, they are not guided by a close reading of the text, by the pious homilies heard in temple, or by doctoral theses in university stacks. They are led by an image, the living, breathing, speaking Rama they've seen plain as day on TV. The printed word may be True, but the illusion of makeup is what really matters.

To prepare himself for the role, Arun Govil did not seek insights from theologians or holy men. He did not even reread the epic — the only time he'd read the Ramayana, in fact, was in his childhood, to please a religious-minded mother. But the actor did train earnestly and hard. He cast about for as many different portraits of Rama as he could find: in temples, in books, in museums, in shrines at the homes of his friends. All the pictures had one thing in common: a facial expression that could only be that of a god. It was a beatifically blank stare, with just the shadow of a smile.

For twenty whole days Arun Govil sat in front of his mirror trying to perfect this expression. If only he could capture the look, he could encapsulate Rama's whole essence. All an actor can do is offer an image, a disguise, a veneer. But in this case the mask and the true face were one and the same. To understand Rama's countenance was to plumb his soul.

Govil realized the hero's face was blank not from absence of thought, but from *abundance* of thought, as if it had no room left for frivolous doubts or fears. This regal impassivity was easy for him to put over. Most Indian actors (even the action stars) strive for a pudgy, fat-cheeked, vaguely clownish look, but Govil (unlike his colleagues) radiates a quiet dignity even off the set. The look of a king comes naturally to him. It took him several weeks before the mirror, however, before he realized that the key to Rama was his smile.

One morning he was sitting in his dressing room, turning his face into a mask, when the sides of his mouth spontaneously turned up just a fraction, and it was precisely correct. "YES!" he cried out, bringing stage hands running. The smile would never leave Govil's lips, not for two and a half years. Love, anger, surprise, remorse — all would be portrayed by ever-so-slight alterations in that faint curve of the mouth. It was not a grin of human arrogance, no smug sign of satisfaction. Simply a smile of inner serenity, of divine self-confidence, the mark of a man who was God's Incarnation and did not fully know it.

It was not only the expression that Govil had to perfect. He had to learn how to carry himself like a deity. What's more, he had to do it laden down by a metal breastplate, weighty arm bangles, and a headdress heavy with fake gold.

"At first it was so uncomfortable that I could barely move," he said. "So I took the costume home and wore it around the house. I'd wash dishes, read the newspaper, talk on the telephone in my full armor and crown. I did this off and on for three months. Eventually they felt almost as natural as my skin." Even now, as he sat cross-legged on a corduroy sofa, he had the unaffectedly upright carriage of a prince.

When a man changes himself into a god every day, he cannot help but be altered by the experience. "I like to think that some of Rama's character has rubbed off on me," Govil said. "I have become a calmer person, more forgiving, less troubled by the difficulties of life. I feel at peace, and perhaps that is the true lesson of the Ramayana. Anyone can find peace if he knows where to look."

But the actor does not take his role for an absolute model. Rama's stony righteousness, his cold, unyielding sense of duty, is too rigid for Arun Govil. "What he does to his wife at the story's end," the star said, "that I could never do. What good husband could? Kingly obligations went against matrimonial obligations, and he was a king first. Perhaps that is why I could not be a king. But," he turned to his wife with a grin that was not divine, "I think I am a pretty good husband."

"An excellent husband, my dear," she said with a laugh. Lekha Govil is a producer and actress who spends most of her time now in classical dance. She met Arun when they shared a stage in a local play, and they have been married for ten years.

"We are equal partners in marriage," she said, "like friends, really. We share the chores. Often if I am cooking dinner, Arun will be vacuuming the rug. So many Indians wear Western clothes, go to Western schools, adopt Western mannerisms, but when they come home they still act in an old-fashioned way. The husband will order the wife around all day long and not raise a finger to help her. It's only 'Get me tea, woman, cook my dinner, go clean my clothes.' They do not want a wife, they want a servant."

"A married couple should be a team," Arun said. "Husband and wife should be equal, but not independent. Too often a woman wants to be so independent that she feels no need for her partner. That is going too far. Marriage is a not merely a bundle of compromises and concessions. It is a harmonious balance with both parties working together, each helping and relying on the other. Rama and Sita were the perfect couple, but the rules of their time are not the rules of today."

Lekha made a mildly disdainful sound with her tongue.

"Perfect couple?" she said. "Hardly. Rama is a fundamentally weak character. He leaves his home when he does not have to, fights the monkey king, Bali, when he does not have to, even gives up Sita when he does not have to. But, at the very end, it is Sita who gets the last laugh."

She did not laugh herself, but was clearly much pleased with the thought.

"How dare Rama doubt his wife?" she asked, amusement giving way to indignation. "How dare he question her fidelity? A husband must trust his spouse absolutely. And how could he possibly subject someone he loved to such a vicious torture as the Fire Ordeal? That is no perfect marriage. Why, if Arun treated me the way Rama treated Sita, I'd hit him on the head with a frying pan!"

"There are many illogical things in every epic," her husband said diplomatically, "things that must be taken on faith."

. . .

It was late when I walked through the modest suburb back toward central Bombay. I was struck by how much and how little the actor resembled the god. An ordinary man disguised himself as a mythical deity, and by this fiction made the god more real than ever before.

➤ ➤ ➤

Film is the ultimate form of illusion. It is blatant untruth gleefully confessed. Audiences flock to the movie houses and crowd around televisions anxiously hoping to be well deceived. They revel in the deception, if it is skillful enough, for it lets them live briefly in a world far more exciting, glamorous, fair, and pleasurable than the one they inhabit.

But the act is often too good. It becomes more real than reality. In countries like the United States, where film is the dominant form of expression, true life just can't compete with manufactured images. Our mental picture of a police detective, for example, owes more to *Dirty Harry* or *Cagney and Lacey* than to Sergeant Ramirez down at the local precinct station. Until fighting broke out in the Persian Gulf and we saw actual soldiers on the news, many of us thought of war in terms of *M★A★S★H, Rambo,* or *Top Gun.* Anyone who has served jury duty knows that our legal system is not full of silver-tongued orators debating for justice, but after *LA Law* and *Perry Mason* we can't help feeling we've just caught the court on a bad day.

India does not have our four-decade obsession with film, but it is fast making up for lost time. Bombay now puts out far more movies than Hollywood. From the lurid, looming cinema hoardings in Madras to the omnipresent posters for coming attractions in Delhi, it is almost impossible to escape the shadow of the screen.

"*Noble Lady,*" one billboard cries out. "She Can Seduce the Impotent!"

"*Agneepath, the Path of Fire!*" another answers. It pictures a burly warrior with a machete above the legend, "I am Krishnan Iyer, MA." His archrival, perhaps, is "Ram Gopal, PhD."

Some artistic, internationally respected films are made in Calcutta, but the vast majority of India's movies come from Bombay. And the vast majority are exactly the same. The poster for one popular feature sums them all up:

"Raping! Killing! Robbing! Kidnapping!" the flyer trumpets

with cheerful abandon. If it added, "Singing!" "Dancing!" and "Making Dumb Jokes!" it could describe any film that has been churned out by the studio over the years.

Bombay blockbusters are nicknamed masala films, because a dish of curry spiced masala contains just a pinch of everything. The films are also a lively mixture — a veritable jambalaya of action, romance, comedy, and cabaret. In a typical sequence the hero may gun down a dozen villains, grab his leading lady for a swoony kiss, get a pie thrown in his face, then jump into a song-and-dance review. The pictures are as formulaic and repetitive as *Rocky IX*, but they do please the crowds.

If the films seem like cookie-cutter copies, so do the stars. Lead actors are almost exclusively light-skinned and baby-faced, sporting identical put-on glares, like overfed school-boys trying to look dangerous. Every actress not relegated to character roles must have her singing voice dubbed by a squeaky stand-in pitched several octaves higher than Alvin the Chipmunk.

Some actors play the same part in every movie, again and again, practically line for line. One star named Ranjeet (he uses only one name, like Madonna or Sting) specializes in rape scenes. Sexual assault is a staple of the Indian cinema, as essential to Bombay flicks as car chases are to American ones. Ranjeet boasts that during his career he has raped every major actress in the business.

In this milieu the serious, serene bearing of Arun Govil's Rama seems all the more godlike. He *must* be a deity (the viewer can't help thinking), he simply cannot be a mere mortal. What other actor could go nearly three years without ever tap dancing, crooning a love song, or slipping on a banana peel?

It was only a few miles from what is now Bombay that the demon Maricha cast his spell of deception over Rama and Sita. The spirit of illusion must have taken root in the soil and flowered two millennia later as a City of Dreams.

Bombay is pure fantasy. It is so wealthy, clean, and orderly it hardly seems like part of India. The hopeful and the hopeless from all over the country come to Bombay to seek their fortune, and many of them actually find it. The others soon discover that the alleys are not paved with platinum, and that illusion can be very cruel indeed.

But cruel or kind, the illusion still dazzles. Bombay is India's Emerald City.

Downtown Bombay has no joubs, the open sewers that border most streets in nearly every Indian city, flowing channels of black dishwater choked by fresh piles of human and animal excrement. The walls and roads of Bombay, unlike the walls and roads of most other Indian towns, are not sticky from urine. Traffic is relatively orderly, and pedestrians do not tempt fate each time they cross an avenue. Taxis not only have meters, they actually *use* them; in other towns, rickshaw-wallahs generally claim that their government-mandated rate cards are "lost" and extort whatever price the market will bear.

The streets of Bombay are largely free of the customary urban cows, goats, beggars, and bullock-carts, but they have distractions all their own. There are shops selling nothing but eggs, either straight from the hen or cooked up as omelettes, because the Parsis who helped build the city love eggs more than air or water. There are curbside artists flaunting portraits of Saudi King Fahd, offering full-scale oil paintings from any photograph while you wait. Each morning I would pass the time of day with these artists as I sat outside the Edward VIII Juice Shop sipping the nectar of fresh strawberries squeezed in an ancient copper press.

There are slow-spoken African merchants and Arab sailors on shore leave anxious to soak up all the whisky forbidden aboard ship. There are red double-decker buses imported from England. There are High Victorian countinghouses. There are fire temples holy to the Zoroastrians — a sect that flourishes here as nowhere else in the world. Outside, the temples are squat and solid as a Federal Reserve Bank, guarded by pairs of Assyrian man-griffins carved of stone; inside, the temples' hidden sancta are known only to the heirs of Zarathustra.

Bombay is an oasis in the desert of Maharashtra; in the vast ocean of India it is an island of comfort and ease. But the coolest, most inviting oasis can turn out to be a mirage, the richest, lushest island may be only a trick of a tired mariner's eyes. For some the promise of Bombay is a realistic dream, for others it is a miserable lie. But Bombay is always, at its heart, a grand illusion.

To call the state surrounding Bombay a desert is no mere figure of speech. Maharashtra is a wasteland in the most literal sense. It is a dry, barren land of craggy canyons and candelabra cacti, with long stretches of sere terrain populated only by a few grizzled trees or haggard shrubs.

The men of Maharashtra wear little white peaked caps, like a nation of waiters or short-order cooks. They build their homes of stone, mud-brick, or thatch, often little more than crude te-pees tossed up to ward off the noonday sun. They paint the horns of their cattle baby-blue to prevent the dusty brown herds from getting lost among the dusty brown hillocks. Perhaps they do it also to add a bright dash of color to the monotone coun-tryside in which they live.

They travel from place to place on overstuffed buses and crawling local trains. The rear fender of each bus is painted with the slogan "Please Sound Horn," perhaps the most superfluous bit of advice any Indian motorist could receive. Maharashtra buses have only one door, so passengers must jump out before the vehicle reaches its stop to avoid being crushed back in by the mob waiting to board. Swaying clumps of travelers cling to the roof and the sides, like parasitic lampreys stuck to the skin of a whale. They are not perturbed by the hulks of overturned ve-hicles that litter each road's margin.

"Turned turtle," they say, as they reach for a better grip.

Jammed halfway out the window on one Maharashtra bus, I abruptly pulled my head in when a dusty truck breezed by to pass on the wrong side of traffic. Its rear bumper had a pious (but unsettling) bumper sticker reading "Help Me, God."

Another time I took a local, a "People's Train," from Man-mad to Bombay. The seating chart showed a compartment meant for six, but I counted a total of twenty-two. Each time another man boarded and tried to squeeze in where there really was no space for him to fit, the other passengers did not protest, did not tell him to find another car, they goodnaturedly pressed their bodies even closer and somehow made room. The room they made for me was up near the steamy roof, hanging from a wobbly luggage rack.

There were three fans on the ceiling, and none of them worked. A man on the rack opposite mine tried to start one of the fans, for it was as hot as it can only get at night, in the tropics, in a small room packed with sweaty farmers. First he wistfully twirled the rusty blade, then began fiddling with two unconnected wires sticking out of the wall. He succeeded only in killing the cabin's lights. Being a small man, he curled up in the luggage compartment and went to sleep. The other passengers smoked their cigarettes in the dark until the train rolled into Bombay the next day.

If Bombay seems like a mirage, that's because it *is* one. The telephones that work, the wide avenues with sidewalks rather than flowing gutters, the aura of shiny, fresh modernity — all of that is not India. For every resident of Bombay, there are seven people who make their homes in the tough, unglamorous scrub of Maharashtra.

It is in the unglamorous scrub of Maharashtra, in fact, that Bombay's dazzling screen fantasies come to life. The town of Goregoan is an hour out of Bombay by train, and Film City is another hour by trishaw out of Goregoan. I went there to watch the shooting of India's current serialized epic, the Mahabharata.

Each Sunday morning the nation is now transfixed by the television again. This saga may not be quite as popular as the Ramayana was, but it still brings all other activity to a halt. Duels from racing chariots, a virtuous maiden rudely stripped in full court, good and evil armies colliding like buffaloes, the gods themselves choosing sides in the world-rattling battle, all over an unlucky throw of the dice by a royal compulsive gambler. The viewing public eats it up with gusto.

On the dusty plains of Film City, a war scene was being staged. I expected a grand Hollywood spectacle, a Cecil B. deMille extravaganza. What I found looked more like a high school play three weeks into rehearsal, a bare-bones production with a Cast of Dozens.

"Action!" the director called out, and a handful of extras who looked like unemployed rickshaw-drivers began dutifully clanking their toy swords about. Their armor was little more than tin foil, the sort of costume a child might wear for Halloween.

The royal cavalry of the Pandavas consisted of six scrawny horses attached to six war-cars made of plywood. The tents of the rival hosts were mere fronting, a few yards of drapery propped up with sticks. A dumpster held an armory of giant maces, each with a head the size of a pumpkin, all made of foam and bamboo crudely covered with yellow cloth in a vain simulation of bronze. There were even artificial people on hand, papier-mâché mannequins in all stages of creation, some dressed in Halloween costumes of their own and ready for decapitation.

Behind a pile of paperboard shields lay one of the series' best special effects, the bed of arrows on which the sage Bhishma was fated to die. The iron cross-frame that supported the actor's body could not be seen from the side, conveying the illusion that he was truly impaled on the shafts' spiky points. "How can it be, *babaji*?" I imagined children asking their uncles in wonderment as they stared more intensely at the television.

The take ended, and the director called a break for lunch. The Cast of Dozens dispersed, with burly grips and stagehands jostling cuirassed warriors out of line behind the mess tent. Boom operators and walk-ons crawled underneath wooden sets to nap fitfully in the shade.

Inside the tent, two stars and the director were discussing the next shoot. Costumes and street clothes hung from the support beams, for the tent served as dressing room, canteen, makeup station, and office. A massive actor (portrayer of Bhishma's enemy Bhima, I guessed) ripped off his sweaty helmet and mopped his face with a towel. He must have been seven feet tall. An obsequious gofer brought him a metal tray full of curry, and the giant wolfishly downed it in a gulp.

I took out my pad to jot down a few notes, and a wispy teenager appeared at my side.

"Go ahead," he said, gesturing to the gargantuan actor, "go on, ask for his autograph."

"No, thanks."

"It's all right, *bhai*," said another camp follower, "he really does not mind at all."

"Thanks, I don't need an autograph."

"No need to be shy," said the first fan. "I, too, was afraid to approach so great a star. But he is very friendly, just like an ordinary man."

"Really, I —"

"No problem, go right up and ask."

I knew I wouldn't be able to convince them that I truly had no desire for Bhima to sign my notebook, so I walked over to the colossus.

His mouth was full of lunch, his right hand as well, so he merely nodded at me and I nodded back.

"You see, boss?" the first fan said as I walked by him on the way out, "You see? Just like everyday people!"

. . .

The actors in the Mahabharata 'and the Ramayana are indeed just like everyday people, more down-to-earth by far than their Hollywood cousins. The greatest epics of India, some of the greatest epics of all mankind, are brought to life by a few underpaid stars and ragamuffin walk-ons in flimsy costumes. And hundreds of millions of everyday people are transported. They do not care that the maces are foam rubber, the armor tin, the arrows splintery balsa wood. For them the ancient stories have never been so real.

Whether written, sung, or staged on TV, the epics are always works of fiction. Rama, Sita, Arjuna, Bhima — they may or may not have been based on historical characters, but all are products of an author's imagination. It is only in the minds of the audience that they become truly real.

It may seem odd at first that Indians should be so easily taken in by illusion. After all, this is no nation of ignorant rubes. Stone Age hunters might be transfixed by a mirror or a Polaroid photo, but Indians were living in gaudy metropolises when Europeans still dressed in bearskins and slept in caves. If Indians are inordinately impressed by shoddy camera tricks, it is not from a lack of sophistication. Merely a lack of guile.

That is not to suggest that they are naive — any such sweeping generalization would be patronizing and incorrect. But I do feel that rural Indians are often more willing than Westerners to accept life at face value. In urban America, by contrast, cynicism and mistrust are second nature; when a New Yorker sees a street performer swallowing fire, he instinctively holds back his dollar because he thinks it must be a trick flame.

Where else but India could an establishment named Cleopatra's Pleasure Palace be merely a vegetarian restaurant? Where else could the Blue Moon Saloon serve up nothing more intoxicating than haircuts? The advertising campaigns of the nation's two largest cola companies illustrate the point nicely. Thumbs Up Cola, which comes in a larger container than its rival, features a picture of a huge phallic bottle and the legend "Bigger IS Better!" Campa Cola responds with a surging, thrusting bottle of its own, above the retort "Taste Is More Important Than Size!" However much the copywriters may have sniggered at their desks, I met few ordinary people who noticed any double-entendre.

. . .

It is this guilelessness, for lack of a better word, that permits Indians to keep their wide-eyed wonder at the marvels of modernity. Like the spanking-new Metro that is the pride of Calcutta.

The subway system of Calcutta is immaculately clean, runs smack on time, and doesn't reek of urine — this in a country where nothing is particularly clean, nothing runs on time, and pretty much everything stinks of piss. Each station has well-tended plants, murals, and even TV sets playing news or movies. The stop below the Indian Museum boasts irreplaceable marble sculptures in fragile glass cases, all completely unmolested. The fare is one rupee, a little over a nickel, about one-twentieth what it costs to ride New York's filthy, unreliable, crime-plagued sewer.

But that is not what amazes the passengers in Calcutta. What holds them spellbound is the escalator down to the tracks.

When I arrived at Kalighat Station, a crowd of all ages was clustered around the escalator's base. Three women in saris were just watching it, hypnotized by the motion, watching the steps climb, fold up, disappear, and pop back up again in a perpetual ellipse. A group of braver teens took turns trying to get on. Each let five or six steps go by before jumping on, waited to get his timing just right so that he would not be sucked into the depths of the iron machine; each rode up five or six unsteady steps before getting scared and scampering back down.

Mothers kept their children several arms' lengths away in case the hungry contraption should reach out and grab them. One balding man in his late thirties, anxious to impress the throng of women, worked up the nerve to go all the way up. He took a running start, jumped with both feet, stumbled, but grabbed both handrails with an unshakable grip, and broke into a wide grin of nervous exultation as he was miraculously carried to the top without walking. He fell down on disembarking, but the women applauded all the same. He trotted down the stairway for another ride.

I walked up as he was standing at the bottom watching the steps intently to gauge the timing of his next leap. I knew I should resist the urge to show off, but I didn't. I brushed through the crowd and effortlessly walked straight onto the escalator, without even looking at my feet! The sari-clad women, hesitant teens, and balding man all stood mesmerized, as if in the presence of a god come down to earth.

If a mortal can ride an escalator to divinity, it is no great stretch for an actor in tin armor to be taken for God Himself.

> > >

Before television, before movies, Indians could still see the great epics in living color. Plays, dances, paintings, and sculpture have always given the Ramayana visual expression, but never were the images so thoroughly convincing. Up north, village amateurs continue to act out parts of the story in gaudy Ramlilas, street theater put on during festivals each autumn. Down south in the state of Kerala, all the characters of classical antiquity dance together throughout the night.

The traditional Kathakali dance lasts from dusk to dawn in the courtyard of a neighborhood temple. These days such performances are extremely rare. The first Kathakali I saw was an open rehearsal in a small wooden house with a corrugated tin roof. Apart from me, the audience consisted of a man looking for a place to sit while he smoked his cheroots and a woman who promptly fell asleep. But the players did not seem to care.

Two drummers pounded on double-sided bongos while two singers droned out a plaintive wail. The star dancer had such a massive gut that he seemed on the verge of giving birth to an elephant, but the limberness of his stocky limbs would have caused envy in anyone half his age and girth.

First he stood stock-still and danced only with the irises of his eyes. Up and down, side to side, sometimes slowly, sometimes fast, round and round in whirling circles, even rocketing about in breakneck figure-eights, the little brown dots kept perfect pace with the racing, pounding, ever-varying drumbeat.

Next, still using his eyeballs alone, he displayed the nine moods of man. Anger, fear, joy, surprise, sadness — his face was an unchanging mask, but there was no mistaking each emotion. Kathakali is more than an exaggerated pantomime, it is a complete physical language. The words and phrases are visual rather than aural, a whole lexicon made up of glances and gestures, turns of the ankle and twitches of the eyebrow.

The pot-bellied dancer was dressed like a hero. I'd earlier watched him putting on his makeup, an elaborate process that can take hours. Each performer must paint his face a bouquet of vermilion, lemon-yellow, black, and aquamarine, must gird on layer after layer of swishing skirts, buckle brass bells onto wrists and feet, tie brass cymbals between forefinger and thumb.

The hero always has his face tinted bright frog-green, and if he is an Immortal he has a white paper halo encircling his chin.

This particular scene showed Rama spurning the advances of the demoness Surpanakha. Women's roles in Kathakali are still usually played by men, so the fair maiden dancer took pains to cover up her chest hair. With a flowing wig and a graceful swirl, the man disguised as a demoness disguised as a beautiful girl swept daintily round and round the full-gutted prince of Ayodhya.

Time and again Rama chased her away, time and again she ran back to embrace him, until he (with a degree of poetic license, for it was Lakshman in the epic) whipped out a gleaming sword and sliced off her nose and ears. As the drums beat faster and harder, more and more furiously, the dancer whirled around and deftly exchanged the maiden's wig for the mask of a ferocious demon. Surpanakha lunged at Rama with a horrifying roar — so horrifying that it woke up the napping woman and made the smoker drop his cigarette — a cry that chilled the blood not only because it was so very loud but because it was the only human voice heard in nearly two hours.

After the show I went behind the sheet that denoted backstage to thank the dancers and (taking a stagehand's whispered suggestion) to give them each a tip. The hero and the demoness both bowed low, batted their eyes in ritualized acknowledgment, and did not speak a single word. They did not have to.

Kathakali, like the Ramlila plays, has brought the epic into people's hearts for centuries. But it has always been very obviously a work of art, an artifice even, a performance that was clearly not real life. Nobody could mistake the silent, fat dancer for Lord Rama, particularly if one had just seen him painting his face green and had dropped ten rupees into his hand. Television has broken down the wall between fantasy and reality, brought gods and demons to life. When Rama speaks not in shrugs and eye-motions but in clear Hindi, when he appears not from behind a strung-up sheet but out of empty air on a miraculous viewing box, the impact goes straight to each viewer's heart.

If Bombay is a dreamland, Kerala is one as well. It too is a vision — not of the future but of the past. Apart from Goa and a few Himalayan territories, it is the only Indian state still covered by jungle. When Rama began his long exile in the now-obliterated Dandak forest, all of the subcontinent may have looked like Kerala.

The tree-covered mountains lie tranquilly on the land like great mastodons sleeping under a blanket of green felt. Every half-mile the jungle changes its face: oar-leafed coconut palms, fan-leafed date palms, groves of teak, groves of mahogany, solid trees covered with vines and thick creepers, spindly trees bent at identical angles, as if they'd all been swayed by the same gust of wind and had forgotten to snap back. There are short, squat banana trees, their fruit clustered in yellow-green bunches, each bunch tipped with a deep purple flower. There are tall, stout jackfruit trees, their limbs sagging from the weight of the watermelon-sized crop. Wherever the railroad tract cuts through a mountain cliff, the living rock drips with condensation from the rain-soaked foliage on top. As the train rumbles by, flocks of startled birds leave their perches and fly above the canopy, silhouetted black in the fading pink sunset.

Villagers cut their rice paddies right into the side of the mountain, like brilliant green stairways climbing straight to a green Heaven. These terraces give way to pipe-cleaner palm trees, chalk-white and no thicker than a young girl's forearm, each shooting skyward for hundreds of feet. Just beyond the town of Bhagavatipuram, I saw a tiny hamlet nestled beneath the swaying palms. The neat, trim houses and the miniature mosque were all painted robin's egg blue, with orange tile roofs, amid a sea of lush vegetable jade. This could not be the same country as the parched plains of Maharashtra and Rajasthan, the cooked expanses of Haryana and Madhya Pradesh. It could only be a dream, dreamt perhaps by a thirsty Bihari farmer during a scorched midday nap, a dream of what India might be like if life were good.

But Kerala's dream extends deeper than scenery. The inhabitants enjoy a harmony and comfort of living wholly absent from many other states. A fifth of the population is Muslim, another fifth Christian, yet Kerala experiences almost none of the religious strife so common throughout the country. The literacy rate is more than twice the national average, with three out of every four adults able to read. Disparity between rich and poor is relatively small, and the grinding, bleeding destitution so common in Orissa, Bihar, or Andhra Pradesh seems several worlds away.

I'm not sure how I persuaded myself to leave the little blue hamlet outside Bhagavatipuram, but leave I did. I had to go to Mattancherry and look at the murals on the walls of the old palace of the rajahs, perhaps the finest Ramayana pictures in all of India.

I took a boat up the backwaters from the railhead in Quilon and was nearly scuttled by another Keralan unreality: the pre-industrial, scarcely feudal boatmen had formed a union and called an impromptu workers' strike.

Kerala, a state with no urban proletariat and no real bourgeoisie, is ruled by unabashed, party-line Communists. What's more, they were freely elected, the very first democratically chosen Communist government in the world. Their philosophy is not even the Maoist brand retooled for peasants rather than factory workers, but the old-fashioned call to arms of Marx and Lenin. A land that has barely discovered capitalism has decided to wrench off chains not yet forged.

It was such a beautiful day that several of the boatmen wanted to be home with their families. The workers conferred for a bit, decided to hold a one-day strike, then changed their minds and shouted a few half-hearted slogans instead. A few more men arrived late, and that shifted the balance. The strike was on again. The newly inspired crew demanded a pay hike, marched in a circle for five minutes, and then trudged home.

"Don't worry, boss," the dockmaster told me. He had never left his chair on the deck and had watched the proceedings with scant interest through half-shut eyelids. "This often happens when the weather is fine at week's end. Some other boat will go, maybe in the afternoon."

Another boat did go, and I sat on its tin roof watching the river. On the water, Arabian dhows with square sails of yellowed parchment lazily eased their way home from the sea. By the banks, fishermen raised and lowered their nets on cranelike wooden frames, an invention brought to Kerala by emissaries of Kublai Khan. On the shore, schoolboys played soccer in sarongs instead of gym shorts.

I eventually got to Mattancherry, in the Portuguese town of Cochin, where the old houses have thick wooden shutters to keep delicate, pale senhoritas from turning brown in the sun. The palace at Mattancherry no longer houses a rajah, but its coronation room of dark lacquered teak displays portraits of all the kings of the last two hundred years. Most of them, I couldn't help noticing, bore the chosen name of Rama.

The glories of Mattancherry Palace are the incomparable murals. There is a wall of Shiva sitting in state, surrounded by apsaras and ever-young nymphs. There is a wall of Krishna sporting with the milkmaids, against a backround of bears, deer, and lions, all copulating with lusty grins smeared across their beasty faces. But the most spectacular murals by far are at the end of a long hallway in a chamber devoted entirely to the scenes from the Ramayana.

The walls are a ceaseless flurry of activity, every inch packed with color and motion, not the space of a thumbnail left idle. Each scene flows into the next without a break, for real life is not divvied up neatly into chapters and paragraphs. The feathery figures are so baroquely styled they seem more Mayan than Indian, as if an artist from Palenque or Tikal had gotten lost in antiquity and been forced to earn his keep in the court of a Keralan king.

Starting on one wall and walking around the room, you can watch the Ramayana unfold before your eyes. In the first scene, three naked queens with basketball breasts and trim, muscular bellies squat over cushions as midwives pull the miniscule babies Rama, Lakshman, and Bharata from between their legs. Without interruption Rama breaks the bow of King Janaka, while Maharishi Vishvamitra strokes his long black beard in wonder. The marriage of Rama and Sita, their betrayal and flight into exile, Bharata's mission at Chitrakut — all flow by in frenzied fresco.

Farther down the wall, Lakshman chops away at the hideous demoness Surpanakha. The evil magician Maricha disguises himself with a deer's body and a human face but leads Rama astray only to his own destruction. Ten-headed Ravana puts on the mask of a mendicant to kidnap Sita and slays the bird king Jatayu in his flight.

Rama, always identifiable by his divine blue-green hue, meets the King of the Monkeys and the King of the Bears. Prince Hanuman leaps clear across the ocean at a bound. The army of furry, long-tailed apes meets the army of night-black Rakshasas in sky-shaking battle, and Sita shockingly — but all that will come later.

Sometimes a too-perfect illusion can be a bad thing. It destroys imagination. The televised Ramayana sets the story right out for the viewer, serves it up ready-made on a platter. Nobody needs to bring anything to it, and nobody takes away anything of his own. When I look at the murals in Mattancherry Palace, or read Valmiki's text, I do not see precisely the same epic as anyone else. Each person must use his own imagination to fill in all the gaps, flesh out the details, conjure up a living picture of how each character sounds and moves. The audience is an active participant, working in partnership with the painter or writer. No two viewings are quite the same, no two readings identical. In the old days, there were millions of different Ramayanas lodged in the hearts of all Hindus. Every Indian, at one time or another, created his own personal epic.

➤ ➤ ➤

The Lord of the Demons had his air-conditioner set high. He prays devoutly for three hours every day, and does not like his ritual to be tainted by sweat.

Arvind Trivedi is proof that appearances deceive. He is a pious Brahmin, one of the most pious I've ever met — and on television's Ramayana he played the evil Rakshasa who almost enslaved the world.

"I'd never thought of myself as Ravana," Trivedi said. "I have always looked up to my elder brother so much that I identify most closely with Lakshman. Have done ever since I was a boy. For a school theatrical, in fact, I once acted the part of Lakshman and my brother played Rama."

On screen Trivedi is swaggering and imperious, with a thick handlebar mustache and curly black wig that make him look less like the Demon King of epic than the Pirate King of Gilbert and Sullivan. In his home, sitting on the edge of his bed after giving me the only chair in the room, Trivedi appeared neither demonic nor piratical.

Mustache and crown had been replaced by thick spectacles and a rosewood rosary. On his forehead was the painted mark of an earnest Shaivite, on his chest the janneu-thread of the twice-born. The apartment was a cramped walk-up in an unfashionable section of town, a flat that would be considered modest even for somebody who was not a big television star. As we talked, his wife slipped in to bring me a tray of vegetarian snacks and slipped out again without saying a word.

"It was almost a sacrament," he said. "To play a part, any part, in the holy Ramayana — I tried to make it an act of religious merit. My preparation for the role consisted mostly of prayer. Each day before the shoot, after putting on my robes, crown, and mock jewelry, I would kneel down to ask Rama and Shiva for guidance. If my performance was good, it is because they inspired me. By bringing this sacred epic directly to the people, we are helping to spread the word of God."

He glanced briefly at the wall opposite his bed. It was decorated with a large photograph of his guru and a colorful poster of the god Shiva. They were the only two pieces of ornamentation in the room.

"I hope and believe," he continued, "that the television serial is raising the spiritual state of India. Hindus are now more aware of their tradition, of their faith. We are reminding our countrymen of who they are. But that places a grave responsibility on the actors. So many people are looking up to us, we must be exemplary role models. Not only on the set, but in our private lives as well."

Arvind Trivedi does not drink. He does not smoke, and he does not eat meat. He does not cheat on his wife. He spends three hours a day in worship. Other actors saw the serial as just another job, but for Trivedi it was always far more. The Ramayana, both as television and as holy text, was a way of life.

Originally Trivedi hoped for nothing more than a walk-on. He asked for the role of the boatman who ferries Rama across the Ganges because he wanted to be a part of the epic and had always admired that character's pure fidelity. The director told him to take a screen test, and Trivedi was miffed; he'd worked with the director before and felt no need to strut for a cameo. But at the studio he was whisked off to wardrobe and suited up in all the make-believe finery of the King of the Demons.

A dozen rival Ravanas, identically costumed, were pacing the carpet of the waiting room, reviewing lines or working out a *Times of India* crossword with studied nonchalance. Four hundred others had already passed through. Trivedi did not even have to read for the part. As soon as he stepped out with wig, mustache, and crown, the director sent all the rest of the would-be Rakshasas home.

By every account, Trivedi stole the show. Critics and viewers agree that he upstaged all the other actors. His trademark was a rich, rolling, derisive laugh, a laugh that dripped smug contempt. He reveled in his newfound celebrity and campaigned strongly for the Hindu revivalist Bharatiya Janata Party. His brother had already used a film career as a stepping stone to Parliament, and Trivedi does not rule out future political ambitions. It would not be the first time that a demon has been elected to government.

I asked him what lay behind his famous laugh.

The actor tilted his head back and croaked out a slow, mocking "Hah! Hah! Hah!"

"That laugh is the key to Ravana's character," he said. "It is the symbol of pride."

In the view of Trivedi, Ravana is not an evil demon at all. He is a man, a heroic man, even a virtuous man, whose only failing is arrogance. That fatal flaw is what brings him low.

"Did you see my episodes?" he asked eagerly. I told him I'd watched most of them on an American cable station aimed at Indian expatriates.

"Which of my scenes did you like the best?"

I said something polite about the banning of Vibhishan.

"Ah, yes, yes," he purred. "Which others?"

The death scene, of course, and the capture of Sita . . .

"Well, at any rate," he said, "you notice that when Ravana laughs, it is always because he is displaying pride. He laughs off good advice and honest warnings, goes laughing into a battle that he must surely lose. It is egotism that blinds him to the truth."

This view of Ravana as an imperfect hero rather than a perfect villain is not unique to Trivedi. It is held by many, particularly among Shaivites and southerners. But now, through Trivedi's portrayal, that is the image of the Lord of the Rakshasas that all Indians have in their minds. For most of them it is a wholly new picture. Only time will tell which vision will last: the ten-headed monster who terrifies small children at village fairs or the man with the Pirate King handlebar, sadly crushed by the weight of his own vanity.

The actor asked me for more of my favorite episodes, asked if my Indian friends had expressed any opinion about his performance, asked if I'd read the reviews that praised him above all the rest of the cast. When I said that I'd seen them, he did not laugh but had to catch himself. Perhaps, like Arun Govil, he had absorbed a trace of his character's nature.

But Trivedi's justified pride in his craft did not strike me as boastful puffery. He hardly leads the life of a self-centered, supercilious star. As I left, he told me that his great wish in portraying Ravana was to help people find God through the epic

Ramayana — the very same God, he said, who lies behind all the religions of East and West. Such a lofty goal is enough to make any man proud.

The King of the Demons is actually an apostle of God. The earthly avatar of God Himself is an unassuming family man, no more, no less. The immortal warriors of epic are papier-mâché dummies, hacked up by movie-set extras wielding wooden swords. If there is any firm, transcendent reality in the world, we humans can never hope to know it. Everything we believe to be true is simply that — belief. We make a leap of faith every time we open our eyes.

> > >

The Upanishads, some of the most philosophical texts in the Hindu canon, tell us that all the world is illusion. They say that Samsara — the universe we mortals inhabit — is nothing but a fantasy, a lie, a trick, so transitory, flighty, and changeable that it can barely be said to exist at all. Life is nothing but a fleeting rush of unfulfilled desires, earthly happiness nothing but a will-o'-the-wisp that vanishes the moment it is grasped. Men, animals, plants, and objects all are created and destroyed in the batting of a cosmic eye: what can a life of eighty years, or any of its events, possibly mean in the limitless vastness of time? Measured against the infinite, any human action is as ludicrously insignificant as the flight of a gnat.

That is why the yogis of old, and the Buddhists who later appropriated much of their theology, called life a mere dream. Every dream seems real for a short time. Even as you're driving a car with no brakes at top speed on the wrong lane of a highway and not hitting anybody, or inexplicably showing up for a crucial business meeting unprepared and completely naked, or flying a jet airplane with a talking bassett hound for your co-pilot, you'd swear your predicament was absolutely real. Human dreams last minutes or hours, then the characters in them fade to oblivion. Could not a dream of God, of the living cosmos, last for eons? Might not we all, as one of the Puranas suggests, merely be characters in the dream of Vishnu?

The aborigines of Australia, for their part, believe the dreaming and waking worlds are equally "real." Nobody ever actually sleeps, the soul merely migrates from one valid, concrete universe to another. If anything, dreams are the more true of the two worlds, for they are a vision of the holy Dream-Time of eternity.

Even in our waking existence, say aborigines, the world is insubstantial and formless, a hazy sea of smoke and mud. Only words and music make the earth real. It is the divine song of the ancestors that created the cosmos, the sacred singing of the ancestors' descendants that keeps Creation intact. Each wallaby, shrub, and rock on the planet became real only when it was named by an ancestor during the Dream-Time, long ago. Each kangaroo, water hole, and eucalyptus tree will cease to exist as soon as men forget its name and its song.

In the beginning was the Word, and the Word was God.

Plato, writing a few centuries after the Upanishads were first sung, came up with a similar concept. Everything on earth, he suggested, is merely an imperfect, unreal image of some divine prototype. Each leather sandal, say, is just a bad copy of some ideal sandal that exists beyond the realm of human sense. And each man and woman is just a faulty facsimile of the One True Person, the perfect Spirit on whose image we are patterned. Reality, Plato said, exists only in the ideal plane.

How, then, can we phantasms find truth? If we and everything around us are figments of divine imagination, how can we gain true existence? The answer, for yogi and Socratic disciple alike, is union with God. By joining ourselves with the only Reality, we become Real.

As for how we achieve this divine unification, that I do not know. If I did, I would be a saint, a maharishi, or a fully enlightened Buddha.

Seven
EVIL

RAMA asked every animal in the forest where Sita had gone, begged information from every mango, every pomegranate, every sandalwood tree. The beasts and the bushes were too frightened of Ravana to speak even a word. Rama ordered the mountains to echo his wife's direction, threatened to tear off their snowy peaks, but the hills remained stonily mute.

"All else I can forget," he raged, "everything else — slander, unjust exile, father's death, everything. But not this. Never this." He shouted harsh words at the gods themselves, warned that he might well destroy all Creation in his wrath.

Lakshman put a hand on Rama's shoulder. "This is not you," he said. "My brother does not repay evil with evil, that is not his way. My brother has suffered before, but never let it affect his good nature. My brother has never been stained with anger. Are you still my brother, or has evil turned you into somebody else?"

"I am still what I am," Rama said, paraphrasing another of his avatars. "But today my bad luck burns like hellfire. If I dove into the ocean, all the world's seas would evaporate in the heat of my misfortune."

"There is no escaping evil," Lakshman awkwardly replied. He felt uncomfortable dispensing philosophy and comfort. "Even the gods in heaven sometimes suffer pain. They accept it, and you must too."

The brothers glumly scoured the forest floor for footprints, practically rolling their eyeballs on the ground as they walked. Their gaze was so intent that they did not see the fearsome Rakshasa until they were each grasped in a mammoth fist.

"Put us down," Lakshman said. Rama's anger had turned to melancholy, and he could not even be bothered to speak a word.

The demon was as big as a hillside but had no legs, no neck, and no head. In his hairy belly was a single eye, and a cavernous mouth full of sharp yellow teeth. The maw gaped open to swallow the brothers, and Rama raised not an eyebrow to resist.

Lakshman cut off the Rakshasa's two arms, which crashed like felled trees to the leafy ground. He did not kill the monster. To coldly slaughter a defenseless foe, even an enemy of undoubted evil, is always an abomination.

The Rakshasa had no head to bow, no palms to press, no knees to kneel, but he offered his thanks all the same. "For sparing me," he said, "I will give you good advice:

"Once, ages ago, I performed austerities and received the boon of long life. I swelled up huge with pride, huge as a mountain, so huge that I challenged Indra himself to fight. The Lord of Storms smashed my head into my chest with one thunderbolt, shattered my legs with another. He, like you, refrained from taking my life, because he too is good. In gratitude for your mercy I tell you this: find somebody just as desperate as yourself, someone just as miserable, just as hopeless. Help him, and he in turn will help you."

For the next few days Rama and Lakshman could not escape the feeling that they were being watched. At every step the forest seemed to chitter and hush. Many times they stood stock still and looked, listened, and sniffed the air, but there was no sight, sound, or scent of any man or any demon. Nothing but the animals of the woods.

They had combed many miles of jungle without exchanging a sentence when an ape jumped down from the trees and kissed their feet. He was no ordinary ape, for not only did he walk upright like a man, but he clearly had a fine sense of royal protocol.

"You are Rama of Ayodhya," the monkey said, "prince of the Ikshwaku clan. I have observed your search, made inquiries about your identity. My name is Hanuman. My master, the one-time king of the Vanars, has something that you may have lost."

He led them through pathless wilds to a secluded hideout in the shelter of a towering white skeleton. When the introductions were over, the Monkey King, Sugriva, brought out a bag of stitched leaves and emptied its contents into Rama's lap.

"I believe," he said, "that these belong to your wife."

Rama stared at the gold necklaces, diamond earrings, heavy

silver and emerald bangles, uncertain whether to cry with joy or with rage.

"They rained from the sky," Sugriva said. "Jewels from heaven — but not from heaven at all. We looked up and saw a woman being dragged off by a furious Rakshasa, a woman cleverly tossing away riches to gain witnesses. I do not know where she is, but I can help find her."

"Speak," said Rama, and the monkey told his tale:

"Long ago," he said, "my elder brother Bali ruled the land of Kishkindhya. A terrible demon was tormenting our people, so he and I went to hunt the monster. We pursued it to a deep cave, and he went in alone. You see, my task was to wait outside, to make certain that the demon did not evade my brother in the dark and escape.

"For one year I stood by the cavern's entrance. I heard cries of anguish, but could not abandon my post. Then one day I saw blood spilling out, cascading down the rocks in a thick stream. I knew that my brother had been killed. If Bali, a far stronger warrior than I, could not stop the demon, then there was no reason for me even to try. Instead, I trapped the monster by sealing up the cave mouth with a large boulder and ran back to Kishkindhya. Against my wishes, the people crowned me king.

"Months passed. I ruled well, I think, and my subjects cared for me. But, wonder of wonders, Bali came back. I offered him the throne, of course, but he accused me of treachery. As it turned out, he had spent that entire year searching the rocky tunnels and finally vanquishing the Rakshasa — the oozing blood I saw had flowed not from him but from the demon. How was I to know, eh? He refused to understand, said I had intentionally plugged the cave hole to steal his crown. He took my wife and turned me out into exile with nothing. I still live in fear of my life."

"If Bali wished to kill you," Rama said, "surely he would have done so by now."

"No, not here," the ape replied. "He cannot enter this part of the forest because of a curse. You see, once a demon bull challenged Bali to fight, even haughtily told my brother to take a day to put his affairs in order and frolic with his women one final time. Cheeky, eh?

"Bali wrestled with the bull and broke its neck with his bare hands. He hurled the corpse high into the air, miles away, and as it flew, drops of blood splattered down into the jungle below.

One drop hit the forehead of a rishi at prayer and disturbed his meditation. The saint laid a ban on Bali, that if he ever set foot among these trees he would die. This skeleton you see belongs to that demon-bull, and I have never dared to leave the safety of its shadow."

The ape dropped to his knees and hugged Rama's legs.

"Help me," he said, "help a wretch who has nothing. Help me regain my kingdom, and I will send millions of monkeys all over the world to track down your wife."

"Have no fear," said Rama, smiling for the first time in many days, "I will lead you out from under the shadow, and let you walk in light. You will be king again. I promise it."

➤ ➤ ➤

In Lanka the King of the Demons was prostrate at Sita's feet.

"I have never before bowed to any woman," he said. "I have never bowed to any man. There is nobody in the universe to whom I would kneel, nobody but you."

Sita said nothing.

"I have wives beyond counting," Ravana said evenly, "and I would give them up for you. I have kingdoms, palaces, mountains of gold. All of it will be yours. Marry me."

"I already have a husband," Sita said, never opening her eyes.

The Rakshasa stood up. "Consider my proposal," he said. "I will give you an entire year."

"And then?"

"If you do not change your mind, I will have no choice but to cook and eat you." He said it as gently as he could. "Please understand, this is not a threat. I would never threaten you. It is merely an honest answer, since I could not tell you a lie."

He pressed his palms together in a sincere gesture of respect, and left. Not until the door had closed did Sita permit herself the indulgence of a tear.

At the gates of Kishkindhya, Sugriva bellowed his challenge.

"Come out and fight!" he roared. "Come out, Bali — or are you afraid?" Sugriva's confidence came easily: behind a thick shrub, Rama was sitting with his bowstring taut.

Bali strolled out, languidly swinging his powerful arms. "Let's go," he said, as his brother lunged forward. For fifteen minutes he battered Sugriva, until the younger ape begged for mercy. Bali then wiped the blood off his fists, shook his head, and walked back to his palace.

Rama apologized to Sugriva as he pulled him from the dust. "I couldn't tell which of you was which," he said, "so I didn't dare shoot. You really do look very much alike."

"Odd," said the ape, massaging his jaw, "we Vanars have the same confusion with men. But I have an idea." Once Bali was a safe distance away he limped forward and called out a new challenge.

"Tomorrow!" he shouted. "We will settle it tomorrow!"

That evening Bali's wife urged him not to fight. She had seen Rama by Sugriva's side and knew there could be no hope of victory.

"Why would Rama wish to harm me?" Bali asked. "I have no quarrel with him. And he is famous for his virtue, he could never be so wicked as to interfere with a fair fight or support a usurper against a rightful king."

Bali stroked his wife's cheek. He knew she did not want to see her former husband die.

"Do not worry," he said. "I have no intention of killing Sugriva. I'll merely humble him again and send him peacefully on his way."

When the two royal apes squared off the next morning, Sugriva had a green creeper tied around his furry neck for identification. As Bali quickly gained mastery in the scuffle, an arrow from the thicket pierced him square in the back.

Bali stared up at Rama in bewilderment. All he could utter was a hoarsely croaked "Why?"

Rama stared back, and for many long minutes had no reply at all.

"I am a man," he said at last, "you are a monkey. I owe you no explanation and no apology."

He knew more words were needed.

"You stole Sugriva's wife," he said. "That is the worst evil any man, ape, or demon can commit."

The Queen of the Vanars did not greet Rama as a deliverer. She lay weeping over her husband's corpse and could not be dragged away.

"Evil," she whispered through her tears, "evil indeed."

How could Rama, the very personification of good, commit an act of evil? How could Ravana, the Lord of the Demons, behave like a true gentleman? These are questions that Indians debate every day, at the dinner table, at the temple, at the tea hut near the village well. Truck-driver philosophers and seamstress theologians come up with many explanations, but never with an answer. There is no answer. Good and evil are not the separate entities we would like to believe.

East and West alike, most of us hunger for a world of clear-cut right and wrong. We like moral certainties. We jump at the chance for a crusade. Each of us thinks of himself or herself as a basically good person. If all of us are righteous souls, where does the world's evil come from?

It comes from us, of course. We, the honest, the charitable, the virtuous — it comes from us. True, there are always a small minority who have no moral sense whatsoever, a tiny cadre of people who can truly be called demons; they may be clinically defined as psychopaths, and they kill or cheat without a shred of remorse. The Charles Mansons and the Klaus Barbies are heinous, but they are responsible for only a fraction of the world's woes. The bulk of human wickedness is far more ordinary. It comes from people who have consciences, who lead normal lives, who try to do what they believe is right. A sadistic commandant may give the order to torture a prisoner, but it is the wage-earning henchman who heats the poker. I have met henchmen, I have met terrorists, I have met people who have done unspeakable things. They are not all evil creatures. And that is a terrifying realization.

If only life were a simple Manichaean struggle between good and evil with battle lines clearly drawn, a fight we could enter gladly and be sure of winning.

When I was a boy, like most boys, I longed to become a knight in shining armor. My heroes were Sir Lancelot, King Richard the Lionheart, and (as the Keralan seer later reminded me) Saint George. I believed that there really had been a time when brave men devoted their lives to the cause of right. I would read Thomas Mallory entire afternoons and evenings, and desperately wish to slip back to those times. It always made me sad to put the book down and look out the window at the mundane world, the world in which "Sir" was what a waiter called my father if he wanted a tip.

I did not bother to think that the Saracens slain by valiant Crusaders were fighting a holy war of their own, knights just as righteous or unrighteous as the thundering chivalry of Europe. Nor did I think much about the women and children slaughtered by the Lionheart for the crime of being Muslim. My heroes had not yet been demythologized. I did not yet know that Lancelot was an adulterer, a *French* adulterer, and a fictional one at that. I did not yet know that King Richard was a homosexual philanderer and a mediocre general at best. But even then the knight with whom I most identified was Saint George. Because he, more than any other, personified the triumph of good over evil.

I longed to ride a pure white horse, slaying dragons with a lance as straight and piercing as truth itself.

It wasn't until much later that I understood what lay behind Saint George's appeal. In most of his iconography the paladin towers over his foe, dispatches it with the effortless mastery of a god. From the famous Bernardo Martorell painting straight on down, the dragon of evil is a tiny, insignificant nuisance cringing beneath the feet of Saint George's steed. It is the ease of the victory that moved me, the inevitability of good's triumph.

What Saint George represented, without my realizing it, was an entire world view in which good *always* beats evil, without even working up a sweat. When he kills the dragon, it is not a titanic clash between equally powerful enemies. For the knight, slaughtering a monster is no more difficult than swatting a mosquito. There is little drama, no chance that the dragon might actually win. Virtue *must* prevail — that is the natural order of the universe. It is an immensely comforting notion of life.

It is also the notion of life that underlies the Ramayana. I don't want to spoil the suspense (and I won't reveal the kicker), but in the end Rama wins. It was fated from the beginning. All the characters know it. Even the Demon King's counselors tell their master that he will lose, and only suicidal arrogance lets him ignore their warning. All Indians know how the epic turns out, yet they cluster around their televisions, radios, and school stages just the same.

Everyone, I think, longs for a world where good always trounces evil. When we go to the movies we know the hero will win out and the villain will be crushed, but we still grip the armrests in anticipation. What are action-thriller films if not morality plays? Does the sadistic drug lord *ever* walk away unpunished? It is the same in most popular forms of fiction: right must defeat wrong, or else we'd feel cheated.

In real life, it is quite often evil that triumphs. In real life, rapists and murderers go free on judicial technicalities, slumlords and stock manipulators flourish as respected members of society. In real life, good, honest, hard-working people lose their livelihoods at the flick of a corporate raider's pen. Perhaps that is why we so desperately seek escape. We ache for a world where good always wins, because that is not the real world we inhabit. We long for Saint George. We long for Rama.

If you look at the icons of these two holy warriors, you notice that both faces wear the same untroubled expression. Both mouths are tinged with the same faint shadow of a placid smile. It is a smile of inner serenity, of divine self-confidence, of quiet contentment, a smile that comes from utter certainty that good is destined to prevail.

Yet even Vishnu Incarnate is not wholly free of iniquity. There are two places in the Ramayana where, by almost any standard, Rama commits a grievous sin. The first is in killing Bali, a moral, rightly guided king, and helping his brother, Sugriva, usurp the throne. Indians searching for a justification say that Bali should not have taken Sugriva's wife, and it is for this crime that Rama punishes him. They do not speculate on why the paragon of virtue chooses to slay the Monkey King dishonestly, with an arrow in the back.

The second instance is at the end of the epic, when Rama betrays the person he loves most. It is an act of great heartlessness. No Indian I know has been able to offer any convincing rationalization.

The explanation — but it is only an explanation, not an excuse — is duty. Rama always obeys dharma, the Law, the unbending code of righteousness. By sticking so closely to the letter of the Law, he sometimes ignores its moral spirit. Rama promises Sugriva his help, and dharma says a vow must be kept, even if (like King Dasarastha's pledge to his tricky wife) it is an unjust vow unwisely made. At the epic's end Rama does not wish to bring Sita pain, but dharma says that a monarch must place his subjects' welfare above all else. As a king and as a husband, he must commit evil actions because the law of righteousness demands them.

If the personification of good is not always virtuous, neither is the embodiment of evil always malign. Except for his sin of pride, not a few Indians have told me, Ravana would be *superior* to Rama.

The Rakshasa Lord is a disciple of the god Shiva, so Shaivites throughout India revere him despite his mortal flaw. In the northern plains, where the cults of Vishnu predominate, Ravana is burned in effigy at raucous village festivals. But in the Shaivite south, people cry at his downfall. When any actor who has portrayed him (whether on television, movies, or stage) walks down the street, small children do not hide their faces in fear. They bounce with excitement, and their parents lift them up to receive a demon's blessing. But the ambivalence toward Ravana goes far beyond mere sectarian boosting of a coreligionist. It stems from a fundamental Hindu belief that the most fearsome evil is nothing more than a perversion of good.

All power, in Vedic philosophy, comes from virtue. Diligent penance and worship amass merit and lead inevitably to generous boons from the gods. Every person in a position of importance must have accumulated a great deal of positive karma, either in this life or in a previous one. There is simply no way for an out-and-out bad apple to do much harm — pure perfidy just isn't strong enough to be anything more than an annoyance. In this view, the real danger is not from pathetic, petty miscreants. Their evil is deep-seated but hardly a threat. Crimes that stem from greed, lust, laziness, or dishonesty are mere peccadilloes, more to be pitied than hated.

"We needn't worry about the everyday rascals," a pandit once told me. "They are weak, because they care only for themselves and are not sustained by any inner conviction. That is why, in a straight fight, virtue will overcome wickedness every time. The only danger, and the source of most of the world's ills, is the good man who has gone astray."

Even Ravana's sin of pride, a sin that has quite possibly caused more devastation through the ages than any other single failing, is seen as a perversion of virtue.

Evil (as Hannah Arendt and others have noted) is essentially banal — but it has also a streak of grandeur.

"Arrogance is part and parcel of any true hero," a Madrasi scholar told me. "It must have limits, and Ravana went beyond these limits. But even the most vaunting vainglory is dangerous only because it is the corruption of a great man's proper self-respect. There is an old Tamil proverb which says that an elephant lying down is still as tall as a horse standing up."

Makhan Lal Sen, an early fighter for Indian independence and a highly respected translator of Valmiki's Ramayana, put it another way. "We Hindus," he wrote in 1927, "are idolaters of greatness, born and bred."

In Islamic and Christian tradition, it was pride that cast Satan from Heaven into the chasm of Hell. Before his fall, Lucifer was the brightest light in all the angelic host.

> > >

The Punjab is a proving ground of good and evil. For the past decade a bloody war has raged there, a war to determine the future of an entire people and, perhaps, of India as a nation. If the Punjab does not gain independence, many Sikhs believe their race will be obliterated. If it does break away, dozens of other states, from Assam to Kashmir to Tamil Nadu, could follow suit, leaving India a chaotic jumble of splintered fiefdoms.

There have been countless atrocities on both sides. Militant separatists bomb trains and buses, murder "collaborators," live high on extortion and threat, assassinate newspaper editors who refuse to trumpet their praises. Police torture suspects, arrest innocent noncombatants as hostages, kill teenage boys to keep them from joining the rebels. In 1991 the Punjab's civil war took more than 5,200 lives — five times the death toll in Lebanon that year.

Here good and evil, like beauty, are in the eye of the beholder. One man's freedom fighter is another's terrorist. Demons and paladins are locked in an epic battle, but there is no way to tell which is which. Every devil is, after all, nothing more than an angel who has fallen.

I do not know whether the Punjab is representative of all lands where people seek independence by terrorism and guerrilla war. I do not know if the same dynamic is at work in Palestine, Northern Ireland, Mozambique, or half a dozen Latin American countries. Perhaps India's northern frontier is a legitimate test case for investigating the universal phenomenon of good and bad, perhaps not. But there can hardly be more clear-cut examples of evil than terrorism and oppression, so the Punjab is as fitting a laboratory as any I know.

The Punjab proves that right and wrong are not the polar opposites we would like to believe. The Punjab demonstrates that iniquity is not virtue's absence but virtue's corruption. The Punjab shows that the world contains a great deal of evil but few truly evil people.

I would have been killed by the militants on March 1, 1990, if not for the blessed incompetence of Indian Railways.

I was trying to catch the overnight Chhattisgarh Express north, to the Sikh holy city of Amritsar. I had no reservation, since the junior clerk mistakenly believed he could not give one without confiscating my passport. Past experience had taught me the futility of arguing with petty bureaucrats, so I looked up the departure time in my train schedule instead.

When I returned to the station the next day, I saw a handwritten sign tacked nonchalantly to the ticket counter: "Bomb blast on the Chhattisgarh Express, 1/3/90." There were two columns of hastily scrawled names under the blunt headings "Those Expired" and "Those Wounded." I later learned that the compartment where my reserved seat would have been was blown clear into the sky at the first detonation.

I rechecked my timetable and found that the train wasn't even supposed to leave for two hours. "Ah," said a conductor when I showed him the page, "it is a misprint in the schedule. The Chhattisgarh Express does not go to Amritsar anyway. You will be wanting the *Chandigarh* Express. Track three. Good day."

That was that. Dozens killed, hundreds wounded, and business as usual. Such occurrences are part of ordinary life in the Punjab. If an attack's death toll is not in the triple digits, it isn't even front-page news. People talk about the daily body count in the same tones that Englishmen discuss the rain.

In my bunk on the Chandigarh Express I slept with the uneasy knowledge that I owed my life to a twofold bungling: an incorrect timetable had sent me to the doomed train, but a thickheaded clerk wouldn't let me book the fatal ticket. A bit more competence on either end would have been lethal. Perhaps it was fated — I had not intended to go to Chhattisgarh, so I was not destined to die that day.

The real issue, however, was not the randomness of death and whether the world is ruled by dumb chance or by order; I may have avoided freak destruction, but thousands die senselessly, unnecessarily, every day. The real question was what sort of person would coolly and deliberately try to murder a train-load of perfect strangers.

It was not a crime of passion, not even a crime of poverty, it was a crime of cold conviction. The bombers did not betray their morals, they acted upon them. They honestly believed that what they were doing was right.

One of my cabin-mates on the Chandigarh Express was a Sikh teenager traveling to Amritsar to become a terrorist. He had grown up in England and spoke in a thick Brixton cockney.

"Me mum ship me off day before yesterday," he said. "Old man wants me t'get training."

"What sort of training?"

"Oh, religious instruction. Also," he lowered his voice, "political."

He was very small and thin, little more than a boy, with a wispy beard and a turban far too big for his head.

"I'm glad I run into yer," he said, " 'tsa good job to talk real English. I mean, these lot 'ere can speak it, some of 'em, but not like us. By the way, I'm 'Archand, but me mates call me 'Arry."

He told me the name of the guru to whom he was being sent, a guru infamous for his close links to the Khalistani militants.

"Me old man says this 'ere guru'll teach me everythin'," Harry went on. "I'm all for Khalistan, but tell yer the truth, I'd rather be back 'ome."

There were several Punjabis in the cabin who most likely shared his desire for Khalistan, the putative Sikh homeland. But Harry said not a word to them. The fragile teen seemed almost afraid of his compatriots, an alien in his own country.

He pointed delightedly out the window at a farmer squatting down to urinate, and complained that the train's lavatories didn't have "proper sitting-down toilets." As he got ready for bed he kept his kirpan, the ceremonial dagger that all observant Sikhs must wear, strapped close to his chest.

"Cor!" he said. "S'bloody cold, eh?"

It was indeed bloody cold. I shivered in three shirts and a sweater. Harry slept with his oversized turban crammed down around his ears for warmth. I heard him coughing all through the night. Once, in his sleep, he mumbled, "No, Mummy-ji!"

When we reached Amritsar the next morning, Harry asked me to help him find the militants' encampment. He'd been in

India only three days and was still intimidated by the touts and the rickshaw-wallahs. He was young, frightened, alone in a strange land, and he looked like he might blow away in the wind. So I got him safely on his way to become a terrorist.

Not all Sikhs pine for Khalistan, but many do. Separatist longings are strongest in those farthest from home, the Sikhs in Britain, Canada, the United States. From a distance, ugly brawls can look like glorious crusades of good against evil. It is much easier to maintain a moral absolutism when war is an abstraction, when the intestines and bits of splintered bone are somebody else's, somebody far, far away. Expatriates send money and arms back to the Punjab, just as Irishmen in Boston and Palestinians in Detroit take up collections for the IRA and the PLO. It is rare to find a Sikh in Toronto who does not support the Khalistani militants, and rare to find one in Hyderabad who does.

Inside the Punjab, most Sikhs long for peace rather than politics. "The police rule by day, the terrorists by night," said Kanwaljit Kaur, a farmer's wife. "One robs in the morning, one in the evening, that is the only difference. The militants come at midnight and take what they want, threaten to kill any of us who resist. The next day the constables beat us up for cooperating with rebels." Like Mrs. Kaur, most Punjabis have little love either for the government or for whatever extremist group might replace it.

Outside of the Punjab, Indian Sikhs generally see the insurgents merely as brutal thugs. They not only deplore the separatists' violent methods, they generally do not even support their cause.

The Partition of 1947 chopped the Punjab in two, half of it remaining in India and half becoming part of the newly hewn Pakistan. Millions of Sikhs dreaded life under a self-proclaimed Islamic government, and almost all fled to India. They settled in Delhi, Bombay, Bangalore — any city or town where they could find work. And work they did; the industriousness of the Sikh people is legendary. "Go anywhere," a turbaned man named Singh proudly told me once, "anywhere in the nation, anywhere in the world, and you will *never* see a Sikh begging." In all my travels, I never have.

Forty years later, these Sikhs of the subcontinental diaspora have built up prosperous communities outside the Punjab. Most of them fear that an independent Khalistan would make them second-class citizens in India, and few relish the notion of picking up and starting from scratch again. They are upstanding citizens and have no love for terrorists.

But even these solid pillars of rectitude can't help feeling a touch of ambivalence. They remember the desecration of the Golden Temple, they know their coreligionists are being oppressed in the Punjab, they are tired of the tasteless "dumb Sikh" jokes that other Indians find uproariously funny. They have been model citizens, fought the wars against Pakistan and China in far disproportionate numbers, helped the nation prosper through their hard work, yet many Hindus still treat them like buffoons or criminals. When they see Khalistanist militants defying all the might of the Indian government, fighting persecution with bullets rather than kind words, even sober, staid Sikhs are moved.

The insurgency is about identity more than politics, and the rebels are battling to maintain every scrap of Sikh culture. Most Punjabis would probably prefer to let their society change with the times, adapt to modernity rather than deny it, but almost all feel the tug of tradition. When they see the militants unabashedly flaunting ragged chest-length beards rather than neat whiskers bound in tight hairnets, when they see men carrying real swords instead of the pocket-size replica kirpans of their Bombay brethren, when they see warriors swaggering with the pride of the Ten Founding Gurus, more than a few Sikhs feel grudging respect.

"This rebellion is little more than a cynical ploy," said Khushwant Singh, "cleverly calculated to stem the tide of assimilation."

Khushwant Singh is a historian, critic, novelist, and teller of jokes. His *History of the Sikhs* is required reading for anyone serious about studying the Punjab. His scathingly humorous quips, culled from his newspaper columns and published in a pirated book that (thanks to India's lax copyright laws) brings him no royalties, are a staple of after-dinner conversation from Calcutta to Coimbatore.

"The Sikh fundamentalists are scared," he told me over coffee, "scared that we will lose our separate identity. Already intermarriage between Sikhs and caste Hindus is not uncommon. We *are* Hindus, really, and well within the mainstream. The distinction between us and the rest is now little more than the beard, the turban, and the last name of Singh."

I remembered a Sikh I'd met in Ayodhya. He had said he considered himself as Hindu as any Brahmin alive. His role model was not Guru Nanak or Guru Gobind Singh (the foremost prophets of Sikhism) but Lord Rama.

"The Khalistanist movement only turned violent in the early eighties," Khushwant Singh continued. "I believe it was a conscious decision. The militants deliberately attacked caste Hindus, knowing full well that there would be bloody reprisals, knowing full well it would lead to government oppression and brutality. They wanted to open a chasm between Sikh and non-Sikh, and the best way to keep communities from intermingling is to stir up hatred. But through it all, their object was to maintain the purity of the Sikh tradition."

Now the hatred feeds on itself, like a mad dog so full of rage it chews on its own foot.

"The youth are unemployed," he continued, "so they turn to crime and call this patriotism. Every police atrocity prompts another act of terrorism, which in turn spurs even greater repression. By the way, how do you know our former prime minister was a test-tube baby?"

We had gone from political science to jokes.

"How?"

"Because right from the start he wasn't worth a fuck. Anyway, you'll find no popular support for Khalistan, at least not outside the Punjab. But the militants have indeed succeeded in driving a wedge between Sikhs and caste Hindus, which was really their purpose all along."

The rebels are fighting to maintain the pristine separateness of their people, fighting not only the police, the army, and Hindu mobs, but fighting time itself. They are fighting to keep the Sikhs pure and uncorrupted, to keep their uniqueness unsullied by compromise. One need not condone their methods, or even support their cause, to respect the moral conviction that drives them to immoral deeds.

The very name of Khalistan is Punjabi for "Land of the Pure."

➤ ➤ ➤

Outside Amritsar's central prison, dozens of men and women squat patiently in the dust. Day after day they wait for scraps of information about family members who may, or may not, be held inside. Each person there has a story, and none of the tales has a happy end.

Prem Singh is a former lance corporal in the Indian army with twelve years of meritorious service. In 1986, he says, policemen burst through his door in the middle of the night, beat his wife with the butts of their rifles, dragged him down to the station, and tortured him for three solid weeks. They hung him upside down and stretched his legs apart like the prongs of a brittle wishbone. They pounded him with fists, chairlegs, the cold steel of pistol barrels, anything within reach. They strapped him onto a kitchen table and administered electric shocks to his genitals, until he felt his manhood fry.

Under the National Security Act, any suspect can be held without trial for one year. Prem Singh watched four seasons change in prison, each day denying that he'd used his military experience to train insurgents. As soon as he was released by court order, the police came again and hauled him off to the dreaded Marmandi torture center. This time the officers demanded a bribe of 25,000 rupees for his freedom. His family scraped together all their savings to save Prem Singh from another session on the kitchen table. Now, waiting here for word of a jailed cousin, he gets shivers just standing within a few yards of a prison.

"I had never been in trouble with the law," he told me, "not even as a boy. At my arrest I was forty-five years old, and not once had I been inside a police station."

Darshan Singh, a wheat farmer, is waiting for word of his brother-in-law and his nephew. About a month before, they were tipped off that the police were looking for them and would kill them on sight. They melted into the countryside. When the police came, Darshan Singh says, they summarily rounded up all the women of the family and carted them away as hostages. The two men had no choice but to turn themselves in, and they have not been heard from since.

Darshan Singh asked his wife and daughter how they were treated in prison, but neither one would answer. They both just looked at the floor. Darshan Singh did not press them. He did not want to know.

Sohan Singh is unemployed, must live off his children although he is barely forty. He used to be a repairer of watches and radios, but now he cannot work. Severe nerve damage has left his hands immobile. Not long ago he was detained and tortured by the police for four straight days. He remembers each hour vividly. They did not accuse him of any crime. They merely used Sohan's pain to force his brother out of hiding.

Like every one of the people squatting outside the prison gates, Sohan Singh now supports the Khalistanist militants. He had never cared about politics until politics became real life. "It's like I was sleeping," he told me, "but now I have been pinched and am fully awake."

His remarks were translated for me — I speak very little Punjabi and he spoke less English or Hindi — by Baljindar Singh, a professor of commerce at Khalsa College. The professor is a big man with a tooth-filled smile, and he firmly supports the fundamentalist insurgency.

"Nothing short of Khalistan will satisfy the Sikhs," he said. "Independence is the only way to end this oppression. We do not mind if perhaps the Indian government retains defense, railways, finance, matters such as these, but we can never expect justice unless we run the state ourselves."

His right hand had only two thick, sausagey fingers. I did not ask whether the deformity came from birth or from incarceration.

"Of course," he said, "there are common criminals masquerading as freedom fighters. Any petty robber can claim to be a Khalistanist, and the police are all too ready to agree. They use it as a dirty brush to tar all of us."

The Punjab is in a state of near-anarchy, yet on paper it has one of the lowest crime rates of any part of India. Almost all gang murders and extortions are perpetrated in the name of Sikh independence, so the police blithely chalk them up to "political violence" rather than ordinary crime.

"This lawlessness would cease under our rule," Baljindar Singh continued. "The true warriors would stop their operations, and the false ones would be revealed as mere hooligans. Since the government of Khalistan would be guided by the Sikh clergy, it would rest on a solid moral foundation."

He saw an old friend standing by the iron gate and raised his arm to wave. At that moment his right hand looked just like a cloven hoof.

There is no torture in the Punjab, said Amil Kumar Sharma. The senior superintendent of police for Majhith District, Sharma administers eight police stations. He is from Uttar Pradesh and came to Amritsar only two years ago. The central government, which now administers the Punjab directly, could not find any competent native willing to take the job.

"By law," he said, "we cannot so much as touch a person brought for interrogation. Any stories of routine abuse are lies, made up by the terrorists to discredit legitimate order."

Superintendent Sharma does not look like a cruel man. His face is round and unthreatening, the face of a man who would rather be liked than feared. He seemed ill at ease as he showed me around what Sikhs say is Amritsar's main torture facility. When he said things that were patently false, his eyes looked sadly apologetic.

"This room here" he said, as he led me down the hallway, "is where we might keep a detainee. As you see, the accommodations are hardly unpleasant."

He opened the door to a clean, sunny chamber with a double bed and a television set. It looked at least as comfortable as most of my lodgings on the road. We both knew it was a farce, that the cell had been specially prepared for inspection by a human rights delegation visiting earlier that week.

"What's this for?" I asked, pointing to a thick metal girder that ran along the ceiling.

"For manacles," whispered a Sikh activist who had accompanied me to the station. "They chain a man to that beam by his feet, leave him hanging there until he says what they wish."

"That," Sharma replied, "why, that is . . . for a curtain. To hang a curtain up in case the detainee wishes privacy."

I asked to speak with a few prisoners, so I could learn about the authorities' kind attention to comfort and privacy firsthand. Terribly sorry, the superintendent said, but this was a center for questioning, not detention. There were no suspects being held here at the moment.

"Interrogation is our only means of solving crimes," he said. "We must bring people here to ask them questions, because they can never talk to us in public. The terrorists have every Punjabi too frightened to say a word. Any villager who comes forward with information is liable to be killed, so nobody will speak when his neighbors are around."

We drove back to the district station in a convoy bristling with weapons. A heavily armored truck stuffed with soldiers led the way, our steel-reinforced staff car came next, and a jeep-ful of officers with carbines pulled up the rear. The superintendent's bodyguards all carried contraband Kalashnikov machine-guns rather than standard-issue Stens.

"We are regularly outgunned by the terrorists," Sharma com-plained, "so we sometimes rely on weapons confiscated from the rebels themselves."

Ordinary policemen (generally Sikhs themselves) seldom en-joy this luxury. The antiquated, heavy-stocked rifles they carry are hopelessly clumsy in a firefight, and certainly no match for the AK-47s that insurgents smuggle in from the armament ba-zaars of Peshawar.

"Look," said the superintendent, "I admit there is some ha-rassment. How can there not be? There is always an implicit threat when armed police show up at a man's house, in your country or in mine. But we are working for justice and order, while the rebels fight only for themselves. If we stooped to their level of atrocity we could wipe them out, but we do not, be-cause we are men of law. It should be clear which side is right and which is wrong."

Back at the station, Superior Superintendent Sanjeev Gupta of Amritsar District served tea and biscuits.

"The complaints are there," he acknowledged, "and not all of them are false. But we thoroughly investigate every charge and punish every guilty officer. Last year fifty-four policemen were dismissed or censured. Fifty-four. Nobody can say we are anything but fair."

Sanjeev Gupta is not a man given to self-doubts. Unlike his colleague Sharma, he has no trace of apology in his eyes. He is a smileless, businesslike man doing a difficult and thankless job. He clearly wastes little time agonizing over the righteousness of his acts.

"Just look at the terrorists' victims," he said, "and you will understand why we cannot be soft. Today, this very morning, I saw the remains of a large family all slaughtered together. Six of them, laid out on the ground, mangled beyond any recogni-tion. The sight of them almost brought me to tears."

It was hard to imagine any tear daring to form in Superinten-dent Gupta's implacable eyes.

"These criminals have the entire population in fear for their lives," he went on. "They perpetrate the most horrific crimes every day. Murder, rape, extortion, theft — these are not freedom fighters, they are brigands. Plain and simple. The public rely upon us, the police, to keep them safe."

On other days, if half of the stories told are true, these walls echo with the cries of men and boys brought in for "questioning." But the only sound in the prison today was the gurgle of tea, poured from a porcelain pot.

The guard who stood by the door went to fetch more biscuits. On the way over, he had explained why Punjab is a uniquely frustrating place to be a cop: "It's these bloody Sikhs," he'd said conspiratorially sotto voce. "Even *they* can't tell themselves apart. What is a victim to say, eh — 'It was the fellow with the long beard and turban'?"

"It is an impossible situation," Superintendent Gupta said, tendering the tray hospitably when the biscuits arrived. "The population will not help us, but what can we do? Just leave the miscreants to their depredations? You face the same quandary yourself in Northern Ireland."

I told him I was not English but American, as if that mattered.

"Well, America then. You show me anyplace, anyplace on earth where terrorism has been defeated by orthodox methods."

I know of no place on earth where terrorism has been defeated, by any means whatsoever. The nations that appear to come closest — such as China and the former Soviet Union — have merely exchanged the terrorism of individuals for that of the state. And Americans, who have the highest rates of violent crime and incarceration of any country in the industrialized world, are hardly in a position to lecture others on law enforcement. It would be nice to believe that evil could be converted by kindness or crushed by force, but this just isn't so. Perhaps all we can conclude is that evil can arise anywhere, in anybody, and that every human being is the ultimate custodian of his or her own soul.

➤ ➤ ➤

The Golden Temple at Amritsar is, to Sikhs, the most sacred spot on earth. It is also the spot where, for a time, the most notorious terrorists in India made their home.

When the Khalistanist movement turned violent in the early 1980s, it was no secret where the ringleaders could be found. They were holed up in the Golden Temple, armed from boots to beards. And not just with kirpans, but with machine-guns, grenades, and even rocket launchers. Some clerics sympathized with the rebels, and those who did not were powerless to stop their shrine from being turned into a fortified lair.

It was the one place in all of the Punjab where government troops could not attack. Any other hideout (no matter how well hidden) would be discovered in time and crushed by the weight of the Indian army. But here, in plain sight, the Khalistanists were assured of victory. If the government attacked, the sacrilege would permanently alienate every Sikh. If it did not attack, the insurgents would be free to escalate their campaign of violence until the state became wholly unmanageable. Either way the rebels could not lose.

In 1984, Indira Gandhi ordered the army to storm the Golden Temple. Three hundred men died. The hallowed walls were pitted by gunfire, the marble floors were scarred by bomb craters, and the sacred pools of water for ritual cleansing were polluted with shrapnel-torn flesh.

Five months later Gandhi was shot by her Sikh bodyguards. Riots raged across northern India. Hindu mobs slaughtered Sikhs in retaliation for the assassination. Sikhs slaughtered Hindus in retaliation for the retaliation. The militants blew up a bus here or there to keep tensions high, but mostly just sat and watched gleefully. Their work was being done for them.

Since that time the Golden Temple has epitomized more than the Sikh faith. It has become the rallying symbol of revolt. For every Punjabi the shrine now conjures up bloody memories of that June morning in 1984. But it still symbolizes Sikhism's kindlier virtues as well as its stern, warlike demeanor. The faith is one of exceptional tolerance, one in which hospitality and kindness to strangers are time-honored rites.

"Welcome, my friend," said a stranger as I entered the Golden Temple.

"Please," said another, "come see the inner sanctum."

"Perhaps you are hungry," said a third, "come eat at pilgrims' kitchen."

They were not the con men and scammers so common at Hindu temples, just ordinary people proud of their faith.

The Sikh philosophy can be read in the mandir's very architecture, as if the tenets of the creed had been baked into the bricks and stirred into the mortar. The four gates are thrown wide open, symbolizing openness to people from the four corners of the world. There are free dining halls, as there are at almost every Sikh temple, for charity is an act of worship. There is only one central shrine, with no image of any deity, for behind all the deities God is One.

Within the walls of white marble, all is serenity. The Inner Temple itself is set in the middle of the sacred lake, an island all of gold. It is reached by a narrow causeway guarded by one enormous barefoot sentry armed only with a long silver staff, but that is quite enough. Pilgrims calmly press across the bridge holding banana leaves full of sweet, oily brown ghee from the free kitchen, filling the air with a smell like that of buttered popcorn.

Inside the sanctum a high priest waves a silver-handled whisk of white horsehair. A drummer and an accordionist play a hypnotic rag. Two acolytes continuously shape saffron-colored wreaths into geometric patterns, orange snakes writhing and multiplying as each devotee kisses the ground and leaves a fresh chain of flowers. On an upper story a lector chants passages from the Abu Granth Sahib, reading from pages larger than pizza boxes, his deep bass voice echoing across the compound.

Next to me sat an old man with a beard so white it was almost translucent. He quietly mouthed the archaic Gurmukhi words that floated down from above. I asked him what the hymn meant, and he was happy to translate:

> One man worships Vishnu, another Allah,
> Some talk of the Extender of Mercy, others of the Merciful.
> Some read the Vedas, others the Qur'an.
> Some wear white, others blue.
> But he who recognizes God's will knows the secret of the Lord.

"This hymn," he said, "saved the Sikhs. When the Muslim Emperor Akbar arrested our Guru Arjun for blasphemy, he demanded to see the holy text of the Sikhs. Arjun offered to point out passages that prove we worship the same God as the Muslims. Akbar said *he* would choose and stabbed his finger into the book at random."

The white-haired man stroked at his silky beard, as if smoothing the feathers on the tail of a duck.

"The emperor chose this hymn," he continued, "and, of course, saw that there was only honest piety. He gave our guru safe passage and fifty-one gold mohurs for the upkeep of the holy Granth. So you see, my friend, Sikhs and practitioners of other faiths have been brothers from the very start."

All the men at the Golden Temple, and many of the women as well, wear heavy kirpans strapped to their chests. But there is not the slightest trace of menace, no hint of animosity. In fact, I don't think I've ever felt more genuinely welcome in *any* house of worship.

There are no longer any terrorists here, but there are still warriors fighting for Sikh identity. They are silent, withered, naked except for loincloths and flowing beards, armed only with sturdy walking staffs and iron bracelets from wrist to elbow. They are "saint-soldiers," the mendicants of Sikhism, and they wander throughout the Punjab engaged in a tireless battle against evil. They bear witness to the plight of the poor and oppressed, shame the powerful into exercising their responsibility wisely, by their very presence reminding all of the unimportance of material things. They wage spiritual warfare every day, warfare to preserve the soul of the Sikhs. The Golden Temple was their fortress long before any Khalistanist insurgent took up a rifle, it will be their fortress long after the shooting stops.

➤ ➤ ➤

Sikhs are no strangers to oppression. They have suffered brutal persecution for most of their history, and it has made them what they are. The creed was born of pacifism and tolerance, but over the tortuous years it enshrined martial virtues in order to survive.

The Sikh faith and people were founded by an accountant. Until his thirtieth year the future Guru Nanak worked as a petty revenue clerk for the nawab of Sultanpur Lodhi, balancing books and keeping scrupulously accurate tax assessments. There had always been something different about Nanak. As a child he had read the Vedas and studied both Sanskrit and Pali to please his Hindu parents, learned Arabic and pored over the Qur'an at a Muslim school to gain entry into the Islamic ruling class, yet neither path seemed to offer all the answers. At the age of nine he once tore off his holy janneu and cried out, "Make mercy your cotton, contentment your thread — it will not break, nor become soiled, nor be burnt or lost!" His classmates only laughed.

Then one day, in the year 1499, long after he had settled down with a wife, two sons, and a comfortably dull job, he found the answer. He vanished for three days and four nights, and when he returned to his family he could do nothing but repeat the words of his revelation: "There is no Hindu. There is no Muslim. There is only one God, and He is the God of all."

For the next two decades Nanak wandered across India preaching his message to any who would listen, and many who would not. He always wore Hindu and Muslim clothes jumbled together so that nobody could guess his faith, and he delighted in exploding hollow conventions. Once he went bathing in the Ganges with a group of devout Brahmins, who tossed water east as a pious ablution. Nanak turned his back to them and began tossing water west. The Brahmins demanded an explanation.

"Why do *you* toss *your* water east?" Nanak asked in response.

"We offer it to our ancestors," they replied.

"I have wheat planted many miles to the west," Nanak said, "and this water is far more likely to reach my fields than your forefathers."

Nanak went on a hajj, the pilgrimage to Mecca that all Muslims must perform if they are able, and one night he sought lodging in an Arabian mosque. He defiantly slept with his feet pointed in the direction of the holy Kaaba, an act of blasphemy, and was roughly awakened by the furious imam. "Please, brother," Nanak said patiently, "try to show me some direction where God is *not*."

The first Sikh guru spent the last years of his life as a simple farmer, advising any who sought out instruction but leaving the propagation of the new faith to his disciples. He died not at the hands of an angry mob or an imperial executioner but peacefully at rest in his bed.

The Sikh nation, however, would not enjoy such tranquility for long. Guru Arjun was born twenty-four years after Nanak's death, and he became the first in a long line of holy martyrs.

Arjun compiled the Abu Granth Sahib, the Bible of Sikhism, and built the original Golden Temple to house it. He turned a dingy little town into a flourishing city and called the city Amritsar. His political capital, Lahore, was named, it is said, for the son of that most Hindu hero, Prince Rama. As the man with the duck-white beard told me, Arjun impressed Emperor Akbar himself with his verses. But Akbar's successor was the vicious tyrant Jahangir, who tried to convert all of India through pain. The word "Islam" is Arabic for "submission," and Jahangir decreed that all his subjects would submit.

Guru Arjun was dragged off to prison and, when he refused

to abandon his faith, was subjected to an inhuman array of tortures. He was seated on a chair of red-hot iron plates that made his skin sizzle like heathenish bacon. He was buried in burning sand with only the tip of his nose permitted to poke out. He was submerged in a vat of boiling water until the flesh nearly melted off his bones. When his wardens thought he could bear no more, they brought him to the river Ravi to ease his blistering body and make it strong enough for further torment. It was the cool water that killed him.

The line of prophet-kings ended a century later with Arjun's great-grandson, Guru Gobind Singh. When he was a boy of nine Gobind watched his father, the ninth guru, have his head chopped off in the main avenue of Delhi. He resolved early that if his people were to survive they would have to learn how to fight. A strong martial strain (present in the faith since its earliest times) had been given new emphasis decades before by Hargobind the Deliverer, but it was Gobind Singh who transformed the Sikhs into a true nation of soldiers.

He was himself a warrior-saint, a master of arrows, swords, and horses. It is said that he could stay in the saddle for days on end, go without food for a week, and then defeat five enemies in hand-to-hand combat. Gobind's military prowess was always tempered with mercy. His medics had standing orders to give the enemy wounded just as much care as fallen Sikhs. His arrows were tipped with pure gold so that the widows and children of his victims would not have to go hungry.

But the guru's people needed more than a good example. On Baisakhi Day, March 30, 1699, they got more. With Mughal armies on all sides and his own ranks decimated and demoralized, Gobind summoned all his people to gather before him. He stepped forward, and the crowd became hushed. Then he drew his heavy sword from its scabbard and called out, "I want a head!"

The Sikhs all looked at each other in amazement, not knowing what to do. Daya Ram, a Shudra, walked over and knelt before Gobind. The guru took him into his tent. When Gobind emerged a few minutes later he was alone, and his sword was red with fresh blood.

"I want another head!" he cried. The people grew agitated, and a buzz of worried whispers ran through them like an electric surge. For several tooth-grinding minutes the Sikhs teetered on the edge of mutiny, and then four men stepped up. Gobind led them to his tent, and when he came back his blade was again stained with gore.

"Now," he said, "it is time for *all* of you to join these five brave comrades in the Baptism of the Sword." The people jumped up, prepared to fight or run, but they burst into tears when the Five Beloved emerged from Gobind's tent unharmed. Each one carried the carcass of a goat whose blood still dripped from the guru's weapon.

Gobind filled an iron tank with spring water and stirred it with his double-bladed sword while his wife added sweet herbs. He gave each man five palmfuls to drink, and gave each the new name of Singh — Punjabi for "lion." The guru needed a powerful symbol for the unity and kinship of his people, a way of tearing down the vestiges of caste and social rank perpetuated by aristocratic appellations, so from that day on every baptized Sikh has borne the same surname.

Over the next few years Guru Gobind Singh watched his four sons fall one by one in battle, and in 1708 he was killed in his sleep by two Pathans. His followers seized the assassins and immediately ripped them to shreds.

With the death of the last prophet-guru the Sikhs entered a century of darkness. Mughal persecution reached unimagined heights, often abetted by the machinations of orthodox Hindus. Throughout the empire no man or woman was permitted even to say the name of the holy Granth, and the Punjabi word *gur* (molasses) was banned from public speech for its similarity to the word "guru." Richly robed emperors riding horses with silver snaffle bits used to hunt down Sikh peasants and kill them for sport.

The Sikhs fought back like lions. Qazi Nur Muhammad, who served with the army of Afghan conqueror Ahmad Shah Durrani, wrote in an elegant Persian manuscript: "If you wish to learn the art of war, come face to face with them in the field. They will gladly teach you a lesson." It is said that during one of the worst campaigns the starving Sikhs, rather than consider surrender, ate meat cut from their own thighs.

To no avail. Banda Singh, successor to Guru Gobind, was captured with all of his army that remained alive. Seven hundred cartloads of severed Sikh heads were paraded through the streets of Delhi, along with two thousand more held aloft on pikes. Banda was dragged along in an iron cage, while the crowd threw excrement and called him a dog-worshiper. The next day Mughal soldiers put Banda's infant son in his arms and promised him his freedom if he would kill the child. He angrily refused, and they hacked the baby to bits before his eyes. Then they cut off Banda's hands and feet, gouged out his eyes, and stuck him with hot pokers until he died.

The wide steppes of central Asia have given birth to some of the most ruthless butchers in human history. Attila the Hun, Tamburlaine, and Genghis Khan (a direct ancestor, incidentally, of the entire Mughal dynasty) are only three of the steppes' most famous children of blood. Now, in the middle of the eighteenth century, marauding horsemen from the dry core of the continent descended on the Punjab. Hordes of Afghans swept aside the waning Mughals and launched several genocidal assaults on the Sikhs. The year 1758 is still known as the *Vada Ghallughara,* the Great Holocaust. It was then that the original Golden Temple built by Guru Arjun was blown to rubble, its sacred pool filled up with the bodies of dead cows. The Afghan ruler Ahmed Shah proudly raised up ghoulish pyramids of Sikh skulls and painted the walls of his mosques with Sikh blood.

But the Sikhs soldiered on, and the Sikhs survived. They lasted because they made war almost an article of faith. One of Guru Gobind Singh's most celebrated hymns reads,

Eternal God, You are our shield,
The dagger, knife and sword we wield.

Their religion had been put in the forge and hardened into tempered steel. For many Sikhs today, battling a hostile government is not an activity that needs any apology. It is not terrorism, not even insurrection. It is a sacred obligation.

➤ ➤ ➤

A few steps away from the Golden Temple is one of the most notorious sites in modern Indian history and the site of the British Empire's greatest shame. At Jallianwala Bagh in 1919 nearly two thousand peaceful protesters were ruthlessly mowed down, without so much as a warning to disperse. Three hundred and seventy-nine of them died. They were killed on the orders of Brigadier-General Reginald Dyer, a man of unbending rectitude, firmly convinced that he was fighting against evil.

The courtyard's brick walls are still pockmarked by inch-deep bullet holes. I looked down a well from which 120 corpses were pulled, and tried to imagine a hail of gunfire so withering that people would jump into the thirty-foot-deep stone pit for shelter. The Bagh is wide enough to hold thousands, but it is reached only by a narrow alleyway. It was in this bottleneck that General Dyer parked his armored car to prevent survivors from fleeing the carnage. A total of 1,605 rounds were fired, and only 26 bullets failed to find human flesh.

Dyer's massacre was retaliation for the murder of four Europeans and an assault on a female missionary. For two months afterward, every Indian passing the street of the attack was ordered to crawl on all fours. When called before a commission of inquiry after the Jallianwala shootings, the general stoutly defended his action as right and necessary to prevent insurrection: "If more troops had been at hand, the casualties would have been greater. . . . It was no longer a question of merely dispersing the crowd, but one of producing a sufficient moral effect."

Dyer was removed from his command, but many Britons both in India and back home supported him wholeheartedly to the end. Admirers even raised £26,000 as a testimonial. Kindly old women, grandmothers who'd never had a malicious thought in their lives, gladly contributed their pocket money to a stone-cold murderer.

In the Martyrs' Gallery by the Jallianwala Bagh's entrance there is a long mural of the slaughter on that bright spring morning. Some zealous visitor has scratched away the general's face, as if obliterating the image might obliterate the evil.

A scraggly-bearded teenager named Lakhbir Singh was poring over the Martyrs' Gallery figures. He said he wished he had been there with a loaded pistol. One shot, right through Dyer's head, *bhai,* that's all it would have taken. He would have had no trouble bringing himself to pull the trigger. As a Khalistanist insurgent, he had pulled triggers before.

"Freedom never comes without a fight," he said. "It is not given to you — you must *take* it by force."

We walked around the Bagh's perimeter, examining the walls for scars of shrapnel. He knew which holes were from gunfire and which from construction scaffolding. Lakhbir Singh spends many afternoons here — not to stoke his memory, for that needs no stoking. He likes to sit in the park and read his high school lessons.

"Gandhi and Nehru," he said, "they promised us a home-land. The Muslims got Pakistan, the Hindus got India, and we got nothing at all. We have been too patient, that is the problem."

I asked who the rebels were, what drew them to the cause.

"We are everybody," he said. "Almost all the boys in my class. Not everyone is so committed, but most support us. How could they not? Sikhs, both young and old, are a religious people, we are not ashamed of it. We will do anything for our faith and for our country."

What about the bombings, the extortions, the murder of innocents?

"That is not us," Lakhbir said, his flat gray eyes hard as shooting marbles. "All that is the work of government agents, or common criminals who merely call themselves Khalistanists. They are a disgrace. We must identify such people — and kill them."

Has he ever killed a fellow Sikh?

"Myself, no," Lakhbir said. "But I have helped . . . disci-pline . . . those who cooperate with the enemy. Traitors must be punished."

There was no rage in his voice, just calm assurance. He was certain, as only a teenager can be certain, that all his actions were right.

Ordinary thieves may rob peasants and burgle banks, but they do not blow up airplanes. Much of the Punjab's violence is indeed perpetrated by everyday criminals, but not the worst of it. When Khalistanist militants put plastic explosive in the cargo hold of a 747 out of Toronto (to take just one recent example), their goals were loftier than mere greed or blood lust. They wanted the world to take note of Sikh grievances. They wanted to save their heritage. They wanted to end their nation's oppres-sion. So they murdered 307 people, many of whom were Sikhs themselves, none of whom had ever done them a bit of harm.

General Dyer's goals had been lofty too: peace and stability, the rule of law, an end to violent unrest, security of life and property. He wanted to cut short a potentially bloody revolt, so he coolly, deliberately cut short 379 lives.

Some three hundred killed in Jallianwala Bagh, three hundred in the assault of the Golden Temple, three hundred in the bomb-ing of Flight 182. The actions are not equivalent, but the arith-metic makes one think.

Man's finest aspirations produce man's most hideous crimes — as soon as the goals come to dominate the methods. Mao Zedong had the dream of creating a perfect human society, of wiping away inequality, hunger, and class injustice; to bring about this utopia he instituted the Great Leap Forward and the Cultural Revolution, events that killed as many as forty million people. Pol Pot tried so hard to stamp out an oppressive feudalism that he exterminated one fourth of the population of Cambodia. Even megalomaniacal dictators like Stalin and Hitler had visions that extended far beyond personal aggrandizement, and that is what made them so dangerous. Their dreams may have been twisted, but they were dreams nonetheless. The most nefarious butchers in history have slept quite soundly at night, lulled by the soothing fantasy that they were striving for good.

Most often, evil lies not in the ends but in the means.

It is easy to dismiss the Punjabi militants as teenage hotheads, unruly kids who have not lived long enough to understand the consequences of their actions. For young people (myself included) death is something of an abstraction, even when viewed every day. It is no accident that most of the world's armies are composed largely of eighteen-year-olds. But many of the Khalistanists' supporters are mature, responsible members of society. They are rational and well-educated, not at all know-nothing ideologues, and they heartily applaud the terrorists' cause.

During the Gulf war, Western observers were sickened by the spectacle of ordinary Palestinians clapping and whistling as SCUD missiles devastated civilian neighborhoods. Advocates for terrorists are, in an odd way, just as morally skewed as the killers themselves. They may not pull the triggers or prime the detonation wires, but they (unlike the teenage guerrillas) have the maturity and the distance to tell right from wrong.

I'd long been more repulsed by the murderers' cheerleaders than by the murderers. It is one thing to commit a crime in confusion or passion — and perhaps spend the rest of one's life repenting — and quite another to defend that evil cold-bloodedly, try to explain it away as the price of war. But in the Punjab I met just such people and was surprised to find myself filled with respect. Many of them are good, decent, moral folk who support acts of violence not out of peer pressure or youthful rashness but out of honest, reasoned conviction. And they, unlike armchair apologists the world over, have the courage to suffer for their beliefs.

The car's rear seat was already full of reverend elders, but they cheerfully encouraged me to pile in nonetheless. They were members of a distinguished delegation that happened to be protesting at the prison, and I hadn't known there were so many of them in the car when I'd asked to hitch a lift.

"Not to worry, my boy, not to worry," said one of the old men. "Plenty of room if we squeeze."

"Please, I don't want to put you out."

"Rubbish," said a second, "no bother at all."

"Yes, yes, happy to have you," said a third. "As you know, hospitality is incumbent upon all Sikhs. The Hindus pray only for themselves, but we pray for the whole world."

We spoke of the insurgency (which they hoped would soon bring the central government to its knees) and the weather (which they hoped would improve shortly, because the Punjab is normally so beautiful this time of year, you know). They urged me to come with them and meet a friend of theirs, who could explain the Khalistanist cause better than they. The first reverend elder, when I said that I came from America, urged me to look up a cousin of his who was the priest of a Sikh temple in New York.

"I do not have his address," he said, "but it is in Queens, he should not be difficult to find." He grabbed a handful of his bushy white whiskers. "My cousin also has a long beard like this — he looks just like me."

Navinder Singh, the friend they took me to meet, is the very model of a modern major-general. Though retired for more than fifteen years, he still looks fit for service. He joined the army in 1938, back when his cavalry unit still rode horses.

"I have fought for India in more battles than I can remember," he said, not as a boast but as a fact. "Believe me, I am not a rash or precipitous man. And a lifelong soldier does not lightly challenge his government."

His light blue eyes had a mischievous glint, and his mouth was always slightly twisted in a conspiratorial smirk. He conveyed the impression of perpetually being on the verge of telling a slightly off-color joke and politely holding back until the ladies left the room. He looked as much like Sean Connery as someone with a shaggy gray beard and a turban ever can.

"Today the Punjab is a police state," said the major-general, his voice turning serious. "It is one enormous jail. Everyone who is not locked up is treated as a potential felon, as a criminal not yet caught. We cannot live like that. It is directly contrary to everything we hold dear."

He straightened the kirpan bulging beneath his armpit and went on.

"Man is free, that is the basis of our entire faith. We do not demand superiority — all humans are equal, whether Sikh, Hindu, Muslim, Christian, what-have-you. But passive acceptance of servitude is a denial of our sacred heritage. A Sikh can be slave to no man."

Major-General Navinder Singh, who once served with the Eighth Cavalry, who once served with the Twentieth Lancers, most recently served two years in prison. He was detained in 1986 after a nonviolent protest and released without being charged in 1988. When he entered his jail cell, he had been retired for more than a decade.

"I wasn't at all political until the early eighties," he said. "Prior to that I was simply enjoying the rest and peacefulness of civilian life. I lived quietly" — his eyes again glinted good-natured mischief — "as a . . . gentleman-at-large."

"A country squire, then?"

"Well, I wouldn't quite say that." Again the Connery grin. "Just an ordinary farmer's son."

Did he hope to become an ordinary farmer's son once more? The major-general turned somber.

"Someday, I pray that it will not be necessary to fight," he said. "But since the desecration of the Golden Temple there can be no turning back. We can never trust the Indian government to treat us with respect — they have not done so in the past, do not now, will not ever. Only with an independent Khalistan will Sikhs live free."

One of the reverend elders was going off to visit Justice Ajit Singh Bains and invited me to tag along. We drove to a hotel where two dozen well-aged political activists were pressing their case upon a harried fact-finding delegate of the European Parliament.

"You will like the judge," he said. "A very fine man indeed."

Justice Bains is the chairman of the Punjab Human Rights Organization, a group that works for independence by all means short of violence. Critics charge he is hand-in-glove with the outlaw militants, but Bains is hardly an outlaw. Until a few a weeks before the storming of the Golden Temple, he sat proudly on the Punjab and Haryana High Court.

"I resigned the bench," he said, "when I realized that the government of which I was a part had decided to wipe out the Sikhs. It is a planned conspiracy to destroy our separate identity, to erase our character as a distinct people. The battle we fight is one of survival."

Justice Bains's group has the same goals as the Khalistanist terrorists, but its ranks are a roster of eminently respectable citizens. They are doctors and professors, lawyers and journalists. The beards of the men are long and gray.

"India isn't a nation," the judge said, "it is an artificial union of at least thirty-two different nations. We Sikhs have our own religion, our own language, our own history and culture. We sing different songs and eat different meat. Like the Kashmiris, the Assamese, the Nagas, and many others, we have no desire to remain part of India. We *are* a separate country, occupied by an alien force."

I asked how the Punjab could survive on its own, a small land-locked nation sandwiched between India and Pakistan, wholly dependent upon two hostile neighbors for trade and transit.

"Sikhs are hard workers," he said, "as you no doubt have noticed. Even today the Punjab is India's breadbasket, the most productive state in the union. Without our water resources being siphoned off to other areas, as is now the case, Khalistan would flourish."

"Besides," said a man at Judge Bains's side, "Mohandas Gandhi, the hero of all the Indians, wrote during the British rule that it is better for a people to suffer hardship under their own governance than enjoy comfort under that of the foreigner."

"Gandhi also," I said, "preached total nonviolence."

The man reached into his briefcase and pulled out a fat chunk of legal documents.

"We have followed all legitimate channels," he said. "As an attorney, I work hard to free all the boys unjustly imprisoned, but the police continue locking them up, torturing them, killing them, so fast we cannot keep up. And when we win a favorable judgment, the authorities simply ignore it. Each and every day I go into court, but there is no justice in the Punjab."

He thumped the sheaf of papers down on the table: petitions

for release from custody, judicial restraining orders, motions to dismiss. On a chair next to him was a crate filled with more of the same. All just paper.

I wished that one of these staid, honorable, righteous souls would condemn the atrocities not only of their oppressors, but of their brethren. I hoped for a ringing denunciation of evil in *all* its forms. All I got was the ritual excuse that any murder of civilians was the work of common criminals or a tragic consequence of war, in any case not the fault of the Khalistanist movement. No crusader, old or young, can abide moral ambiguity.

There is a saying of Guru Gobind Singh that runs: "When all other methods have failed, then it is right to pick up the sword."

Eight
RACE

$\mathcal{T}$HE summer monsoons came and went, and still the Monkey King had done nothing to find Sita. He spent every day and every night behind the locked doors of his harem, attempting to satiate his insatiable thirst for wine and for women. When Hanuman tried to stir his master to action, Sugriva turned him away with a belch and a giggle.

Rama, having retired to the forest after installing Sugriva on the throne, was becoming impatient. After four months of inaction, he sent his brother back to Kishkindhya with a message for the king. "Do not threaten him," Rama said, "merely remind him of his duty." But Lakshman brought his bow nonetheless.

The palace guards would not let Lakshman past the gate. They had standing orders never to disturb the ruler with such pettiness as matters of state. Lakshman gave his bow a mighty twang, and the reverberations shook the solid bronze doors on their hinges.

After some hurried rustling within, a hastily clad Vanar came out. It was not the king but his wife, Tara. The Sanskrit adjective used to describe her is *stanabharalhasa,* for which we unfortunately have no English equivalent. The closest translation is "slightly stooped over from the burden of her breasts."

She apologized to Lakshman for her husband's shabby behavior. "You must forgive him," she said, "for he has no self-control whatsoever. He is only a monkey, a slave to his animal passions. But do not worry — he has given the order, and tomorrow morning millions of Vanars from all over India are arriving here to begin the search for Rama's wife."

Lakshman went away wary but content. As soon as he was gone, Tara prodded the Monkey King out of his stupor.

"What, eh, again so soon?" he stammered. "Well, if you like —"

"No," she said, "the time for that is over. You must summon all your troops and get them to Kishkindhya by daybreak."

Theking sent Hanuman, who ran with the speed of a zephyr. Three million Vanars came from the Anjana Hills, ten million from Shitachala, millions beyond counting from dark mountain caves where no human has ever ventured, charcoal-black apes from the southern coast who eat nothing but coconuts, apes from the nether regions with fur the color of fire. Millions of Bhallukas came too, for the bears were vassals to the king of the monkeys, and they followed Hanuman back in a heavy-pawed, lumbering mass.

The next morning all the valley surrounding Kishkindhya was filled with the serried ranks of apes and bears. Sugriva, trying hard not to show his hangover, walked out on the palace balcony and gave them their marching orders.

"You must search the entire world for Sita," he said, "search every hole and every crevice in each and every land. Go to the east and search among the Mandaras, who have long ears as hard as iron that they use to protect their eyes, who have only one foot but can hop faster than most men can run. Go to the tribe of eastern Rakshasas, who have bristling hair and yellow skin, who live on uncooked flesh. Go to the race that is half man and half tiger, who live half in the water and half on land. Go across the sticky red Sea of Blood and search among the Bird People.

"Go west across the Ocean of Milk, which is white like the clouds in spring. Search the land on the other side, where the Rakshasas are ugly and huge as mountains; every day they are burnt up by the terrible heat of the sun, and every day they dive into the milky sea to be restored to vigor. Search in Kerala, in Andhra, among the Malaya ghats. Go to the Sea of Fire, where the fish come out in the net fully cooked.

"Go north, to the Himalayas, where the tops of the mountains kiss the sky. Go to the jungles of Assam and the deserts of Rajasthan, where there is no hill or tree or anything at all. Go to the land where the women have faces like horses. Go to the Land of Eternal Silence, where no sound ever has been or ever will be heard.

"Search all of these places well, Vanars, and come back in one month. But do not come back without Rama's wife."

Privately he took aside Anganda, Bali's son, whom he had made his own heir. He gave him the most difficult task, to search the wholly unexplored regions across the Southern Sea. All anyone knew was that south had always been the direction of death. But the Monkey King gave his nephew not only a picked band of Vanars as his posse, he also sent along his most trusted servant, Hanuman.

It was a bird who told this band where to go. In fact, it was the brother of the Bird King, who had fought with such bravery (and such futility) to prevent Sita's abduction. A wizened old thing, he had once flown so close to the sun that it had burnt up his feathers, and he told the Vanars they would find Sita on the island of Lanka. But to reach this island, he said, they would have to cross one hundred miles of open sea.

Anganda asked which of his cohorts could leap that far. One of his captains said he could jump twenty miles, another said he might be able to reach forty, but even forty miles would bring them no closer to Sita.

"I can do it," said Hanuman, and it was no idle boast. "My mother was a Vanar, but my father was the Wind God. Once, as a boy, I thought the sun was a ripe piece of fruit, and I leapt three hundred miles straight up to try to grab it. Lord Indra, angry at my childish impudence, hurled a thunderbolt that sent me crashing down to earth.

"I was not badly hurt — a broken jaw, nothing to speak of. But my father the Wind was angered by Indra's slight. He ceased to blow, and all life came to a standstill. The waves of the seas melted, the crops roasted in the field, and human beings started to die. Soon there would not have been enough men left to offer the sacrifices that feed the gods themselves, so Indra appeased my father by granting me a boon: that I might never die except by my own will.

"But that is history. Now it is time to jump."

He braced himself against the side of a mountain, all the muscles in his body coiled into springs of compressed energy, every hair in his hide standing on end from concentration. He beat his tail against the rock three times, let out a ground-shaking roar, and bounded off into the sky.

Thick-trunked trees uprooted by the shock plummeted into the sea with great splashes, and the petals of ten thousand plucked flowers wafted softly into the water. Hanuman clawed and pawed his way through the air, churning up huge waves full of sharks and crocodiles in his wake.

In mid-flight a fearsome naga-serpent reared up before him. "I have a boon from Brahma," she said, "that none may pass this way without being devoured. You cannot avoid being caught, it is fated. But if you can wrench yourself once from my iron jaws, you may go free."

Hanuman swelled himself up to the size of an elephant. "You cannot open your mouth wide enough to swallow me," he said.

She opened her maw wide enough to engulf two elephants. Hanuman made himself enormous, as big as a Himalayan peak. The naga effortlessly stretched her mouth wide enough for two Himalayan peaks.

"It's no use struggling," she said, "Brahma has decreed that no creature can get by without being swallowed. You —"

Before she'd even finished speaking the words, Hanuman had shrunk himself down to the size of a sparrow and flitted in and out of the serpent's bite.

"Good day," he said, and continued on his way.

Old Lord Ocean greeted Hanuman as he flew by. To help the Vanar on his mission, the god of the sea raised up an island of trees heavy with fruit and cool shade. The ape thanked the deity for his gift, but he was in too much of a hurry to stop and rest.

As Lanka drew closer he saw (just in time) two eyes poking above the waves. He knew they belonged to a crafty demoness who captured her prey by seizing their shadows. Hanuman shrunk himself as small as a gnat, so tiny that he cast no shadow at all. He then flew into the Rakshasi's ear, swam through her veins, and tore her heart to shreds.

When he alit in Ravana's kingdom, the Vanar was not even tired. He stared in amazement at the towering city, for the demons' capital was far more resplendent than any place his monkey eyes had ever beheld. The houses were seven stories high, so tall they looked like man-made mountains. The gates were cast of pure burnished gold. Once night fell, Hanuman took on the form of a brown tomcat and wandered the well-tended streets unnoticed.

He crept past the sentries, past Brahmins chanting their midnight mantras, past the three-tusked elephants who guarded the Demon King's door. Hanuman poked his feline whiskers behind the harem curtains and blinked his green eyes at the sight.

The entire chamber was filled with languorous, half-slumbering beauties in varying states of undress. All were high-born maidens who had freely chosen to be Ravana's concubines. They slept draped over one another, one woman resting her head on another's ample breasts, a third making a pillow of the first's round buttocks, so closely intertwined that it would have been impossible to tell just which limbs belonged to whom. In the center of it all lay Ravana, idly caressing a different wife with each of his twenty hands, and for each consort within his embrace two more lustily tried to squirm their way forward, sometimes moaning out his name in their sleep, sometimes passionately kissing one another while dreaming that the lips were those of their husband, sometimes even —

— Well, at this point Valmiki gets so caught up in the minutiae that he loses track of his story for nearly an entire chapter. Modern readers would doubtless find such arcane details of ancient life tedious. At any rate, Hanuman looked throughout the harem with most sincere diligence but did not find Sita anywhere.

He searched all over the palace grounds, and when he came to a walled-in forest he found her. He knew it was Sita, because after many months of fasting she was still the most beautiful woman he had ever seen. He knew that everything Rama had done — killing fourteen thousand Rakshasas in the Dandak forest, murdering Bali to place Sugriva on the throne, sending millions of Vanars on a tireless quest — had been done for her. When Hanuman had started on his mission he had silently scoffed at the foolishness, that any man should risk so many lives merely for the sake of one woman. Now, when he saw Sita sleeping by the tree, he realized that if Rama should destroy the entire world and all of its inhabitants to save his wife, it would be a fair exchange.

The Vanars were not born monkeys. Originally they were men, every bit as human as any Kshatriya prince and among the subcontinent's oldest inhabitants. They are arguably more truly Indian than Rama himself.

In archaic Sanskrit the word *vanara* meant simply "forest

dweller." It could equally well describe a man, an ape, or a three-toed sloth. Scholars say that in antiquity the invading Aryans may have used this word as a derogatory term for the indigenous Dravidian people whose land they had conquered.

At the time the Ramayana was first sung, the tall, light-skinned Aryans treated their smaller, darker, hairier subjects with disdain. They invented the caste system to prevent any contact with the Dravidians. *Arya* is Sanskrit for "honorable," while the term *anarya* means both "dishonorable" and "of another race." They despised the native people, saw them as barely human. They called them "monkeys."

It was nearly a thousand years later that Valmiki finally wrote the epic down. During that time the origin of the racial slur had been forgotten. An ugly metaphor had softened into harmless myth. For the Indians of Valmiki's day and for Indians today, the Vanars were neither more nor less than genuine, honest-to-goodness apes — fur, tails, and all.

The two races, Aryan and Dravidian, never became one. The historical Aryans (as opposed to the imaginary ones of fascist myth) were neither blond nor Nordic-featured, but they were quite clearly a people apart. They probably looked much like present-day Iranians, who are their most direct descendants; "Aryan" and "Iran" are variants of the same root word. In India these newcomers came to see any physical interaction with members of other tribes as the grossest of pollutions. They instituted the world's earliest and most comprehensive form of apartheid.

In the southern part of the subcontinent, where Aryan domination never truly took hold, the Tamils are still proudly Dravidian. In the north, caste set up a nearly unbreachable firewall between the children of the conquerors and the children of the conquered. Some ethnic mixing did occur over the ages, but to this day, in many parts of India, one can often tell a Brahmin from a Shudra merely by the shade of his skin.

Although the bloodlines remained largely separate, the two cultures united in a gleeful commingling — a wanton union that eventually gave birth to the Hindu faith. Indian civilization may have been fathered by the Aryans, but it was conceived and gestated in a Dravidian womb.

When the Aryans first crossed the Indus River in the misty depths of prehistory, they gloried in violence and slaughter. Hindus today celebrate nonviolence. The Aryans were ravenous meat eaters, with a particular relish for beef. Hindus today (even those who savor a good drumstick now and then) hold vegetarianism as a moral ideal — and of course would never think of eating cow flesh. The Aryans worshiped the ancient steppe-gods Indra and Varuna. Hindus today almost never pray to the Master of Thunderclouds or the Lord of the Waters; they bow down to Shiva and Vishnu, gods barely mentioned in the Vedas at all, pre-Aryan divinities (some scholars say) who patiently waited through the centuries and won out in the end. It was in the Dravidian south that the Shaivite and Vaishnavite sects first gained dominance (around the time King Alfred ruled England) and converted India from Buddhism back to the Hindu religion.

The Aryan contributions to Hinduism were primarily caste and the Vedas — no trifles, certainly, but not the entirety of the faith. Their original doctrine was mere legalistic Brahminism, a pharisaical practice wholly wrapped up in dry ritual and ceremony. Although Jains, Buddhists, and bhaktas spurred reform, some say it was the Dravidians who gave this pagan polytheism its heart, who turned it into a modern religion. They may well have absorbed the invaders' beliefs, adapted them, and made them their own.

India has always swallowed up her conquerors over time. First the Aryans, later the Persians, Greeks, Huns, Afghans, Mughals, Britons, and a hundred other tribes along the way. India can never be assimilated into somebody else's civilization. She is too big, too ancient, too self-assured ever to fall victim to *that* sort of imperialism. Even Rudyard Kipling once warned his countrymen, "Asia is not going to be civilised after the methods of the West. There is too much Asia, and she is too old." India's land may be ruled by aliens from time to time, but never her mind, never her soul.

In the end, it is always India that does the digesting. She takes what she wants of each conquistador's culture, gobbles it up, and spits out the rest. From Muslims she took pilafs and purdah; from the British, cricket, democracy (after a fashion), and an incomprehensible love of bureaucracy. The Taj Mahal itself — the very symbol of India in Western eyes — was built by the emperor of a foreign dynasty who spoke a foreign tongue, and it is still a mausoleum sanctified by a foreign faith.

India has never been a melting pot, or even (as the Canadians prefer) a salad bowl. It is more like the bazaar where the stew and the salad ingredients are bought: an exuberant, disorderly display of every color, flavor, and price, of vegetables, grains, and meats, of scents and spices mixing only in the scented air. It is a profusion, a confusion, but never a fusion.

India is more of a conglomeration than a country, a hodge-podge of hundreds of cultures, languages, and peoples held together only by an idea. I am not sure just what that idea is. It is not only Hinduism, since India is home to Jains, Sikhs, Buddhists, Parsis, Christians, and more Muslims than any two nations in the Arab world. It is not shared history, for even the sprawling Ashokan, Gupta, and Mughal empires never covered all of India. It is clearly not language, for Indians speak over forty major and two hundred minor tongues.

There is greater racial diversity in India than in most entire continents. Any comparison is inherently subjective, but North America, South America, and Australia (not to mention Antarctica) seem to pale by comparison. Even Europe can't claim more than a dead heat: a Kashmiri is just as different from a Keralan as a Spaniard is from a Swede. Natives of both Barcelona and Stockholm at least worship the same deity and use the same alphabet.

But somehow a nebulous sense of "Indian-ness" does exist, and it binds together Gujaratis, Orissans, and Nagas who might seem to have nothing at all in common. Perhaps it is this elusive, undefinable (yet very real) link that has allowed the subcontinent's multitude of races to live in some rough semblance of harmony for four thousand years.

➤ ➤ ➤

Kishkindhya still stands, after a fashion. Far from shunning their identification with the apes of epic, some Dravidians have proudly embraced the Vanar legacy. In the fourteenth century a southern people set out to recreate Kishkindhya and even founded their capital on the spot (near the modern-day town of Hampi) where Sugriva's city was believed to lie buried. The Vijayanagar Empire, one of the most powerful and magnificent in all Indian history, was a bold attempt to bring the glories of the Monkey Kingdom back to life.

It started, as many things do, with money. The town had been more or less independent for thirty years, but no overlord seemed to notice until the two brothers who governed it had the audacity to mint their own coins. In 1360 the Muslim sultan who claimed the entire region as his own ordered all Hindu bankers killed and their progeny barred from money changing for two generations. But the brothers had built impregnable walls around their city, and the new kingdom stood.

Vijayanagar's first humiliation came half a century later, not from gold but from a goldsmith's daughter. The king had heard rumors of an incomparably beautiful girl living near the border of the Bahmani Empire, and he sent envoys to ask for her hand. He collected spouses the way some men collect postage stamps; according to an Italian traveler who was the first foreigner to visit Vijayanagar, the monarch had no fewer than twelve thousand wives. Apparently he had inherited not only Sugriva's capital but the Monkey King's legendary libido as well.

The goldsmith's daughter rejected her royal suitor. Perhaps she was aware that upon the monarch's death at least two thousand of his consorts were expected to perform suttee, ritual suicide either by burning or burial alive. Naturally the king swept down on her village with a vengeful army, but the girl had already fled to the court of the Bahmani shah.

The Muslim ruler had sparred with Vijayanagar before, once even infiltrating the royal banquet hall with a squad of picked soldiers dressed up as a troop of jugglers. But now the time was right for a crushing blow. His well-disciplined troops routed the Hindu forces, and he gloatingly demanded as the price of peace the royal princess of Vijayanagar for his wife. He married the goldsmith's daughter off to his own son, and a war that broke out over lust ended in a double wedding.

But the hills of Karnataka were rich in rubies, emeralds, and diamonds, the shores teemed with pearls, and Vijayanagar quickly grew strong again. Soon it held unchallenged sway over all the southern portion of India, from one sea to the other. Its foremost port, Goa, was on its way to becoming one of the major hubs of the world. Its capital was home to half a million souls, larger even than Rome. As the ambassador of the Muslim sultan of Herat admitted, "The city is such that eye has not seen nor ear heard of any place resembling it upon the whole earth."

The empire's wealth was not evenly distributed. A Russian traveler named Athanasius Nikitin wrote, "The land is overstocked with people; but those in the country are very miserable, while the nobles are extremely opulent and delight in luxury. They are wont to be carried on silver beds, preceded by some twenty chargers caparisoned in gold." One sixteenth-century visitor was told that the king collected nine tenths of his subjects' income as taxes. Commoners who committed any petty crime were summarily executed: beheaded in the market-place, impaled by a wooden stake, or trampled under the feet of regal elephants.

It was an immensely cultured society but a rough and raucous one as well. Dueling was not only legal but officially licensed and encouraged. Prostitutes serviced their customers in the pub-lic plazas and temples, and profits from government brothels paid the wages of a ten thousand—man police force. Even the vegetarianism so prized by Dravidians was honored mostly in the breach; a Portuguese merchant was amazed to find the citi-zens of Vijayanagar happily eating not only venison, mutton, hares, partridges, doves, quail, and sparrows, but also the flesh of pigs, cats, rats, and lizards. Today the meat of such unclean animals is consumed only by the casteless "tribals," aborigines who predate both the Aryans and Dravidians.

Vijayanagar had an almost Aztec thirst for blood sacrifice. Each of the sheep cut up for shanks in the bazaar was butchered on the steps of a temple, its blood and woolly head offered up to a sticky red idol. On one festival day the king person-ally presided over the ritual slaughter of 250 buffaloes and 4,500 nanny-goats. But the metropolis's citizenry had a roman-tic streak as well. Abdur-Razzaq, a Muslim diplomat, observed: "Roses are sold everywhere. These people could not not live without roses, and they look upon them as quite as necessary as food."

The dynasty was ended (as fate would have it) by a prince named Rama, and with it died the glory days of the resurrected Vanars. As king of Vijayanagar, he alienated both his subjects and his fellow monarchs with his insufferable haughtiness. He took over Muslim mosques and turned them into stables for his cavalry. When vassals humbly expressed their allegiance by kiss-ing his hand, Rama Raya would ostentatiously summon a water-bearer to wash his fingers of the stain. By the time the super-cilious sovereign reached the ripe age of ninety-four he seemed unlikely ever to die, and his enemies banded together for a bold assault on the man who ruled half of India.

He was carried into battle on a golden litter, large buckets at his side filled with pearls and gold nuggets to dole out to soldiers who fought with exceptional gallantry. But when the well-trained Muslim warriors charged, Rama Raya's litter-bear-ers fled to avoid being crushed under the leathery feet of circumcised elephants. The king himself was too senile to walk and was dragged before the attacking monarch to have his head struck off with a single blow.

The Islamic artillery fired devastating salvos of copper and gold — the gunners had loaded their cannons with bags of hefty Hindu coins. The history of Vijayanagar ended as it began, with a shower of money.

The Muslim army rested for three days, then pillaged Vijayanagar for five straight months. A traveling merchant who passed through the ghost town shortly afterward wrote that the site was inhabited only by lazy tigers, their bellies full of the meat of men.

For two centuries the tradition of Hinduism in India — the Vedas, the caste system, the Shastras, the Upanishads, the Puranas, the whole bit — had been preserved from Islamic annihilation. India's culture had been defended and nurtured until new standard-bearers could arise up north. The Aryan tradition had been sheltered from a brand-new foreign invasion. And it had been kept alive by the Dravidians, by the Vanars, by the monkeys.

The new Kishkindhya lies in ruins now, yet it is not dead. The ceilings and pillars of long-godless temples are blackened from cooking fires, the soot of a hundred generations. Squatters make their untidy beds beneath the empty altars, breast-feed their babies in the shattered colonnades. Some of the shrines are still sanctified, centuries after their builders were buried. At one temple a glum old man and an unsmiling young woman are joylessly being married, knotting together the fringes of their garments as trumpeters blow salutes and relatives toss handfuls of flowers. At another mandir eight-foot-tall icons of Rama, Sita, and Lakshman — polished black stone with glittering mother-of-pearl eyes — wear white robes newly woven by earnest devotees.

I spent several days wandering through the surreal necropolis of the resurrected Vanars. I climbed across a wide expanse of open rock face on which, through the ages, penitents had piled up small mounds of pebbles to memorialize their prayers. I chatted with the guardian of Sugriva's Cave, an old man who sits patiently all day in a little cleft in the cliff, calmly watching over the spot where Sita's jewels were stashed.

I watched sculptors and masons restoring the grandeur of a

time-battered palace, cutting up the very same boulders their ancestors had quarried, using crude chisels to chip fantastic images out of the hard gray rock underneath the baking sun. At Vittala Temple, where each pillar resonates with a different pitch when slapped with an open palm, where the walls are so skillfully joined that they still hold together without a single dollop of mortar, I marveled at the mastery of a huge, impossibly ornate juggernaut carved of granite five hundred years ago. In a collapsing shed by the slow, green river I marveled at the passing of a huge, impossibly ornate juggernaut carved from teakwood a few decades ago, now abandoned as too decrepit to roll, left to disintegrate like Vijayanagar itself in unnoticed rococo splendor.

But it is the vanaras, the "forest-dwellers," animals of all types, who dominate this Vanar city. There are one thousand images of Hanuman here, testament to the greatest monkey of all. The figures carved into lintels, ceilings, and archways are not the standard Hindu array of humanoid gods and angels. They are ducks, boars, and fish, elephants at play and griffins at bay, camels and ogres and bug-eyed, bug-eating bullfrogs. Today most of the shrines are occupied not by humans but by striped chipmunks that scamper straight up stone walls and lazy lizards that bask in the noonday heat.

Where divinities appear, they take on their beasty incarnations. A thirty-foot icon of the divine pachyderm, Ganesh, is hewn out of a single elephantine boulder. Vishnu, most commonly worshiped through his human incarnations Rama and Krishna, here is Narasimha the Man-Lion. He towers above the plain, stares from a dozen dark capitals, gnashing his teeth and tearing up enemies with bloody claws. But Narasimha (like all of Vishnu's personalities) is ultimately a preserver: there once was a demon who could not be killed by any man or beast, so Vishnu took a form that was neither human nor animal to save the world.

Most of the humans etched into Vijayanagar's walls are laughable buffoons. Every tableau dances with waddling dwarfs, feeble graybeards, grotesquely fat men with lecherous leers. The main exception is at Ramchandra Temple. Here scenes from the Ramayana line each surface: Rama battling Ravana, Maricha disguised as a deer, Lakshman humbling Surpanakha, all still tinged with traces of their once-lustrous colors, visible for an instant when I light a match.

Yet even this story, an Aryan story, a conqueror's story with a hero from the north, is chiseled out with a uniquely Vanarish slant. Most of the episodes emphasize the apes over the men. When Rama splits seven palm trees with a single arrow, it is to prove his valor to a judgmental Sugriva. An entire panel is devoted to the magnificence of the royal court of Kishkindhya. In the scene of jubilation at Sita's return, Rama's queen is overshadowed by the bevy of beautiful ape-women in the Vanar king's harem.

One sure way to rob a racial slur of its sting is to embrace it wholeheartedly. In America, men and women whose parents had been crudely termed "colored" now wear the name "people of color" with pride. Rappers like Ice-T, Ice Cube, NWA, and the Geto Boys defiantly label themselves "niggers." And not only slurs of race: homosexual activists boldly march under the banner of "Queer Nation." With this idea in mind Salman Rushdie named his Prophet after a medieval demon — and was disastrously misunderstood by people who hadn't bothered to read his book.

The Dravidians, consciously or unconsciously, seem to have done it right. Whether the Telugu warriors who built Vijayanagar or the Tamil moviegoers who cheer more lustily for Hanuman than for Rama, they defeat contempt with self-respect. Man is, after all, merely an ape with an attitude.

≻ ≻ ≻

"Different race," said the professor, "different epic."

Gnanam Sambandam, literary critic and Tamil scholar, was talking about the Ramayana. "The story is the same," he said, "but we have brought the details in line with our own sensibilities."

The southern version, written by the twelfth-century poet Kampan, diverges from its Sanskrit predecessor mainly over sexual politics. Rama does not simply win Sita as a prize, for instance. "We Tamils are romantics at heart," the professor explained, so Rama must see his wife-to-be from afar and break King Janaka's bow for love rather than glory. A married woman should never be sullied by another man's touch, so Ravana carries off the entire cave to avoid polluting Sita by as much as the brush of a fingertip. Tamil men are unable to stomach the notion of a female berating a male, so Sita's tortuous fire ordeal at the epic's end becomes a self-chosen expiation for her slander of Lakshman during the episode of the magical deer.

"We alter some instances," Sambandam said, "but never change the epic's meaning. Even the weak parts — like that atrocious Uttara Kanda." He was referring to the tale's apocryphal last chapter, a shocking depiction of heartless betrayal and a world turned upside down. "Positively blasphemous, that. The Aryans, like their cousins the Greeks, are not troubled by a bit of immorality in their deities. We Dravidians hold our gods to a much higher standard."

Professor Sambandam is a little man with a big beard and a belly so neatly spherical it looks like he's swallowed a bowling ball. He clothes his erudition in a dingy sarong and a curry-smeared undershirt. As we talked he rolled morsels of *pan,* pinching out the betel nut, spices, and banana leaves from plastic bags, Tupperware containers, and a little black canister that once held 35-millimeter film.

"So much Tamil consciousness-raising is mere know-nothing populism," he said. "Demogogues even condemn the Ramayana as not only foreign but scandalous and improper, merely on the basis of a few randy incidents." And they are indeed few. Ravana's harem scene notwithstanding, the Ramayana is hardly the Kama Sutra. "Even if there are some spicy bits, what of it? After all, you do not judge your Bible solely on the Song of Solomon. Every palace has libraries, throne rooms, courtyards, and banquet halls, but these rabble-rousers look no further than the bathroom."

It was monsoon season, and a torrential thundershower broke out instantly and pelted down rain in solid sheets. It poured like a storm of forty days and forty nights, but stopped cold after less than forty seconds. All electricity in the house died and did not come back for half an hour. Professor Sambandam took absolutely no notice.

"We Tamils have a puritanical streak," he said, sitting in the dark. "So when Ravana falls it is not just through arrogance but through lust. Between raging egotism and true divinity is only a hairsbreadth difference — pride causes the Rakshasa's death but not his disgrace. It is his unlawful passion for another man's wife that brings him shame."

He popped another leaf-wrapped betel nugget into his cheek. From time to time throughout our conversation he would delicately lift his bushy gray mustache and wipe his mouth with a piece of cloth.

I asked him why Aryans and Dravidians had lived side by side yet separate for longer than any other two peoples on earth.

"Caste!" he said. "The greatest racial barrier ever known." Professor Sambandam is a Brahmin himself and could therefore claim Aryan descent, but he considers the caste system a shameful anachronism. "Of course, you Americans are no different. People from New York look down on people from Los Angeles, people from Los Angeles look down on people from New York, and both look down on people from anyplace else. Once, when I was on a lecture tour in America during Mr. Kennedy's term, there was one student in my class who sat in the back of the room, shunned by the other young men. He was tall, handsome, muscular, bright — the very picture of an ideal man. He sat alone because his skin was the wrong shade."

I wanted to tell him that things had changed since then, that thirty years in America was a much longer time than thirty years in India. I knew it was so, but for some reason the words stuck in my throat.

So I asked him instead about the Vanars.

"They are metaphorical, of course," he said. "How else could monkeys talk, eh? Hanuman, the Prince of Apes, provides a model for all men. No literary character anywhere in the world compares with Hanuman. He is loyal, trustworthy, always scrupulously —"

Gnanam Sambandam abruptly leaped up and hurried out of the room. Several times during the course of our conversation he had scurried off without explanation, whether answering a call from the kitchen or finding a new grandchild to bounce on his knee. Each time he would return fifteen minutes later and pick up in mid-sentence.

"— honest, always willing to sacrifice himself for his master. Hanuman is a saintly person, courageous, exceptionally learned, and absolutely celibate."

The stream of innumerable grandchildren who filed across the professor's lap testified that he himself had upheld celibacy more in theory than in practice.

"It does not matter," he continued, "that in the epic Hanuman has a tail. He has much to teach us, whatever our race. For Aryan, Dravidian, even American, we are all much the same.

You Westerners exaggerate the differences, say Indians are funny because we dress in dhotis and haggle in the bazaar. But you yourselves wear scanty bathing trunks and get discounts by clipping coupons out of newspapers. Both of us bargain, only we Indians do so with our God-given mouths."

The little girl on his lap hopped down to the floor, shouted that she was going to play next door, and scampered out of the room.

"So many politicians try to stir up race hatred," he said, barely noticing. "They cannot govern properly, so they try to distract the people with discord. I know plenty of political men, ministers of state, and many of them are not even fit to be garbage pickers. I'm not sure they could even manage *that* task competently."

He spit a red gob of betel juice into a handkerchief and lifted his mustache to wipe his lips.

"Racial differences should be an opportunity," the professor said. "We should learn from each other, let the talents of one complement the talents of the other. Without the Aryans, we would not have the epics or Vedas. Without us Dravidians, there would be little *but* the epics and Vedas. Shaivism, Vaishnavism, the very puja ceremony — you know, I wrote a nine-hundred-page book proving that the puja is southern in origin, but who has read it? — why, even vegetarianism is all Dravidian. We should all learn from Rama, and we should all learn from Hanuman as well."

It is so easy to paper over race divisions with platitudes. People should not be judged by color or ethnicity, we're all the same under the skin — platitudes (like clichés) are banal because they are undebatably true. But racial harmony is not created by mutual back-patting, hand-holding, and singing folk songs round the campfire. As Professor Sambandam suggested, people of different traditions should do far more than merely tolerate each other.

Instead of minimizing our dissimilarities, we should revel in them. In India, in America, in Europe, all over the world, racial minorities are ostracized or oppressed, patronized or pampered, but seldom appreciated for their own merits. They are encouraged to assimilate into the mainstream, or kept deliberately separate for electoral ends. They are given reserved seats in legislatures and endowed chairs at universities, but all too often it is their *presence* that is required rather than their ideas. We should celebrate cultural diversity not because it is Politically Correct and makes us feel fuzzily open-minded, but because all peoples have much to learn and much to teach. The homogenization and pasteurization of culture sterilizes even those of us who are born milky white.

From kindergarten through high school I learned virtually nothing about the world beyond Europe and America. Academic tokenism had put George Washington Carver on a historical level with George Washington, but it was (as Carver might have put it) small peanuts. I was ordered to respect the heritage of African-Americans, but I was never told about the glories of the Zulu and Ashanti empires or the medieval splendor of Timbuktu. I was ordered not to see Arabs as camel-driving terrorists, but I was given not a single *sura* of the Qur'an to read, assigned not a solitary line from the master philosophers al-Ghazali or al-Ash'ari.

I don't recall even being ordered to respect the cultures of Asia — Political Correctness apparently does not extend across the Pacific Ocean. If current curricula are any guideline, W.E.B. DuBois made far greater contributions to world civilization than Confucius or the Buddha. From first grade through twelfth, there was not one mention of the Sung dynasty poets, *The Tale of Genji,* the Lotus Sutra, the Mahabharata. China, Japan, Korea, India — all just a jumble of places where take-out food comes from.

Race has been made a political football in academic circles. There are too many books by white people (say the Correct ones), too many white professors — assign a dozen works by blacks and Hispanics or we'll boycott your campus. They have the right problem and the wrong solution. Gabriel García Márquez and Yukio Mishima belong in the canon because they are brilliant writers, not because they conveniently fill a particular ethnic quota.

Every day we in the West close our eyes to the wisdom and the beauty of four millennia, because it comes from societies we make little attempt to understand. The Ramayana, like the *Odyssey* or *Paradise Lost,* is a cultural treasure, not of one particular race but of all races. It tells us much about India, but just as much about ourselves.

➤ ➤ ➤

The lands of Hanuman are still very different from the lands of Rama. Southern India, the Dravidian heartland, is home to a race that has adapted but never succumbed. When I traveled about the Vanar territories I was struck by the differences between India's two great nations.

Karnataka — where bright crimson flame-trees blaze amid the pea-green rice paddies, where bullock-carts are piled high with dripping stalks of sugar cane rather than drab brown mounds of northern wheat, where farmers spread their straw on the highways to have it threshed by the passing traffic — was the center of Dravidian empires even before Vijayanagar. From the eleventh through the fourteenth century, the Hoysalas reigned supreme. Their temples still stand at Halebid, Belur, and Somnathpur, each a holy orgy of fabulously ornate soapstone carving, each so stunningly elegant as to make any Aryan artisan weep with envy.

I darted from one sliver of shade to the next, because at noon the paving stones of Belur's courtyard will fry bare feet like raw cutlets. I noticed one blank spot left on an exuberantly baroque column. The temple guardian told me it had been deliberately left unadorned, the only bare spot in the entire sacred complex, an empty panel reserved for whatever artist might think himself superior to the Hoysala masters. In the eight hundred years since, nobody has dared take up the challenge.

The Telugu-speakers of neighboring Andhra Pradesh like their curries ferociously hot. Their cuisine is quite possibly the spiciest in the world, and they treat Aryan tenderfeet with good-natured contempt. "Like eating paper," they laughed to me of the foods of the north.

I have a taste for fire, and after the blistering dishes of Burma and Thailand I thought I was ready for anything, but Andhra cooking is a whole other matter. To avoid being labeled a lightweight I would swallow wicked vadi peppers, secretly chewing them with my tongue rather than my teeth to mute the burn, all the while trying to plaster a nonchalant look on my face as the noxious toxins corroded the lining of my stomach. My hosts would hungrily gobble down two vadis for my one. "Hindi food is so bland," they would say, "Telugu food is much better, eh?" I would nod. People in Andhra Pradesh could drink straight battery acid without singeing their taste buds.

. . .

Goa, the foremost port of the Vijayanagar empire, has long been inhabited by a race far more alien even than the conquerors of antiquity. In 1510 the Portuguese arrived under Afonso de Albuquerque, and the next hundred years were Goa's golden age. Merchants of all nations and all faiths, every color and shape — Venetians and Gujaratis, Malays and Spaniards, Bengalis and Armenians — came here to trade, swindle, buy, sell, bribe, borrow, extort, and steal.

With its whitewashed walls and orange-tiled roofs, Goa still feels more Iberian than Indian. Its churches are full of elderly black-robed women fanning themselves during Latin Mass, its alleys full of cashew vendors hawking necklaces of brown nuts strung together with twine. On the evening of Good Friday I drank sweet port wine in a Goan cafe with a balcony so narrow it could not accommodate both my shoulders at once, and I watched the cursing innkeepers roll drunkards out onto the cobblestones to sleep off their intoxication in the warm, salty air.

On Easter Sunday I went to the Basilica of Bom Jesus, where the faithful kiss the silver casket that holds Saint Francis Xavier's mutilated remains; one hand, one toe, and much of the guts were long ago sent to Yokohama, Lisbon, and half a dozen other cities as holy relics. When I told this to a Hindu tourist from Bangalore, she had to stifle a smirk at the ghoulishness of Christians.

In 1961 the Indian army took over Goa without wasting a single bullet. The European administrators left gracelessly, but they carried away the knowledge that they had arrived on the subcontinent earlier and been kicked off it later than their one-time rivals the Brits. At Se Cathedral, just after Easter Mass, I sneaked into the abandoned attic to see what the conquered conquerors had left behind. Decaying wooden saints tossed haphazardly to the ground, a collapsed roof beam, several heavy pews in need of repair, and, frosted with gray cobwebs, a shelf of unread books. They were in Portuguese, now intelligible only to older Goans, for even most Catholics of Iberian descent have forgotten the tongue of their forefathers' race. I turned a page gingerly, as if touching a butterfly, and still it turned to dust in my fingers.

Kerala has always been a joyful mix of races. The Malayalam language and culture are four-square Dravidian, yet Muslims and Christians — many of them descendants of colonists from Arabia, Portugal, Persia, or Holland — make up nearly half the state's population. In Trivandrum, Hindu children scamper around the arches of a pale pink mosque, while down the road Islamic girls and boys play tag among the headstones of a Roman Catholic graveyard.

There have been Christians in Kerala almost as long as there have been Christians. It is said that Saint Thomas the Apostle, "Doubting Thomas," fled here with his disciples shortly after Jesus' death. Certainly communities of Syriac Nestorians were reciting the Lord's Prayer a thousand years before Prince Henry the Navigator taught his captains how to sail. Even in the predominantly Hindu towns one still sees churches, beef butchers, and priests with gold crucifixes. In Ernakulam I passed a storefront with the sign "St. Jude's School of Driving." There could be no more appropriate deity for Indian highways: Jude is, of course, the patron saint of lost causes.

Even the illnesses of Kerala are all its own. The sticky, humid climate breeds ailments virtually unknown farther north. In any Keralan village it is not uncommon to see a man with shins swelled up Popeye-like from elephantiasis, a woman whose skin is covered with bumps and protrusions as if she were a drippy wax candle, a child with an arm puffed up like a log and a hand like a big brown cauliflower. Not all of life's oppressions come from other people.

On a wall in Ernakulam's sister-city of Cochin there is a graffiti mural in the form of a four-frame cartoon. It is a picture of Rajiv Gandhi turning into a tank. In each box his nose grows pointier and more haughtily upturned until it becomes a gun barrel; his complexion goes from coward-white to envy-green to battle-khaki. As a northern Hindi-speaker, Gandhi had never been wildly popular in the lands of the Vanars. But race might well have worked against him even if he'd spouted Malayalam and craved coconut curries.

"We see things differently here," said a desk clerk at Ernakulam's Grand Hotel. When I asked him why southerners didn't burn effigies of the demon Ravana in their street plays of the Ramayana, his eyes strayed to Rule 4 on the poster of house regulations: "Residents are not allowed to bring into the hotel any guests having contagious diseases/ unsound mind/ suspicious character." But he answered all the same.

"We love Ram," he said, "but we in the south also love Ravan."

"Because he is Dravidian?"

"Perhaps, perhaps not. But Ram is like the government, and Ravan is a rebel. We southerners always like a rebel."

After four thousand years of subjugation to an Aryan world order, Dravidians are entitled to root for an underdog.

There are dozens of Indian races quite distinct from the Hindi-speaking mainstream. There are aboriginal Bhils and other "tribals," there are Himalayan Buddhists, there are Nagas and Bengalis and Assamese — the list goes on and on. But in the battle against Aryan cultural dominance, the standard-bearers are certainly the Tamils. As I made my way through the state of Tamil Nadu — from the pilgrimage towns of Madurai and Rameshwaram to the pilgrimage towns of Mahabalipuram and Kanchipuram; past vast herds of cattle with bells on their horns, being driven by young boys into neighboring Kerala, because no butcher in the state is willing to slaughter them; to Madras, the capital of all Dravidia — as I made my way I knew I was still in India, yet at the same time I was in a wholly different country.

The monsoon season comes earlier down south than up north. We did not know that this particular cyclone would be the deadliest one India had seen in over a decade, one of the deadliest this century. We did not know it would kill nearly one thousand people and leave hundreds of thousands more homeless. But a macabre joke making the rounds of Madras that afternoon said the government in Delhi collected taxes from the Tamils and all it sent back in return was bad weather.

Pandits with shaved heads and white dhotis tried to outrun the storm on mopeds. Office-wallahs furiously pedaled their Hero bicycles, holding the handlebars with one hand and their umbrellas with the other. Minutes after the first raindrop, the streets of Madras had become brown muddy rivers. Water pelted down from the sky like machine-gun fire, like baseballs in a batting cage, like the relentless crush of a hydraulic press.

The rain bombarded Madras's larger-than-life movie hoardings, titanic 3-D signboards where gargantuan villains and heroes physically reach out to grab passing motorists. At the end of the row of posters was an eye-grabbing public service announcement: "Avoid Accidents — Don't Look at Hoardings Like This One." Just before it was an advertisement for a film with Eddie Murphy, only here the actor was painted with straight hair and sepia skin: America's most famous black movie star had been turned into a Tamil.

It rained all that day and all that night and all the next day and all the next night. Cars slewed through puddles of brown water up to their mud-caked chassis, and motor-rickshaws stalled out in the middle of intersections that had become lakes. There was nothing to do but wait the storm out, so I bought a bottle of Mughal Monarch whisky and sat down to wait.

"Why do you drink *that* brand?" asked an indignant man in the chai-house where I'd taken refuge.

I wasn't quite sure. Mughal Monarch is pretty foul stuff, wholly unrecognizable as whisky unless you read the label. But the same could be said of Aristocrat, Gold Mohur, Black Knight, Two Dogs, or any other locally brewed travesty that passes for Scotch in India. All I could answer was that it got the job done.

"Have some of *this,* my friend," the man said, pulling out a bottle of Bagpiper Gold. The black-bearded figure on the label looked more Sikh than Scot, but I seldom turn down a shot of liquor.

It was awful. No worse than my own Mughal Monarch, but awful nonetheless.

"The Mughals," said the man, "oppressed our people ruthlessly. I will drink nothing that bears their name. And what do Muslims know about drink, eh?" He tossed the spent butt of his cigarette on the dirt floor and crushed it with the calloused sole of a bare foot. Then he sent a boy out to buy us beer, and the child demanded two rupees extra for venturing out in the rain.

The boy returned with several bottles of Knock-Out and Hercules. Despite their names they were weak brews that tasted like fermented cat urine. I stuck with the Bagpiping Sikh.

"We do not hate our overlords," said my drinking companion. "Mughals, Englishmen, and *always* the bloody Aryans. We do not hate any of them. We just do not wish to become them."

He wore a flesh-colored hearing aid in his right ear. But it was colored for a white man's flesh.

In Madras I lodged at the Dasaprakash, an old-fashioned hotel for people who are pious, sober-minded, and exceptionally Tamil. For the convenience of guests there is a Shiva temple just off the the main lobby. Not a scrap of meat is served in any of the inn's three restaurants, not a scrap permitted in any of the rooms: northerners may go about eating the reincarnations of their own grandparents, but most Tamils (like the Vanars of epic, who lived on fruit, berries, and nuts) scrupulously shun the flesh of any animal. The hotel is known throughout the south for its seriousness of purpose; when I later mentioned to people at the other end of the state that I'd been staying at the Dasaprakash, they would invariably give an approving nod and ask if I was a vegetarian.

I had intended to lodge at a different place, a ramshackle Victorian boardinghouse with a century-old coat of blue paint that was peeling like the burnt skin on a sunbather's back. The man who drove me there would not hear of it. "I think this place is not so hygienic," he said delicately, "and we must be careful of your health, my friend."

He was a stocky man with thin hair and thick spectacles. He worked for a local newspaper whose editors I was in town to meet, so he'd borrowed the only air-conditioned car in the pool to get me safely settled in. When we stepped out of the artificial chill and into Madras's miasma of humidity, his glasses, those of his assistant, and those of his driver all simultaneously fogged over. "What is more," he said, lowering his voice as he wiped the condensation from his lenses, "there seem to be a number of disreputable persons here. I think this is not suitable lodgings for an upstanding gentleman such as yourself."

Of course I was all the more intent on staying, but an overfed rat picked that moment to scurry across the floor. I agreed to board at the Dasaprakash instead, for the sake of my spiritual well-being.

The Dasaprakash has two banquet halls, the site of some of the most scrupulously upright social events in Madras. After I checked in, I checked them out. The first hall was booked for a wedding, the second for what a bold sign unashamedly proclaimed "The Puberty Celebration of A. K. Ganesh." Naturally, I went to the second hall first. I was curious to see whether social anthropologists were correct about coming-of-age rites transcending cultural barriers — perhaps the staid, proper Madrasis had gathered to watch little A.K. drink himself sick and have furtive sex in the back of a borrowed car.

Actually, a Dravidian boy's initiation into manhood is an earnestly serious ritual, not a debauch but a display of mature self-discipline. It involves (among other things) the consumption of small amounts of cow urine and excrement; how many American males would have the will to accept adulthood under such terms? But I had arrived too late to witness the ceremony. The only activity in the room was that of a wooden ceiling fan listlessly churning up the baking, lifeless air that precedes a monsoon.

I looked in at the first banquet hall, but Dravidian weddings are much like any others. Women in saris thick with gaudy gold filigree primped self-consciously and rearranged their flower garlands. A brass band dressed in black, red, and silver beat out a tune of conquest rather than romance, but nobody seemed to be listening. Just outside the door was a pathetically skinny horse on which the groom had made his grandiose entrance. The unsteady steed waited patiently, almost crushed beneath a blanket of sequined coverlets, and I wondered if its bent back would break when mounted by the same rider with a full wedding meal in his belly.

➤ ➤ ➤

The most definitively Tamil festival of all I did not see in Tamil Nadu. I did not even see it in India. About three years before I set foot on the subcontinent I was in Malaysia, in the seaside city of Penang, where descendants of Tamil plantation workers outnumber both the native Malays and the Chinese immigrants. It was there that I saw the human spirit put itself to the ultimate test in the procession of Thaipusam.

They feel no pain, I was told, but it hurt me just to look at them. It was a time of celebration, I was told, but the principal celebrants seemed none too jolly. This was a day they had been eagerly awaiting all year, a day they would remember fondly all their lives. So I was told.

I was in Penang to write a story for a Japanese newspaper. The story had nothing to do with Indians, nothing to do with Hinduism, it was a piece about the execution of a mentally retarded drug courier — and when I eventually returned to Tokyo the paper decided it didn't want the story after all. But now I was in Penang, my work done, and as I was walking back from my last interview I ran into a man with his back full of fishhooks.

His bare flesh was laced with dozens of deeply anchored barbs, each tied to a long, sturdy cord that lay coiled on the ground. From his arms, legs, chest, and even forehead hung heavy brazen ornaments: pendulous bowls of burning incense, clanking bells, polished balls of shiny metal there just for painful decoration. An older man and two children were pushing in the last few hooks, tugging after each insertion to make sure every prong was firmly rooted.

I asked why. The Human Pincushion said not a word. Perhaps it was due to his religious trance, or perhaps to the thick metal rod that stuck through both his cheeks and skewered his tongue in between. One of the children answered for him. The Tamil god Muruga (also worshiped by Bengalis as the Lord of Thieves) had granted the Pincushion a great favor, so he now was repaying the deity for his kindness.

The main avenue of Penang, normally clogged with exhaust-spewing cars and buses, tonight was clogged with people. Dozens and dozens of flagellants decked out just like the Pincushion were drawn up in a circle, each man attended by his family, friends, and well-wishers. Each had his hide similarly flayed, each wore the same unblinking, zombielike stare into nothingness.

Big wooden carts the size of Volkswagen minibuses stood waiting, mobile shrines laden with fruits, cakes, garlands, spices in great piles of color, flickering candles, exuberant icons, bouquets of fresh flowers heaped up in fragrant bales. Four men pushed each carriage out, straining to turn the creaky, ungreased wooden wheels.

"Will the carts be pushed all the way down this street?" I asked the child.

"No, no," he said, "they will be *pulled*."

At this point men started tying the juggernauts to the cords streaming out of the flagellants' backs.

"You don't mean *they'll* pull them, *that* way?" I asked.

"Yes, yes," he said. "It's all right," he said as an afterthought. "When the road is too steep, some people will also help push from behind."

"Where are they going?"

"There." He pointed to a temple at the top of a big hill far in the dusky distance.

Soon all the penitents were saddled up. Those who had not been hitched to the wheeled shrines took on towering metal kavadi frames — skeletal pyramids covered with banners, ribbons, spinning pinwheels — and balanced the heavy loads on their lacerated shoulders.

Slowly, painfully, and (for the onlookers) festively, the procession started off on its long march. The Human Pincushion and his comrades set the pace, leaning forward at 45-degree angles against their burdens, the rough cords taut as bowstrings, the vicious barbs imbedded snugly in the meat of their backs. With each man's every labored step, the hundreds of spots where the hooks entered his skin rose up like little tents of flesh. All around the marchers, thousands of joyous merrymakers sang and danced, played drums and flutes, banged tambourines and stomped happy feet. The men with the steel kavadis whirled, bobbed, and writhed in tortuous circles as the unencumbered crowd shouted out its encouragement.

All through the night the party roared, old uncles dancing with young nephews and nieces, cousins with cousins, strangers with strangers, and even before full darkness descended, people began lighting oily torches that spat yellow flames into the night. It must have been a sight from the mountaintop temple: a curvy gold snake of fluttery light stretched out for miles, slowly slithering its fiery way up the hill.

From the center of the crush, it was a shifting collage of food, incense, shouting voices, grinning faces, dancing lights, dancing feet, and silent, somber men with sharp pieces of metal jutting out of their limbs. When dawn broke and the holidaymakers filed off to grab an hour or so of sleep, they ended the festival by smashing coconut shells on the ground and setting the mounds of hairy husks ablaze. When the light of day illuminated Penang at dawn, it revealed empty streets strewn with the debris of a wild festival and a line of newly lit bonfires to warm the morning air. The only inhabitants of the city left standing were the monkeys, who picked carefully through the carnage for a festive breakfast of their own.

India is full of monkeys — big black-faced langurs, gray-brown macaques with tails like question marks, wrinkle-browed apes with bright red buttocks, always stealing food from tables and playing raucous games of tag in the treetops. Monkeys, we know, are comical creatures. Always scampering about purposelessly, chittering frantic sounds that mean nothing, loping from place to place with a clownish bounce. They look vaguely human but lack the basic dignity even of such lower animals as lions, bulls, and elephants. They are our closest relatives, but (as when Uncle Zeke crudely picks his teeth and belches all through Christmas dinner) we find their kinship faintly embarrassing. To our anthropomorphizing minds they seem silly, childish, wholly devoid of self-respect or self-control.

Ironically, self-respect and self-control are two of the Dravidians' foremost traits. Few other peoples could have proudly held on to their distinct cultural identity through three thousand years of disparagement. Few other peoples could have displayed the calm patience to deal with their conquerors by outlasting them. Few other peoples could steadfastly refuse to eat any meat whatsoever out of religious conviction. And few other peoples could pull Thaipusam juggernauts with harnesses stitched into their flesh.

The poet Valmiki, in all likelihood, never met a Tamil in his life. The only Dravidians he knew would have been Shudras, dispirited through generations of oppression. Had he traveled south even once, perhaps Hanuman, Sugriva, Bali, and the rest would have been men instead of apes.

> > >

Just as the Vanars weren't born monkeys, the Rakshasas may not have been born demons. Every nation has its mythological ogres and bogeymen, its djinns and its afrits, its trolls and its banshees. In most cases the evil spirits are loathsome parodies of humanity: less civilized and less physically appealing, but stronger and harder to kill. In short, they are man's universal caricature of the Other.

Psychologists might say that demons are merely the personification of all we fear, our haziest terrors all rolled into an easily identifiable form. Undoubtedly true, but perhaps they are something else as well. Perhaps when demons were born (as J. A. de Gobineau has suggested) they were the enemy race just over the next hill.

The Rakshasas of Indian epic embody most of the worst stereotypes that one race can have about another: they are foul-smelling, horribly ugly, and inhumanly violent, half-naked cannibals with fat bellies and coarse hair on their backs. But most of all, they are black. Black as the darkest horrors of night, black as evil itself, black as the inhabitants of Lanka then and now.

The Sinhalese, the people of present-day Sri Lanka, claim to be descended from Aryan forefathers. Maybe, maybe not. But whatever their lineage, by Valmiki's time they had already created a thriving civilization essentially cut off from the Aryan culture of northern India. Some Indian skeptics deny that this is the Rakshasa kingdom of epic, saying that Lanka (like Ayodhya) was never meant to be a real geographical place. Maybe, maybe not. But the Ramayana clearly identifies the demons' homeland as a very large island one hundred yojanas off the subcontinent's southern tip. There is only one such island on any map, and from the earliest history its name has been Lanka.

The Aryans (in all likelihood) had little or no contact with the Sinhalese, but they obviously had heard of an advanced nation in the middle of the sea. Valmiki portrays Lanka as a highly cultured, urbane, sophisticated kingdom, every bit as resplendent as Ayodhya itself. He says it is as beautiful "as heaven itself," with gates of gold and thresholds inlaid with rubies and sapphires. "Everything therein," the poet writes, "was immaculately neat and clean."

Nor are the Rakshasas here all barbarians. In contrast to their brethren in the Dandak forest, the demons of Lanka are "neither very tall nor very dwarfish, neither very stout nor very lean, neither very fair nor very dark." They are, in brief, not composite evil, but ordinary people. Perhaps even extraordinary people. Hanuman, in his spying expedition, finds the Rakshasas "sweet of speech, and wholly pious." They may not be Aryans, but they do not seem to be one bit inferior. Valmiki even writes that in their community the Vedas and the Shastras are regularly chanted by holy Brahmins.

Yet in the next breath, the poet again lambastes the Lankans as hideous black-skinned cannibals. Their fantastic city is not even their own creation, but the gift of the god Vishvakarma. The Aryans, it seems, could not truly stomach the notion that any other race might be capable of advanced civilization.

It would be hard to imagine a people less demonic than the Sinhalese. Even a decade of civil war (in which they have both suffered and perpetrated horrible atrocities) has not made them brutal. Their virtues are not the harsh, forbidding virtues of a warrior-nation, and their vices are not the vices that come from cruel hearts. I could say much about the kindness of the Sinhalese, but one instance will suffice.

I was diving off the shore of Nilaveli, having rented a dubious-looking scuba tank and regulator from an even more dubious-looking pillager of coral. The reef was swarming with black-and-white zebra fish, shocking yellow lemon-fish, phosphorescent blue-green robins, lumbering Napoleons as big as bear cubs, fish two feet long and pencil-thin and translucent as lightly smoked glass. All were quite unafraid of humans — perhaps the only benefit of the devastation of war is that it saves a country from the devastation of tourism.

It was late afternoon when I used up my air. I climbed on board the little skiff I'd hired, but the boatman was unable to start the motor. We spent over an hour fiddling with the engine. Each time he'd poke a wire into the machine to make it cough, and I would pull up the ungainly cinder block lashed to a twisted log that served as a homemade anchor. Each time the motor would sputter and die, and I'd toss the concrete and wood back to keep us from drifting farther out to sea. The boatman had only one hand, and as he slapped and prodded the motor hopelessly, he steadied himself against the keel with his stump.

At sunset we swam to Pigeon Island, an uninhabited atoll a few hundred yards away. I wished I'd been smart enough to bring a canteen of water or matches for a signal fire, and I resolved never to be so stupid again, if there was an again. In the morning, when the current was less strong, the one-handed boatman and I would have to attempt the long and unlikely struggle to the mainland. Better to go by drowning than by slow dehydration.

I don't think I've ever been so grateful to hear any sound as I was when, several hours into the night, I heard the hum of an approaching engine. The following moments were a quick sequence of shouts from us, the beam of a flashlight from the fishing boat, an embarrassed nod of thanks from the man with one hand, and pledges from me to name my firstborn after each one of our rescuers.

Back in Nilaveli the owner of my lodging house told me what had happened.

"When a man does not return in time for dinner," he said in

a kindly tone, "it can mean only two things: either he has taken up with a woman, or some mischief has befallen him. I happen to know all the women in this town, so it must have been the latter."

He poured me more arrack, the local liquor distilled from palm and coconut. It tastes like diesel fuel, and when improperly brewed kills several wedding parties each year, but at this moment it might have been Dom Perignon.

Up above us a family of monkeys chased each other from tree to roof. As each one jumped across the gaping void, he seemed to float interminably in midair, to soar for effortless ages before landing safe on the other side. For a moment, the notion of Hanuman leaping over the ocean at a single bound did not seem a mythical conceit.

"I made some queries," the proprietor said, "and many townspeople became rather worried. Several had seen you go out toward Pigeon Island, but nobody had seen you come back. Your boatman has a reputation for, er, for, ah, not spending every night at his house, so his absence was not missed. But we grew quite concerned on your account, and several fisherman decided to have a look-see."

I thanked him again, and he cut me off with a dismissive shake of the hands. "Don't think about it," he said with a shrug. "Why, what else would anyone do?"

Others might have done the same, others might have done nothing, but this much is sure: when I was rescued from shipwreck, my deliverers were none other than the Rakshasas. Had Valmiki ever met anyone from across the Southern Sea, perhaps the people of Lanka would have been men instead of demons.

Nine
RITES

THE demonesses guarding Sita taunted her unmercifully.
"Good eating here!" said one Rakshasi, pinching Sita's left breast.

"The drumstick's mine!" another cackled.

"Oh, no!" said another, raising her voice in mock anger. "I called the drumstick days ago."

They were a hideous assortment of polyglot ogresses. Some had only one eye, some had long necks like sinuous snakes, some had thick hair all over their bodies, some were dwarfish and humpbacked, some tall and yellow-eyed, some had the faces of tigers, deer, buffaloes, or jackals, some had the feet of cows, camels, or horses, some had the ears of a dog or a donkey and the dangling nose of an elephant. All were drunk on wine mixed with fresh blood.

"You are divvying up the feast too soon," said the least intoxicated Rakshasi wardeness. "Last night I dreamt I saw Ravana riding naked on an ass, drinking oil from a cracked vial. A woman dressed in red, her garment all caked with mud, was dragging him away by a rope tied around his neck." The demoness did not have to explain the meaning of her dream. It was a clear portent of who would live and who would die.

Late that night, once the guards had gone to sleep, Hanuman crept down from his perch. He whispered in Sita's ear, and since he whispered in pure Sanskrit she knew he had come from her husband. When he gave her Rama's ring as proof of his identity, Sita could barely keep herself from crying out with joy. But she would not accept the ape's offer to carry her home on his back.

I might fall off, she objected; besides, you can't take on the whole Rakshasa army; besides, it is not right for a married woman to touch another man's flesh. Hanuman stared dumbfounded through each hasty excuse.

Finally Sita admitted the real reason for her refusal. "I cannot return with you," she said, "because it is Rama's duty to rescue me. A husband must defend his wife, that is his dharma. I cannot shame Rama by letting another man perform his appointed mission."

Hanuman reminded her that if it came to war, millions of people would die.

"Better that millions of millions die," she said, "than that I should cause my husband to break holy dharma."

Hanuman silently thanked the gods that he was only a simple monkey and that such knots of theology were beyond his unraveling.

While creeping out of the palace, Hanuman happened to awaken a band of royal bodyguards, and soon the whole city was up in arms. The Vanar fought off hundreds of the demon soldiers, and whenever archers shot their quills at him the son of the Wind God easily jumped out of range. He swelled to a huge size, and crushed dozens with each swipe of his gigantic paws.

Ravana's son Indrajit arrived on the scene in a car drawn by four horses with sharp yellow teeth. He recognized Hanuman and knew from his spies that the ape was fated never to die except by his own consent. So when Indrajit cast his magic net at the Vanar, he ordered his weapon not to kill but to bind.

He dragged Hanuman in chains before the King of the Demons and kicked him to the floor.

"Hah! Hah! Hah!" Ravana bellowed. "So this is the best that Rama has to send against me. A monkey? Hah! Hah! Hah!"

Hanuman said nothing.

"I have heard," Ravana said, putting his face right up to the ape's nose," that you Vanars greatly value those ridiculous tails of yours. Perhaps that is the source of your foolish recklessness. Let's find out, shall we?"

He picked a flickering torch off the wall, and set the Vanar's tail on fire.

Hanuman choked back his scream, sat still in agony for several long minutes, and when the pain had burned away Indrajit's magic spell, he knew what to do. He shrunk himself small enough to slip out of his shackles, then whipped his blazing tail about like a firebrand to set the palace aflame. He ran through the streets of Lanka leaving a burning trail behind him, and before making the great leap back to India he extinguished his fiery appendage in the Southern Sea.

Back in Kishkindhya, all the Vanars rejoiced with Hanuman on his return. They got drunk on fermented honey and gobbled up all the flowers in the royal botanical garden, but King Sugriva did not mind. For the first time in many months, he saw a smile on Rama's face.

Ravana asked his counselors for advice. All of them obsequiously parroted the words he wanted to hear.

"Who could challenge you?" they said.

"Ravana must bow to no man," they said.

"A king can never give up his prize," they said.

All except Vibhishan, Ravana's youngest brother.

"Rama has done you no harm," said Vibhishan. "Kidnapping Sita was an act of evil, it cannot help but bring about your downfall. The bad omens are right before your eyes: for months now the sacrificial fires have not flared up when fed with oblations but have only given off foul smoke and sparks, as if the gods were rejecting our very offerings. Every holy rite is tainted. Reptiles infest all the temples and sacred places. Ants and cockroaches crawl over the curd left before every altar. Cows no longer give milk, elephants no longer sweat, horses refuse to eat. Mules shed human tears and cannot be cured by any spell or science. Ravens, jackals, and vultures laze about the palace walls, calmly waiting for their feast.

"Do you not see these things, my lord? As your servant and as your brother, I beg you not to ignore the warnings of fate. Do what is right, and let Sita return to her husband."

"Coward!" Ravana shrieked. "No weakling is any kin of mine!"

Burly guards tossed Vibhishan out of the council chamber, and all the courtiers of Lanka felt thankful that they hadn't been naive enough to speak their true minds.

> > >

Rama and his army of Vanars reached the Southern Sea at dusk. They looked across the ocean and saw whales and Timingilas — great Devourers of Whales — dancing between the waves.

Raising his head to the salty breeze, Rama addressed the wind: "O Breathing Air," he said, "cast your gentle caress over Sita in Lanka, then blow the same gust past my face so I can feel the touch of her skin against mine."

Lakshman, standing next to his brother, rolled his eyes.

At that moment Vibhishan, having flown over the sea with his demon magic, alit on the shore and started walking toward the camp.

"Look," said Sugriva, "a Rakshasa noble is coming to be killed."

Vibhishan explained who he was, told how he had abandoned his wife and children, abandoned his station and master, because he could not fight an unrighteous battle.

"Why are we wasting time talking?" Sugriva asked. "Kill him and be done with it."

Rama put up his hand, and the Vanar captors held their blows.

"He is a Rakshasa, an enemy," Sugriva reasoned. "Even if everything he has said is true, the man betrayed his own brother, his own king, his own race. How can we possibly trust him not to betray us as well?"

Rama was too kindhearted to remind the Monkey King of his own role in fratricide.

"Friend or foe," he said, "this man seeks my protection. He may be evil, he may be good, but since he is a suppliant I cannot possibly turn him away. It is my duty, my dharma, to aid any creature who comes to me in need. That is all there is to say."

So Vibhishan joined the Vanar host, but still Rama's army had no way of crossing the sea.

Rama knelt down on the sandy beach and prayed. For three days and three nights he prayed to Lord Ocean, prayed that the sea might grant his troops safe passage to Lanka. He prayed so hard that the sand underneath his feet began to melt into glass, and on the dawn of the fourth day his prayer was answered.

Lord Ocean arose from his element, algae-green and huge as a tidal wave, spraying all the Vanars with his frothy white foam.

"I will calm my waters," he said, "and make them flat for you to pass. But you will still need something solid on which to walk. Build a bridge across my body, and I will hold it up safe and dry."

So the apes descended on all the forests near the shore, tore up trees and boulders and carried them down the beach. Under Rama's direction they heaved each load farther and farther out onto the stilled ocean. After five days of ceaseless labor, they had constructed a span ten yojanas wide and a hundred yojanas long.

In later ages — almost up to our present day — a Hindu who crossed any of the Black Waters would immediately lose his caste and fall lower than the lowest tanner of cowskins. But Rama lived before such a time, so he joined his soldiers in a lusty cheer and marched out across the uncrossable ocean.

Two Rakshasa spies brought their report back to Ravana. The king complimented his agents on their skill in evading detection, but the demons could not accept their master's praise.

"We were captured," the first spy said, "and the loathsome monkeys wanted to kill us."

"But Rama would not let them," the second continued. "He said he had nothing to hide — why, he even gave us a guided tour of the camp before sending us safely back home!"

"He is approaching," said the first spy, "with his troops in the classic Garuda Vyuha formation, his army drawn up in the shape of a great eagle poised to swoop on its prey."

At this point one of Ravana's courtiers ventured an honest opinion.

"My lord," he said, "in the fields just outside our walls, asses are born of cows, and mice of mongooses. Tigers are mating with cats, and dogs with swine. The world as we have known it is out of joint. All your knowledge of the Vedas and the Shastras is futile without simple moral sense. You must give Sita back."

Ravana made a sound midway between a laugh and a snort.

"Must?!" he cried. "Must? I *must* do this? No, no, my friend, a king does not know the word 'must.' Why are you all so afraid of this Ayodhyan beggarman, this hermit, this orphan exiled by his own father, this ragamuffin leader of a pack of flea-bitten monkeys?"

The spies and the courtiers all looked at their feet.

"The question, in any case, is irrelevant," Ravana said, more calmly. "I cannot bend, it is not in my nature. A man's fate is carved into his very soul, it shapes his character, it guides his every action. Even if I wished to do so, I could never back down."

He looked out of the window, out to the sea.

"I will fight this battle," said the king. "I . . . *must* fight this battle. And," he added, his eyes narrowed to sharp blades of sight, "I will win it."

<hr/>

The Ramayana is more than a folk epic, it is a holy text. Merely listening to the deeds of Rama, one of the most important gods in the Hindu pantheon, brings merit to every believer. But to understand Valmiki's tale even on the level of myth, to appreciate it purely as literature, one still must know a bit about Hinduism. Formal rituals do not often enter into the narrative: Rama's prayer to the Sea God is one of the very few places in the original text where the hero's worship is described. But every solemn ceremony — from the marriage of Rama and Sita to Dasarastha's funeral to the coronations of Sugriva, Rama, and Vibhishan — is at heart a religious rite. And every event in the story, from Dasarastha's pronouncement of exile to Rama's wandering as a hermit to the final battle between the Vanars and the Rakshasas, is shaped by religion, every action is the unfolding of a different spiritual principle. There is no dividing the plot from the gospel.

India has never maintained the West's absolute schism between the sacred and the profane. For Hindus, worship is not a form of prayer, it is a way of living. Christians may put on their Sunday best to take communion or listen to a sermon once a week, but Hindu theologians see holiness in *any* action done well. Plowing a field or cooking a good meal can be a daily sacrament. Even in today's outwardly secular society, few aspects of Indian life are not wholly immersed in religion. The very name of the faith comes from the monotheistic Zoroastrians of Persia, who coined the term "Hindu" after their word for Indians; the inhabitants of the subcontinent had never felt it necessary to give their doctrine any label. They distinguished only between those who accepted the authority of the Vedas and those who did not. Theirs was not any sharply defined creed but simply the way the world worked.

Most of us in the West think of Hindu theology as an impossibly intimidating subject, as far above the common person's ken as the intricacies of quantum mechanics. There are many reasons for this. Much of our impression of Eastern religions comes not from genuine Hindus or Buddhists but from muddle-minded pseudo-swamis giving out pamphlets at airports, or from New Age bookstores where the Rig-Veda is shelved next to the healing crystals. Moreover, it is indeed daunting to set aside the entire Judeo-Christian intellectual framework that underlies everything we believe. And, yes, many aspects of India's ancient philosophy are complex enough to make Wittgenstein or Kierkegaard wince.

I am certainly not going to try to explain the entirety of Hinduism. Being neither a scholar of theology nor even a Hindu, I'm simply not equipped. But I *can* sketch out the rough contours of the faith and shade in a touch of detail here or there with an amateur pencil. I offer only the preliminary disclaimer that any attempt to encapsulate such a varied and complex religion must necessarily be a gross simplification.

The core of the faith, the root from which all the rest grew, is an ancient polytheism brought to India by the invading Aryans. The gods themselves have changed: gone are Indra, Agni, Varuna, all the hoary divinities of the steppe. In their place are Ganesh, Parvati, Kali, Devi, Lakshmi — a pantheon of younger deities born on Indian soil. Rama is among the youngest of all: while his story dates back to the depths of prehistory, he was not widely worshiped until the fifteenth century.

The Hindu gods are very much like their Greek and Roman counterparts — all were, of course, descended from the same ancient Aryan pantheon. They are merely supernatural beings who can make human lives easier if properly placated or pour down a torrent of woes if given offense. The Rig-Veda, a collection of hymns to appease various deities, is still (alongside the Gita) the holiest text in the Hindu canon.

What these devas grant is not salvation in the next life but favors in this one. For the vast majority of Hindus, faith is directed largely to the here and now rather than the hereafter. Sadhus and particularly devout pandits look for union with the Divine, but most Indians know they will have to live through countless incarnations before breaking free of the cycle of rebirth. When they toss rupees at a temple icon, they generally pray not for spiritual redemption but for a full plate of rice and lentils.

Most of the Vedas are intensely this-worldly, asking the gods for comfort and material well-being. The oldest of these hymns date to the time of the Aryan invasion, about 1,500 to 1,200 years before Christ. Even though the specific gods invoked are no longer widely revered, the Vedas themselves are the central element of every Hindu prayer.

In epic times it was believed that great acts of piety irresistibly *compelled* the gods to grant generous boons. Virtue brings power, says the law of divine justice. But whenever a man grew *too* virtuous, his mushrooming stock of merit became a threat to the gods themselves: if the saint used his psychic power he might prove equal to the forces of Heaven, and if he kept his expanding store of spiritual strength bottled up he could incinerate the whole world with its brilliance. To protect the earth (and the human race on whose devotion all immortals depend) the gods would be forced to defuse a rishi's explosive holiness by granting his dearest wish.

This is why so many characters in the Ramayana, from saints like Vishvamitra and Agastya to demons like Ravana and Indrajit, are given boons. Any man, no matter how unkind his heart, could wring concessions from Heaven by a display of iron will. Yogis who gave up food and water, foreswore the delights of the flesh, lived on nothing but air and pure thought, were said to gain gifts of impossibly long lives and incredible physical abilities. Today there are no rishis who live ten thousand years or make mountains tremble with a glance. Some would say all this proves is that the holy men of today are not as holy as those of old.

The boons asked and granted now are the humbler boons of ordinary life: success in an examination, a plentiful harvest, birth of a son rather than a daughter. In every temple the god's idol is treated just like a divine monarch capable of dispensing regal largesse: the statue is awakened in the morning with bells and songs, bathed with scented water, often dressed in fresh robes. During the day it is fed with oblations of fruit or rice, paid tribute with flowers and coins. At night it is put to bed, with chanted hymns as a lullaby. Periodically, like every monarch, it is entertained with displays of music and dance. On festival days a mobile image of the deity is taken out of the shrine and sent on a royal progress through its domains.

During my time in India I saw many forms of worship in many temples, and no two were precisely the same. At Meenakshi Temple in the southern pilgrimage town of Madurai, I watched the devotees lining up for afternoon puja. This daily rite, the central ceremony of Hinduism, can be performed at home or in a mandir. A price list above the shrine's inner sanctum gave a wide range of options, depending upon whether the celebrant wanted a private or public rite, upon the number of chanting Brahmins, and upon the sort of musical accompaniment. Those who could not afford their own puja salved their souls by tossing sticky lumps of butter at huge stone idols of the triple-breasted Meenakshi and her husband Shiva until both statues looked like the spitball-crusted ceiling of a grade-school cafeteria.

The cavernous halls and labyrinthine corridors of the temple were shrouded in thick clouds of incense, the dark corners full of napping sadhus using their thickly matted dreadlocks as pillows, cradling their cobra-shaped walking sticks as they slept. One mural in the temple's Thousand-Pillared Hall showed Shiva impaling an army of gray-skinned, black-bearded Jain monks on vicious spikes, a proud allegory of Hinduism's medieval reconquest of India. A few yards away an equally proud (if less well schooled) sign read "This way to bothroom, letrine, urine." Neither one seemed out of place.

At another Dravidian temple, Kamakshimman by name, nobody spoke a word to me as I scooped a handful of holy water like hearty pea soup from the algae-heavy bathing tank, stared up at the exuberant circus of figures atop the goparam pyramids, and strained to make out the forms of Hanuman and Nandi pent up behind screens for their midday siestas. But when I inadvertently wandered into the room where the idol was kept, I was chased away by two angry old men who did not cease their haranguing until I'd left the temple complex. In the north, members of all castes and all faiths are usually permitted inside the inner sanctum, but at many Tamil shrines the mere presence of meat-eating, ritually impure non-Hindus is seen as a terrible insult to the divinity's dignity.

On the other hand, at the Bengali temple of Kalighat (from which Calcutta takes its name) I was virtually dragged before the central altar by a throng of earnest devotees. Some were honestly eager to share their faith with me, but most were baring their secrets for the sake of filthy lucre. A man daubed red chalk on my forehead, and demanded baksheesh. Four children needlessly identified the shrine's door, knowingly offered to "watch" my shoes, pulled me inside, and demanded baksheesh. A pandit muttered a hasty blessing over my head, and demanded baksheesh. A foreigner is an easier mark than most, but temple-wallahs do not live on foreigners alone.

It was with some trepidation that I entered the shrine; if there is any deity one would not wish to offend it would be Kali. She is the wrathful aspect of Shiva the Destroyer, possibly the most bloodthirsty divinity in any extant religion. Her eyes blaze with fire, and she wears a necklace of human skulls still dripping with brain marrow. As Durga she smiles while killing a different victim with a different weapon in each of her hundred hands. As recently as the mid-nineteenth century, the Thugee cult (from which we get the word "thug") used to roam the roads of north India strangling unwary travelers to feed Kali's appetite for slaughter.

At the Kalighat altar the big, black stone goddess juts her tongue out in a primeval victory cry, her chin and cheeks red with the gore of her enemies. Worshipers push forward to leave blood-red flowers by the idol's toes. If my presence there was a desecration, nobody seemed to care.

Outside I walked barefoot through the blood and the mud and the trash and the excrement of the temple courtyard. By the front gate a man was dismembering goats. Kalighat is one of the few temples in India where animal sacrifice is still commonly performed. On the guts-slippery pavement there was a pile of eight unskinned legs and two shaggy heads, the portion reserved for Kali's pleasure. The butcher and his son were unraveling a long string of pale intestines, separating the salable meat from the useless viscera, rinsing a blue-green balloon of an organ under a water pump.

I could understand the faithful honoring Kali out of fear, trembling as they knelt before her, praying to be spared her wrath. But this is not the way she is seen. Devotees view the goddess as a kind, merciful, and loving deity, the nurturing Mother of All. I asked several people at Kalighat to explain this, and received only pitying stares. "She is the dear Mata," said one woman patiently, "the giving Mata, who cares for each of her children."

There is, of course, another woman in Calcutta who is called Mata by her disciples. I would not have thought Mother Teresa could have anything in common with the death-dealing goddess Kali. But the God of Mother Teresa might be wholly unintelligible to a Bengali, and He is also a deity of blood: a lowly carpenter nailed to a cross, dripping blood from his forehead, palms, feet, and chest, blood that the faithful ritually drink every week, cleansing blood that washes away every sin, blood whose shedding saves all humanity. Only the fine line of cultural squeamishness divides the gruesome from the glorious.

There is another level, however, on which the gods can be understood. To many Hindus they are separate, individual beings, but to others they represent different aspects of the One True God. I discussed this deeper, symbolic stratum of the pantheon with a man in a sweat-stained Nehru suit who paid particular devotion to the Monkey God, Hanuman.

Down the street from Kalighat, Hanuman has a little shrine. This most perfect of Vanars is seen as the chamberlain of the gods, the keeper of the doors of heaven. In ancient times Agni, the God of Fire, served this function; the early Aryans placed sacrifices in Agni's fiery "mouth" and saw the gifts physically borne up to the skies in the form of black smoke. Today many people feel more comfortable addressing their prayers to the easily approachable Ape God than to such august and terrifying divinities as Shiva or Vishnu. Like Roman Catholics seeking the help of patron saints, Hindus look to lesser gods for intercession.

"First we go to Hanuman," said the man in the Nehru suit, "then to the higher devas. If you want to ask your boss for a raise, better first to sound out the secretary, eh?"

Every Tuesday is sacred to Hanuman, so the shrine that day was thick with weekly favor-seekers. Shaivites often prefer to use Ganesh as their intermediary, for the elephant-headed immortal is Shiva's favorite son. But many Vaishnavites cherish the Monkey God as a model of devotion, for his unquestioning loyalty to Vishnu's avatar Rama. They see him as a perfect example of a dutiful disciple. A common street mural throughout the country shows Hanuman tearing open his bloody chest to reveal, engraved on his beating heart, the images of Rama and Sita.

"Must pray first to Hanuman," said the suited man, "or else perhaps the prayer will get lost." He was, it turned out, a well-educated person, a former civil servant, so I asked him about the deeper meaning of Hindu polytheism.

"The Supreme Being is like a bureaucracy. No, no, do not be alarmed," he added hastily, for I must have lifted my eyebrows at this apparent blasphemy, "certainly it operates more efficiently, but along the same principles. You see, each of the gods has his own function and responsibility. Just as we civil servants have a Ministry of Defense, a Ministry of Finance, what have you, on the spiritual level there is the war god Kartikkaya; Lakshmi, the goddess of wealth; Sashthi for childbirth, Manasa for snakebite, Sitala for smallpox, and so forth."

"But aren't the gods, like the ministries, distinct entities?"

"Yes and no. The ministries have different offices, but all are part of the very same government. If you wish to receive a driver's license, do you send off your application addressed merely to 'The Government, New Delhi'? Of course not. You mail it to the Bureau of Motor Vehicles. But surely you would not doubt that it is the government which issues the license."

For many Indians, polytheism is an intellectual convenience, a symbol to make the underlying pantheism easier to comprehend. Perhaps that is why Hinduism contains the only major form of polytheism (apart from Shinto, which never extended beyond Japan) to survive into the twentieth century.

I asked the Nehru-suited man if polytheism might be the key to Hinduism's tolerance of the deities of other religions. At an unassuming shrine on a Bombay street, for example, I once saw five Hindu icons beside a Madonna, a crucifix, and a portrait of Zoroaster, all equally garlanded and adored. Can Hindus (I asked) pray to the Buddha and Jesus Christ because they see all divinities as aspects of the One True God?

"We have wide-open minds," he said. "We will worship anything. It can't hurt, and maybe it will help. At the very least it can bring peace of mind." But he did not like an analogy I raised, Khushwant Singh's metaphor of Hinduism being a boa constrictor that swallowed up any faith it encountered.

"No, no," he said, "we do not eat other gods, we do not take them away and destroy them." He mused for a moment. "I prefer to think of Hinduism as a garden," he said, "a lush, beautiful garden filled with all manner of ancient trees and lovely flowers and birds singing joyful songs. A garden eternally in bloom, in whose fertile soil any type of plant can take root and blossom."

Modern Hinduism is, of course, much removed from the ancient Aryan paganism. It is far more than simply paying homage to the appropriate deities and being rewarded for one's sacrifice. Perhaps the clearest distinction between a primitive and an advanced religion is the concept of universal ethics: pagan faiths emphasize ritual correctness over absolute right and wrong, while sophisticated creeds hold a worshiper's state of mind more important than the oblations he offers up at the altar.

A vital component of Hinduism's sophistication is the doctrine of karma. What karma means is simply that there is justice in the world, that every good act will be rewarded and every evil act punished, either in this life or a later one. Karma is the mechanism through which God functions, the device that gives all men and women their just deserts.

The word *karma* is Sanskrit for "action," or, to be more precise, any action with a moral overtone. Everything we do, think, or feel accumulates positive or negative karma. Helping a blind person across the street, for example, builds up good karma, while kicking a Brahmin in the stomach amasses a very large store of bad karma indeed. It is a fundamentally optimistic doctrine, for it holds that good deeds inevitably lead to happiness and bad deeds to misery.

Central to the doctrine of karma is the belief in reincarnation. As every earthquake, civil war, or cyclone reminds us, the world's stock of adversity is dealt out with no regard for virtue. Quite often — some would say usually — long-suffering saints are given only greater hardships, while conscienceless blackguards revel in luxury. If there is a fair settling of scores, it certainly does not happen in this life alone.

It is karma that determines one's reincarnation, karma that decides one's destiny. A pious, hardworking seamstress may be reborn as a Brahmin. A dishonest businessman may come back as leper, or perhaps (if his crimes are especially heinous) even as a goat, a dog, or a snail. We ourselves create the karma that creates our lives.

Even the events in our daily routine are the result of karma. Every illness, every accident, every winning lottery ticket is the payment for some past act. Sometimes misdeeds are punished in the same lifetime: in the Ramayana, because King Dasarastha killed a hermit boy in his youth, he is forced to send his own son into exile.

Virtually every religion has some concept of an afterlife, whether here on earth or on another plane. Christians, Muslims, Buddhists — all hold the spirit to be eternal. It is difficult to see how one can believe in any omnipotent deity without also believing that something exists after death. Greek philosophers such as Pythagoras, Empedocles, Pindar, and even Plato (that apostle of cold logic) believed in a metempsychosis, or "transmigration of souls" virtually identical to reincarnation. In the Hindu view, the very life in our bodies — the soul, the spark that separates a human being from an inert mass of flesh and bone — cannot be killed. It can only be recycled. The soul is a part of God, and how can any fraction of God ever be said to die?

The universe itself, Hindu doctrine holds, goes through an endless chain of lives. Each cycle of creation begins with a Golden Age, a heroic time of miracles and magic, a time when all things are possible. The events of the Ramayana take place in the most recent golden age, which is why various characters can live to be thousands of years old without causing any surprise. As the cosmos ages it deteriorates, through Silver and Bronze Ages, until it reaches the Iron Age, the age of Kali, and is eventually destroyed by Shiva and created anew. The Kali-Yuga is a time when all morals are forgotten, when trust vanishes from the earth, when cheating and murder are commonplace, when men return to the level of beasts. Needless to say, in Hindu cosmology all of recorded history has taken place within the current age of Kali.

The Greeks and Romans divided the world's past into the very same metallic ages, but perhaps this merely indicates that the idea goes back to the same Aryan root. Still, as a matron in a coffeehouse in Mysore pointed out to me, the notion of Creation destroyed and remade is not merely myth. We had been discussing reincarnation, and she pulled a newspaper out of her handbag.

"Look at this, if you please," she said, and I did. It was an article describing a current archaeological theory about the demise of the dinosaurs. Sixty-five million years ago, between the Cretaceous and the Tertiary eras, the giant reptiles who had ruled the earth for eons all mysteriously died. The hypothesis is that an asteroid six miles across landed just south of Jamaica, crashing with a force ten thousand times as powerful as all the world's atomic weapons combined. The impact (so the theory goes) tossed up a dust cloud that blotted out the sun, killing most plant life and cooling the atmosphere, so that all the dinosaurs starved and froze in a cosmic instant. "Look," said the woman, "the ages of earth are not speculation, your own Reuters News Agency proclaims it scientific certainty."

This view of the cosmos as a living entity stems from the fact that Hinduism is (on a more abstract level) not polytheism, not monotheism, but pantheism. God is not a being who lords over the universe, He *is* the universe. Creation is not His handiwork, it is a part of His very essence. Everything that takes place, whether it be two meteors colliding in space or two sparrows fighting over a mate, is merely an expression of God's will. This is really the natural conclusion of a belief in predestination: if God knows and ordains every action, then all the cosmos is but a working out of His plan. One may well ask whether this robs our human, mortal existences of any independent meaning, whether thieves and philanthropists share equally in this divine unity. It is a question that pandits and rishis have pondered for millennia, a question they will ponder for millennia to come.

The method by which a person unifies his own spirit with the divine spirit is yoga. The religious yoga of a devout Hindu has little relation to the stretching and relaxation classes which go by that name in America — about as much relation, perhaps, as receiving holy communion has to munching Triscuits: the latter action is similar, but stripped of all meaning.

Yoga is a wide range of physical and mental techniques used to liberate the soul from its fleshly prison. It was through yoga that the sages of antiquity won their fabulous boons from the gods. A young yogi I met in Nasik helped me understand a bit of what this means.

It was almost four o'clock, so the temple was full. The world was created at four in the afternoon, and one day at four in the afternoon Shiva will destroy all Creation. It is a time of day that superstitious old women dread, and more than a few others feel a bit uneasy. I was sitting just outside the temple gate when Lal approached me with an unusual question.

"Pardon me," he said, "but is it true that Americans bear what is called a 'superiority complex'?"

"Some do. Like some Indians."

"Might I inquire to which nation you belong?"

I told him I was an American and that (for what it was worth) I did not think I personally had a superiority complex, though others were free to disagree.

"Ah," he said, much relieved, "I am happy to hear this. My brother told me otherwise, but I had never met an American so I could not be certain. It would be sad if one nation believed it truly knew all answers." At first I thought he was making fun of me, but there was not a shadow of sarcasm in his voice.

He was a tall, stringy man in his late twenties, with eyes that always stared. Lal dropped down next to me and sat comfortably in a full lotus position. He taught yoga to children, he said, and was always looking for new sources of knowledge.

"The physical contortions are the easiest part," he said, "especially when an individual begins young. That is why I like to instruct children, their bodies are so flexible it is no effort for them at all."

To demonstrate, he twisted his limbs through half a dozen pretzelish poses: standing upright with one leg tucked on his opposite hip, standing on his head with the soles of his feet pressed together, lying on his back with his heels hooked over his neck. He barely broke the train of conversation when switching from one posture to the next.

"Yoga is all about developing self-control," he told me. "First it is necessary to gain mastery over one's own body, to make it do precisely what the mind wishes." The yogis of ancient times, it is said, so completely dominated their flesh that they were able to subsist on air alone, to sit without batting an eyelid for centuries. There are still confirmed cases of fakirs walking through white-hot coals without so much as blistering their toes.

"Far more important," Lal continued, "is the mastery of one's own mind. That is a thousand times as difficult, but it is what truly matters. Physical discipline is merely a prelude to mental discipline. That is what brings spiritual power, and eventually spiritual enlightenment."

He told me of his own guru, a man 108 years old who was still so strong that once, when he slapped Lal on the forehead for lack of concentration, the young yogi spent four days in bed with a throbbing headache. One hundred and eight, it should be noted, is a particularly auspicious number in Hindu numerology.

In a sense, the whole Hindu faith is a search for power. A believer seeks power over his environment by offering up Vedic prayers to the gods, by amassing positive karma through good deeds, by submitting to fate with the devotion of a bhakta. But yoga offers a more direct path. It lets diligent practitioners unlock the ultimate power, the power we all carry within.

Lal seems an unlikely candidate for Master of the Universe. Though a Brahmin, he is a wool dyer by trade. He is proud of his profession, and eagerly reached into his shoulder bag to show me swatches of fabric from his latest batch. Yoga is a hobby to which he devotes most of his free time, but he would never give up dyeing. Creating the finest shades reminds him of crafting his own karma. It is always a challenge, he said, always a puzzle, to get the colors just right.

"Nobody can escape karma," he said. "It is like trying to throw away a stone: you can toss it hard or softly, hurl it so high in the air, but still it will always fall back down to earth. You can cast it into the ocean, but the waves will bring it back to shore. A man can act however he pleases, but he cannot control the outcome of his actions."

That is where yoga comes in. We cannot alter the results of karma, but through rigid self-discipline we can prevent bad karma from accumulating in the first place. The physical side is indeed the easiest: it is not very difficult to restrain oneself from acts of murder, rape, or robbery. But to rid ourselves of the emotions at the root of these crimes — emotions like anger, lust, or greed — to expunge these thoughts from our minds, to root them out of our very souls, *that* is a hard battle indeed.

If an earnest yogi can so dominate his body as to rest comfortably on a bed of nails, by dominating his mind perhaps he can truly gain Mastery of the Universe.

I got a glimpse of the pantheistic unity of the cosmos that yogis attempt to reach at a little village in Madhya Pradesh. It was during the festival of Holi that I saw, clear as a reflection in a cold stream, the God inside us all.

On Holi, straight-faced farmhands and dour dhobis become as playful as kindergarteners. Throughout the north it is a celebration to mark the end of winter and the return of balmy days. Gray-haired aunts and white-haired grandmothers, fathers who barely know how to smile, giggling sisters, sniggling cousins, uncles almost too fat to move — all observe the holiday by dousing each other with brightly colored water.

Some throw water balloons, some shoot water pistols, most toss buckets of water tinged with dye or glittering with slivers of ground mica. Some even hurl cans of unadulterated paint. Friends, relatives, and total strangers stalk each other through the streets and inner courtyards, edging against storefronts and calculating fields of fire, shrieking with glee as they splash each other with all the colors known to man.

By midday I'd been hit enough times not to care anymore. I joined the gang of teenage boys who ruled the town's streets. They quickly showered me with blue and green dye and, once I was completely stained, welcomed me wholeheartedly into their band. Every boy's face and hands were already masked with color. We pelted all the cars, houses, and pedestrians we could find, and every victim accepted the bath with good humor. That, after all, is what the rite is all about.

For the week after Holi, most of the population of northern India goes about its business spattered with indelible splotches of paint. Clothes can be changed, but it takes many washings to rinse all the dye from one's skin and hair. Every town's walls are streaked with rainbow smudges. Even the animals are not safe — goats, cows, and dogs walk about with hides stained red, yellow, and purple, sometimes until the monsoon rains come to wash it all away.

When I got back to my room at the end of the day, I looked in the mirror and saw God staring back at me: my skin, just like the skin of Lord Rama himself, was a delicate shade of blue.

> > >

Underlying every Hindu idea is the concept of dharma, the unchangeable Order of the Universe, the divine Law which human beings can ignore at their own peril but can never thwart. The word itself defies translation. It means That Which Must Be Done, That Which Regulates the Cosmos, That Which Is Eternal, just about anything else one cares to write with First Letters Capitalized.

Dharma, which controls everything, maintains everything, is a force rather than a personality. It is occasionally anthropomorphized as a divinity (the father of the hero Yudhishthira in the epic Mahabharata) but is never actually worshiped. Only obeyed.

On an individual level a man's personal dharma is simply the way he ought to live his life. This is the basis for the entire caste system: the bulk of the Indian population is willing to accept a subservient status because of the belief that every individual has a particular function in society, a function ordained and predestined, a function that cannot and should not be changed. Indians may not accept their fate uncritically or without questioning, but (by and large) they do accept it. The dharma of a dhobi is to wash laundry, that is his path, that is the place he has been assigned in the universe. Every time he cleans a dirty undershirt, he is carrying out the holy will of God.

Most Hindus accept the doctrines of their faith — dharma, karma, yogic unity, and the rest — without worrying too much about the whys and wherefores. Few Christians, likewise, spend their time pondering the difference between transubstantiation and consubstantiation in the eucharistic host. But there is a whole other realm of Hindu belief, a speculative, metaphysical side of the religion embodied by the Upanishads. If not for this lofty, philosophical strain, the creed probably could not have survived.

C. S. Lewis once wrote that all religions must combine both "thick" and "thin." The thick aspects are the rites and rituals, the shows and ceremonies accessible to every peasant at a gut level. Without these, religion is merely an intellectual exercise with no magic or emotional pull. Christianity has the Mass, Hinduism the puja, ablutions in the Ganges, sacrifices of goats at the Kalighat temple.

The thin side is the abstract deliberation, the rational attempt to understand the workings of the universe. Without this, religion is no more than pagan witchcraft. Any faith lacking either thick or thin is destined to flounder. The logical Deism of eighteenth-century Europe, espoused by such geniuses as Voltaire, Jefferson, and Franklin, highhandedly shunned all thick elements as "superstition," and did not outlive the Enlightenment. For the same reason Unitarianism will probably never become a denomination of the masses.

On the other side of the ledger, the ancient Aryan polytheisms died out in Greece and Rome largely because they ignored the thin. Philosophy was divorced from religion, and as the intellectual elites grew more sophisticated they lost respect for the primitive pantheons. In Homer's day the gods were revered, but by the time of Aristotle and Anaxagoras they had become a pathetic joke. Aristophanes practically made a career out of poking fun at the immortals. Long before the coming of Christian monotheism, most serious thinkers throughout the Mediterranean already held their own faiths in some degree of contempt.

In India, however, the gods survived by growing up. Around

the time that Socrates argued and Democritus mocked, Hindu sages developed a speculative philosophy within the framework of the existing religion. The gods could still be taken literally by the illiterate population, but they could also be seen symbolically by the intelligentsia. The new metaphysics made no attempt to supplant the old pantheon. It filled a different need, served a different constituency, and together the two complementary strains kept Indra and Agni from joining Zeus and Hermes in the limbo of dead immortals.

It is precisely because they look for God in different places that these widely divergent camps can coexist peacefully in Hinduism. Through Vedic rites a worshiper seeks the blessings of *external* divinities, gods who reach down from heaven to aid men and women on earth. Through yoga, meditation, and study of the Upanishads, an inquiring mind searches for the *internal* divinity instead.

The God sought in the Upanishads is an all-encompassing "presence" rather than a personal deity. He (or It) is most often called Atman, the Self, the Universal Soul.

In one famous Upanishadic discourse, a young yogi asked his father to explain Atman; if He is everywhere and all-powerful, why can He never be seen or felt? The sage slowly peeled a fig and took one of the tiny seeds in his palm. He asked his son where a fig tree comes from.

"From that seed," said the boy.

The old man shook his head and split the seed open. "What do you see inside?" he asked.

"I see nothing," his son replied.

"From that nothing" said the sage, "a stout fig tree will grow. Atman is the void in the center of every seed." He then took a pitcher of water and sprinkled in a handful of salt. After it had dissolved, he told his son to drink the water and describe its taste.

"It tastes salty," said the boy.

"Show me the salt," said his father, and the other looked at his feet. "That is Atman," the old man said. "Atman is the salt which invisibly permeates the whole glass.

"Atman is within you," he said. "Find your Self, and you have found Atman."

This abstract, otherworldly quest for the One Spirit is the side of Hinduism that Westerners most commonly associate with the faith. Perhaps this is the reason so many of us find the religion difficult to understand. Anyone, Indian or Western, who claims to truly comprehend all the subtleties of the Upanishads is either a great scholar or a great fool. The vast majority of Hindus leave metaphysics to the pandits and the sadhus. This, the thinnest of thin creeds, has never been a large part of folk belief. Any search for moksha, for release from the cycle of rebirth, for spiritual union with the Universal Self — such a quest is only open to the holiest of the twice-born. Virtually all other Hindus are destined to suffer many rebirths before they can even set off on this path, and their worship is therefore more concerned with living as comfortably and honorably as possible within this Realm of Illusion.

Oddly enough, it is the thin side of the faith, the deeper, more philosophical strain, that may be most in line with our Western beliefs. I once had dinner at the home of a highly orthodox Brahmin, and when we discussed theology I could almost have been talking to an Episcopalian vicar.

Pandit Kumar, a member of a priestly jati, was a retired judge who had moved to Varanasi on leaving the bench to be closer to the faith of his clan. It was his son Sanjay who introduced me to the family guru, Baba Raghunanden Das of Ayodhya. His daughters cooked up a delicious vegetarian meal, and his sons joined me to eat it, but Pandit Kumar himself did not come in until after we had finished. He is too much of a traditionalist to dine in the presence of one who is not twice-born and had diplomatically arranged to be called away on "business" to save me from embarrassment.

"The entire universe," he said, once the curds and curries had been cleared away, "was created solely by God's infinite love. God *is* love, pure, boundless, all-encompassing love, love for every creature and every stick and stone."

I raised the medieval argument (from Aquinas? Augustine? I couldn't remember, but was sure I hadn't come up with it on my own) that if God has any love at all, the cosmos *had* to be created as an object for that love. If God wished to give, to help, to ordain (and that, both Eastern and Western creeds teach, is His very nature), then He inevitably had to establish something apart from Himself as a recipient. The very existence of Creation, then, implies the existence of a caring God.

"Yes, yes," said Pandit Kumar, "the universe had no choice

but to flow into being. And our quest, as children of love, is to reunify the divine spark inside us with the Universal Self, to let our soul rejoin its beloved parent."

I asked about the multiplicity of immortals in the Hindu pantheon (which even the metaphysical Tenth Upanishad numbers at 3,003), asked how to understand them in relation to the One God.

"God is One," Pandit Kumar said, "but He has many aspects. Even the Holy Trinity of Brahma, Shiva, and Vishnu is three separate divinities, but still one God. All the devas great and small, they are merely reflections of the One Spirit."

Like Christian angels, the profusion of Hindu deities can be taken as actual superhuman beings subservient to the One God, or they can be understood as symbolic projections of that same divinity. Either way, it is a far cry from the paganism of antiquity.

"Everything a man needs to know," said my host, "can be found somewhere in the Vedas. God *is* the Veda, He *is* the holy Word, but that was not enough. God wanted to give mankind a living example, so He incarnated as Rama and Sita. Not just as Rama, mind you, for God is neither male nor female. We call Him 'He' out of convenience, but of course there is no gender to the All-Present. So He became the perfect human couple, both man and woman, to show us how to live our lives."

Christ too is the Λογοσ, the Logos, the Word; and as the human Jesus, He too is the Word made flesh. Pandit Kumar's contention that Sita is as much a divine avatar as her husband is unusual but certainly not heretical; the great popularity of posters showing a divinity split right down the middle — half Rama and half Sita, or half Shiva and half Parvati — shows that such an abstruse belief is not limited to bookish intellectuals. Jesus, of course, had no female counterpart, but the fact that many Christian denominations now ordain women as ministers marks the fading of a two-thousand-year doctrine that only a man could be the mirror of God.

I asked Pandit Kumar if he thought the same God lay beneath Eastern and Western faiths. Like almost every Brahmin to whom I have put that question, he nodded in vigorous affirmation.

"Of course, but of course!" he said. "There is only One God anywhere — how could there be more? If Muslims and Christians were not worshiping the very same being that we worship, they would be praying to nothing, and I do not believe that is so. It is only the names that are different. We call Him by the name Shiva, Ram, Brahma, Prajapati, or perhaps Atman. You may say God, Christ, the Lord, and so forth."

He picked up a glass of water and took a sip.

"In English you call this 'water.'" he said. "As you know, in Hindi it is *pani*. The Chinese call it something else altogether. But wherever you go in all the wide world, water or *pani* is the very same substance."

In one of the Upanishads, Indra asks Prajapati where to find the One Self. Look in a vessel of water, Prajapati says, and what you see therein is Him.

Many observers have noted some superficial parallels between Hinduism and Christianity. Both trinities are made up of a Creator (God the Father and Brahma), a Spirit (the Holy Ghost and Shiva, whose presence permeates the entire cosmos) and an Incarnator (Christ and Vishnu, both of whom become human beings to save mankind). In this last Person the link is particularly striking:

Christ, as the Book of Revelations tells us, is "the Alpha and the Omega, the Start and the Finish." Krishna, perhaps the most widely revered of Vishnu's avatars, proclaims in Book Ten of the Bhagavad Gita: "I am the beginning, the middle, and the end. I am the letter A." As presented in the Gita, Krishna is far different from any previous Hindu deity. He is a personal savior, a messianic deliverer who will bring all men and women salvation if only they choose to give Him their devotion. Krishna, Christ — there is even an eerie similarity in the very names.

Both religions, perhaps more than any other two faiths, are based upon the cleansing of sin. Christians wash away their mortal taint with the water of baptism, Hindus scrub off pollution with ablutions in the Ganges and other holy rivers. The crucial difference is that Christians merely accept purification from God, while Hindus actively work to obliterate their own iniquity by building good karma. Westerners think of Hinduism as a creed of passivity, but in theological terms *we* are the passive ones and *they* the go-getters.

It would be sophistry, however, to call Christianity and Hinduism kindred faiths. They have entirely different lineages — one belongs in the family of Middle Eastern monotheisms with Islam and Judaism, the other in the clan of Asian pantheisms with Buddhism and Jainism. What similarities exist — and there are far more differences than similarities — are probably more coincidence than true convergence.

Similar or different, though, all religions are merely symbols through which man tries to understand God. All the rites and rituals, all the dogma and myth, all the stories of Abraham offering up Isaac, Christ rising from the dead, Muhammad smashing the Meccan idols, Rama battling the demons of Lanka — all are mere symbols, nothing more and nothing less. We humans have no way of comprehending God intellectually: a being of omnipotence, omniscience, and omnipresence is wholly beyond anything we can imagine.

Perhaps God lies not in the plethora of faulty symbols that men have concocted through time, but in the common reality these metaphors clumsily seek to express. Beneath it all, every faith boils down to this: there is a moral power governing the universe, a power whose primary requirements are that we return its love and treat our neighbors with kindness. As for what this power is and precisely how we can do its bidding, *that* is where the faiths diverge.

If Christianity and Hinduism, creeds about as different as any two ever practiced, can have the same core (and even some of the same symbols), then perhaps all religions do indeed seek the same God.

It is not metaphysics, however, that grabs the Indian soul. An ordinary peasant draws scant comfort from the search for Spirit or meditation on divine union. In response to the cold, dispassionate rationality of the Upanishads, there arose (as early as the first century B.C.) several highly emotional sects paying deep, gut-level devotion to Shiva or Vishnu. These bhakti cults are still the most widely practiced form of Hinduism.

In a sense, Hinduism has become a monotheistic faith with more than one Supreme God. Practitioners can be Shaivites or Vaishnavites — or even both at once. Since all Hindus accept Shiva and Vishnu as different sides of the same being, their choice of which form to honor is largely a matter of personal preference.

Almost all of the deities currently worshiped in India today are intimately associated with one of these two Supreme Gods. Kali, Durga, Parvati, and Devi — the powerful and terrible mother goddesses — are the "wives" of Shiva, but they are more accurately the female manifestations of his wrathful, destructive nature. Ganesh, the munificent god with the head of an elephant, and Kartikkaya, the indomitable god of war, are Shiva's sons. In his own form, Shiva is venerated as no Vedic god ever was: as a personal, omnipotent savior who gives his devotees everything they could wish and asks in return only unconditional love.

Vishnu also has his affiliated deities: Lakshmi, the goddess of wealth and good fortune, is his wife; Hanuman, the Monkey Prince, is the servant of his avatar Rama. But Vishnu is most commonly worshiped through his various incarnations. As the Sustainer of the holy trinity, he has taken mortal form nine times to preserve the world from destruction. In addition to his better-known avatars, such as Rama, Krishna, and Gautama the Buddha, he has saved the cosmos in the shapes of a man-boar, a man-bird, a man-lion, and a comical dwarf. In his tenth and final incarnation, yet to come, he will be a rider on a pale horse, wielding a blazing sword, freeing the world of an unholy domination.

Our world *must* be saved for us, the bhaktas hold, for nothing in life simply happens of its own accord. Everything is planned by God. In the Ramayana, when Vishnu accepts birth as Rama he bids the lesser divinities to father the entire Vanar nation to help him in his fight. An entire race is brought into being simply to help a hero defeat a demon.

The bhakta's ideal, formulated in the Bhagavad Gita, is a selfless, unreserved, unconditional adoration far above any other type of love. In theological terms it may be called *agape*. It is a love superior to that of a man for a woman, above that of a parent for a child: it is the love that only a true worshiper can have for the true God. This is a sentiment alien to the old Vedic commerce of sacrifice for blessings. Vishnu (especially in the forms of Rama and Krishna) values his devotees' hearts, not their tallies of dead goats.

The Gita offers all bhaktas an easy road to earthly happiness and eternal salvation. Where the Upanishads teach that karma can be overcome by eliminating human activity and concentrating wholly on the development of the mind and the Spirit, such a withdrawal from the mundane realities of everyday life is beyond most people's capacities. We can't all run off to the forest and spend the rest of our days in unbending meditation. The Gita says we do not have to. We can escape the results of karma simply by detaching our minds, by not caring whether we gain or lose from our actions, by steadfastly doing our individual duty without greed, hate, sorrow, or pity — so long as we do it all while placing our trust in God. Tend the crops well and leave the rest to the Almighty: it is a path of enticing simplicity.

A segment of the epic Mahabharata, the Gita takes the form of a discourse between Krishna and the hero Arjuna. On the eve of battle, Arjuna wishes to forsake all violence and live at peace with his enemy. The god talks him out of it. He is a warrior, Krishna reminds him, and his divinely ordained purpose is to kill other men.

If every human action is part of God's plan, we do not sin by carrying out His will. By recognizing that we act purely as His agents, that all our deeds are merely Him working through us, we become partners in His grand design. Only when we try to thwart God's strategy by ignoring our appointed duties, or when we foolishly claim our acts (and their inevitable karma) as our own — only then do we suffer just punishment for our unavoidable iniquities.

Krishna persuades Arjuna to trust and to kill. In Rama's very first childhood battle, he is taught the same lesson by his saintly mentor. At the start of the Ramayana, during the prince's martial training, he is attacked by a dreadful demoness. The rishi Vishvamitra tells Rama to slaughter the Rakshasi without compassion: "You must not shrink from killing her simply from the consideration that she is a woman," the sage says. "An act may be cruel or sinful, yet it should be performed by a ruler for the protection of his subjects. This is the eternal rule of conduct."

Rama, unable to overcome his inherent kindness, merely chops off her nose and ears. But the demoness keeps charging, harder and harder, despite the arrows, until the prince has no choice but to shoot a bolt straight through her heart. The gods reward Rama for abandoning chivalry by showering him with divine arms. He is merely God's tool, so he commits no sin.

The bhakti cult of Krishna, unlike that of Rama, goes beyond *agape* to *eros*. In layman's terms, lust. Actual devotion to Krishna is based less on the Gita than on the Brahmavaivarta Purana, a collection of myths celebrating the god's idyllic life as a cowherd beloved by legions of beauteous milkmaids. Even after he marries Radha, the most dazzling of the gopis, Krishna still must tend to all the other maidens' libidinous needs. On one particular evening he satisfies 900,000 women, turning himself into 900,000 men to accomplish an amatory feat that would strain the powers even of an exceptionally vigorous immortal.

Some humorless fundamentalists try to portray the gopis' love for Krishna as a platonic one, a devotion untainted by any trace of carnality. Sure. The texts themselves are sometimes unabashedly frank, detailing each of the gymnastic positions favored by the god and his lovers, even chronicling the number of their orgasms. Nobody who has read Part IV, Chapter 15, of the Brahmavaivarta Purana (to take but one lengthy example) could possibly say that Krishna and the gopis were just good friends.

But the legends are not pornography, the stories are not told to arouse giggly concupiscence. They are holy writ, the stuff of earnest faith. The descriptions of divine orgies are not meant as titillation, but as metaphor. We debased humans cannot possibly comprehend the pure, spiritual bliss of God's true love. It is something infinitely more powerful than any emotion we have ever encountered. To help understand just what such a love might be like, the bhaktas evoke the most intense (and most fleeting) bliss that mere mortals are likely to know — unbridled, unabashed, sweat-soaked copulation.

Nor is this carnality merely the safe, respectable cohabitation of wedlock. Krishna's exploits are doubly adulterous: not only is he married himself, but the gopis are all wives of cuckolded cowherds. The very illicitness of their union serves to emphasize the passion. A bhakta's love must know no limits, must be powerful enough to overwhelm any convention, law, or taboo. We must be willing to surrender every scrap of honor, virtue, and self-respect to our Lord, to strip our souls bare, to offer ourselves up without holding anything back. We must become spiritual sluts for God. And the reward for our total submission is unimaginable ecstasy for all eternity.

There is an Indian expression to describe a man who chases skirts when his wife isn't watching. "He is Rama at home," the adage goes, "but Krishna in the street." The prudish paladin of the Ramayana and the lusty libertine of the Brahmavaivarta Purana are both guides for life, both manifestations of the same God.

Not all bhakti sects have the erotic intensity of the Krishna cult, but all seek the same transcendent emotion. Even the more staid devotees of Rama are sometimes moved to fever pitch. On

Rama's birthday in early April, the pitch was so feverish that I was nearly stampeded by a mob of ardent faithful burning with a passion for prayer.

The town of Nasik, about a hundred miles out of Bombay, is believed to be the place where Rama, Sita, and Lakshman made their ashram in the Dandak forest. Worship of the Ayodhyan hero has been strong here for centuries. For lodgings I chose the Dasarastha Hotel over the Rama Guest House, and I ate at a little restaurant across the street from the Hanuman Saw Mill.

Pilgrims from all over Maharashtra were gathering at the Temple of the Black Rama to celebrate the festival of Rama-navami. So many of them had flocked to the shrine that riot police stood about anxiously, their vicious bamboo lathis at the ready. Several dozen schoolchildren in paramilitary white uni-forms with red berets regulated the flow of human traffic, glee-fully blowing their silver whistles with only occasional pauses to fill their lungs with more air. Children and whistles, I mused with my fingers stuck in my ears, should always be kept far apart.

In the courtyard a guru was haranguing his audience to model their lives after those of Rama and Sita. Beneath the overhang of a stone portico, a small group of elderly men and women sat singing hymns to the accompaniment of drums, flutes, and tiny brass cymbals. Peasant women, in from the countryside for the big day, circumambulated the mandir while tossing finely ground mica into the sky.

Rama was born, legend says, at the stroke of high noon. As twelve o'clock approached, the crowd grew noisier. Kids smashed coconut husks on the steps of the shrine. A low mur-mur of "Sri Ram, Sri Ram" welled up through the masses. The worshipers pressed forward — men at one of the temple's doors, women at the other — surging ahead as the sun crept slowly closer to its zenith, each person aching to be the first one inside.

At the stroke of noon, drums deep within the shrine began to roll like thunder. The pack of devotees let out a joyous shout, tossed flower petals and little globules of white sugar. The para-military prepubescents gave up any attempt to maintain order and blew their shrill whistles with gleeful abandon. Police guard-ing the temple doors let worshipers in three at a time.

The closer one got to the top step, the tighter the bottle-neck grew. Men shamelessly squirmed and shoved, pushed and poked, jostled and jabbed to get in front of their comrades. It was more brutal than a Tokyo subway. For twenty minutes I bore the blows with as much good humor as I could muster, but then I started to hit back. An elbow gouged my kidney, and I responded with a fist to the offending man's jaw. A knee slammed into my abdomen, and I answered with a backhand strike to a stranger's solar plexus. By the time I reached the door my blood was up, I found myself perversely savoring the roughness of the melee. When I entered the holy sanctum to march past the looming black icon of Rama, I had to choke back a hearty obscenity just leaving my lips.

There is much to be said for the cathartic effect of an occasional brawl. Controlled mayhem such as slam-dancing or tackle football can purge the soul of much pent-up violence. But the Kala Rama temple (it seemed to me) was not an appropriate place. Even as I savored the rush of adrenalin that accompanies both giving and taking pain, I felt ashamed to be a part of the scrum. Beating up on other people solely to gain entry to the house of God — there could hardly be a greater hypocrisy.

And yet in a sense the struggle outside the temple was every bit as much a religious rite as the offering of flowers at the altar. A bhakta's faith is no shallow, safe credo. It is a flame burning deep within the soul. The near-riot on the mandir's steps in Nasik served to stoke this flame, to rekindle its ardor, to build it into a fervent blaze of holy passion.

Nasik also boasts the very cave from which Rama's wife was abducted by the King of Demons. Well, not the cave itself, precisely, but the spot where the cave would have been if Ravana had not scooped up the whole mountainside (in one variant tradition) and carried it off to Lanka. Beneath a two-story house of brick and yellow plaster is Sita's Cavern, a tiny chamber deep in the earth, of dubious antiquity but indubitable holiness.

It is reached by squeezing down a steep tunnel much like those of the pharaonic tombs at Luxor, then crawling through a level passage on hands and knees, then sliding on one's stomach (unless one is a very tiny person indeed) through a rough-hewn chute with the circumference of a dog-kennel door. Sita's Cavern demonstrates the ecumenical unity of India's two rival bhakti cults: the airless den itself holds three black Vaishnavite icons of Rama, Sita, and Lakshman, but the room upstairs contains a shrine to the Shaivite god Ganesh, and an antechamber in the twisty rabbit warren sports a lingam holy to Shiva.

Outside the Sita Gupha, a Hindu heretic showed me a photograph of God. It was a grainy enlargement of what appeared to be a spark of light, and the man assured me that this was an actual snapshot of the Almighty. He did not tell me whether he had taken the picture himself, or how the photographer had persuaded his model to pose for the session. But he did pull out a complex diagram demonstrating that the human soul is actually a small organ in the brain, located midway between the thalamus and the cerebellum.

He wore a Brahminical janneu-thread and a wide, white grin, and he spoke in a high, squeaky voice. He said he was a cosmetics salesman by trade, and a Shaivite bhakta by faith. I label him a heretic not for his photo and chart — such oddities put him outside the mainstream but not outside the pale. I call him a heretic because, in our theological discussion, he stoutly maintained that Shiva is the Sustainer in the Hindu Trinity and Vishnu the Destroyer.

"How can that be?" I asked. "It is Shiva who will destroy the universe at the end of our era, Shiva who has destroyed it countless times already. It is Shiva who wreaks devastation in the forms of Kali, Rudra, and Durga."

"Yes, yes," he said, "but primarily Shiva grants boons to those who worship him, gives blessings to all who ask. It is Vishnu who comes down to earth to kill: as Rama in the Ramayana, he kills the demon Ravana; as Krishna in the Mahabharata, he kills the entire Kaurava army. He is a great god, but his place is only to destroy evil."

I refrained from reminding him that Krishna never kills anybody in the Mahabharata but merely urges others on to their fated slaughters. As an outsider challenging a believer about his own religion, I knew I already sounded quite enough of a smart-aleck.

"What about his incarnation as Vamana?" I asked instead. According to legend, Vishnu once saved the world in the form of a dwarf. A demon had won possession of all the earth as a boon, possession that was destined never to be wrested from him by force. Various gods blustered and threatened, but they knew they were powerless to overthrow what dharma had ordained. Vishnu assumed the unassuming avatar of Vamana and went to the demon as a harmless, jolly buffoon. He asked a small favor, a trifle really, just a grant of as much land as he could tread in three dwarfish steps. The demon, proud of his own generosity, was happy to agree. So Vishnu-as-Vamana took three paces that spanned the entire world, and sustained the cosmos for another age.

"Ah, yes," the heretic replied, "but what about Vishnu the Maiden?" I hadn't heard that story, so he went on. "You see, one time a Rakshasa prayed to Shiva for a boon, for the power to turn anything to ash with a touch. Shiva granted the wish — for he is the most generous and most giving of all divinities. It was foolish, but no matter.

"In any event, as soon as the blessing was given, that treacherous demon tried to touch Shiva! What an ungrateful wretch, eh? But Shiva was too clever for him, shrunk down to the size of a flea and hid inside a mango. None of the gods could fight the demon, for he could turn any of them to dust with a fingertip."

For a moment his voice was drowned out by the cries of vendors from the market across the street, bazaaris selling peppers and peanuts, lentils and licorice, cloves and coriander, fiery red watermelons and sober red dyes for the robes of Shaivite swamis.

"That is when Vishnu took on the shape of a beautiful maiden," the heretic continued. "He — or perhaps I should say 'she' — danced with the Rakshasa, teased the rascal unmercifully, always sliding up close and then darting away just before the poor fellow could touch her. That is often the way of women, is it not?

"In any case, Vishnu led the demon to imitate every motion she made in the dance. She twirled about, the demon twirled about. She kicked her heel, the demon kicked his heel. She touched her head, the demon touched his head — and immediately turned to ash. So you see, even though it is always for a good cause, Vishnu is the Destroyer after all."

The Hindu faith is broad enough to encompass an enormous range of heterodox beliefs. "Heresy" is a term that has little actual meaning in India, because (apart from acceptance of the sanctity of the Vedas) there is nothing even approaching a unified, cohesive Hindu doctrine. The man outside the Sita Gupha held a view outside the tradition of his religion, but he was a heretic only in a Western sense. Most Hindus would see him merely as a devout bhakta, a misguided one perhaps, but still a soul walking steadily down the path that leads to God.

➤ ➤ ➤

At dawn, Rameshwaram is already alive. The housewives here start the day by tossing water on the dust outside their doorsteps and decorating the damp ground with geometric patterns of sprinkled white powder. Their husbands have already left to set up their stalls of amulets and charms. Most of the people bustling through the darkened streets, however, are not inhabitants but pilgrims. To Vaishnavite and Shaivite bhaktas alike this is perhaps the holiest town outside of Varanasi. This is the piece of Indian soil closest to Lanka, the place where Rama prayed to the Lord of the Ocean, the spot from which he built his fabulous bridge and marched his army of monkeys across the sea to make war on the Demon King. This is also (according to one later tradition) the site where Rama, avatar of Vishnu the Almighty, bowed down and worshiped Shiva.

Looming over the whole village, a huge black mountain against the fading blackness of the sky, is the Ramanathaswamy Temple. From someplace deep within float the chanted melodies of the day's first puja. Later that morning I would wander through the mandir's Thousand-Pillared Hall: past idlers sleeping, eating, or gossiping beneath columns carved in the shape of divinities with crocodile eyes and tiger tails; past attendants painting fresh designs on the leathery foreheads of temple elephants, who reach out their trunks to accept donations from bemused worshipers; past altars to Nandi (the very sort of Golden Bull against which the Old Testament and the Qur'an both fulminate), each pair of gilded horns garlanded with flowers whose scent, it is said, can intoxicate a true believer as quickly as strong wine.

The most interesting part of Ramanathaswamy Temple, however, is a life-sized crèche. It shows Rama and Sita praying before a Shiva-lingam by the shore of the ocean while monkeys and demons look on in reverent awe. Later that morning I would watch pilgrims kneel before the shrine to leave banana-leaf baskets filled with coconut husks, persimmons, and red-petaled flowers; I would watch worshipers worshiping Rama worshiping Shiva. But now, at dawn, the sights of the temple remained locked behind great wooden doors, only their sounds drifting eerily through the morning air.

At dawn the seaside barbers of Rameshwaram give their first shaves of the day. They do not own scissors, only straight razors. Their customers are almost all pilgrims, so there is little demand for a purely cosmetic trim. The dirt floor of the long, frond-roofed hut is thickly littered with black and gray hair. When I entered, two barbers were already at work on a pair of fresh scalps, whose owners chatted together as casually as if they'd been sitting side by side on a bus.

A signboard gave the price list: "For Chin, 5 Rupees. For Head, 8 Rupees." I decided to save the extra three rupees. Not knowing the Tamil for "*Don't* cut all my hair off, don't even *think* of it, *just* a shave, that's *all*," I merely rubbed my half-week cheek bristles with vigor. The barber splashed some cold water on my face and began scraping away with a rusty straight-edge of great antiquity that had already depilated countless crania. It was not the most comfortable shave I've ever had, but he did not leave so much as a single nick.

At dawn the bathers in the warm Southern Sea make their first daily ablutions. Whole families shaved bald by the barbers smear their heads with ocher sandalwood paste to keep off the rising sun, then wade into the ocean to pray. Old tribal women with rubbery earlobes stretched down to their chins by the weight of heavy earrings, penitents bearing the marks of their individual sects daubed boldly on their foreheads, children splashing in the gentle waves — all bathe side by side.

A pandit leads fifteen pilgrims in a series of chants, then takes them knee-deep into the sea. Frail grandfathers who needed no razor and pretty teenage girls blushing at their baldness all scoop up handfuls of salty water to pour over their smooth heads. On the beach, two Brahmins and their wives knot the hems of their robes together, and each pair builds a lingam out of sand. Once they have blessed it with prayers and flowers, each couple picks the holy mound up and dumps it into the ocean.

After the Ramayana's final battle, a popular southern legend has it, Rama and Sita performed a puja ceremony to thank Shiva for their victory. Rama sent Hanuman off to the Himalayas to bring back a lingam for the rite, but the monkey could not return by the appointed hour. Sita, unconcerned, built a lingam of her own. She molded the phallic icon out of sand and bowed down beside her husband to offer prayers before it.

Does this act, as some fundamentalist Shaivites claim, indicate that Vishnu is an inferior deity to Shiva, that Rama is not the Lord of the Universe? I think not. What it says to me (as a layman and a non-Hindu, but as someone with a keen interest in the subject) is that all the deities worshiped by man are different faces of the same One God, and that this One God is a part and parcel of each of us. Maybe that is what the yogis of Upanishadic times meant when they spoke of "realizing the godhead" within each of our souls. If a human incarnation of God can bow to a divine manifestation of God without sacrificing either his humanity or his divinity — if a man like Rama can both pray to God and *be* God at the very same time — so too, perhaps, can we all.

Ten
WAR

EN billion battle cries shook the earth. Every monkey and every demon let out a wild whoop of blood lust and charged headlong into the fray. All the weapons invented by man or by monster hacked and chopped and swung and sliced: discus, spear, arrow and sword, axe, hammer, mace and club, trident and dagger, javelin and lance, *bhalla*-weapon, *prasha*-weapon, *gada-*, *tumara-*, and *shakti*-weapons, every instrument ever devised for the dealing of death.

Soon vast stretches of the ground were soggy with spilled blood, and the air was so full of dust kicked up by the melee that warriors could no longer tell friend from enemy and had to ask each opponent his race before striking a blow.

The number of corpses was enormous, but it was only a fraction of the number actually killed. Rakshasa soldiers ate their victims as fast as they mowed them down, and Ravana had given orders that all of his own dead be thrown into the sea to keep the enemy from joying at their reckoning. Those who could see the world of spirits might have watched Yama, the God of Death, cast his thread like a noose around the necks of millions and drag each man's soul kicking and screaming off to the nether regions.

The Vanar general Neela squared off against the Rakshasa general Prahasta and killed him with a massive stone. Akampana showered Hanuman with arrows like a torrent of monsoon rain, but the monkey struck him down with an uprooted tree. Atikaya, a close kinsman of the Rakshasa king, came at Lakshman wearing impenetrable armor given by Brahma, so the Ayodhyan prince slew him with a Brahma-arrow whose point was an all-penetrating diamond.

From far in the distance, Rama spied Ravana. In the tide of

battle the Demon King was a swirling eddy of destruction. He moved forward at a furious pace, obliterating everything in his path. A casually flung arrow of his sent the Vanar monarch, Sugriva, crawling away in agony. General Neela shrunk himself down to the size of an insect to escape the demon's wrath, but Ravana roasted his hide with a quill of fire. Hanuman jumped in front of the Rakshasa, smacked him full in the jaw with all the cyclonic power of the Wind God's son. Ravana only laughed.

"After such a punch," Hanuman said, "it is an insult both to me and to my divine father that you are still alive."

"Hah! Hah! Hah!" boomed the demon, and floored the ape with a thunderbolt crack of his fist.

Lakshman drew his chariot to a halt.

"When you are done playing around with monkeys," he spat, "come and fight with a man."

Ravana fired off a hailstorm of arrows, but Lakshman parried them with *khura, ardhachandra,* and *bhalla* weapons. He shot back three flaming bolts of his own, which pierced the demon's neck and made him woozy with pain. Ravana got out his Brahma-discus, enormous and gore-caked and clanking with bells. He hurled it straight at Lakshman's chest, and the prince fell backward into the red mud. But as the Demon King grabbed the limp legs of his supine victim and prepared to drag him back to the city, he felt a looming shadow block the sun from his neck. He looked up into the face of Rama himself.

"You have fought bravely," the Ayodhyan said, "and it is too bad that I must kill you. But right now you are wearied from combat, and it would not be just for us to fight. Go home, salve your wounds, and get a good night's sleep. Tomorrow, once you are fit and well rested, come back for your death."

Ravana flew back to his city in a magic chariot built by the craftsman of the gods. He stormed across the moat filled with sharks and crocodiles, through the high golden wall encrusted with gems, and into the palace built upon a thousand pillars.

"Wake Kumbhakarna," he ordered his chamberlain.

Kumbhakarna, the Demon King's brother, had been asleep for half a year. He was enormous, as huge as a tall mountain, too vast to fit inside the palace's largest audience hall. He slumbered in a cavern outside of town, and the servants sent to fetch him were tossed against the cave walls by the force of his snoring.

They struck at his chest with fists, clubs, and maces, but they could not wake the giant. They blew conch shells and trumpets, they pulled at his bristly hair, bit his nose, poured boiling water into his ears, all in vain. Not until they brought in ten thousand bull elephants to trample on his limbs did Kumbhakarna start to stir.

His mighty yawn blew the men and elephants clear out of his lair. He blinked his red eyes, and the servants brought in cart-loads of buffaloes, deer, and boars, with two thousand vats of fresh blood to wash it down. Kumbhakarna devoured it all in a matter of minutes.

From the day of his birth Kumbhakarna had devoured every-thing in his reach. Animals, men, Rakshasas, everything. The gods feared that the earth would soon be depopulated, so they prayed to Lord Brahma, and Brahma put the giant to sleep. But Ravana also prayed to Brahma and reminded the Creator that Kumbhakarna was His own grandson. All he asked was that his brother's sleep not be permanent, and Brahma granted the re-quest: Kumbhakarna could break his hibernation for one day out of every six months.

He thundered out of his cavern, shaking the very earth with every footstep, and plodded toward the battlefield. The journey would have taken a horseman on a swift mount all afternoon, but Kumbhakarna made it in six great paces. When he reached the Rakshasa lines, he was stopped by Indrajit, King Ravana's magician son.

"Wait, Uncle," said the sorcerer. "Me first."

Indrajit wore gloves of blasphemous cowhide, he spat in the faces of gods and got away with it. Once (empowered by a boon from Rudra) he had even taken Indra himself prisoner, releasing him from captivity only as a favor to Lord Brahma. In return the Master of Creation had given him the blessing of invisibility and the gift of magic.

Ravana's son strode into battle at the head of a corps of picked soldiers, arrogant demons riding on elephants, tigers, giant scor-pions, mules, camels, vultures, snakes, boars, lions, and jackals. He struck down the Bear King, Jamvuvan, the Vanar heir, An-gada, and several million apish infantrymen.

Rama, having just restored his brother to health with a potent balm from the Himalayas, watched his men dropping like har-vested wheat, slain by a warrior who was not there. The Ayodhyan fitfully twanged his bow, but he could not find a target. And then, without warning, he and Lakshman fell victim to the demon's spell:

Indrajit showered them with naga-weapons, arrows that turned into venomous serpents just before they hit their mark. The nagas took great bites of the heroes' flesh, injected their poison deep, coiled themselves around every limb to hold the pair immobile. Rama and Lakshman lay helpless on the ground, half-drowning in their own blood, captives of the magic net of snakes.

Vibhishan, Hanuman, and the other warriors formed a circle to defend their master, and Indrajit sped away laughing a ghostly laugh.

"He needs time to replenish his sorcery," said Vibhishan, who could see his invisible nephew but was not powerful enough to challenge him. "He will soon be back."

Rama and Lakshman writhed in agony under the *naga-pasha,* and all the strength of the Vanar host could not rip the snakes off their tortured bodies.

"When we are free," Lakshman grunted through his gritted teeth, "I will slaughter every Rakshasa on this whole damned island."

"No," said Rama, still just barely smiling despite his unbearable pain, "it is not right to kill a whole race for the sins of one man. With the death of Ravana, this butchery will end."

Indrajit returned, this time visible to all who cared to see. He was dragging Sita by her long black hair. Before Rama's powerless eyes, he unsheathed his vicious sword and slit her delicate neck.

Every ape and every bear jumped forward to grab him, but he was already gone. Sita's corpse vanished with him. The two brothers strained against the net of snakes with every muscle but could not loosen even one coil.

"I'll send you to the special Hell reserved for woman-slayers," Hanuman shouted to the empty air. "There you will be shunned and abused even by the poisoners of wells and the murderers of Brahmins."

Lakshman stopped his struggling, and slowly began to cry.

"There is no justice," he moaned. "There is no dharma. There is no reward for virtue, no punishment for vice. If this can happen, then religion means nothing at all. We all should cast off right and wrong, just pile up booty, live by rape and plunder. If such a thing can happen, there is no meaning to life."

Rama wanted to dissuade him, to restore his faith, but no words arose from his heart.

Vibhishan spoke and put their fears to rest. "It was only an illusion," he said, "merely a magical trick. Ravana would not allow Sita to be killed — he has risked everything he possesses for her. This is just a ploy to gain time, while Indrajit prepares his final sacrifice of invincibility."

At that moment all the troops felt a cool breeze across their backs, from the wingbeats of a bird so immense it filled the sky. The bird was Garuda, the eagle avatar of Vishnu. At its approach the serpents of the naga-pasha slithered away in terror, for the eagle is the sole nemesis of the snake.

"Who are you?" Rama asked reverently of his deliverer.

"Do not ask who I am," the bird replied. "You will know me soon enough. Understand only this: in saving you I also save myself, and in saving you I save the world." He flew away, but this time his wings did not stir even a particle of dust.

Kumbhakarna the giant came out at a leisurely, relentless amble, assaulting the earth with each massive step. He scooped up and swallowed everything in his path, Vanar and Rakshasa alike, all just food for his rumbling stomach.

Hanuman leapt high in the air to pour stones and logs on the demon, but Kumbhakarna casually swatted him down like a summer gnat. Hanuman crashed to the ground and began vomiting blood.

Neela, Anganda, and their toughest band of stalwarts all attacked the giant at once, but their strongest blows felt to him like a gentle caress. He waved them away as if shooing off insects too puny even to kill. Sugriva hurled a mighty boulder, but the rock splintered harmlessly against the Rakshasa's cliff of a chest.

Lakshman stepped before him. "When you are done playing around with —"

Before he could finish, Kumbhakarna had contemptuously swept him out of the way with the back of his hand. His next bit of meat, he had promised himself, would be Rama himself.

Rama, for his part, did not waste time with idle boasts. He strung his bow with two wind-arrows, which cut off the giant's hands faster than thought. Two quills with blades like scimitars hewed away Kumbhakarna's legs above the knee. The towering demon screamed as he fell, and Rama filled his gaping mouth with arrows. His severed head knocked down a section of the city wall, and his trunk tumbled into the ocean to create tidal waves on the far Indian shore.

Lakshman, meanwhile, had gone hunting for Indrajit. With the defector Vibhishan as his guide, he found the invisible sorcerer. Indrajit was within minutes of completing his incantations, a rite that would make him unchallengeable in all the Five Worlds. He had lit his sacrificial fire on the field of battle, offered up a pure black goat, and watched as Agni, the God of Fire, consumed the oblation to bear it up to Heaven. As the magician prepared to utter the rite's final words, Lakshman issued his challenge.

"How dare you?" Indrajit cried. "I will incinerate you all, like a bonfire reducing cotton to ashes." He saw his uncle Vibhishan in the chariot and understood how Lakshman had seen through his invisibility.

"Traitor!" he shrieked. "To fight against one's own race, king, and family — what fouler deed could a man commit? Even if my father were the vilest criminal ever born, it would still be my duty — and yours — to stand by his side."

"Justice knows no family," Vibhishan said priggishly before his nephew cut him down with a hundred arrows.

Indrajit took to his own chariot and whipped his horses into a frenzy. "Not so brave now, eh?" he mocked Lakshman. "Come fight me now, without your hired Rakshasa eyes."

He circled around and around, filling the prince with sharp quills.

"Your arrows are gentle," Lakshman gasped. "They feel good against my skin. Please, send me more."

He could not see Indrajit, but he could hear the creak of the demon's carriage wheels, the beat of his horses' hooves, the twang of his bowstring, the rasp of his hot breath. Lakshman cleared his mind of all other thoughts, filtered out all the other sounds of battle, blocked out the pain of the bolts ripping straight through his torso every second. He closed his eyes and concentrated until he could single out Indrajit's wheels, horses, bow, and breath from all the other wheels, horses, bows, and breaths, and then he began to fight back.

Indrajit fired an arrow given by the god Yama, and Lakshman splintered it with one from the god Kuvera. He shot back a Varuna-weapon, which the magician deflected with a dart from Rudra. For hours they exchanged blow and counterblow. Then Lakshman took out his most powerful missile, the very arrow with which Indra had once defeated the army of the Asuras and established Aryan dominion across the whole world. With Indra's own instrument he decapitated Indra's captor.

➤ ➤ ➤

Overfed vultures perched on Ravana's flagstaff. They had been feasting on his victims since the battle began, and the Demon King laughed with confidence when he saw them. They would have fresh meat very soon, he thought, very soon. The scavenger birds themselves cared nothing for the duel's outcome. Either way they would be fed.

"Let us begin," said Ravana.

"Indeed," Rama replied.

The Rakshasa fired off a volley of bolts with blades shaped like the mouths of lions and tigers, like the heads of vultures and hawks. The prince shot back Agni-weapons, arms of fire: some flared like bonfires, some like meteors, some like planets, and some blazed with the brilliance of the sun. Ravana shot naga-weapons, and Rama responded with Garuda-weapons, which turned to eagles and grasped the bile-spitting snakes in their talons.

The duelists drew closer and took out heavier armaments. The King of the Rakshasas hurled his twelve-belled Brahma-discus with the force of a reaper, but Rama caught it and broke it over his knee. Ravana flung a triple Shula-trident of black steel, and Rama shattered it with a shakti sent by Indra. All the other warriors stopped their purposeless combat and gathered side by side to watch the only battle that mattered.

Again and again Rama hacked off his enemy's ten heads, and each time another ten sprouted in their place. Again and again Ravana slashed his enemy's blue-green flesh, but even when all his aquamarine skin was stained red with blood, Rama continued battling on. They fought for a day and a night and a day. At the second dusk, both equally exhausted, they agreed to withdraw until the next morning.

That night, as Rama prepared to collapse into merciful sleep, Maharishi Agastya came before him in a vision. The maharishi, who had turned Rama from a wandering hermit back into a warrior and given him the gift of divine arms, now came bearing one more gift.

"What I have for you," he said, "is a weapon that will assure you of victory."

Rama bowed his head and held out his hands to receive the sword, spear, or mace.

"Not that sort of weapon," Agastya said. "You have plenty of those already, and what good have they done? The weapon I bring you is more powerful by far. It is a piece of knowledge, and one you already know."

Rama looked confused, as well he might.

"This whole war," the sage went on, "has been a conflict of one divinity against another: the discus of Brahma against the dart of Rudra, Agni's javelin against Varuna's axe, the gift of god against the gift of god. Futile, a waste of time."

Rama could not argue. For all his slaughter, Sita was still locked tightly in his enemy's dungeon.

"The cosmos is not truly ruled by a pack of squabbling deities. It merely appears that way to us mortals, when we look at the world and see its seemingly meaningless anarchy. But behind all the faces, behind all the stories, all the gods are but One God. God is Brahma, He is Vishnu, and He is Shiva. He is the Sun God, the Wind God, the Fire God, the Water God. He is Yama, the God of Death, and He is Prajapati, the God of Creation."

The maharishi looked into his pupil's eyes.

"That God," he said, "is also you yourself. He is me as well, and every other living being, but at the moment He is most directly you, Prince Rama of Ayodhya. He is called by many names in many lands, worshiped under many different images, but what does a name or an image matter? Know that all the gods of the world are One, know that the One God is also you, and this knowledge will give you the power to do anything you wish."

He raised Rama up from the ground.

"If it makes you more comfortable," said Agastya, "think of this wisdom as a weapon, the most devastating and wonderful weapon ever forged. Think of it as the all-conquering Arrow of God."

➤ ➤ ➤

At dawn both armies massed for the final duel. The man bowed to the demon, and the demon bowed to the man. Then Rama thought one word of prayer, and the Arrow of God sliced through Ravana's heart.

The epic battle of the Ramayana is still being fought in Lanka today. Vanars and Rakshasas — Tamils and Sinhalese — are at this very moment engaged in mutual slaughter. Their war is no chivalrous contest, no game of glory. It is not a noble clash of good and evil, nor even a righteous struggle between equally honorable foes. It is only a chaotic, bloody melee of fear and betrayal and inhuman brutality. Perhaps it all was different in the days of legend. Or perhaps, at its heart, this is the very nature of war.

Like Ravana's fight with Rama, the Sri Lankan civil strife grew out of blind arrogance and lust for power rather than deep-seated hatred. The two races had often sparred over the centuries, but for several generations prior to the conflict they had lived in relative harmony. Only a common greed for the political spoils of independence set them at each other's throats. And as in the mythical battle, once weapons were drawn they could not be resheathed without drawing blood.

Sri Lankans are naturally not as tied to the Ramayana as their subcontinental cousins, but links to the epic run deep nonetheless. Pilgrims still visit Sita Eliya (the site of our heroine's captivity), the islet near Manaar where Hanuman alit, and a hill near Galle that is believed to have been thrown there by the Monkey God in his rage. But the strongest tie of all is the very land itself: Lanka was a battleground then, it is a battleground now, it has been a battleground for most of the time in between.

Death for death, body for body, Sri Lanka is one of the bloodiest spots in the world today. The nation has fewer inhabitants than Mexico City, but in the three years prior to my visit some 30,000 people had been slain. This may not match the carnage of the wars of larger countries, but for a tiny island like Lanka it spells utter chaos. During that period the body count was far higher than those of Lebanon, Cyprus, and Northern Ireland put together.

During much of the past decade the land trembled under

an eight-way shootout: government troops, right-wing death squads, Sinhalese terrorists, at least three separate Tamil armies, a Muslim militia, and an invading force sent by the Indian military fought a running battle of each-against-all. At times the entire country was a free-fire zone.

By 1990 this anarchic donnybrook had weeded out all but the two heartiest contenders. The government crushed the terrorists and then disbanded its covertly supported death squads. The Muslim militias dissolved. The Liberation Tigers of Tamil Eelam sent the Indian troops packing, and with them all rival Tamil bands. For thirteen months a cease-fire between these two held, and all Lankans breathed a collective sigh of relief. But war is not often the sort of game that ends in a draw. It goes on and on, not until one side has won, but until the other realizes it has lost. When I arrived in Sri Lanka, the land was reveling in a rare moment of peace. By the time I left it had fallen yet again into business as bloody usual.

In the Ramayana, heroes duel with fantastic weapons sent by the gods. Every Agni-dart and Rudra-trident is a boon bestowed by a deity upon a warrior who has merited it by diligent penance. The greater a soldier's piety, the more devastating his divine arsenal. This fundamental justice makes epic war a trial of virtue rather than mere violence, perhaps even makes it a fair and righteous way to settle earthly wrongs.

Today, of course, any link between military prowess and moral purity is mere coincidence. Lanka's warriors have their own miraculous arms: laser-sighted sniper's rifles, wire-guided missiles, plastic explosives nearly as fearsome as any Brahma-shakti. The invading Indian army even had at its disposal the region's only Atomic Arrow of God. The tools of war have lost none of their puissance since legendary times, but the men who wield them are no longer paladins.

No two rival bands of wolves, chimpanzees, or humans can share precisely the same stretch of jungle, and the island of Lanka is a small jungle indeed. The bestial savagery of modern combat should come as no surprise: when we go to war we shed our thin skin of humanity, because in our muscle and sinew we humans are still savage beasts.

➤ ➤ ➤

The Brigadier, a friend of a friend who put me up for a night, lives in a small southern town. He is a big, hearty, jovial fellow, the model of a generous host, and a man who has committed unspeakable crimes. He knows this, he admits it, and if the need arose he would do it all again.

"You can't fight guerrillas by the Marquess of Queensberry rules," he said. "In war you must do what you have to in order to win, to survive. Once the firing starts, all those pretty rules go right out the window. You set aside morality until the fighting is over, and only then can you take the law back. Because if your brutal enemy is the one who wins, neither law nor morality will *ever* be allowed to return."

The Brigadier described his career thus: a lawyer by profession, a government soldier by necessity, a lay priest by election. He considers himself a lawyer first. After helping crush a radical Sinhalese insurrection in 1971, he had personally defended in court the very same terrorists he'd captured in the field.

"Like John Adams," I suggested. "He was a leader of the American movement for independence but served as defense attorney for British soldiers charged with the Boston Massacre."

"Yes, quite," said the Brigadier, not at all certainly. "You must annihilate the foe," he said, his voice more sure, "not let up until he is destroyed, but then (and only then) you must rehabilitate him. To hold a grudge is merely to perpetuate the cycle of violence. Must be generous in victory. MacArthur (a fine general, that, I shook his hand once, in my youth), he soundly thrashed the Japs, but once the war ended he helped them rebuild."

My host brought out a bottle of Scotch. Not Ceylonese Scotch, mind you, but actual Scots Scotch. The Macallan, no less. I was quite pleased. Not merely because it had been months since I'd consumed any alcohol which hadn't been brewed in somebody's back yard, but also because I hoped it would let the Brigadier tell me his whole story. He had done more in the war than just his soldierly duty, that was clear not from what he said but from what he did not say. When I asked him for the raw details of his campaigns, he always subtly changed the subject. I didn't relish the prospect of trying to drink a 220-pound infantry veteran under the table to get him talking, but at least the liquor wouldn't be rotgut.

After the fourth tumbler, I asked the Brigadier how he could reconcile his military service with his duties as a Buddhist alderman. He admitted no inconsistency between a violent life and a doctrine of nonviolence. "We must defend our religion," he said, "or we will have no religion left." A pure goal can sanctify impure actions. But perhaps the incongruity bothered him sometimes, as he ordered executions in the morning and marched in *perahera* processions in the afternoon. Though the Brigadier had served as the chief lay priest of a major temple for the past twenty-four years, I saw not a single icon or religious painting anywhere in his home.

A servant announced that dinner was prepared, and we sat down to eat. We were joined by a member of Parliament and by a haggard middle-aged woman who was clearly the Brigadier's mistress. She was introduced to me as "Mrs. Amerasekera, a neighbor," but the tone in which she addressed the staff was not the tone of a guest.

"We are defending a fragile way of life," said the Brigadier as his cook divvied up a platter of rice noodles. "These Tamils would turn our little island into another India."

Mrs. Amerasekera shuddered. "Wretched place," she said with a wince. "Filthy, impoverished, horribly backward. Beggars everywhere. I've been there several times, and always *so* happy to get back home."

"No wonder the Indians were so anxious to invade us," joked the Brigadier. "After the squalor of home, the jawans must have seen their tour of duty here as a vacation."

I agreed — with perfect candor — that Sri Lanka was unquestionably far more pleasant than most of the subcontinent.

"Of coursh," sloshed the MP, "cant blem th' Tam'ls." He'd been clearly intoxicated when he arrived and had gotten steadily more so as the evening progressed. He noted, correctly, that the Tamils had enjoyed a privileged position under British rule, and at Independence they had not only lost this special status but also suffered discrimination at the hands of the majority Sinhalese. "Not t'excuse the buggers," he said, "but we oughttahav treat'd 'em better early on."

Mrs. Amerasekera shook her head but held her tongue. She had obviously had this conversation before.

The Member of Parliament had taken off his shoes and socks, and unbuttoned the middle two buttons of his shirt. His hair stuck out in at least four different directions. In a rapidly deteriorating voice he told me how he'd barely escaped assassination last year, when a right-wing Sinhalese terrorist had thrown a hand-grenade into his limousine. He had survived (he said proudly) by jumping out the window and curling up inside a drainage pipe.

A cordless telephone by the Brigadier's side buzzed, and our host stepped out to the hallway. "So much business," said Mrs. Amerasekera, "it never stops." Since retiring from active duty a few years ago, the Brigadier has run a private security firm providing clients with armed bodyguards and arsenals for personal protection.

"We just can't keep up with demand," Mrs. Amerasekera continued, "and constantly must turn customers away." The problem is not in supplying the weapons, but the men to wield them. Most of the best youths are already in the government army, in the rebel bands, or dead.

Through several curries and sambars, and another bottle of Scotch, the Brigadier took three more calls on his portable phone. Each time it rang, Mrs. Amerasekera and the servants looked just a tiny bit worried.

The MP by this time was completely unintelligible. At first I thought my own facilities might be impaired, but I managed to carry on an apparently lucid conversation with Mrs. Amerasekera about Pali, Sinhalese, and Malayam scripts. Whenever the MP addressed a question to me I could only guess at an appropriate answer. He bobbed his head appreciatively, but I have no idea whether we were communicating or simply trading mutual gibberish. A typical interchange went like this:

Him: "Mgjsdsldk sldkvn, Przdt KKdlkgsdfy aamsdlkfk kldfjsldkj?"

Me: "Yes, I think President Kennedy was our finest postwar president."

I hoped that the Brigadier was getting as drunk as his guests. By midnight the MP had passed out on the couch, Mrs. Amerasekera had retired for the night, and the Brigadier had become more expansive. He admitted, without actually saying so, that he had led one of the notorious southern death squads.

"We'd bring suspects in once the evidence was clear," he explained, "and after a few clouts they'd start confessing everything. But would that stand up before a judge? Of course not. What can one do? The problem must be . . . taken care of."

For most of the 1980s, the southern half of Sri Lanka was wracked by terrorist attacks from the right-wing (or Marxist, depending on whether you believe actions or rhetoric) Sinhalese militants of the JVP. Orthodox methods to combat the insurgency had utterly failed. At one point the movement could count on 300,000 terrified collaborators. The tide was turned by a vigilante militia, mostly soldiers and policemen out of uniform, covertly encouraged by the central government. These death squads, often under such meaningless pseudonyms as the People's Revolutionary Red Army, broke the back of the rebellion in the winter of 1990. Many ruthless thugs were exterminated — and many innocents as well.

"Let me show you something," the Brigadier said, reeling over to his desk and coming back with a bound notebook. "Some jottings for my memoirs, should I ever write them. They would make a good book, don't you think?"

I skimmed his account of the campaign, a flippant narration of ambushes, shootouts, and duels of grenades. The Brigadier's nemesis was a cagey one-legged rebel leader, eventually captured in his lair because he could not run away. The journal was full of phrases like "We encountered a bevy of black-shirted gents pouring forth a torrent of Billingsgate language, but our valiant warriors drove them back with ripe rounds of lead."

"That is the side of war I enjoy," said the Brigadier, stabbing a finger at the page. "The glorious excitement of an open fight — I *do* enjoy it, why not admit as much?" I remembered a rather cruel young commando leader who'd shared my bus seat that morning. "It is rather curious," he had said, "that only a single letter turns the word 'laughter' into 'slaughter.'"

"But today the battle is not fair," the Brigadier continued. "I hate to fight dirty, but I cannot hold back my hand if the enemy hits low. Or if the enemy might possibly win."

He gulped down the last amber swallow of whisky.

"In Vietnam," he said, his voice more sober despite the drink, "you Americans did terrible, terrible things. And for you it was not even a war of survival. When the battle got too rough you could just leave, as you finally did. The Tamils as well, they can always run back to India. But we Sinhalese, we Lankans, we cannot leave. There is no place for us to go. This island is the only home our people have ever known. Whether threatened by terrorists of my own race or rebels of another, I have no choice but to fight with every means at my disposal."

He went back to the desk and came back with a photo album. I flipped through the pages of glossy snapshots of the Brigadier's victims. Picture after picture showed bodies ripped to shreds, limbless torsos bathed in blood, corpses coldly laid out in rows, human beings reduced to red piles of hamburger meat.

The binder's cover was engraved with a fluffy kitten and, in flowery script, the word "Memories." Manufacturers of photo albums do not provide for the fact that not all of life's memories are happy.

"Think fast!" said the Brigadier, and I felt the barrel of a pistol pressed against the back of my skull.

Fortunately, I have enough friends with macabre senses of humor that I did not instinctively flinch.

The Brigadier laughed and slipped the hefty automatic back into a shoulder holster hidden beneath his cardigan.

"That's what it is like," he said. "You never know when you might get your bullet — or from whom."

He sat down in the chair next to mine and stared straight through my eyes.

"I've had cases," he said solemnly, "where the JVP has forced a man to hold his own wife down so a dozen of the terrorists could rape her. One right after the other — and he had to *watch* as he pinned her hands back, watch them violate her until she bled, for if he disobeyed, the guerrillas had threatened to kill all his children.

"Everyone in the village knew who the criminals were, but not a single soul would come forward to testify. Each knew that if he opened his mouth, the terrorists would inflict the same torture on *his* family. Tell me, my friend, how can any legal authority deal with *that*?"

I had no answer for him. A man who has never faced the destruction of his world cannot lecture one who faces it every day. But as I lay awake that night under the roof of a hospitable murderer, I did wish I could tell the Brigadier one thing I'd learned about war:

If you destroy your enemy by adopting his methods, by modeling yourself on him, by *becoming* him, you have not really survived at all. *He* has.

➤ ➤ ➤

Sri Lanka does not feel like a nation under siege. Most of the country (the southern and western portions of it, at least) seems positively idyllic. The land once called Ceylon, which hangs below India like the dot on a fat exclamation point, is separated from the subcontinent by much more than water. Though their average annual income is only four hundred dollars, Lankans' life expectancy is seventy-one years and their literacy rate is an astonishing 87 percent. I expected a maelstrom of violent confusion but found a soft-spoken, slow-paced nation far less turbulent than its looming neighbor. The cease-fire *must* hold, people told me again and again, it *will* hold, the war is certainly over, because Lanka is naturally an island suited for peace. So many of them said it with so much desperate hope that I thought, just perhaps, it might turn out to be true.

Colombo, the capital, is like an Indian city put through a washing machine. Its streets are wide and orderly, spick and span, not full of children pissing merrily into overflowing gutters. Its temples are islands of serenity rather than whirlpools of holy bedlam. Its stores are casually full of all types of Western products: Coke, Sprite, Fruit Loops, and Toblerone chocolate stacked next to cans of pickled rambutans and cartons of water-buffalo milk.

A barbershop proudly offers "Disco" and "Shaggy" haircuts. Outside its door a man sells piles of coconuts with bright orange husks. At a liquor store, shelves are stocked with Stolichnaya, sake, and claret from Saint-Emilion. A poster on the wall advertises a tastefully displayed carafe of "Thunderbird — The American Classic." Until coming to Sri Lanka, I'd never seen T-Bird sold in any bottle too large for a wino's pocket.

From the perfect palm-fringed beaches near Dondra (where fishermen perch on bamboo stilts just beyond the breaking waves, waiting patiently for fish to bite their baited hooks) to the shady green jungles and ocher bamboo groves of the Kandyan mountains (where young girls and old crocodiles bathe side by side in the sluggish brown rivers), the country does not have the look of a land at war. Arab traders once found Lanka so blissful that they thought it must surely lie next to Eden; the land's most famous mountain is named Adam's Peak, because the Muslim travelers believed that was where Adam stood when he looked back on his Paradise Lost. Today much of Lanka still has the feel of a serendipitous garden. The very word comes from Serendip, the Arab name for the island of Lanka.

Life is simple here. On the creaking Lankan trains, the passengers' luggage often consists of a bunch of pineapples or a large jackfruit, tied with twine to create a makeshift handle. On the platforms of a dozen little stations, two goats with paper loading tags around their necks are the entirety of somebody's baggage.

In one small provincial village I visited, a woman in a broad-brimmed Victorian sun hat and frilly lace dress rode daintily on a bicycle. When she turned her head, I saw that leprosy had left her face blotchy, like the skin of a carp. The local boys laughed as she pedaled by, but I was struck by her dignity — a tragically deformed woman had ignored the taunts of her neighbors and proudly put on all her best finery for a civilized afternoon's outing. Comical or inspiring, one thing is certain: on that day the woman had more important things to think about than war.

In another town I learned why Lankan electricity never seems to work. Residents tend to blame their daily power failures — one of the only dysfunctions of a well-functioning society — on the destruction of war. Often, I found, it has a more mundane explanation. Half a dozen men gathered beneath the control box of an overhead power line were hitting the device with sticks. A red emergency light was flashing, one of the men explained, and if they could stop its flashing the emergency would disappear. Eventually they succeeded in smashing the box, and all went away happy.

Even the local newspapers paint a picture of a country that has no news. On the first morning I happened to take a count, the Colombo broadsheet *Daily News* ran no fewer than eight separate front-page stories on the details of President Premadasa's day. The *Sun* ran forty-seven international wire service pieces in its meager twelve pages, as if important things were happening in every nation except Sri Lanka. There *was* one article about the Tamil guerrillas' hold on Lanka's northern territories — from the Reuters news agency. Lankans had to have word of their own civil war sent to them from London. The text's very appearance branded it as a story that didn't matter: it was printed in a mishmash of styles, with each letter a different point size and no two aligned properly, Bodini bold and italic typefaces freely intermingled, like a kidnapper's ransom note.

The only real scoop of the day came from a rival tabloid, the *Island*. It had nothing to do with war. Two men, the article reported, had pleaded guilty to selling "faecally contaminated ice cream." The judge fined them each a little less than $130 and warned them that if they were caught putting excrement in their desserts again he *might* have to consider shutting their chain of restaurants.

.   .   .

On a beach near Galle the unreality of the war was brought home to me by the sight of two little boys playing with home-made bows and arrows, laying the stick-quills flat on the sand and pretending to shoot them in midflight. They were clearly imitating the battle scenes of epic in which Rama (or, in the Mahabharata, Arjuna) defends himself against enemy archers by splitting each incoming arrow with a bolt of his own. It is a common game among children of the subcontinent: according to the Minto Hospital in Bangalore, during the weeks when episodes of the television Ramayana portrayed the war in Lanka, arrow injuries increased threefold. More than one hundred kids were accidentally shot in the eye, a third of them totally blinded.

I did not know whether these boys had seen actual war. The cease-fire (the one between the Tamils and the government, at least) had held for nearly a year at this point. Perhaps to them mortal combat truly was no more than a pleasant game.

When I was their age, I too played war games. My weapons were plastic instead of wood, toy machine-guns and grenades instead of toy bows and arrows. At that time my country was also at war, my father was an air force captain, and I was living on military bases. But those bases were always in the safety of Indiana and Michigan rather than the jungles of Vietnam. War was something far, far away, something one might see on television, something vaguely related to what Daddy did for a living, but something that could never have anything to do with real life.

The first time I came under actual gunfire, I was an adult. I was in the Philippines — I had gone there only to do some scuba diving and visit a girlfriend's family, but I was caught up in an abortive coup d'etat. What struck me most about battle was its utter chaos. Soldiers, rebels (and, of course, one foolish American without the good sense to stay inside) might maneuver carefully for advantage and stake out entrenched positions, but each time the bullets started to fly, every man merely dove for cover. Insurgents would ask me if I'd seen government patrols around the corner, and loyalists would ask for information on the mutineers' pass signs. Then a helicopter gunship thunders into the sky and nobody on the ground knows whose it is and artillery booms echo from all sides and nobody knows whether the copter is the attacker or the target and now frenzied machine-gun fire in front in back left and right and everyone crawling under cars into alleyways or flat against the ground and the copter leaves and small-arms fire trickling off and silence and people go about their business once more.

One fire-fight left a long stretch of Quezon Boulevard smeared reddish brown with human guts. A little farther on, a man's brain had been blown clear out of his skull. It sat, pink and wrinkled, on the hot asphalt. When the shooting stopped, a band of young boys emerged from hiding and began to poke delightedly at the naked brain with sharp sticks.

Perhaps children always see war as a game. A friend of mine who grew up in Vietnam remembers how, while the guerrillas and the government troops were kidnapping village teenagers to serve in their armies, he and the other younger boys would play soldier with rifles made of sticks.

➤ ➤ ➤

Throughout Lankan history, even before Lankan history for that matter, the Rakshasas and the Vanars have been periodically at war. The battle between the Sinhalese and the Tamils was raging when Valmiki wrote his epic, it raged through the centuries before the Portuguese arrived, and it still rages today. Perhaps the two races are simply destined to be bitter enemies. Or perhaps Sri Lanka is too small an island ever to be shared.

The Sinhalese are, by their very name, Lion People. It was the son of a lion (legend says) who first brought them to Lanka. The ancient Sinhalese epic Mahavamsa tells how the race was created: Once, as a northern Indian princess was traveling in a caravan, a lion jumped from the jungle to devour all her bearers. Every servant and soldier fled upon hearing the beast's roar, but the princess sat mesmerized. "Very fair was she," the chronicler notes, "very fair — and very amorous." She was inflamed by the animal's ferocity, by the untamable power of his strong, sleek limbs. She followed the lion's tracks back to his lair and there mated with him as if she were a jungle cat in heat.

In time she bore a son and a daughter, children with the strength of lions and with hairy paws instead of hands and feet. When he reached manhood the son killed his feral father, shooting arrows into the beast's head at will because the old lion could not bring himself to raise a claw against his beloved offspring. Then the son reclaimed his ancestral throne, married his sister, and sired sixteen pairs of twins.

The eldest of these children was Vijaya, the first mythical

king of Lanka. He was a violent, unruly youth — so lawless, in fact, that his father had to exile him for the good of the kingdom. Vijaya took seven hundred of his retainers and crossed the Black Ocean to a place that knew no law. He landed in Lanka (the monkish mythologizer writes) on the very day that the Buddha left earth for Nirvana.

The land was inhabited only by nagas and demons. It was a demon (or rather a demoness) who gave him his crown. Kuveni, a yakkha spirit, had been preying on his men in the shape of a female dog. Vijaya saw through her disguise, seized the demon-bitch, and threatened to strangle her on the spot. Overpowered, she transformed herself into a beauteous sixteen-year-old maiden and did his bidding from that day onward. Once his physical needs had been adequately tended to, she took him to a wedding feast where the invisible spirits were all gathered together, and (like Vibhishan betraying his demon nephew to Lakshman) pointed out her hidden kinfolk so that Vijaya could slay them one by one.

She was a devoted consort to him, but when it came time to found a dynasty Vijaya sent for a wife from India. He loved her deeply (the lion-man told the demon-woman), but humans and yakkhas could never truly be united. Disgraced and heartbroken, Kuveni returned to her own people. Without saying a word, they killed her as a turncoat.

Historically, we know that both Aryans and Dravidians settled in Lanka during the five or six centuries before Christ. There was a certain amount of intermingling, but by the third century B.C. the Sinhalese had a definite vision of themselves as a race distinct from the Tamils ("Damilas," as they called all Dravidians) of southern India.

When Valmiki wrote his epic poem, the Sinhalese and the Aryans were second cousins far removed. They had common ancestors and practiced largely the same religion, but they had been cut off from each other for so long that no direct ties remained. The Aryans may (or may not) have felt some vague sense of kinship with the Lankans, possibly more of a kinship than they felt with the Dravidians; but in their view the Sinhalese were still an alien race living at the end of the earth.

This ambivalence runs straight through the Ramayana. The Rakshasas are generally portrayed as bloodthirsty demons, but Ravana's kingdom is also described as a highly advanced civilization. Various demons, from royal Indrajit straight down to the lowly wardenesses guarding Sita, use the term "un-Aryan" as the bitterest insult in their vocabulary. Valmiki specifically notes that some Rakshasas are Brahmins — an utter impossibility if the nation were not Aryan. Modern-day Sinhalese may bristle at the identification, but despite their northern Indian roots they are quite clearly the Rakshasas of epic.

Even now the Sinhalese subtly link themselves with the demons of antiquity: Vibhishan, the brother of Ravana, is still worshiped as the island's guardian deity. He has been revered since prehistorical times, and would-be mothers still offer up prayers for offspring to the Rakshasa prince.

What most decisively separated the Sinhalese from the Tamils, however, was not bloodlines but faith. About half a century after Valmiki's death the Sinhalese converted to Buddhism, and Lanka's recorded history began.

The nation's capital, for over a thousand years, was at Anuradhapura. The city, like so many seats of ancient empires, lives no more. All that remains are the unburning stones and the noncombustible brick. But when I wandered through the ruins of Anuradhapura, I wandered through an architectural library of Lanka's past. The nation's whole story was spread out before my eyes, though I lacked the erudition to read more than a few chapters.

It was a king named Tissa, grandson of Anuradhapura's founder, who accepted the conversion. The great Buddhist emperor Ashoka, who ruled more of India than any other monarch before the British Raj, had sent missionaries throughout Asia to help spread the Sakyamuni's teaching. To Lanka the emperor sent his very own son and daughter. The son taught King Tissa how to follow the Eightfold Path of Righteousness, explained the mysteries of moksha, persuaded him to devote his whole nation to Buddhism. The daughter brought a cutting from the sacred boh tree under which the Buddha himself attained enlightenment.

She planted that cutting, and it is now the oldest cultivated tree in the world. It sits in the center of an Anuradhapura temple, nearly twice as wide as it is tall, squat and square like a gnarled old gnome turned to wood. Its branches are strewn with a patchwork of multicolored banners, flags that with every flap send a devotee's prayers into the wind. On the day I visited, six bald Tibetan nuns were eating their lunch beside its trunk. Though adherents of a sect deemed unorthodox by Theravada

Lankans, the nuns quietly enjoyed their meal under the shade of the sacred banyan.

The Buddhist state of Anuradhapura flourished. King Tissa built a system of canals and reservoirs to provide water in the dry season, and today heat-wearied townspeople still while away their afternoons by the banks of the artificial Tissaweywa Lake. The hydraulic technology was so advanced that the gradient of many watercourses was held precisely to six inches per mile.

The new kingdom's success, however, aroused powerful envy. The first Tamil conquerors were a pair of brothers, who journeyed to Lanka to sell horses and somehow managed to make themselves kings. A later Dravidian monarch named Elara ruled (the Mahavamsa concedes) "with even justice toward friend and foe," but justice did not earn him peace with his Sinhalese neighbors.

Buddhist rule was restored by Gemunu the Wrathful, a warrior-king and reincarnated monk. His mother was barren, the story runs, so she directed her maternal love to caring for an elderly saint upon his deathbed. When the holy man finally passed away, he prayed to be reborn in the queen's sterile womb. The miraculously conceived infant would have a princely appetite for warfare but a monkish passion for the Buddhist faith.

Gemunu earned his Wrathful sobriquet in childhood, when he proved to love battle more than his own family. The boy's father asked him to promise that he would live in peace with the Tamils, that when he inherited the crown he would not seek to reconquer Anuradhapura from its new Hindu masters. Gemunu stormed out of the room and contemptuously sent his father a set of women's clothing. Until the old king's death, Gemunu refused to speak even a word to him.

The day he ascended the throne, Gemunu the Wrathful went on the warpath. He forged a spear with a Buddha relic inside, so that every Hindu he cut down would be slain by the force of the Sinhalese faith. Five hundred holy bhikkus marched alongside his troops.

He killed the alien king of Anuradhapura in a duel fought on the backs of elephants. He crushed thirty-two other Tamil potentates, to unify all Lanka for the first time "under one umbrella." Only then, once all the killing was done, did Gemunu the Wrathful discover the true meaning of his religion.

Like Rama after the slaying of Ravana, Gemunu gave the fallen enemy king the funeral rites befitting an honored comrade. He sat on his throne in the Brazen Palace and wept hot tears, "remembering," says the Mahavamsa chronicler, "that his actions had wrought the destruction of millions."

His monks tried to comfort him, saying that he'd killed only one and a half men: one Tamil Buddhist and one Dravidian who was partially converted. "Unbelievers and men of evil life were the rest," the court sages said. "Their deaths are no more of a loss than the butchering of beasts."

But Gemunu felt that loss to the end of his days. The splendors of Anuradhapura are a testament to his grief. He filled the city with towering bell-shaped stupas and magnificently frescoed temples, a desperate attempt to atone for his life of wrath. By fighting and winning a bloody war of faith, Gemunu had learned that all true faith seeks to create rather than destroy. In his old age the reincarnated monk was a man of nonviolence once again. When I climbed the crumbly steps of Mirisavetti Dagoba or Ruvanvelisaya, I thought I felt a trace of his sadness seeping out of the stones.

For the next millennium — through the rise and fall of the Roman Empire, through the crucifixion of Christ and the revelation of the Qur'an to Muhammad, through the reign of Charlemagne and the Dark Ages of Europe — the Sinhalese kings of Anuradhapura fought the Dravidian kings of South India.

Sometimes Tamil warlords would invade Lanka merely for plunder, sometimes they would seize control of the capital for a whole generation, and from the fifth century onward they always maintained a foothold on the Jaffna peninsula. Sometimes the Sinhalese would forge military alliances with Aryan monarchs of the subcontinent, stage counterinvasions of Tamil Nadu, import northern Indian mercenaries to help fight their unending campaign. When, in 1987, the Sinhalese president of Sri Lanka asked the Hindi-speaking prime minister of India to send troops against the Tamil rebels holed up in Jaffna, he was merely perpetuating a coalition formed by both men's distant forebears.

Sometimes the Dravidian onslaught reached far beyond Anuradhapura, clear down to the other end of the island. The most celebrated Hindu temple in Lanka is in Dondra, at the nation's southernmost tip. Its stubby pillars jut plaintively from the ground, the only physical remains of the Tamil mandir constructed nearly two thousand years ago. But next to the ruins is a relatively modern shrine to Vishnu, whom the local Sinhalese Buddhists still worship as the patron deity of their province. Its walls are painted with scenes of the Ramayana's Lankan episodes: Hanuman's leap, Ravana wooing Sita, and (of course) the eternal fight of the Vanars and the Rakshasas.

Occasionally peace reigned long enough for both races to turn their enmity inward. Bitter discord arose between various orders of Sinhalese monks, conflict that not infrequently escalated into violent skirmishing. At Anuradhapura one can still see the bhikkus' latrines, each stone squatting-trough and urinal carved with the images of other monasteries, so that the monks could piously piss and shit on their rivals' homes.

In the eleventh century Anuradhapura fell for the last time, to conquistadors of the Dravidian Chola Empire. The Sinhalese raised a new capital farther south at Polonnaruwa. It took two hundred more years for this city to be razed. As in the Ramayana, the invading Vanars finally crushed the Rakshasas on their own home soil.

Herds of cattle graze serenely amid the ruined temples of what were once the thriving metropolises of Anuradhapura and Polonnaruwa, and gray-furred, black-faced monkeys with tails like question marks swing from the limbs of the finely carved statues. On one Polonnaruwa lintel I saw a bas-relief of Ravana in battle, his ten heads and fifty arms a metaphor for invincible power: the king of the Rakshasas is so mighty that his sword-hand seems everywhere at once, he is so stoutly impervious to injury that he seems to have more than nine lives. But a multitude of limbs and lives could save neither Ravana nor the Sinhalese kingdom from destruction. When the Tamils sacked Polonnaruwa in 1215, the Golden Age of Lanka ended forever.

Later Sinhalese rulers never regained the power of these medieval monarchs. Squabbling princelings lorded over their bailiwicks at Kotte or Kandy but never again held sway over a united empire. Unable to win the respect of their subjects and neighbors by war, they looked elsewhere for prestige. They found it in a tooth.

Buddha teeth, actual teeth from the very mouth of Gautama the Buddha himself, are the Southeast Asian equivalent of splinters from the True Cross. If all the wooden chips in European reliquaries are authentic, then Christ was crucified on a cross the size of a California redwood, and if all the Buddha teeth are genuine, then the Sage of the Sakyas had the mouth of a killer whale. But the molar that came to be known as the Kandy Tooth has been so widely adored for such a long time (at least since A.D. 328) that it may, just possibly, be the real thing.

It is still revered wherever Theravada Buddhism is practiced. Kings and queens of the Burmese, Mon, and Thai royal houses have sent brooms made of their own hair to sweep the ground beneath the Tooth's altar. When the Portuguese conquered Lanka in the sixteenth century (claiming they'd "inherited" the deed to the whole country from a converted Sinhalese king with the lusty baptismal name of Don Juan), they saw the Tooth as the most important obstacle to propagation of Christianity. They seized it from its temple, turned down a ransom offer of 300,000 gold ducats, and delivered it to the papal Inquisition to be burned as a heathenish abomination. Not until much later would they learn that a clever bhikku had kept the holy relic safe by handing over a monkey's incisor in its place.

A story from the Glass Palace Chronicle — a medieval history of the Burmese court at Pagan — shows just how vital possession of the Tooth became to establishing a Lankan king's legitimacy. For a time it replaced battle as proof of dominion, and far more powerful rulers were willing to treat the keeper of the holy relic with humble deference:

An early Burmese monarch, who wanted to build his raw kingdom into a true center of Buddhism, looked to pious Lanka for inspiration. The chronicle identifies him as Anawrahta, the founder of the empire of Pagan, but since Anawrahta's great-grandson was still searching for a tooth-relic, this seems unlikely. The chronicler probably confused him with a later ruler, who bore the king-sized name of Siritaribhavanadityapavara-panditasudhammarajahadhipatinarapatisithu. No kidding.

Such a regal moniker could hardly fail to engender hubris, and Siritaribhavanadityapavarapanditsudhammarajahadhi-patinarapatisithu decided he needed the Buddha Tooth for his very own. Many a cotton-throated courtier must have silently cursed the monarch whose name could scarcely be stuffed into one human mouth, but none dared object. After all, the king had an army (the chronicle states) of 72 million soldiers, a number about equal to the combined populations of Europe, Africa, and North and South America at the time.

The sacred Tooth united the whole Theravada world in faith, and Siritaribhavanadityapavarapanditsudhammarajahadhipati-narapatisithu decided to honor the harmony, peace, and charitable spirit of the Buddha by waging a war to capture it. His head overflowed with bloody plans for extracting the Tooth by brute force, when a spirit appeared to him in a dream. Why not, the spirit said, simply ask for it politely? The notion had never occurred to the king. He sent lavish gifts to Lanka, humbly begged for the relic, and (in a matter of speaking) his wish was granted. The tooth magically replicated itself so that both devout countries could have a worthy object of devotion.

Transporting a genuine Buddha tooth is no easy business. For starters, it would be highly disrespectful to touch even the carrying case of such a holy item with such base instruments as human hands. Both Burmese and Lankans take the symbolism of height very seriously indeed; it is exceptionally rude to stand above a social superior, so a tooth from the very head of the Buddha could never be physically lower than any portion of any carrier's anatomy. In order to get the replicated tooth into the boat, the Sinhalese monarch (for no underling would do) placed a golden chest full of jewels on top of his head and waited for the holy molar to float in of its own accord. He then waded out until he was neck-deep in the ocean and could slide the casket on board the waiting ship by bowing his forehead. The ship sailed for Burma but turned back at the sight of Siritari-bhavanadityapavarapanditsudhammarajahadhipatinarapatisithu waiting haughtily in a silken howdah atop a tall elephant. Not until the king of Pagan repeated his fellow monarch's neck-deep-in-the-brine-with-treasure-chest-on-head ceremony did the tooth consent to follow him home.

Pagan is now a ghost city, just as dead as Anuradhapura and Polonnaruwa. The replica tooth was housed in Shwezigon Pagoda, by the banks of the Irrawaddy in the center of Burma, but there is no trace of it there today. A monk taking his afternoon nap in the shade of the pagoda's doorway once told me that it disappeared centuries ago, perhaps when Genghis Khan's horde torched and looted the great capital. The aged bhikku did not even possess a tooth in his own mouth, but he did not seem to care.

As for the original Lankan Tooth, it is still venerated at Kandy. I didn't set eyes on it — *that* is permitted only on the rarest of festival days. But I was, very briefly, in its physical presence. During morning puja every day, four musicians beating drums and piping on flutes circumambulate the shrine, while devotees line up on the balcony to lay wreaths of flowers outside the altar's chamber. Two enormous monks stand guard at the door, making sure that nobody gets too close to the gold reliquary that enshrines the Tooth inside dozens of caskets, like a Russian stacking doll.

The Kandy Tooth is still a symbol of war and of peace, still an icon of Sinhalese pride in the face of Tamil belligerence. Soldiers with heavy machine-guns and high-powered sniper's rifles ring the roof of the Temple of the Tooth, vigilant to ward off the one attack that could devastate their countrymen's morale. And every prime minister since the island gained independence has prayed at Kandy to mark his legitimacy as the ruler of Lanka.

➢ ➢ ➢

For miles north of Trincomalee, there is scarcely a single house that is not missing a wall or a roof. Every building of substance, whether a home, a temple, a mosque, or a school, has been bombed to varying degrees of rubble. The poorest fared the best here, ironically, since their palm-leaf huts were easily rebuilt and they did not face the threat of being crushed under falling masonry. Just outside town I passed a grim, matter-of-fact funeral procession of a dozen men walking, a dozen on bicycles, and four stoic pallbearers sweating under the burden of a hastily slapped-together coffin with a lid that didn't fit.

The war may be invisible in the Sinhalese south, but throughout the Tamil north and east it is an inescapable fact of life.

Trincomalee itself is a quiet town, but this is not the quiet of peace. It is a leaden silence, a cold silence despite the summer heat, a waiting-for-the-other-hobnailed-boot-to-drop silence. Here, as in the outskirts, most of the houses are punched with bomb holes. The colonial Dutch orange-tiled eaves have been shattered to shards of baked clay, and the joubs choke with sewage because there is nobody to clean them.

The streets are brimming with armed men. Government troops with green berets on their heads and golden Sinhalese lions stitched onto their shoulders lounge behind sandbag bunkers. Policemen in short-sleeved khaki uniforms with ridiculous peaked caps and Chinese 84-S rifles shuffle nervously in their shoes, like security guards at a suburban shopping mall. Marines from a nearby naval base, their sea-blue tunics embroidered with neat silver anchors, chunky carbines slung loosely under their armpits, sip warm colas. And, looking more like professional soldiers than any of them, guerrillas from the Tamil Tigers casually prowl the alleys with grenade launchers cradled to their jungle-camouflaged chests.

Rival government and rebel patrols cruise the city on foot or in jeeps, each pretending to be in firm control, each carefully avoiding any contact with the enemy to avoid shattering the illusion that *they* are Trincomalee's only masters. Every fourth or fifth intersection has a roadblock, but the fatigue-clad guards do not bother to search any of the sparse traffic passing by: with the cease-fire permitting both sides to roam about fully armed, what hidden danger could they possibly find? None of the soldiers stationed in town seems to be performing any clear task, but all walk with the unique swagger of men carrying loaded firearms.

There may be confusion over which army dominates the streets, but there is none over which commands the loyalty of the people. Large red banners with the emblem of a roaring tiger fly everywhere — stretched across windows, above cigarette and confectionery stalls, on poles behind the carts of vendors who hawk flavored goat's milk tinted yellow, green, or bright pink. Any empty wall is painted with slogans cheering on the Tamil Tigers or posters of fallen rebel heroes.

War is a constant here, a permanent condition even when the fighting ceases, a backdrop to ordinary existence. It is so much a part of people's lives that sometimes they hardly remember it is there. One day at noon I went to the New Central Liquor Restaurant to buy some arrack, and the barman turned me away with a concerned warning: "To drink so early in the day is not good for your health," he said as a jeepful of soldiers rumbled by outside.

The local cinema in Trincomalee was showing an American flick barely two years out of date. It was *Heartbreak Ridge*, a Clint Eastwood film. A war movie.

≻ ≻ ≻

"Our own government behaved like a foreign army of occupation," said the bishop. "In 'eighty-six and 'eighty-seven their helicopters often dropped bombs on unarmed civilians, I saw it with my own eyes."

The Reverend Dr. Deogupillai, Roman Catholic bishop of Jaffna, is no friend of the Sinhalese authorities. As one of the very few "respectable" people willing to speak out against the government he earned the nickname "Tiger in a Cassock."

"The root of the war," said the bishop, "is the fact that we Tamils are now second-class citizens. Back in colonial days, when English was the official language, Tamils and Sinhalese were subordinate but equal. And the good Lord has given us great cleverness and determination, so under the old system we did quite well."

During the British times, certainly, the industrious Tamils held a disproportionate number of the country's choicest jobs. This inspired a majority backlash at Independence, and until 1979 all government business was conducted solely in Sinhalese. Tamils are still effectively locked out of most important official positions. Nepotism is so common in the ruling class that most of the nation's prime ministers have been close relatives, and the initials of the governing UN Party are said to stand not for United National, but for Uncle-Nephew.

I was surprised to learn, from the bishop and from others, how many of the Tamil Tigers are Christian. The best guess is something around ten percent. The bishop supports neither the Tigers' goals nor their methods, but he said that they have treated his congregants better than any of Lanka's other armies. I asked if his political activism was inspired by the controversial doctrine of holy rebellion currently sweeping many Latin American archdioceses.

"I am not concerned with Liberation Theology," the prelate replied, "just with liberation."

A black-robed priest came in, to remind the bishop deferentially that it was almost time to get ready for the Requiem.

"A service I perform far too often," said the Reverend Deogupillai. "Each death is an individual tragedy, of course, but each also brings us closer to the death of our whole race. So many Tamil youths have been killed that there aren't enough young men left to provide our girls with husbands. Many women must become spinsters, and the birthrate is already dropping precipitously. I honestly do not know where the next generation of Tamils will come from."

"And war is only the worst of our afflictions," added the priest who had just arrived. "Poverty is also a heavy load to bear."

"We Tamils have not been blessed by nature," the bishop

agreed. "Down south, you can drop a seed in the ground, walk away, and practically overnight it grows into a fruit tree all by itself. Up here in Jaffna, you can sow it, water it, nourish it every day — and still the plant will die."

"Almost the only crop we have in plenty is the palm tree," said the priest. "But it is a strong tree, a hearty tree, and once it sends its roots into the soil it can never be ripped away."

He let the metaphor hang in the air for a sober moment.

"We have only the palm," he continued, while the bishop straightened his collar, "so we grind it up for sambar to eat, ferment it for toddy to drink, and ferment it still more for arrack to forget."

"To forget what?" I asked.

"Maybe," he replied with a laugh, "to forget that we have nothing else to eat or drink."

The hour of the Requiem was approaching fast. The bishop and the priest hurried off to the church, to say Mass for another victim in a war that was supposed to have been over.

I had come north to hunt for Tigers. Despite the cease-fire, no hired car would drive to Jaffna for love or money, unless perhaps the love was exceptionally deep or the sum of money exceptionally large. Buses had refused to travel the route since the mid-1980s. But after several days of poking about, I learned that the government, as a goodwill gesture, had quietly reopened the rail connection that had been shut for the past few years. When I bought my ticket in Colombo, yet another power failure had left Fort Station a blind black lair, and a shirtless clerk squinting at scribbled orders by the flicker of a yellow candle made me repeat my destination three times to make sure he'd heard it right.

The train jolted to a start and jolted to a stop at each platform, often in between as well, like the car of a student driver learning how to use the clutch. Both sides of the tracks that stretch to the north were littered with the hulks of wrecked carriages. A few hours out of Colombo, I saw two bombed-out wheelhouses and a caboose sitting in the middle of an acre-wide pool of moonsoon rainwater; their rust had turned the whole pond a deep orange. Not much farther on, villagers were picking apart another wreck for scrap metal. The train's carcass had been nearly skeletonized, but the scavengers searched optimistically among the twisted steel bones nonetheless.

The man in the seat next to me always pretended to be asleep when the conductor walked by. If asked a question in Sinhalese, he told me, his accent would mark him as a Tamil. His light blue eyes betrayed an ancestry at least as much Dutch as Indian, but the war had forced him to choose only one heritage.

Everyone up north hated the government, he said, because it sent soldiers in street clothes to raid homes in the night. Everyone up north hated the Tamil National Army and the Eelam People's Revolutionary Liberation Front, two Indian-sponsored rebel groups, because they were merely ruthless thugs out for their own enrichment. Everyone up north hated Rajiv Gandhi's "peacekeeping" army, because it harassed innocent people and was interfering where it had no right. The officers were decent enough, he said, but the ordinary jawans were unbearably rude, spoke neither Tamil nor English, and smelled very bad.

As for the Tigers, the blue-eyed man was circumspect. When I asked him about them, he looked out the window at three country women hanging their laundry to dry on a fence of barbed wire. Some people support the Tigers, he said, some do not, but at least nobody could accuse them of banditry.

In the compartment's doorway, two teenage boys stood talking while they passed a cigarette back and forth. They were about the same height, about the same age, and both had scalps shaved nearly bald. One was a novice monk, the other a conscript foot soldier, separated only by a change of clothes.

Just beyond the town of Vavuniya, the country begins to look much like Tamil Nadu. Women wear red bindis on their foreheads, and the children who jump in through the windows at each station sell roasted vadi peppers and other vegetarian snacks rather than spicy sausages on sticks. Even the dry scrub of the landscape, so different from the wet, tropical lushness of the south, seems to say that this territory is part of India rather than Lanka.

The monk, the soldier, and all of the remaining Sinhalese got off at Vavuniya. We were leaving the land of the government and entering that of the Tigers.

Every station from this point on bore a neatly stenciled Tiger insignia, every school and public building proudly flew a Tiger flag. Once the train jerked to an abrupt halt, and a column of Tamil guerrillas boarded each compartment to search for God-knows-what.

Most of the "soldiers" were young boys carrying AK-47s

more than half the length of their bodies. They could not have been more than twelve years old, but they were the oldest twelve-year-olds I had ever seen. I nodded amicably to one of them when he filed past. He didn't nod back, didn't even smile — but he didn't shoot me either.

I'd known that the Tigers had been recruiting children because there weren't enough adults to fill the ranks, and this had been my main fear in traveling north. I wasn't much afraid of being captured and held hostage: there had been cases of Westerners kidnapped or killed, but these had all been the work of the disbanded EPRLF militia. The Tiger leadership was smart enough to realize that it had far more to lose than to gain by mistreating an American, so I was not particularly worried about a bloody-eyed rebel commander tossing me in irons. What gave me shivers, however, was the idea of a tantrumy child poking my ribs with the barrel of a machine-gun.

The Jaffna I visited was quite a different place from the Jaffna of six months earlier or (as it would turn out) six weeks later. It was, for a brief time, liberated territory.

A row of tanks under dropcloths guarded Elephants' Pass, the narrow causeway linking Jaffna Peninsula with the rest of Sri Lanka. The train station was patrolled by a platoon of "Lady Tigers," special units composed entirely of women. They wore the same feral uniforms as the men: camouflage with slashing horizontal stripes instead of conventional blotches, the same sunlight-and-shade pattern that nature gives jungle cats to hide them from their prey.

The only authorities there were the rebels themselves. Tamil infantrymen filled the streets and coffeehouses, rode two at a time on frail motor scooters, pedaled bicycles down the main thoroughfare with their rifles slung across their backs. Small martyrs' monuments — usually a model of an AK-47, the Tigers' weapon of choice — seemed to dot every intersection. Even the schoolgirls skipping home from afternoon classes proclaimed their loyalties in their dress: at nearly every school in town the uniform consisted of a white blouse, white skirt, white socks, white shoes — and a gaudy black-and-yellow Tiger-striped necktie.

Along the main avenue, the most prosperous businesses were all funeral parlors. Death, it seemed, was Jaffna's only growth industry. The undertakers' trade was clearly booming, but competition was intense. Each storefront displayed its urns and coffins in big showcase windows, like suburban auto dealerships. Each trumpeted its services with blaring neon signs: "Embalming, cremation, caskets!" read the banner outside one cheery establishment, inexplicably named the White House. "Tombstones, wreaths, all funereal needs! Hearses for hire, day or night!" If Crazy Eddy were a mortician, this is how he would advertise.

The old statehouse and government buildings still stood (some of them), but the Tigers were Jaffna's only law. The rebels administered their land — and collected their heavy taxes — from little offices hastily opened in houses, shops, and schools. At a traffic circle downtown, forty-seven cars and trucks waited patiently to buy their "safety inspection" stickers from men holding rifles instead of wrenches.

At every Tiger outpost a portrait of Vilupillai Prabhakaran, the guerrilla generalissimo, hung in a position of honor — chunky, baby-faced, grinning like a genial uncle rather than a stone-killer. I carried his photo at all times, to avoid being shot. Whenever I was stopped by a rebel patrol, I whipped out the picture and was permitted to pass with handshakes and pats on the back. If I'd ever mistakenly displayed it to soldiers of the government or to rogue EPRLF remnants I would most likely have been executed, but in Jaffna any armed man I met was almost certain to be a Tiger.

The owner of my hotel, the only reputable establishment in town, was overjoyed to see me. I was the first overnight guest he'd had in a long, long time. It was so difficult, he said, to keep the staff properly trained ("not to mention properly paid, *baba*") when there were no customers. Over the past few years his inn had been shelled, strafed, and commandeered by the Indian army. Once he went six whole months without a single visitor. He never could bring himself to shut down, because the damn war can't last forever, you know, and business is *certain* to pick up once the fighting ends. Maybe this cease-fire will be the one that lasts. Yes, maybe it truly will.

A few steps away from the hotel was Jaffna Fort, the scene of the city's heaviest fighting. Most of the old Portuguese quarter had been bombed to rubble, the Iberian yellow and white stucco walls all turned to chalk. Beneath the ramparts facing the sea (the sea over which Hanuman leapt, over which Rama and the Vanar host marched, over which generations of Tamil invaders sailed their ships of war) sat an abandoned dogcatcher's cart full of thin mongrels. The animals may have been collected to be sold for food, or perhaps they were victims of a rebel effort to stamp out rabies by rounding up strays. They had not yet started to eat each other, but if left there long enough they would.

The mass of twisted wreckage next to the fort (a Tiger officer told me) used to be the Central Police Station. I'd hardly have known it was ever a building at all. The only discernible remains were some collapsed steel girders sticking up from a brown heap of brick, and a concrete statue of a former prime minister with the head neatly shot off. A unit of guerrilla soldiers (the oldest about thirteen) was guarding the demolished structure. One of them was talking to a friend of his, a schoolboy in blue shorts carrying his lunch in a pail and his textbooks in a satchel. I could not decide whether the pair looked like two children or like a child and a miniature adult.

The guerrillas' central command headquarters was not difficult to find. Every taxi driver knew the way. When I entered the unfortified compound, I was not even searched for weapons or explosives. Security is tighter at any New York nightclub.

But, then, why shouldn't it be? When rebel leaders came to HQ they invariably brought formidable armies of bodyguards. In any case, only a fool would attack a Tiger in Jaffna.

I had managed to get invited to the command post through an introduction arranged by a friend of a friend of a friend. I was not permitted to meet Prabhakaran — the supreme commander never appears in public and almost never submits to interviews. But I'd been promised a chat with Anton Balasingham, a top Politboro member and the insurgents' chief theorist.

When I arrived at the camp I was told that Balasingham was still at a vital conference in the eastern provinces. A functionary served me tea and politely suggested that I be so kind as to come back in a couple of days.

"I would offer you something to eat," he said, "but this is Friday, so we have no meat today."

"Just today?" I asked. In India, Tamils are generally strict vegetarians.

"Have you ever heard of a tiger who did not eat meat? As for myself, I like nothing so much as a good piece of bully-beef."

He had only three teeth in his mouth, and I couldn't imagine how he chewed his tough, blasphemous cow-flesh jerky.

"Why Friday?" I asked. "Relic from Portuguese times?"

"No idea," he said. "I would eat meat every day, but my wife refuses to cook it."

I questioned him about the years of Indian occupation. The last troops from the subcontinent had pulled out only two months before, forced to withdraw by a miscegenational union of the Sinhalese government and the Tamil Tigers.

"Every day there was constant gunfire," he said. "One never knew whether it might be mere target practice or our country-men being killed. During the occupation people would only work three days each week, they'd stay safely in their homes for as long as they could. Now they can go to work all five days. As for my relief now that the Indians are gone, it is too great for me to express in words."

He told me that when the civil war broke out he had quit his longtime job as a clerk in the Public Transportation Office and volunteered to serve the Tigers in whatever capacity he could. Many of the older residents helped in little ways, he said, by acting as lookouts or smuggling food to safe havens.

The functionary's only son was a Tiger soldier. The old man pulled out a photo of a young man in striped fatigues, with an assault rifle loose in his arms and a small glass vial strung around his neck. I knew that the vial (which all Tiger fighters, women and children included, are required to carry at all times) con-tained a single dose of cyanide. No Tamil rebel may ever be captured alive.

I asked the desk man if he was proud that his son had become a killer, that his child would most likely die of a bullet or a poison tablet. There was more sadness than apology in his voice when he answered.

"It was his decision, not mine," said the old man. "Every day I worry for his safety, and every night that he goes out on a mission I cannot sleep until the dawn. I wish he could have a happy life, as I have had, that he could raise a family.

"But this is war, this is not peace. So, yes. Yes, indeed, I am proud."

I went away, and when I came back several days later the chief theorist was indeed at the camp. Anton Balasingham wore a white shirt and white sarong, black-framed glasses and a black goatee. He looked like a man of thought more than of blood.

"We have studied every modern guerrilla movement," he said. "The Viet Cong, the Shining Path, the PLO, the Eritreans — we try to learn from all and take the best methods of each. But we emulate none, for our cause is unique."

Balasingham helped found the Liberation Tigers of Tamil Eelam while teaching social studies in London during the late 1970s. I could easily understand why men like the functionary and his son became rebels, men whose only decision was whether or not to help defend their people in a war they did not create. But what was the motivation of the men who stirred up that war in the first place? How great must an oppression be before it justifies the universal devastation of battle?

"We did not unleash this strife," the theorist said, "*they* did. It was the government that dropped bombs on innocent civilians, the government that strafed whole neighborhoods from the air. All we did was fight to protect our homes."

Ironically, it was the Lankan government's foolish 1987 air campaign that indirectly helped the Tigers triumph. Even high Sinhalese officials now admit it was a bad mistake. Before the bombing of Jaffna, Tamil insurgents had been quietly armed and trained by India, but in deference to their patrons they had kept their rebellion relatively low-key. In 1987, however, India responded to the bombing with a mission of her own, flagrantly violating Lankan airspace with a massive drop of humanitarian aid and supplies. The impotent Sinhalese government had no choice but to sit and watch: its air force had no jets, and its only antiaircraft guns dated from the Second World War.

Mindful of how it would look for the leader of the non-aligned world to be engaged in bald imperialism, Rajiv Gandhi did a turnaround: he offered to use his influence over the rebels (and his military muscle) to end the civil war. Lankan President J. R. Jayewardene knew he had no chance of taming the Tigers on his own, so he grasped at the opportunity.

At first the Tamils welcomed the Indian troops as protectors. "We even put garlands around their necks," Balasingham said, "we called them our saviors." But within two months the Indians launched a lightning offensive against all the rebel militias.

"They were in no sense of the word a peacekeeping force," the theorist said. "As defined by the United Nations, a peacekeeping unit is impartial, generally carries only small arms, serves only to maintain the status quo. It is certainly not a party to the conflict. The Indians were quite clearly no peacekeepers but an alien army of occupation." He neglected to mention that it was the rebels themselves, by reneging on a promise to disarm voluntarily, who triggered the Indian crackdown.

The Tigers battled on for three years — India's longest war since Independence. Sri Lanka has been called India's Vietnam. By the time new Prime Minister V. P. Singh decided to cut his losses and retreat in 1991, 1,200 Indian soldiers, 700 Tigers, and nearly 10,000 Tamil civilians had lost their lives.

By this time the Lankan government was being assailed from both sides: Sinhalese radicals of the JVP had used the Indian occupation as a rallying cry and started a wave of terror in the south that left 17,000 people dead. The government could not fight a war on two fronts — and its Indian bedmate of the rebellion's dark night looked far less attractive in the sober light of morning. Ranasinghe Premadasa, the new president, made an alliance with the Tigers that left each army supreme in its own part of the country. The Indians were told to leave, the government crushed the JVP, and the Tigers began stalking and devouring their one-time brothers-in-arms.

I asked Balasingham how he felt about the internecine slaughter of Tamil by Tamil, about the civil war within the civil war.

"As our leader Prabhakaran said," replied the goateed guerrilla, "it is sad that we are forced to kill our own blood brothers. But the other groups are not patriots. They are all merely quislings, stooges of the Indians, and traitors to their very own people."

The fractious Tamil armies could have stepped right out of Monty Python: there is a scene in the movie *Life of Brian* where the hero tries to join the Judean People's Liberation Front and is nearly throttled for his trouble.

"Fuck off!" says the guerrilla leader. "We're not the Judean People's Liberation Front. They're our worst enemies in the world."

"Then who are you?"

"We're the People's Front for the Liberation of Judea!"

During the 1980s, Tamil loyalties were split between the Liberation Tigers of Tamil Eelam, the Eelam People's Revolutionary Liberation Front, the Eelam Revolutionary Organization of Students, and the People's Liberation Organization of Tamil

Eelam. All were Marxists, all were revolutionaries, and all (at one time or another) were mortal enemies. After some initial cooperation they ended up attacking each other (and the Indian-sponsored Tamil National Army) with greater violence than the Sinhalese.

Now the Tigers have wiped out all their rivals and are soft-pedaling their half-hearted Leninist rhetoric. Balasingham cited Che Guevara and Mao Zedong only for strategy, not ideology. When he quoted the Chairman he did not mention class warfare or the dictatorship of the proletariat, only the famous simile of a guerrilla army swimming like a fish through an ocean of friendly peasantry. The events of the past year in Eastern Europe and the Soviet Union, Balasingham conceded, showed that socialism must come through democracy, if at all.

"We are a people's army," the theorist said. "That is our ideology — whatever will help the people. Communists believe in world revolution, while we merely fight for our people. That is why we chose the tiger, the ancient symbol of Dravidian pride, for our movement's emblem. We give up comfort, we even give up traditional Tamil vegetarianism. We eat monkeys, snakes, lizards, rats, anything that moves. In the jungle, one does whatever one must in order to survive."

I asked about the future, and whether the bloodshed was finally over. Prabhakaran had recently urged the government to join him in ending the war "by the principles of dharma rather than violence." I asked Balasingham whether this cease-fire was a breathing space before the final showdown or the beginning of a true, lasting peace.

"I believe that Tamils and Sinhalese can live together in harmony," he said. "For many years we lived side by side in the same cities, and we can be good neighbors again. Of course, we Tamils cannot give up our weapons until the political climate changes. But I do have hope that this day will come soon. We have been carrying rifles for seventeen years now, and our arms are weary. We are tired of wars and of killing."

I left the camp believing him, mostly. Not just because his arguments were convincing, or because I'd heard the very same sentiments from the great majority of the people I'd spoken to in Jaffna, Trincomalee, and all over the northeast. Not just because the Tigers apparently enjoyed almost universal support among the Tamil masses, or because they seemed to treat noncombatants more humanely than the government, the Indian troops, the JVP, or any other armed force in Lanka had for decades.

During his campaigns against the Japanese and the corrupt Kuomintang, Mao convinced observers as shrewd as Edgar Rice Snow that he was nothing more than an honest patriot defending China. Then, during the Great Leap Forward and the Cultural Revolution, he sent up to 40 million Chinese to their graves. I did not trust Balasingham simply because he sounded reasonable and his enemies were an unsavory lot. Nor could I support his separatist goals, for the Tamils do indeed have a homeland in the south of India, and the Sinhalese have never had any home other than this tiny, idyllic, and terrible island.

What impressed me about the theorist was not his rhetoric but his sacrifice. The man with the neatly trimmed goatee would clearly rather be debating dialectics in a cozy London living room than gnawing on rat bones under a lean-to in a raging monsoon. That, rather than anything he said, made me believe he truly wanted peace.

A few days after I left the Tiger base camp, Lanka exploded again in war. And it was the Tigers themselves who started it.

Just before dawn the rebels launched a sneak attack on twenty-four police stations. The constables had standing orders to surrender rather than resist, so as not to jeopardize the fragile cease-fire. The Tigers accepted their surrender, then blindfolded them, marched them into the woods, made them lie face down on the ground, and emptied the magazines of their assault rifles into the officers' backs. Only one man, Piyeratna Ranaweera by name, survived to tell the story. In Batticaloa the Tigers used human shields to attack government positions. They forced civilians to march ahead while rebel cadres hid behind them to ambush sentries.

I was on the morning Batticaloa-Colombo train when hostilities broke out. The very next Batticaloa-Colombo train was stopped by Tigers, and two dozen "suspicious" people were dragged off to the forest. Whether a white foreigner with a notebook full of information on the insurgency would have qualified as "suspicious" I can only guess.

Every flight out of the country was booked solid by terrified Tamils fearing the inevitable Sinhalese backlash. All internal travel halted until a temporary truce was arranged, five days and 376 deaths later.

During the next year there would be many more surprise attacks, more bombings, more surreptitious slayings of enemies' families. Eventually, in May 1991, the Liberation Tigers of Tamil Eelam would even assassinate Rajiv Gandhi himself.

I flew away from Lanka in a magical chariot built not by the heavenly craftsman Vishvakarma but by McDonnell Douglas. As the island of Ravana grew smaller outside the window, I could not help thinking that the war had turned Lanka's inhabitants — Sinhalese and Tamil alike — into demons after all.

Eleven
LOVE

RAVANA lay dead, his ten faces wet from the weeping of his wives. Vibhishan, as his sole surviving kinsman, had the obligation of preparing his brother's body for cremation. The new king of Lanka refused.

"He was an evil man," Vibhishan said. "Let his spirit forever roam the Hell of the Unburned."

Rama would not countenance such an impiety. "Hatred extends to death," he said, "and no further." He respectfully turned his eyes away from his fallen enemy. "Your brother was a brave warrior. Give him the funeral he deserves."

So the Rakshasa Brahmins wrapped Ravana in a single piece of red silk and laid his body on a golden bier. Vibhishan led the procession of mourners — courtiers shedding crocodile tears, bards extolling the dead king's glories, cosseted concubines limping along on tender feet unaccustomed to walking. The high priest sacrificed a goat, skinned it, and made a coverlet out of its pure white fat to wrap around Ravana's heads. Once the prayers were concluded, all the demons and the monkeys tossed reverent handfuls of rice on the corpse, and Vibhishan set his brother on fire.

Only then, when he saw his foe go up in flames, did Rama unstring his bow.

Sita waited patiently. She had waited several years already, waited patiently when there had been little hope of rescue, waited even when she had thought her husband dead. If Rama did not see fit to summon her just yet, she could wait a little longer.

After the funeral of the old Rakshasa monarch and the coronation of the new one, Hanuman finally appeared at her prison.

He swept aside the wardenesses and asked Sita if she wanted him to put her hideous Rakshasi guards to death. She would not hear of it, and by way of explanation told him the story of the tiger, the hunter, and the bear:

Once a tiger was chasing a woodsman through the jungle (she said), and drove him into the canopy of a tall tree. The tiger could not climb, so he pawed at the trunk, tried to shake his prey loose, roared at the man to come down and be eaten.

The animal's bellows woke a big brown bear who had been slumbering on an upper branch. Toss down the hunter, the tiger said to the bear, for man is the common enemy of us both. The bear refused. This person has sought refuge in my tree, the beast called back, and whatever crimes he may have committed in the past, it is now my duty to protect him. With a friendly nod to the hunter, the bear went back to sleep.

The tiger was hungry and would not go away. I will eat, he growled to the man, but my meat does not have to be human. Push that bear off his perch, and I will let you go free.

The hunter was happy to oblige. He climbed up to his snoring host, and gave a mighty shove. But the bear instinctively grasped the tree limb with his claws and kept his balance.

See how your generosity is repaid, the tiger roared up to the bear. You offer your friendship, and this wretch betrays you at his first chance. Toss the villain down, and your vengeance will be my feast.

No, said the bear, I shall not. I cannot break my dharma simply because this man has broken his. It is never right to repay evil with evil.

As soon as she entered the palace, Sita longed to race through the pompous corridors and hurl herself into the arms of her love. Instead she followed Hanuman to one of the guest suites and waited some more.

"Wouldn't you like to rest first?" the ape asked.

"There will be plenty of time to rest later," she replied. "All I want is to be with my husband."

Hanuman hurried off to seek permission, but returned with a new sari in his hands. Rama would not grant her an audience until she had bathed and put on fresh clothes.

"How considerate he is of my comfort," Sita said to herself, and hardly cried as she tried to believe it.

Rama, meanwhile, turned things over and over in his mind.

Duty wrestled with passion, and duty naturally won. At length he gave the order for his wife to be summoned. All the court brightened at his word. Vibhishan clapped his hands to call the chamberlains, commanded them to lay out a banquet such as Lanka had never beheld, to fetch the finest musicians and dancers in all the land, to give the palace a fresh coat of paint and festoon all its windows with aromatic wreaths, to —

"Leave it be," Rama interrupted, his face dark with what on an ordinary mortal's visage would have been a frown. "Why go to so much bother, only for a woman?"

Lakshman, Hanuman, and Vibhishan all stared at each other in disbelief.

Sita was brought in, but before she could lock herself in the embrace for which she'd waited years, Rama raised his hand and stopped her cold.

"I have avenged the insult done to me," he said. "I fought this war for myself, not for you. The demon who dishonored my wife is dead. Ravana has used you, so you are of no further use to me."

She did not know whether to protest, rebuke, or plead. "But where shall I —"

"Go where you like," he said, his steady voice betraying not a trace of rage, "anywhere you wish, just so long as it is far away. Your sight is unbearable to me, like sunlight to a man nearly blind."

Sita turned away and spoke four words to Lakshman in a voice no louder than the whimper of a field mouse.

"Brother," she said, "build me a pyre."

Rama turned her request into a command with a brief nod. Nobody in the assembly hall dared to utter a syllable. Lakshman voicelessly fumed as he dragged great logs and dry kindling across the marble floor of the audience chamber, but he could not make his brother return his angry glance.

The bonfire was lit, and Sita walked up to the crackling flames. She stared deep into the withering inferno and called out to the God of Fire:

"If I have ever given my husband the least trace of offense," she cried, "then I do not wish to live. But, Divine Agni, if I am chaste, then let your flames protect me."

The only sound in the room was the sinuous snap of the fiery orange tongues licking the air. Their heat singed the hem of Sita's sari and caused thick beads of perspiration to roll down her cheeks. With barely a moment's hesitation to ponder what she left behind, Sita slowly walked into the blaze.

Rama looked across the great hall to see that time had come to a halt. All the courtiers and servants were still as statues, with Lakshman, Hanuman, Sugriva, and the rest frozen fast in place. Even the flies and mosquitoes hung unbuzzing in midair, and through the windows Rama saw that outside not a leaf on any tree was rustling in the breeze. The only moving things in the chamber were the whips of fire calmly engulfing his wife.

It was with some surprise that Rama looked down from his throne to see five strangers standing before him. Their eyes did not blink, their feet hovered one inch above the ground, and their garlands were not coated with dust. In short, they were gods.

"We are Brahma, Shiva, Varuna, Indra, and Yama," they said, although Rama could not see any one of them open his mouth. "A deity such as yourself cannot act in such a manner."

"I had thought I was a man, the son of Dasarastha," said Rama, with a touch of wholly inappropriate sarcasm. "Tell me who I really am."

"You are Vishnu," the divinities said in unspeaking unison. "You are the Preserver. You are Us. You are God."

They vanished, and the court came back to life.

At that instant Agni, the Fire God, emerged from the bonfire carrying Sita on his shoulders. She was completely unharmed, though her garments had turned flame-red.

"Listen, all who would hear!" the old Vedic god of ritual purity bellowed. "This woman has not sinned against her husband in thought, word, or deed. She is perfectly chaste, as unsullied as the day she was born."

Rama ran and grabbed Sita in his arms. Their kiss was so fervent as to make newlyweds blush. And the king's customary thin arc of a smile widened into a delighted gaping grin.

➤ ➤ ➤

As it happened, the Fire Ordeal marked the end of Rama's fourteen-year sentence of exile. Before he left Lanka, Rama was paid another visit by the Sky God, Indra.

"We are well pleased with your acts," said the divinity. "Choose a boon, and I shall grant it."

Rama asked that all his fallen comrades — every Vanar and Bhalluka killed in the war — be restored to life.

"It is too much," said Indra, "for these animals were created solely to assist your struggle, but nevertheless I shall grant your request." He nodded his head, and several million dead apes and bears began to rise groggily from the battlefield.

To keep him from taking another fourteen years to get back to Ayodhya, Vibhishan gave Rama the magical chariot that Ravana had ridden to war. In the course of one afternoon the miraculous carriage flew Rama, Sita, Lakshman, and their chosen guests over the Southern Sea and straight across India. The Vanars stayed behind in Lanka, to feast and pass the time with their newfound Rakshasa brothers.

As Rama and his party sped above earth and water, they retraced the path of all their wanderings: the Black Ocean, which Hanuman had leapt in a single bound; Rameshwaram, at the subcontinent's southern tip, where Vibhishan had defected to the party of truth and where the apes had built a bridge over the waves; Kishkindhya, the Vanar capital, where Rama had killed Bali, placed Sugriva on the throne, and seen the evil in his own heart; Nasik, where the demon Maricha had tempted Rama into the forest while Ravana spirited Sita away; and Chitrakut, where Rama, Sita, and Lakshman had devoted themselves to hermits' austerities.

When the party landed in Ayodhya, the regent Bharata came out to meet them in his tattered penitent's garb. After fourteen years, he again wore Rama's sandals on his head to demonstrate his submission. He joyfully put the shoes on his brother's feet and begged Rama to take back his throne.

For the coronation, fast-running messengers collected holy water from the four oceans and the five hundred sacred rivers. All the other ritual items were quickly brought to the palace: cowrie shells, honey, clarified butter, fried rice, a lucky elephant, swords, bows, a chariot, a perfect tiger skin, kusha grass, a lion with four prominent canines, fresh curds, lithe dancing girls, well-adorned prostitutes, and a yellow bull with a large hump and horns wrapped in gold.

Rama was languorously bathed in scented water by seven beautiful virgins. Brahmins, warriors, merchants, and ministers then annointed him with oils and precious essences. The high priest Vaisista seated the new king on a golden throne encrusted with gems and placed on his head the crown of Manu, the first ruler of men. Sugriva and Vibhishan, both monarchs in their own right, held up white umbrellas to shield Rama from the sun. At the moment of his coronation, the earth grew rich with crops, the trees heavy with fruit, and the heavens rained down wreaths, gemstones, and song.

Rama ruled wisely for ten thousand years. During his reign the world was a blissful place. While he was king, no woman became a widow. Disease and hunger were unknown, and ferocious animals stayed far away from every village. Thieves gave up their profession, liars told the truth, and the old never had to perform funeral rites for the young.

*　*　*

The Ramayana is India's greatest love story. If there is a special heaven set aside for legendary lovers, then Rama and Sita must be dancing an eternal *pas de deux* there alongside Romeo and Juliet, Tristan and Isolde, Pyramus and Thisbe, Sid and Nancy. Throughout the subcontinent the names of the prince and princess of Ayodhya are still synonymous with perfect matrimonial bliss. How ironic that they weren't even in love.

Not in a Western sense of the word, that is, or in the sense that modern citified Indians are coming to expect. A traditional Hindu union like that of Rama and Sita is based on duty rather than desire. Even today most Indian marriages are arranged by parents, with the bride and groom often not even meeting until the wedding day. But now, for perhaps the first time in history, significant numbers of people are discovering romance. Love — burning love, crushing love, knot-in-the-pit-of-your-stomach love — is no longer a mere abstraction of courtly poets.

That is not to say that Indians have ever been strangers to this uniquely human emotion. There were always scandalous couples who defied their parents' wishes and eloped, always secret paramours who made surreptitious trysts in midnight-dark rice paddies, always those rare lucky pairs who managed to marry for passion rather than propriety. But these were never more than a happy few.

For most Indians, love was a sort of warm, contented affection for one's spouse of many years. The only permissible physical relationship between a man and a woman was the bond of marriage, and the only real purpose of marriage was the raising of a family. In the small towns and villages where the bulk of the Indian populace lives, this is still largely true. But in the cities, educated women and men are demanding much more.

Students go out on dates without a spinster aunt as a chaperone. Office-mates see a movie together after work. On a Sunday afternoon young Lotharios stroll in the park and duck behind convenient trees to wheedle kisses from their giggly sweethearts. They talk of love as a birthright, as a thing their grandparents couldn't begin to understand.

Yet the Ramayana is still the standard by which every love affair is judged. Not all Indians choose to model themselves after Rama and Sita (just as most Americans don't mimic Ozzie and Harriet), but to hundreds of millions they are still the ideal couple. A scholar I met in Varanasi suggested to me that the two great Sanskrit epics together represent the home life of all Indians. The Mahabharata — a tale of cousins cheating each other out of inheritances, uncles killing nephews, an eldest son gambling his wife and four brothers into slavery — portrays families as they really are. The Ramayana shows a family as it *ought* to be.

In a traditional arranged marriage, the strongest bond is simple obligation. Through four millennia a husband's foremost task has been to protect and provide for his wife, a woman's sole responsibility has been to run a household and serve her man. If the two parties happen to care for each other, so much the better. But primarily they are partners in the business of raising a family.

Rama wins Sita by his own effort, but (in the Valmiki original, if not in the later Tamil adaptation) he does it for glory rather than love. When he breaks the bow of King Janaka to earn his bride, Rama has never spoken a single word to Sita, never even set eyes on her. Sita follows her husband into exile not because she adores him but because it is her dharma to be at his side. After ten years of marriage they come to love each other, but their actions are still motivated by duty. Rama may be genuinely grief-stricken at Sita's kidnapping, but he invades Lanka to redeem his *own* honor; Sita may be tormented by her husband's absence, but she rejects Ravana's courtship only out of iron-willed rectitude. The prince of Ayodhya will not even take his bride back until ordered to do so by the Fire God himself. Husband and wife alike are slaves not of love but of right.

Why, it may be asked, do millions still accept such a seemingly sterile existence? Why do they willingly — even eagerly — give up all hope of romance in exchange for mere stability? One simple answer is that for most Indians, mere stability is a fine thing indeed. Life in the Gujarati scrubland is seldom easy, and a hardworking rice farmer may find a loyal, steady helpmate worth a dozen fleeting heartthrobs. But many of the people who enter arranged marriages are hardly impoverished peasants. Lots of well-to-do, well-educated men and women, men and women with the freedom to choose any partner they wish, still find their spouses through a matchmaker.

Those who do not happen to know a matchmaker simply browse the classified ads. Nearly every local newspaper regularly publishes an advertising section of "matrimonials." Men cite their jobs, annual incomes, and any physical or sexual defect that could be grounds for divorce if concealed. Women (or their relatives, for no properly bred woman would broadcast her own availability) offer dowries of "450,000 rupees cash" or "five acres choice land, and jewelry." *All* list their caste and ancestral region.

Some demand a photograph, but good looks are far less important than the right birthday: every ad, virtually without exception, requests an exchange of horoscopes. After all, beauty is transitory, but fate is eternal. Only after an astrologer determines the bride and groom to be compatible will a marriage take place. Even the most secular, modern-thinking couples generally have their birth stars plotted before tying the knot.

Whether they found each other through the matrimonials or the network of old gossips, most arranged couples I met appeared to be happy. Or, at very least, content. But no married person can speak with utter candor in the presence of a mate, so I went to a coffeehouse in Mysore where men gather to pass the midday hours away from their wives.

"The choice of a wife," one elderly gentleman explained to me, "is the most vital decision a man will ever make." When he had introduced himself, he'd given me a business card that read simply:

Mr. N.N. Menon
Registered Freedom Fighter
A Politician since 1935 against foreign rulers in India

I'd asked him how one registered as a freedom fighter, but he had not wanted to talk about Independence. That, he said, was a long time ago.

"A wise fellow," Mr. Menon said, "must be quite certain that his spouse has a temperament, upbringing, and personality compatible with his own, because he will have to keep company with her for the rest of his days."

"One may talk of love at first sight," interjected a man who had been sipping his coffee from the saucer rather than the cup, "but what use is all that? Fine for youths, for persons in adolescence, but hardly a basis for a lifelong match. Real love, the kind that lasts, does not burst out uncontrollably, like weeds in a garden. It develops quietly, over many years of married life."

At the table next to ours, three obese men were shoveling bread and dhal down their throats and letting out sonorous belches. The sounds of gastric distress were like the mating songs of sick whales.

"Just look at Rama and Sita," Mr. Menon went on. "Theirs was a union far stronger than any young puppy love. And even in today's so-called love marriages, both parties generally come from the same caste and background. It is only natural: most of the ladies whom one encounters day to day will most likely belong to one's own social set."

This certainly was true of Rama and Sita. He was a Kshatriya prince, she a Kshatriya princess, and the match was advantageous to both families' dynasties.

"After all," agreed Mr. Rao, the fourth man at our table, "everybody gets along better with those of a similar upbringing. A laborer will not want a schoolteacher for a wife, nor would a boy from the village wish to marry a girl from the city. How different can it be in America?"

It *is* different in America. There may not be many Rockefellers marrying trash collectors, but between the very top and the very bottom of society just about anything goes. Men whose grandfathers emigrated from Sicily date women whose grandmothers still live in Stockholm. Investment bankers cohabit with caterers. Los Angeles cinematographers marry Boston lawyers and fly across an entire continent on alternate week-ends.

Then again, America's divorce rate is approximately thirty times that of India.

"Some of my acquaintances have arranged marriages," said Mr. Menon, "and some found their own brides. Those who went through a matchmaker are almost all better pleased."

"I have been married for seventeen years," said Mr. Rao, "seventeen happy, peaceful years. I first saw my bride outside the temple on the day of our wedding, and have never looked at another woman since."

An old blind beggar shuffled into the coffeehouse, wailing a hauntingly beautiful song, which he accompanied by rhythmic taps of a rupee coin against the bottom of a battered tin bowl. When he had finished, each of us put a few rupees in his palm. He bowed and then shuffled off. I couldn't understand all the words of his song, but it was something about a boy who drowns himself for the love of an unattainable girl.

"In my case," said the man who drank his coffee from the saucer, "an arranged marriage was the only option. I am Sindhi, and where could I find a Sindhi woman without the aid of a matchmaker?" The Sind is now part of Pakistan, and virtually all Hindus fled the territory at Partition. For forty-odd years the Sindhis have been scattered throughout India, a people with a distinct culture but no ancestral homeland. Bloodlines and family tradition are all that prevent them from melting into historical oblivion.

Marriage is a microcosm of India on the move. In starting the gradual shift from negotiated unions to "love" matches, Indians are again trading security for opportunity, routine contentment for the wild extremes of joy and misery, the chicken in the hand for two turtledoves in the bush. They are taking enormous risks in giving up the preordained solidity of their parents and grandparents. We in the West, who have been taught to trust our own instincts in making big decisions, can hardly appreciate the terror that such a choice entails: in what is generally the most important judgment of any individual's life, he lets himself be guided not by logic, not by duty, not by the advice of his family, not by fate, not by infallible astrological omens, but solely by the whisperings of his heart. The risks are great — but so too are the rewards.

> > >

All too many Indian women undergo the Fire Ordeal to this day. All too many have their honor tested in the blazes, their bodies caressed by the scorching fingers of Agni, the God of Flame. Every year thousands of young brides die in "kitchen fires," many (if not most) of which have been deliberately set by their husbands. Murder may carry less social stigma than divorce.

An arranged marriage is seldom an equal partnership, and the woman is almost invariably the less equal partner. Many Indian men see their wives solely as a source of dowry income and unpaid labor; they keep the women cut off from friends and parents, treat them like menial servants. If a bride does not produce a son within the first few years of wedlock, sometimes a groom's entire family will conspire to do away with her. Rather than raise eyebrows with a divorce (and give back the dowry), all too frequently they make a fresh start with a match and a pool of spilled kerosene.

Many husbands routinely beat their mates, and a battered wife has little choice but to suffer in silence. If she leaves she will most likely spend the rest of her life alone: in rural villages remarriage is generally impossible, for a Hindu bride is expected to be a virgin.

But Indian women are not always the powerless pawns that their theoretically inferior status might indicate. After extensive fieldwork in Tamil Nadu, the renowned anthropologist Louis Dumont concluded that "the subordination of the wife is more a matter of form, asserted at the beginning of the marriage, than a basic fact." Often women will assert their hidden power in subtle ways, so as to maintain the illusion that their husbands are really in control, but sometimes they are far more straightforward. While passing through a small village in Uttar Pradesh I witnessed one such instance — in the middle of the town's busiest intersection.

A woman rushed into the center of the traffic circle, grabbed a small man by the hair on his head, and yanked him off his bicycle onto the ground. She smacked him twice on the jaw, then took off her shoe and used it to pummel his face. When he slid to his knees she started kicking him with all the strength she possessed. Every car, rickshaw, and pedestrian stopped to watch the spectacle, to point and laugh. A policeman pushed his way through the ring of onlookers, but he made no effort to stop the woman.

The husband did not strike back, not even when the blood started pouring from his nose and mouth; he just cowered on the ground and tried to fend off the blows. He was not a large man and did not appear to hold back his hand out of chivalry. His wife was hardly an imposing figure herself, but her rage was terrible to behold. She looked like a meek, shy hausfrau who had finally been pushed too far. As she punched, slapped, and stomped on her fallen man, she shouted through her tears, "How could you? How *could* you? How *ever* could you do it?"

Some wives escape the dull drudgery of home through extra-marital affairs. Infidelity is probably most common among the urban elite, where a woman is more likely to mix with strangers and less likely to be thrashed for any transgression. At a posh cocktail party in Madras, a man who'd had several too many gin and tonics was giving me a boozy dissertation on all that was wrong with Indian society and the world at large. When he heard I was retracing the course of the Ramayana, he made a bitter grimace.

"It's a boring, shitless epic," he said. "Pardon my language. I am sickened by its popularity, embarrassed that my country-men still are captivated by such rubbish."

I asked what specifically he disliked about the tale.

"Why, everything!" he said. "It's all just a pile of unrealistic, goody-two-shoes nonsense. Now the Mahabharata, *that* is a far better work. What with Miss Draupadi servicing five different men all at once, now *that* is more what real life is actually like."

He drained his drink, spat the ice back into the glass, and grabbed another from a passing tray, all in one fluid motion.

"Rama is a fool," he said angrily. "To stay loyal to Sita for so very long — a bloody useless simp. Today everybody is fucking each other's wives. Excuse my language. But why be ashamed? Nobody remains faithful anymore."

"Even in the villages?"

"Even in the villages. Even women you wouldn't think could ever imagine such a thing. Even women you would never sus-pect, unless you happened to know it for a fact, unless you hap-pened to find out purely by accident."

He staggered off to the bathroom, picking up another drink on his way. The party's hostess came over and put a hand on my arm.

"Don't mind old Ganesh," she said in a low voice. "He's drunk again, so you can't believe anything he says."

"But is what he says true?"

She paused a moment. "No, no," she said. "Just the ramblings of a paranoid old drunkard."

There is a great deal of pain in arranged marriages, on both sides. Women clearly suffer more, but their enthusiasm for the institution remains undiminished. And not just peasant women who have no other choice: I know quite a few Westernized, cosmopolitan Indian women — lawyers, journalists, well-educated professionals in full control of their lives — who have willingly left their choice of spouse up to matchmakers. When I ask them why, they speak of duty to their families, ties to tradition, hunger for stability — and a haunting fear of never finding the right man on their own. In the view of many, the only thing worse than being bound in an empty, loveless marriage is *not* being bound in an empty, loveless marriage.

> > >

Not all arranged matches are empty or loveless. Some bloom into blissfully harmonious romances, some blaze and smolder as lifelong seductions. After all, the Kama Sutra is an Indian text.

The Taj Mahal, the very symbol of India in Western eyes, is the world's greatest monument to love. It was built by a heartbroken Mughal emperor at the death of his adored wife. In the courtly gardens of the Taj, I met an old man who might well be Shah Jahan reincarnate.

His hair was snowy white, his mouth had not a single tooth, and his dark walnut skin was creased like crinkly wax paper. He wore a long black formal frock coat in the heat of the afternoon, leaned on a weathered teak walking stick, and gazed at the world through thick glasses with smart cherry-red frames. His name was Mr. Krishnan. If he had not actually existed, he would have been dreamed up by Gabriel García Márquez.

'I have come here at least once a week for seventy years," he told me. "My wife and I used to sit by that fountain in the shade. Sometimes she would cook a basket of samosas, and we would spend the hours feeding them to each other. She was always at her loveliest in the light reflected off the walls of the Taj."

The light *is* different here, just as to painters the light in Venice is unlike light anywhere else. Perhaps the walls of the mausoleum reflect not only light but love.

"When my wife died," Mr. Krishnan went on, "I began coming to the garden each and every day. I felt closer to her here even than in our home, because this was where we shared our happiest moments. For nearly two decades I walked about the hedges each afternoon, by myself but not quite by myself. When I sit by the fountain and shut my eyes, I can still taste the samosas."

Their two children have long since moved away, to Delhi and to Chandigarh, but Mr. Krishnan could never bring himself to abandon Agra. He has left the city only three times in his life, and on each occasion he felt unbearable pangs of loneliness that did not subside until he sat in the gardens of the Taj once again. In recent years the government has begun charging an entrance fee for the monument. It is two rupees — about a dime — but Mr. Krishnan cannot afford such a daily extravagance on his civil service pension. Now he visits only on Fridays, when admission is free. "All the other days of the week," he said, "I spend eagerly looking forward to Friday."

The Taj is always overrun with tourists, and on Fridays even more so. Most of the gawkers are Indian, but there are also Germans, Brits, French, Americans, Japanese, and Aussies by the busload. Mr. Krishnan does not mind. He does not even seem to notice.

Mr. Krishnan has no favorite time of day to see the Taj. He has been here countless mornings, when the sunlight bounces off the white marble — marble inlaid with semiprecious stones and then sanded smooth as fresh butter — with such brilliance it hurts your eyes. He has been here countless evenings, when the sun turns into a blazing red comet, paints the mausoleum yellow, then orange, then pink, then deep purple before dropping from the sky to make room for the moon. He has been here countless nights, when the crowds have all gone and the site is silent, when the air is so crisp and clean you don't even notice the swarms of mosquitoes from the mud flats of the Yamuna River below, when all you can do is stand spellbound by the contrast of the pure, man-made whiteness of the alabaster minarets against the deep and infinite blackness of the heavens.

Mr. Krishnan has seen the Taj at all hours and from all angles. One of the custodians is a friend of his, and once let him climb up to the gilded dome at midnight. He has explored the structure from top to bottom. Many times he has descended to the tomb far beneath the exquisitely tiled floor, its dead air hot, humid, and thick with the trapped sweat of centuries. Although a Hindu himself, he always speaks the name of the Islamic holy place with hushed reverence. God is love, he says, and this is most certainly a temple of love.

"Shah Jahan did not plan to be buried here," said Mr. Krishnan. "The Taj was meant to be a mausoleum only for Mumtaz, his dear lady. Do you know what the name 'Mumtaz' means? It means 'excellent,' and she was indeed the most excellent of women. As for his own tomb, the shah intended to build an exact replica of the Taj, but all in black marble instead of white. A perfect mirror image, for the wife is a perfect reflection of the husband."

Beneath a tree to our left, a family of Sikhs had spread out a blanket for a picnic. The father was happily lifting his baby daughter up above his head with one hand, bouncing her in the air to make her laugh. The mother was unpacking a small case of food: curries in metal pails, breads wrapped in tin foil — and a basket filled with delicate brown samosas.

"Why was the black Taj never built?" I asked.

"A sad thing," Mr. Krishnan replied. "The emperor Jahan was deposed by his wicked son Aurangzeb. He was imprisoned over there," the old man pointed up the river to Agra Fort. "For years he would sit in his cell, unable to do anything except stare out of the tower window at the city he once ruled. But I like to believe that every day when he stared downriver at the Taj, he was cheered by the sight of his dear wife's resting place."

Mr. Krishnan's gaze strayed to the marble dome, and he was silent for a solid minute.

"But one good thing arose from this tragic situation," he said. "Because Shah Jahan could not build a separate tomb for himself, he was buried here in the Taj alongside his lady love. Whenever I think of them, side by side for all eternity, I cannot help but feel happy."

The afternoon was waning, and Mr. Krishnan had to go home to take his heart medication. After we'd shaken hands and started to walk away, he turned around and called out to me:

"May God bless you with happiness — may you get married very soon!"

➤ ➤ ➤

Marriage, in a rigid traditionalist view, is no more than the cornerstone of family. A union without children is no true union at all. How ironic that Rama and Sita, the perfect couple, went fourteen years without producing any offspring.

Westerners think of themselves as individuals, but most Indians see themselves first as members of an extended family. A person's own wishes generally take a back seat to the duties owed one's parents, children, grandparents, and siblings. For orthodox Hindus, family ties have a truly religious importance: Rama unquestioningly accepts Dasarastha's ban of exile because the highest piety of a son is filial obedience. A person without a family is cut off from society, adrift all alone in a turbulent world.

Estrangement from kinfolk is one of the bitterest mishaps an Indian can endure. Many Americans think little of moving away from their hometown, visiting relatives on the occasional Christmas or Thanksgiving, dropping a periodic birthday greeting and sporadic vacation postcard. To most Indians, this would be an amputation. One's family is an extension of oneself, a part of one's identity. I have Hindu friends even in America who live in their parents' houses long after marriage or who travel across nine states several times a month just to spend a weekend back home.

A Bengali father on pilgrimage to Ayodhya once gave me a speech that could have come from *King Lear*. Children today are all ingrates, he said, just opportunistic parasites. He raised four daughters, gave them modern educations, all the advantages, found fine husbands for each of them, and now they treat him like a beggar. As long as he was doling out money they were deferential and polite, but now that he's a poor pensioner they can't even be bothered to visit. Children today have forgotten the examples of Rama and Sita, the Bengali man said. He had come to Ayodhya, the home of Rama and Sita, to pray for the return of his family's love. If his prayer was not granted, he planned to renounce all his daughters, renounce everything he'd ever held dear, and put on the rags of a hermit.

In nearby Faizabad I played confessor to an embittered rickshaw-wallah. In hopes of a bigger tip, he'd been complaining about how tired his legs became at the end of a day. I surprised him by offering to switch places: I'd do the pedaling and he'd sit in the passenger seat, on condition that he truly played the part of a passenger by telling me all his life troubles.

"You will find it so difficult," he laughed. "Rickshaw-man's job is hard work." But we traded seats nonetheless.

It *was* hard work, hard both to propel the lumbering vehicle forward and to control its unwieldy momentum. I gained a new appreciation for the legions of skinny boys and grizzled grandfathers who pump the pedals fourteen hours a day.

The rickshaw-wallah had hulking shoulders and brawny legs as thick as logs. The gray hair growing out of his ears was so thick I wondered how he was able to hear. He said that he generally enjoyed his job because it had kept him fit and healthy for nearly fifty years, that he earned enough money to keep his family fed, and that his wife had proved herself by giving him three sons. But still he was not happy, he said, because of his brother.

"He went off to America," the beefy man said, "to Boston, U.S.A. So many years ago. Asked me to come join him, but I have seen American television on videotape — 'Dallas,' you know it? I want to see America, but there every man is sleeping with the other man's wife. I love my wife, I do not want to be sleeping with the other women, and so I cannot go."

Like a good rickshaw-wallah I did not correct him, did not argue, just nodded my head and kept on pedaling.

"Now, ten years later," he went on, "my brother is so rich. He has about, oh, a hundred million dollars. And now when he comes to India, my brother will not visit me. He will not even talk to me, because I am a poor man. He thinks I will be asking him for money. But I do not want his money, just my brother."

Abandonment of one's family is, to Indians, an abomination. That is why the epic character of Vibhishan is both honored and detested today. In the Ramayana he forsakes his evil brother Ravana, after first trying and failing to turn him back toward the path of virtue. Vibhishan sacrifices everything he holds dear for the sake of right, deserts his clan and his race to fight at the side of the divine Rama. To some, this makes him a brave hero. But to many Indians it makes him a villain more foul than any in the entire epic.

Ravana and the other demons (the criticism goes) may be wicked, but at least they are honest, they play by the rules. They are honorable foes — that is why Rama gives Ravana full regal rites at his funeral. Vibhishan, however, is nothing more than a traitor. He may have picked the right side, but the very act of *changing* sides was a violation of dharma. No man should *ever* betray his brother, no matter how brutal or tyrannical he might be. No man should *ever* desert his family, no matter what vile deeds they may have committed. Loyalty to one's kinfolk is always the height of holiness.

This is perfectly in line with the philosophy of the Bhagavad Gita. Here Arjuna, like Vibhishan, must choose between kin and conscience: loyalty to his brothers demands that he fight an unholy battle, but stubborn morality makes him shrink from the slaughter of so many strangers. As the god Krishna tells him, personal conscience is not a reliable guide. Fallible humans can never comprehend the universal good and evil of the cosmos. We can't see the whole picture, so our notions of morality are by their very nature flawed. Perhaps the injured puppy we save from death will infect our whole village with rabies, perhaps the young milkmaid we kill with a stray arrow would have given birth to a genocidal dictator. Only God knows the full ramifications of our actions, so we must simply follow our own personal dharma and trust that He will sort things out for the best.

Vibhishan's desire to help Rama is laudable, but his first duty should have been to aid his brother. The television version of the Ramayana paints Vibhishan as a minor hero, but Valmiki's text is far more ambiguous. Sugriva, the Monkey King, urges that the defector be executed, for any man who could betray his own brother would never be a trustworthy ally. Rama, however, takes the Rakshasa prince in and welcomes him as a true friend. As God Incarnate, he cannot turn away anyone who seeks his love and protection. And Vibhishan, for his treachery, is rewarded with the crown of Lanka.

But the crime of familial disloyalty strikes deep at the Indian psyche. The freedom fighter and Ramayana translator Makhan Lal Sen cannot contain his bile during the Lankan chapters: when the unquestionably perfidious Indrajit berates his uncle for joining Rama's camp, the learned editor says in a footnote, "Indrajit's words should be written in letters of gold." And when the Rakshasa prince attempts to defend his desertion, Sen parenthetically fulminates, "Thank God that brothers like Vibhishan are still rare in the world, but one is enough to disgrace the whole race."

➤ ➤ ➤

India wears calluses on your soul. So much bestial poverty, so much routine destitution, and those lucky enough to escape misery often escape only by the margin of a single meal. India makes you into a hard, cynical person, and if you're already hard and cynical it makes you even more so. You find yourself shoving aside six-year-old beggars because they don't look quite wretched enough to deserve your spare change. Soon — very soon — you no longer feel any shame for your hardness.

Consciously or unconsciously, you formulate rules for your altruism. I, for my part, always gave money to lepers, and seldom to anyone else. A person with four sound limbs and two good eyes (my reasoning went) has no business begging. But when charity is doled out by formulas of calculation, it is no longer true charity. It is mere accountancy.

What sustains so many hopeless existences? What keeps the legions of the luckless from tossing themselves off the nearest bridge? For many, I found, the lifeline is love.

The beggars of Calcutta are no more ubiquitous than the beggars of Delhi or Allahabad or (for that matter) New York City. But they do seem to be far more genuinely woeful. Panhandlers in other cities are often frauds, like a fit-looking man in Nasik who asked me for money to buy food: I gave him half of the pomegranate I was eating, but he tossed the fruit away with a dirty scowl and a muttered curse. In the nation's capital I was approached at every street corner by women clutching grime-smeared infants; I gave one mother five rupees — more than I'd spent on my *own* dinner that evening — and she practically spat in my face. No sooner had the note left my pocket than six other women with babies materialized out of nowhere, like vultures flocking to a freshly slaughtered carcass. The incident repeated itself each time I gave money to a healthy person until I started limiting my donations to bona fide lepers.

The beggars of Calcutta are uniquely miserable because so many of them *are* bona fide lepers. Partly because it is the largest city in the commonwealth, partly because it has a Communist government that claims (implausibly) to take care of its teeming proletarian masses, mostly because it is the home of Mother Teresa's free hospital and mission for lepers, Calcutta attracts the halt and the palsied from all over India.

Advocates of the homeless in America like to say that streetpeople in Washington or Newark live in Third World conditions, and even compare their plight to that of the street-people in Calcutta. Utter nonsense. The shantytowns on the banks of the Hudson are mere shadows of the shantytowns on the banks of the Hooghly. America's beggars deserve far better treatment, but most of them would be laughed out of the gutter in Calcutta: they generally have two good hands each.

Along Chowringhee Road (the name by which residents still call the city's main thoroughfare, although street signs have labeled it Jawaharlal Nehru Road for decades) no man with all his limbs would dare put out a begging cup. Each hand that stretches out toward the passing pedestrian is missing several fingers, each face that moans a plaintive prayer is lacking a nose, an ear, or an eye.

Unlike the querulous mothers-with-children, lepers are immensely grateful for anything one may drop in their laps. They have to be. Most people toss their coins with eyes averted, never speaking a word or slowing their pace, giving change not out of kindness but as the price of passage, like motorists chucking quarters into a highway toll basket. They hurry on without turning their heads, as if leprosy were a disease transmitted by sight.

I, too, felt squeamish at first, and (although I've been told that the illness is not easily contagious) I never felt particularly comfortable touching an infected person's skin. But I did make a point of looking each mendicant in the eye and exchanging a word or two while I fumbled for my pittance of a handout. Most times I felt that the leper appreciated the human interaction at least as much as the dirty, crumpled banknote.

Calcutta's central avenue is a long, chaotic bazaar of activity. Old women constantly sweep the sidewalks clean with witches' brooms made of rude twigs. Footsore rickshaw-wallahs pull their fares at a slow trot, for Calcutta is the last major city on earth where carriages are drawn not by bicycles, horses, or motors but by unshod human feet. A second-story studio offers instruction in "Western Dance: Break, Disco, Jive, Jazz and Ballroom!" I was curious to find out just what "jive" dance might be — but not curious enough to push my way past a man happily urinating into the doorway, right next to an empty public toilet.

In the street, huge nannying billboards ("A little care makes accidents rare!" "Cigarette smoke is DEATH, no joke!") scold drivers to lead cautious lives. Gray-uniformed schoolchildren are shuttled home for lunch, six of them crammed into a tiny box on the back of a battered tricycle. Curbside vendors try to sell anything under the sun. "Look!" a woman calls out. "Cheap! Real silver! Real sapphire! Last price!" It is neither cheap, nor real silver, nor real sapphire, nor her last price.

And always there are the lepers.

Calcutta has no Hilton Hotel, but on Sudder Street it has both a Histon and a Shilton. I saw a particularly sorry-looking leper sitting on the pavement outside the Histon and sat down to talk with him about his life. He spoke only Telugu, so we had to communicate through three intermediaries: another beggar translated the Telugu into Bengali, a shopkeeper translated the Bengali into Hindi, and (since neither the shopkeeper nor I spoke Hindi with perfect fluency) a Sikh conversant in both English and Hindi (as well as his native Punjabi) helped out on the odd hazy sentence.

One of the leper's hands was a mere pancake of flesh, the other had only melted traces of fingers. Both his feet were encased in custom-cobbled boots far too tiny to contain toes. His legs had makeshift wooden splints to keep them from disintegrating. He had only half a nose.

He had been perfectly healthy until the age of thirty. "Just as strong and healthy as *you*, my friend," he said with a wicked grin.

He used to be a carpenter in Andhra Pradesh. When his hair had just started to turn gray, the disease made itself known. His flesh began to rot. He lost all sensation in his extremities, would carelessly burn, smash, or chop off his digits without even noticing. Several times his limbs became gangrenous, and the only tipoff he had was the foul stench.

His mother refused to let him into her house: she had watched her husband die of leprosy and had vowed never to catch it herself. His sister sometimes put out food for him, always on a special plate that she handled only with a rag wrapped around her hand. His old friends always walked on the other side of the street, pretended not to hear when he called out their names.

He came to Calcutta for treatment at the clinic, but the medicine did not work. For the past six years he has been trying to scrape together enough money to get back home. He would walk if he could, hitchhike if anybody would take him. Even if he had the money, he is not sure he'd be allowed a seat on any bus or train.

I asked him if there was anything in the world that made him happy. With a vigor I'd never have guessed his putrescent frame possessed, he leapt up and let out a hearty holler. From around the corner a plump woman with a bright-eyed child came running.

"*This,*" said the leper, putting an arm around his wife's neck, "this is what makes me happy."

She too had the illness and held up her left hand to show four stumps of fingers. They had married when both were in the early stages of the disease, but her condition had stabilized while his had gotten steadily worse.

The husband gleefully tousled his son's hair with his pancake-hand, tickled the boy playfully with his vestigial club. The child is perfectly sound — as sound as his father was until the age of thirty — but leprosy is generally spread by close physical contact. One day, in all likelihood, this boy also will have pancake-paws and custom-cobbled boots.

The beggar kissed his wife on the forehead, and a pleased smile crept across her face. They were a family, she said, and for that they felt lucky.

Once a very wise man was asked for proof of the power of love. It shall make the blind man see, He said, it shall make the deaf man hear, it shall make the leper leap.

➤ ➤ ➤

Forty years ago V. S. Naipaul wrote that an Indian woman's ambitions in life were wholly negative ones: *not* to be unmarried, *not* to be childless, *not* to be divorced. For the bulk of the female population, this is still the case. A recent poll asked women to name their role models, and more than half chose Sita as their ideal. To follow the path of Sita is to live vicariously through one's mate. The highest piety of a woman (such a view holds) is to serve her husband — that is why Sita gladly follows Rama into harsh exile. A man gains virtue by action, a woman by helping her man to act.

A woman who does not try to emulate Sita has traditionally been shunned as a hussy. Even today, to whisper that a someone "is *hardly* Sita, you know" is to say that she sleeps around. An Indian woman who engages in sex outside of marriage is generally seen as a common prostitute — and if she doesn't happen to demand money for her services, well, *bhai,* she must be a fool as well. Outside the big cities, at least, Sita's path is the only path worth treading.

Any other path is not only scandalous, it is vaguely unpatriotic. "*Our* women are different," sniffed many an Indian, both male and female, when I asked about the possibility of a woman not wanting to settle down with a husband and kids. Wanton wenches, slatternly strumpets, shameless jades who refuse to bind themselves to a man — they have no place in proper Hindu society. That may be how females behave in depraved, degenerate nations across the Black Water, but never here in Holy India.

Yet nobody who has seen the temple carvings at Khajuraho could ever accuse India of prudery. I'm no Puritan and no ingenue, but I learned a thing or two there; the reliefs at these ancient shrines display some positions and techniques I'd never even imagined, feats I *still* don't think the human body is capable of performing. I am told that there is also such a thing as pornography in modern India — a soft-core publication by the name of *Debonair* (a French word, of course) — but the closest I saw was a magazine entitled *Women of Socialist China,* in a Communist bookstore in Madurai. Shelved among the volumes of anachronistic Soviet propaganda ("Munich: Mistake, or Cynical Calculation?"), it had a feature photo spread with the arousing heading "Capable Women of the Countryside." All the lovely lasses were safely foreign — and even so, Bob Guccione need not fear the competition.

In Amritsar I met a medical doctor in a state of exultation about his triumph over the temptations of the flesh. On the train ride up from Delhi he had shared a sleeping compartment with two nubile French girls.

"I knew that French women favor free love," he told me, "and I prayed to God that I might be spared seduction."

With his buck teeth jutting well past his lower lip, he looked like a timid rabbit that wouldn't dare raid an untended cabbage patch.

"One of the girls had a cough," he said, "and as a doctor I knew it was my duty to offer her some medicine. But I feared she might take this as an invitation to . . . to carnal relations, and so I lay in my bunk uncertain what to do. Finally my professional ethics got the better of my morals. I gave her a vial of elixir, quickly jumped back to my own bed, and pulled the covers over my face. I prayed hard to God, prayed that He save me from temptation, and do you know what happened?"

His eyes shone with joy as he came to the story's conclusion.

"The merciful God protected me. He heard my prayers, kept *both* the French girls securely in their own bunks, and I passed the whole night in safety."

And yet. Indian women are not merely bedmates and cooks, housekeepers and mothers. Surprisingly large numbers of them manage to become doctors, lawyers, university professors, and even political tyrants. Women have ruled each of the three nations that made up India before Partition: Benazir Bhutto in Pakistan, Begum Khaleda Zia in Bangladesh, and Indira Gandhi in India itself. Sri Lanka's Sirimavo Bandaranaike, as far back as 1960, was the first female prime minister of any country in the world.

True, all of these women won their offices through the popularity of their martyred husbands or fathers. They succeeded or failed on their own merits, but rode to their inaugurations in the hearses of their men. True, their very gender propelled them to the political stratosphere, for back-room power brokers promoted them as unthreatening, compliant figureheads. When the dominant Congress Party tried to run the wholly inexperienced Sonia Gandhi as their candidate for prime minister in the wake of her husband Rajiv's assassination (she had the good sense to decline, for now), it was only following a well-established tradition. But how does this compare with the state of women in American politics? It is a virtual certainty that no woman will be elected president until well into the next millennium. As of September 1992, only two out of one hundred senators are female, and all the congresswomen with any true influence can be counted on the fingers of one hand.

We may well ask which is the more liberal society, one that lets women build on the success of their men, complete it, make it whole, even (as in the case of Indira Gandhi) perhaps come to rival it, or one that shuts women out of real power altogether? Apart from Corazon Aquino and Violetta Chamorro, every female premier of a Third World nation has come from the Indian subcontinent. In political terms, at least, Sita's heiresses are not faring all that poorly.

In the epic as well, Sita is no mere cipher. Valmiki writes

that "by her religious and yogic powers she can protect the world — or reduce it to ashes." She could free herself from the clutches of Ravana, but she deliberately chooses inaction because that is her dharma: she was born to be not a warrior but the wife of a warrior.

Her virtue is more subtle than that of her husband. Bashing up demons is easy, it requires no thought. Her task is less obvious but no less vital: to make her man complete. Without her aid, in fact, Rama cannot be the Supreme Deity. God is beyond gender, is both male and female, so Sita is an integral part of her husband's divinity.

In Ayodhya there is a temple, Janaki Mandir, devoted wholly to the worship of Sita. It is a baroque, gaudily painted place, frequented primarily by women. In the shade of one of its archways I spoke with a well-dressed woman whose card read "Dr. Mrs. P. R. Shankar, Lady Doctor." I asked whether she, as a sophisticated, educated professional, still looked to Sita for guidance.

"It is very difficult," she admitted. "Sita might not even be the sort of person I would have as one of my friends. She did not assert herself as an equal of men, was content to walk two steps behind. Personally, I would *never* walk two steps behind *anyone*."

The Lady Doctor grinned a broad grin.

"But it is not a question of liking her or disliking her," she went on. "Sita is the female side of Ram, the feminine aspect of God. It is hard to emulate her, particularly for a career woman such as myself. But she has much to teach every one of us. Her patience, her kindness, her devotion, and her overwhelming love for all living things — no woman should be ashamed to learn these traits from Sita."

> > >

Mrs. Tami Bhandari sits in her kitchen all day, though she has not cooked in years. There are servants for *that*. From morning to night she holds court in a corner, her white hair wrapped in a white headcloth, her nearly spherical body wedged behind a sturdy wooden table laden with stacks of ledgers and piles of sewing.

"Must be down here to keep an eye on things," she says, "else the whole household would go to the dogs." The "things" are a stately old manor with twenty-foot ceilings and a sprawling ornamental garden full of unruly hedges. The household consists of Mrs. Bhandari, eight or nine servants, and the occasional fortunate guest.

Mrs. Bhandari has always been the absolute mistress of her fate. She has been married twice, but has never taken marching orders from a man. It is impossible to imagine her crooning blandishments and running to fetch slippers.

"My first husband considered himself quite an important character," she says. "Notions of lording it over the house, and all that. I'd have none of it. Kept him from getting too high and mighty. There were already far too many people quaking at his command — after all, he was the mayor of Amritsar."

She was born when the century was in its infancy, and the world was a very different place. Her grandfather, a Parsi from Bombay, moved to the Punjab and set up an ice factory many decades ago. The Amritsar of her youth is not the Amritsar of today, what with high-noon gun battles and midnight death squads. "The young thugs have been too coddled," she says with a frown. "They live by thievery and murder, for the simple reason that they *can*. Quite right — I would, too, if anybody was damn fool enough to give me food and money for nothing.

"But," she adds wistfully, "India was never an honest country. Always so many rajahs stabbing each other in the back, and suchlike."

I ask her about the iron bracelet on her wrist, the kara that all observant Sikhs must wear. She is not a Sikh, and wears it only to ward off arthritis. Somebody once told her that the holy metal cures every infirmity, and she hadn't particularly believed it, but when she put on the kara all stiffness mysteriously vanished from her aged fingers. As a Parsi married twice to Hindus in a city of Sikhs, she must mix and match her cultures: she normally speaks Farsi, Urdu, or Hindi but deigns to utter Punjabi ("a coarse language, that") when giving the servants their orders.

Mrs. Bhandari pays her staff well — the equivalent of one hundred dollars a month, plus food, and she is willing to give an advance "if someone wants to buy a bicycle, or a new dress for his wife." She runs the house with a fist to match her bracelet, but every gardener, bearer, and dhobi has been with her for over a decade. She warns me not to leave any of them a gift or tip, to avoid breeding indolence. When I ask her how to contact the Khalistanist rebels, she orders a silent, bald manservant to act as my chaperone. "He's quite all right," she whispers conspiratorially, waving the man out to find a rickshaw, "a bit daffy, though. Not young, I think, but I've never asked."

A small green lizard scurries across the kitchen wall like a badly animated cartoon, scampers as effortlessly as if on level ground. It hides behind a light fixture, basking in the yellowish heat, darting out every now and then to gobble up an insect attracted by the bulb's weak glow.

One night at dinner, after a third afternoon spent chronicling atrocities, I ask Mrs. Bhandari why she chooses to remain in war-ravaged Punjab.

"Leave?" she snorts. "Why should I? Let the robbers drive me from my home? From all I have loved?"

I ask what it is that she has loved.

"This is where I was married," she says, her voice becoming dreamier. "Not once, mind you, but twice. This is where I raised my family. They are what I have loved, and therefore they are what I *am*."

A snap of her fingers brings a servant running to reload our plates with dansak.

"This epic you are following," she continues, "it says the same thing. Here in the Punjab — the *old* Punjab, mind you, not this chopped-in-two job of today — we have the two cities of Lahore and Karachi. Both, of course, now in Pakistan, right across the border. Named for Lava and Kusha, the twin sons of Sita. She makes the ultimate sacrifice for them, as well as for her husband, and why? Because of love."

The old woman clasps my hand for emphasis and stabs her folded spectacles in the air.

"I," she says, "even I, who am not even a true Hindu, who am a worshiper of fire rather than of painted icons, I am moved by the tale. Sita speaks even to me. She demonstrates the true power of love.

"Surely," Mrs. Bhandari says, withered lips twisted into a coquettish half-smile, "you have known love yourself?"

Yes, several times. And not long after I left Amritsar, I went down to Goa to meet someone I loved very much. She loved me as well — why else would a woman travel three thousand miles to spend her two-week vacation watching her man talk philosophy with sadhus and lepers?

We have since taken our separate paths. If blame must be assigned, it must be assigned to me: she wanted us to get married, but I could not silence the voice that commanded me to keep voyaging far, far away. Sins of lust may sometimes be forgiven, but sins of wanderlust are beyond all redemption.

I like to believe that the love we shared was far stronger than whatever emotion may exist between giddy groom and bartered bride in an arranged marriage. But can something so transitory truly be strong? She and I have parted ways and gone on to other lovers, while a hundred million couples who met only on the day of their wedding still lead contented lives together.

Perhaps any comparison is just apples and mangoes. Perhaps it's the fault of language, which shelves both conditions under the catchall heading of "love." There are many different kinds of love, as many as there are different people, and the love of Rama and Sita is a drive as close to duty as to romance.

It is not a love that arises from the satisfaction of physical or emotional desires — most of us, with our chains of blithe couplings and uncouplings, have experienced *that* type of love often enough. *That* sentiment, perhaps better labeled "romance" or "passion," is what we in the West generally mean when we say "love." But Cupid's sting wounds the heart, not the soul. It is, fundamentally, a selfish longing: we yearn to be with a loved one for the simple reason that it makes us happy. A fine, fine thing, yes — but not the sort of love that makes the world go round.

The love celebrated in the Ramayana is a completely different breed. It comes not from the fulfillment of individual wants, but from their sublimation. It can exist side by side with romance (and for contented couples in both East and West it generally does), but it does not rely on mere fleeting cupidity. It is a love that requires surrender of the self. It is a love that leads to the procreation of children and the preservation of the species. It is a love that makes us whole.

Indian society views single people with wary suspicion. A man or woman alone is incomplete, just half the equation. Only upon marriage does a person become a full member of the community. The gods themselves are married: Shiva has Parvati, Vishnu has Lakshmi, Krishna has Radha, the whole pantheon is a cotillion of couples. But each divine pairing is far more than the union of two separate beings. Every goddess is merely the manifestation of her husband's female attributes. The fearsome she-deities Kali and Durga are worshiped independently as wives of Shiva, but they are also personifications of the other side of his character. They are said to "flow from him," to be part of his very flesh, his very essence, just as the first woman came from Manu's rib.

We humans, too, need a mate to be complete. In biological terms, the only fundamental difference between any two humans is gender: black or white, tall or short, smart or stupid, all these are merely differences in degree, not in type; every person has varying amounts of color, height, and intellect, but no male has a womb and no female has testes. A man and a woman together form a microcosm of the whole human race.

I, personally, see nothing wrong with living an incomplete life. In fact, I rather enjoy it that way. I like the vicissitudes of independence, and at this particular stage in my life I have not grown bored with meteoric romance. I prefer to be an unfinished man, for now, because I prefer freedom over stability and excitement over comfort. But most Indians don't see it that way at all.

Most Indians crave completion. It is, after all, the perfect human condition. An unmarried person is only half of an undiscovered whole, and it is nearly every Hindu's wish to be part of such a whole. That, and not such trivialities as lust or passion, is the reason for marriage.

There is a love which binds a man and woman together, which lets each be the fulfillment of the other. There is a love which takes two individuals and fuses them into a single unit. There is a love which makes every man or woman the embodiment of all men and women. There is a love which, by joining human with human, also joins the human with the divine.

This is the love that Rama and Sita shared, this is the love that keeps India alive.

The arrow of Cupid strikes deep, but not so deep as the Arrow of God.

Twelve

ENDINGS

$\mathcal{T}$HAT which I am about to relate did not happen. It could not have happened, it must not have happened, because if it really did happen, then what would be the point of this whole tale? The thing which did not happen is this:

A few months after returning to Ayodhya, Sita began to feel ill in the mornings. She started to crave the most ridiculous foods — lentils with sugar, bananas in goat blood, pickled fish. She was (it soon became apparent) pregnant.

At first Rama was overjoyed. He'd spend hours with his lips pressed to Sita's belly, whispering Vedic verses to her womb so that the baby would be born well schooled in the way of righteousness. Then, at one of his weekly council meetings, the king happened to inquire about the current topics of conversation in the street.

"Your subjects are all well contented and loyal," said one courtier, a bit too hastily.

"Yes," Rama said, "but what do they talk about?"

For a very long time nobody said a word. Then one sourfaced old counselor broke the silence.

"They talk about your wife," he said bitterly. "They consider it most strange that Her Highness should never conceive during fourteen years of wandering, yet somehow return from Ravana's captivity heavy with child. They laugh that commoners must follow the moral example set by their monarchs, so husbands will just have to tolerate their wives taking lovers. That, my lord, is what the people talk about."

Again duty warred with love in Rama's heart, and again duty won. He did not want to believe it, deep down he truly did not believe it, but his subjects believed it, and that is what mattered. A king, he told himself, must never place his personal wishes above those of his people. A monarch's duty, his path, his righteousness, his dharma, is to serve the men and women of his nation.

Perhaps Rama forgot the difference between a true leader and a pandering demagogue. Perhaps the hero, who had braved ten million demons in mortal combat, turned coward in the face of his own subjects. Or perhaps an unbending code of righteousness ought, every now and then, to bend.

Rama summoned his brother, told him to take Sita and abandon her in the depth of the forest.

"Do not talk to me of good and evil," he said, putting his hand up before Lakshman could utter a word of protest. "This is not a matter of right or of wrong. It is merely a thing that a king must do."

The next day Lakshman, still wearing an implacable scowl, invited Sita on a picnic in the woods. When they were far in the wilderness he told her that she could never return. Sita did not cry. She did not scream, beg, or complain. She just sat down and waited. She'd had practice at that.

Sita hadn't been waiting very long when an old gray hermit approached and offered her shelter.

"Who are you?" she asked her benefactor.

"My name is Valmiki," the old man replied.

➤ ➤ ➤

Years passed. For the kingdom of Ayodhya, they were bad years indeed. Crops failed, hunger grew, plagues and pestilences lay heavy on the land. Livestock gave birth only to scrawny runts, and the udders of milch cows dried up to withered sacks of skin. Brigands and murderers proliferated like mosquitoes. The sun could seldom be bothered to shine.

India, once the richest of all nations, became the impoverished country she is today.

One day a Brahmin came before Rama with tears in his eyes and a dead boy in his arms.

"This was my son!" he ranted. "Dead! Dead of the fever! A pious child, the son of a pious father, from a line whose ancestors never committed the tiniest of sins!"

All the courtiers droned murmurs of sympathy.

"It is your fault!" the Brahmin shouted at Rama. "You killed my son! In a state with a virtuous monarch, such a tragedy could never have occurred."

The chief of protocol casually ordered guards to have the man killed, but Rama commanded them to stay where they were. He told the Brahmin to put his son's corpse in a vat of oil to keep it from decomposing, and promised to see what he could do.

He gathered together the wisest men in the kingdom, all the sagest scholars and seers and pandits and priests. He asked them to tell him what was causing such misfortune in his domains. They conferred and puzzled and finally determined the source of the jinx to be a certain Shudra reaching above his caste to practice religious austerities.

Rama went alone to the ashram of Samvuka (for that was the sadhu's name) and found the holy man lost in meditation with a smile of spiritual ecstasy etched on his time-worn face. The king asked the hermit but two questions:

"Were you indeed born a Shudra?"

"Yes," the sadhu replied, "I was."

"And do you indeed seek God?"

"Yes," the sadhu replied, "I do."

Rama took out his sword and chopped off the old man's head.

The calamities only multiplied. Rama, in desperation, decided to perform the Ashwamedha, the great horse sacrifice.

This rite, if properly consecrated, destroys all past sins. It can be undertaken only by a king willing to give up all the wealth he possesses, but it alone (among all holy rituals) has the certain power of granting a man's dearest wish.

Rama let loose a perfect black horse and commanded Lakshman to follow and protect the stallion as it roamed freely for one whole year. During this time the monarch provided a ceaseless feast for all his subjects and uncountable guests from abroad. Rama built palaces for visiting kings of neighboring lands, constructed spacious barracks for foreign knights, raised comfortable hostels for alien tradesmen and farmers. Brahmins assembled from all over India to be showered with gifts of rice and rations, silk and scriptures.

At the end of one year, the horse returned for its sacrifice. Priests ceremoniously slew thousands of sheep, chickens, goats, boars, geese, squirrels, bullocks, fish, and reptiles, offering up the entire animal kingdom as an oblation to Heaven. It was Rama himself who slaughtered the pure black steed.

He made three slow slices on the horse's neck and cradled the stallion in his arms as it died. For one night, from sunset to sunrise, he lay beside his victim pouring his moral impurities into the beast's ebbing soul. At dawn the priests dismembered the body, crushed its bones, and set the corpse on fire. Rama stood over the roasting marrow and sniffed in the odor of his salvation.

During the seasons of festivity, legions of minstrels and musicians had congregated in Ayodhya to play for the reveling crowds. There were all manner of skilled mummers and honey-throated bards, but the most celebrated performers of all were two small boys. They were twins, named Lava and Kusha, and they spent every day singing the story of Rama's exploits. They sang, in perfect Sanskrit, the verses of the epic Ramayana.

When Rama got word of the remarkable twins he ordered them brought to the palace at once.

"Who taught you these couplets?" he asked.

"Our guru, the hermit Valmiki," Kusha answered. "He received the whole saga, all 24,000 slokas of it, in a tragic vision."

"Ever since we could speak," said Lava, "he has made us memorize the story one verse at a time."

"Who is your father?" the king asked, his voice breaking.

"We have no father," said Kusha.

"But our mother," said Lava, "is a hermit woman by the name of Sita."

Rama looked in their eyes and recognized his sons.

The king sent a regal delegation to escort Sita from the forest. When she arrived at the palace with Valmiki by her side, Rama welcomed his wife and her protector with courtesy, if no great warmth.

"I am prepared," he said, his voice buttery with magnanimity, "to let you return to my side. You may be my consort once again."

The court broke out in a chorus of applause, but Sita displayed not a hint of emotion.

"Of course," Rama continued, "after spending some years in the company of this man Valmiki, you must once again prove your chastity. I have little doubt that you will triumph as before."

He waved his hand for a bonfire to be built, but Sita said no, she had a better way:

She called out in a clear, high voice and asked Mother Earth Herself to vouch for her purity.

"Holy Mata," she prayed, "Sacred Mother of All, grant this request: If I have always been sinless, if I have never so much as thought of a man other than my husband, then swallow me up and let me return to your bosom."

A low rumble shook the ground, and the earth opened up a yawning chasm below Sita's feet. As she tumbled back down into the soil that had given her life, she wore a smile of quiet serenity.

Rama, for the first time in his mortal existence, began to cry. He sobbed uncontrollably and did not stop for weeks. His own thin arc of a divine smile never returned.

He did not take another wife. He did not tend to affairs of state. He ruled Ayodhya for several thousand miserable years, during which time the proud kingdom disintegrated in ruin. All the inhabitants filtered away. The capital was populated only by Vanars and Bhallukas, who gradually forgot their powers of thought and speech.

Rama died alone, mourned only with the howls and screeches of monkeys.

I've always liked this ending better. It is entirely apocryphal, having been written centuries later than the rest of the text by an anonymous poet who was certainly not Valmiki. I prefer it because an easy conclusion is too, well, easy. In real life nobody simply lives happily ever after. And in real life heroes often turn out to be less than heroic. Most Indians are familiar with this Uttara Kanda chapter but feel somewhat uncomfortable about it. One of the major vernacular retellings — the Hindi version of Tulsi Das — excises the episode entirely. And quite understandably: it completely subverts the meaning of what went before.

Here Sita rather than Rama is the true embodiment of virtue, here she is the one who triumphs in the end. Here good and evil are turned so thoroughly topsy-turvy that an avatar of God kills a saintly penitent simply for the sin of piety. Here a craven paladin banishes his only love, the woman for whom he'd sent millions to their deaths, all on account of bazaar gossip. In a twisted way it makes perfect sense: the iron Law of dharma dictates that spirituality is the province of Brahmins, that a wife's fidelity ought not be sullied by so much as a whisper. But strict adherence to the law leads to destruction of the law — a subversive thought if ever there was one. I do not know why this appeals to me. Perhaps I am just a subversive at heart.

I asked Guru Baba Raghunanden Das, the Ayodhyan hermit who has not left Hanuman Cave in half a century, just what this Uttara Kanda means. It is a cautionary tale, he said, an episode that did not really happen but could have.

The whole epic (the solitary sage continued) is a lesson in duty. This is as it should be: every man and every woman must follow dharma, too many people today forget this basic truth. But blind, unthinking devotion to obligation is not enough. Without love, duty is hollow. We must do what is right, but our rigid sense of righteousness must be humanized with emotion. If the path of virtue were always perfectly illuminated, what need would we have for the light of God?

So this pessimistic denouement never truly took place. Through trust and love Rama and Sita, the greatest hero and heroine India has known, lived out their lives as happily as two people can. By following their example, so too can we all. And as Valmiki concludes his narration:

"The man who desires a son or great wealth, the king who desires victory over his adversaries, he has only to listen to the story of Rama. By hearing it, every woman will be blessed with fertility. Anyone who listens to this tale — and listens with due regard — will gain health, longevity, and absolution of sins. All who read or heed its message will meet no obstacle in life."

A Few Words of Explanation and Thanks

The explanation: I have changed some of my sources' names, to spare them embarrassment, social ostracism, or (in at least three cases) the threat of death. Since this book is intended for a general rather than an academic audience, I have omitted diacritical marks in transliterating Sanskrit and Arabic words; also, rather than maintaining a pedantic consistency in nomenclature, I have modernized the spelling of certain epic characters' names while permitting others to keep their archaic forms.

The thanks: To Suzanne Gluck, my agent, without whose help this book never would have been started; to Betsy Lerner and Henry Ferris, my editors, without whose guidance it never would have been finished; to Peg Anderson, my manuscript editor, without whose sharp eyes it would have been riddled with foolish errors; and to the rest of the people at Houghton Mifflin and ICM.

I would also like to thank Terra Brockman, for support, encouragement, and structural damage; Sanjay Pandey, for invaluable help in translation; Charles Lindholm, for averting my academic excommunication; and Ravinder Kumar, Tom Jannuzi, Rama Balachandran, Barbara Crossette, Maureen Aung-Thwin, Louis Kraar, Ramashray Roy, Philip Lutgendorf, James Benson, and Colonels Lohtia and Perera, for setting me straight in the research, writing, and fact-checking.

Most of all, I would like to thank the various Indian and Sri Lankan people whose lives and words I have borrowed in these pages. Their kindness, hospitality, and patience made my travels possible, and their stories made the book a reality.

Also available from Touchstone

These books are available at your local bookshop, or can be ordered direct from the publisher. Just fill in the form below.

Price and availability subject to change without notice.

SIMON & SCHUSTER CASH SALES,
PO Box 11, Falmouth, Cornwall TR10 9EN

Please send cheque or postal order for the value of the book/s, and add the following for postage and packing:

UK including BFPO - £1.00 for one book, plus 50p for the second book, and 30p for each additional book ordered up to a £3.00 minimum.

OVERSEAS INCLUDING EIRE - £2.00 for the first book, plus £1.00 for the second book, and 50p for each additional book ordered. OR Please debit this amount from my Visa/Access/Mastercard (delete as appropriate)

CARD NUMBER ☐☐☐☐☐☐☐☐☐☐☐☐☐☐☐☐

AMOUNT £ .... EXPIRY DATE ....

SIGNED ....

NAME ....

ADDRESS ....

....